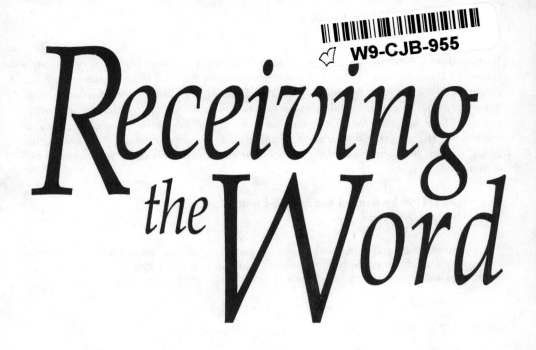

Receiving the Word

HOW NEW APPROACHES TO THE BIBLE
IMPACT OUR BIBLICAL FAITH AND LIFESTYLE

Samuel Koranteng-Pipim

BEREAN BOOKS

P.O.Box 195, Berrien Springs, MI 49103-0195

Berean Books *seeks to restore among Bible-believing Christians the spirit of the early Bereans (Acts 17:11), by subjecting contemporary views to the Bible as advocated and exhibited by the foremost Seventh-day Adventist theologian, Ellen G. White. In addressing today's critical issues, each book adopts a serious tone, provocative style, and a reassuring outlook. These books are for all who seek the lordship of Jesus Christ in their lives, the sole authority of His inspired Word as their infallible guide, the proclamation of the everlasting gospel as their life vocation, and the revival of primitive godliness as the most urgent need in their churches.*

For your own copy of *Receiving the Word,* or for additional copies, contact your ABC Christian Book Center or mail your prepaid order ($10.95, plus $3.00 shipping and handling in the U.S.A.) to:

Berean Books, P. O. Box 195, Berrien Springs, Michigan 49103-0195

FAX: 616-471-4305; Internet: 105323.612@compuserve.com; CompuServe: 105323,612

Library of Congress Card Number: 96-95095

Koranteng-Pipim, Samuel
    Receiving the Word: how new approaches to the Bible impact our biblical faith and lifestyle / Samuel Koranteng-Pipim

        1. Bible—Evidences, authority, etc. 2. Bible—Inspiration. 3. Bible—Hermeneutics. 4. Bible—Criticism, interpretation, etc. 5. Hermeneutics—Religious aspects—Christianity.
I. Title
BS480.K67 1996   220.1´3
ISBN 1-890014-00-1

Cover Design by Randy Siebold

Printed in the United States of America

Dedicated to

Enoch de Oliveira (Brazil)—*A Custodian of the Word*
Gerhard F. Hasel (Germany)—*A Teacher of the Word*
Paul K. Nsiah (Ghana)—*A Student of the Word*
Larisa Petrovna Ivanisheva (Ukraine)—*A Servant of the Word*
Charles D. Brooks (USA)—*A Preacher of the Word*

They represent the large number of dedicated Seventh-day Adventist
church leaders, scholars, laymen & women, and preachers
around the world who, despite tremendous odds,
have had the courage to stand for
biblical convictions.
Acts 17:11

Table of Contents

Foreword
by
Dr. Paul Yeboah

Published works that speak with compelling eloquence do not need introductions; they constitute their own introductions. Such is the case with respect to Samuel Koranteng-Pipim's *Receiving the Word.*

Therefore, instead of employing this page to highlight the merits of this timely work, I will direct my comments to the author himself, commending him for his courage in writing this book and alerting him to the kinds of interesting reactions his work is likely to generate. I offer my comments from the vantage point of one who has been closely acquainted with the author in his evangelistic work in Africa, Europe, and North America:

Samuel, at a time when some prefer not to debate issues, your book evidences that: (1) you prize the quest for biblical truth over the pursuit of theological tranquility; (2) you neither believe in the myth of theological neutrality nor the political expediency that encourages it; and consequently, (3) you have chosen not to maintain the *status quo* of silence on the divisive issue of biblical authority and interpretation. These characteristics of your work make it invaluable for anyone seeking to understand some of the current theological developments in the Seventh-day Adventist church.

But in today's climate of theological pluralism and its culture of indifference to truth, you need to be reminded that those who dare to call others to biblical accountability, particularly on forbidden issues, are seldom tolerated. Thus, while your book will be a blessing to thousands of earnest truth-seekers, you must also expect some negative reactions against your work, and even against yourself. Such a barrage would be mounted even if *Receiving the Word* had not been written by an African. For whenever error is exposed, it always finds ways to vent its wrath against the message and the messenger of truth.

With this in mind, I urge you to take counsel from advice given by William W. Adams to Mr. Robert Shank some three decades ago. These words are memorialized in the introduction to Shank's provocative book against the long held position of "once saved always saved" (see Robert Shank's *Life in the Son* [Springfield, Missouri: Westcott Publishers, 1961], xviii-xix). To personalize the advice, I will replace Mr. Shank's name with your own:

"Samuel, unless human nature has recently and radically changed, there are some who will do their utmost to give your book the 'silent' treatment. Some will be too learned to acknowledge that they have not known all there is to know on the subject. They will consider that their first obligation is to their personal academic reputation and professional interests. With great scholarly dignity, they will carefully ignore your book.

"Some will loudly denounce your book merely because you dare to call in question some of their customary interpretations and to challenge their accustomed doctrinal position. They will label you a heretic or a novice. Let me urge you to ignore all criticisms of yourself, and all criticisms of your book that amount to mere general disapproval and denunciation. This will be the resort only of men who are incapable of presenting any serious reply to your interpretations and thesis. Negative criticisms that fail to demonstrate objectively that your interpretations are incorrect will not deserve serious consideration or serve the cause of truth.

"Some will consider that 'unity' is more important than truth and that, right or wrong, conformity to tradition and popular opinion is the only wise course. Men so easily become enslaved by vested interest in the *status quo,* and many will refuse to venture the risk of honestly searching for the truth at the possible expense of comfort.

"Some, thank God, will read your book with growing provocation and an insatiable hunger and determination to see the study through to a conclusion that is unquestionably Biblical. They are the ones (I pray they may be many) who will profit from the reading of your book and form an honest effort to refute it. Whatever the ultimate verdict, their knowledge of the Scriptures will be increased and their lives and Christian witness will be enriched because of your book.

"Samuel, there may be other responses to your book which neither you nor I can foresee. But this much is assured: all genuine scholars and searchers after truth will be compelled to take your book into consideration."

My earnest prayer is that every reader of *Receiving the Word* will be led to take an uncompromising stand for God's truth—no matter the cost. It is this truth alone which can truly set us free (John 8:32).

Thank you, Samuel, for challenging us to receive the Word and live by it.

Chicago, Ill.
October, 1996

To the Reader

Receiving the Word has an innocent title; but it deals with an explosive issue—biblical inspiration and interpretation and their impact on our faith and practice. Since the subject matter is contentious, readers must be aware of the two dangers confronting anyone who seeks to address the issue. On the one hand is the risk of becoming cowardly, hesitant, people-pleasing, waffling, and compromising. On the other hand lies the danger of becoming headstrong, judgmental, unkind, abrasive and dogmatic. In the name of "love," the first option risks not speaking the truth; in the name of "truth," the second fails to speak in love.

In this book we have done our best to speak the truth in love. Still, we anticipate varied reactions to this work. For those unaware of the internal sophisticated challenge to our distinctive doctrines and lifestyle, this book will be a disturbing eye-opener. For those seeking to understand the underlying causes of recent theological conflicts in the Seventh-day Adventist church, this volume will provide a probing explanation. For those who believe in the "progressive" ideas of theological liberalism and its method of higher criticism, this book will present a biblically compelling alternative. And for those who have always accepted the Bible as God's inspired, trustworthy, and solely-authoritative Word, this work will be reassuring.

Receiving the Word adopts a serious tone, bringing a probing style to this sensitive issue. The following paragraphs will explain why.

Immediate Context

One of the best things to happen to the Seventh-day Adventist church in recent times has been the intense discussion over such issues as abortion, polygamy, divorce and remarriage, fighting in wars, women's ordination, and homosexuality. These discussions have brought into the open a major crisis that has been ignored and even denied during the past several decades.

This crisis has to do with the conflicting views within the church over the nature, authority, and interpretation of the Scriptures. It has divided North American Bible scholars into "conservative" and "liberal" camps. The issue has also created conservative and liberal Adventist institutions, influenced by their respective thought leaders.

A Divisive Issue. Because of the polarization between theological conservatives and liberals, a cordial but uneasy fiction exists among our pastors, administrators, and theologians. Although they belong to the same church, institution, even theological faculty, and although they are pleasant and amiable whenever they meet, yet there is a great gulf that separates them.

This crisis has also left many students in our institutions confused. It has produced a generation of preachers, Bible teachers, church leaders, editors and publishers who are unsure of some of our historic beliefs and practices. It has also shipwrecked the faith of many youth and new believers, whether they be in Seventh-day Adventist classrooms or churches.

A Forbidden Issue. But despite its baneful results, very few of our Bible scholars are willing to address candidly this forbidden issue of conflicting methods of Bible interpretation. Even when they attempt to discuss the cause of their disagreements, they do so only at a superficial level. In this way, they escape being labeled as "dogmatic," "ultra-conservative," or "fundamentalist"[1]— epithets often hurled at Bible-believing scholars who refuse to adopt the unscriptural views of their "progressive" counterparts.

Moreover, church leaders and institutional heads often hesitate to tackle the forbidden issue, even when they are aware of how it is eroding confidence in our Bible-based faith and lifestyle. They fear that Adventist Bible scholars would brand them as reactionary "theological police officers" slowing down the acceleration of "open-minded investigation of truth" or even stopping the traffic of "academic freedom" or "freedom of individual conscience."

A Global Church Issue. As the published works and influence of these North American thought-leaders are spreading abroad, this contentious issue is threatening to fracture the worldwide Seventh-day Adventist movement, not along cultural lines, but according to prevailing attitudes regarding the authority of the Bible. This may explain what some have perceived as a growing polarization between "the church of the West" and "the rest of the church."

For example, shortly after the 1995 General Conference session in Utrecht, the Netherlands, an Adventist scholar in ethics wrote: "The vote refusing the NAD [North American Division] permission to ordain its women is the real 'tip of the iceberg,' the iceberg being the clash between *scriptural literalism,* a view largely held in the developing world—Africa and much of South America and Inter-America, and a *principle-based approach* to Scripture followed in areas where the church has matured for a century and a half" (i.e., North America, Europe, and possibly Australia). This professor states that "many African converts, not far removed from bigamous exploitation of women, are naturally drawn to an interpretation of Scripture ['scriptural literalism'] that affirms a millennia-old sentiment toward women."[2]

The undertones of cultural arrogance in the above comment were perhaps unintended. The same can be said of another article to which the above-cited author directs his readers. The second writer, until recently the editor of a church publication for pastors, suggested that those who do not subscribe to the so-called "principle-based approach" cannot handle a high level of abstract thinking and are comparatively immature:

"Most people have not learned to reason abstractly," he wrote. "This is why the *literal approach* is so appealing. Children begin with concrete and literal understandings of life. It is not until around 10 years and older that they can begin to conceptualize and reason in the abstract. If people learn only the *proof-text method* of Bible study they will never develop a principle-based approach and *will always remain children in their understanding*. The method that rules in the coming years will determine whether the Adventist church *will continue to grow and mature or whether it will always remain in an infantile state*."[3]

Statements of this kind from responsible thought leaders of the church raise some crucial questions.

Critical Questions. What do the expressions "principle-based approach" and "literal approach" really mean? How are these approaches different from the two conflicting methods that have polarized Adventist scholars for three decades and more—liberalism's higher criticism (the historical-critical method) and the traditional Adventist plain reading of Scripture (the historical-grammatical method)?[4]

Should one accept as an established fact the assertion that some parts of the world church are more "mature" in their understanding of Scripture than others? If so, what is the nature of this "maturity"?

Can we explain the polarization between "the church of the West" and "the rest of the church" on certain theological issues on the basis of culture and some undefined concepts of principle versus literal methods of interpreting the Scriptures?

Finally, to what extent do conflicting approaches to Scripture contribute to the identity crisis in certain parts of the Adventist church? In short, what is really at stake in this crisis over biblical authority and biblical interpretation?

The Crisis of Identity

The editor of *Adventist Review* describes the crisis as "The Fragmenting of Adventism."[5] On the other hand, an unofficial Adventist publication hails this "fragmentation" as "A *Gathering* of Adventisms"—i.e., mainstream, historic, evangelical and progressive Adventisms.[6]

Still, *Christianity Today,* the largest evangelical magazine in the United States, peeked into our church recently and on seeing the distinct factions and theological conflicts between "traditionalist," "evangelical," "liberal," and "charismatic" Adventists in North America, perceptively concluded that our church is experiencing "an identity crisis."[7] This article notes that "the present confusion is in direct contrast to the confidence of Adventism's pioneers," who "knew exactly who they were. They were God's 'remnant church.' 'A special people, with a special message, for a special time!'"[8]

"What Is Going On?" Formerly, when someone asked "What is going on?" the answers were: "Jesus, our loving Savior, is coming very soon"; "our Lord and heavenly High Priest is transforming lives and bringing about revivals in our churches"; "the 'present truth' of the three angels' messages is being received in all parts of the world."

But today, when someone asks, "What is going on in Adventism?" the response often goes like this: "Some church scholars are challenging the distinctive doctrines of the church"; "some churches are rebelling against the decision of the worldwide church"; "some church leaders have lost the courage of biblical convictions"; "some 'reformers' are teaching that the church has become 'Babylon' or is in apostasy."

The replacement of optimism with pessimism in some parts of the world, together with the fragmentation of the church, are indications of Adventism's current crisis of identity. Our General Conference president recently observed: "In many of the more developed and sophisticated areas of the world, I sense that an increasingly secular value system is negatively impacting many of our members. I sense a *growing uncertainty about why we exist as a church and what our mission is.*"[9]

Our present identity crisis is not only about the *nature* of worldwide Seventh-day Adventism, but more significantly about the *future* of Seventh-day Adventism worldwide. The crisis is not just about whether it will remain a *united* church, but more importantly about whether there will be a *church* to be united. The crisis facing the church threatens to undermine the unity, identity, and mission of our church.

Response to the Crisis

The present volume, *Receiving the Word,* attempts to explain the root cause of the identity crisis and to explore how it relates to the conflicting views over biblical authority and interpretation.

Title of Book. Our title comes from Acts 17:11, where Paul commends the Berean Christians for their fidelity to the written Word. Their example, in that they "received the Word with all readiness of mind, and searched the Scriptures daily, whether those things were so" (Acts 17:11), suggests that there can be no useful *searching of the Scriptures* (i.e., no meaningful interpretation of the Bible) without first *receiving the Word* as God's inspired, trustworthy, and authoritative message.

This basic assumption of Christian theology appears in Article 1 of our "Fundamental Beliefs," which calls upon Seventh-day Adventists to accept the Holy Scriptures, the sixty-six books of the Old and New Testaments, as God's infallible and authoritative revelation of His will on every issue of doctrine and practice.

But there are disturbing indications that this important theological *foundation* of our church is slowly being chipped away. Already *cracks* in our theological foundation—our historic views regarding Scripture's inspiration, trustworthiness and authority—are evident in the challenges mounted from within against such doctrines as the substitutionary atonement of Christ, the sanctuary, the church as "the remnant," the Spirit of Prophecy, the second coming, and the Sabbath.

Another indication of the widening cracks is the confusion in our church over issues such as the Genesis creation account, homosexuality, abortion, polygamy, women's ordination, clean and unclean meats, Christian dress, and the use of alcohol.

These uncertainties about theological beliefs and practices may be traced to the inroads of higher criticism (the historical-critical method of biblical interpretation), which in recent decades has gained increasing acceptance among many of the church's thought-leaders.

General Unawareness. Unfortunately, many church members and leaders may not even be aware that our theological house (our doctrinal beliefs and lifestyle) is in trouble, let alone realize that the cause of the problem is due to cracks in our theological foundation (our view of, and approach to, inspired Scriptures).

One perceptive scholar explains why this often happens: "The problem is that most students of the Bible do not have the time to dig into the foundations of the various approaches [to the Bible]. We are tempted to adopt that approach to the Bible whose visible structure appeals to us, and to forget that, if we adopt a theology someone else has constructed without testing the foundation, we do so at our peril."[10]

Those who realize that cracks exist in our theological foundation generally make either of two ineffective responses to the problem.

1. Attitude of Indifference. Some exhibit "administrative ostrich-ism," burying their heads in the sand, pretending that the problem is not real, or even if real, that it will vanish by default or inaction.

This response forgets that such proverbial ostriches not only bury their heads in the sand but also lay eggs which will sooner or later hatch into many more ostriches. In other words, indifference breeds indifference, with fewer and fewer people willing to do something about the situation.

2. Cosmetic Changes. Instead of mending the cracks in the foundation, some give more attention to painting the crumbling walls with new and bright colors, re-arranging the furniture, changing the carpets and curtains, and installing modern technological gadgets to make the house more comfortable and "user-friendly." Thus, instead of our thought leaders abandoning the unbiblical method of higher criticism, some simply substitute new names for this scripturally-discredited method.[11]

The dangers of this kind of response are like those described in Jesus' parable of the man who built his house on the sand: "The rain came down, the streams rose, and the winds blew and beat against that house, and it fell with a great crash" (Matt 7:27 NIV).

An Alternative Response. This book does not recommend either of these two courses. Instead, we shall attempt to clear away the sand from the ostrich's head and also seek to go beyond the cosmetic changes—the theological furnishings, paint, and gadgets. We shall attempt digging through the dirt to the foundation—what scholars refer to as the assumptions or presuppositions—and discover the cracks that have resulted as otherwise talented architects of Adventist theology have slowly chipped away parts of the foundation.

In this effort, we shall seek to spotlight the conflicting methods of biblical interpretation currently operating in the church, illustrating them with representative published works of some thought leaders—works which are all in the public arena where they continue to have influence.[12] We shall also point out ways by which the crumbling foundations may be repaired.

Purpose of Book

General Objective. The apostle Peter urges Christians: "Always be prepared to give an answer to everyone who asks you to give the reason for the hope that you have. But do this with gentleness and respect" (1 Pet 3:15 NIV). *Receiving the Word* is one Bible student's answer to the crisis of biblical authority and interpretation in the Seventh-day Adventist church.

Thus, the book is not simply an attempt to correct misconceptions regarding the approach to Scriptures supposedly held by Seventh-day Adventists living outside regions where the church has "matured for a century and a half."[13] Rather, it is one Adventist's effort candidly to address a forbidden issue that has polarized North American Bible scholars for decades into "liberals" and "conservatives," a growing crisis that is being felt beyond the boundaries of North America.

In this respect, *Receiving the Word* may be viewed as a response to a recent call by the Adventist church to "develop and implement plans to teach the world membership principles of biblical interpretation," so that pastors and teachers may be encouraged "to make presentations defending the Bible as authority."[14]

Specific Objectives. We offer this volume, therefore, to readers with the following specific objectives:

(1) to create an awareness among Bible-believing Adventists—whether laymembers, students, or leaders—of the nature and implications of liberalism's approach to Scripture, so that they may be prepared to respond to it effectively;

(2) to offer some answers to our young people—including students of religion and theology—who, because of doubts and skepticism created by some of their pastors and Bible teachers, are presently confused about important issues regarding the authority and interpretation of the Scriptures; and

(3) to invite Adventist thought leaders who are convinced and crusading advocates of the contemporary liberal methodologies to reconsider their assumptions and attitudes regarding God's inspired Word.

Author's Intentions. Pursuing such an investigation has its risks, which may explain why some responsible scholars and leaders have steered away from this explosive issue. Is it not more sensible and expedient to go peacefully on with one's life and professional career than to jump into the midst of a theological storm?

There are times when silence is a betrayal of Christ and His cause. Such is the case with respect to the issue of biblical authority and interpretation. It may be politically expedient to remain silent; but how can the "theological watchmen of Zion" (cf. Ezek 3:17-21) explain their silence when the future of God's church is at stake? Can they remain silent when the historical-critical method continues to ruin the faith of innocent students in the classrooms and unsuspecting believers in the pews?

Following months of heart-searching, we decided to address this sensitive issue by offering a biblically persuasive alternative to some of the incorrect or inadequate answers from some contemporary thought-leaders. We do not offer this book as the last word by an Adventist on the subject of biblical hermeneutics. Rather, we intend simply to ascertain whether or not our theological foundations are still sound.

Believing still what we stated in the preface of *Searching the Scriptures,* that it is better to discuss an issue without settling it than to settle an issue without discussing it, and believing also that to disagree with friends is not to dishonor them, we pray that this work will not only clarify some of the hermeneutical issues behind the church's current crisis of identity, but will also provide some criteria for evaluating any new approach to biblical interpretation.

Organization

The nature of the subject addressed in *Receiving the Word* requires that readers not simply read the book, but that they study, deliberate, and act upon it. With this in view, I have arranged the main body in three major divisions.

The Main Body. Section I (Chapters 1-3) gives a wider background to the crisis over biblical authority and interpretation among Seventh-day Adventists. It defines the problem, illustrates the kinds of responses being offered, and outlines the choices available to Bible students.

Section II (Chapters 4-6) focuses on the Adventist scene, explaining the nature of the crisis by documenting the *what, who, why,* and *how* of the battle over the Word. It attempts to show why the new methods of interpretation are leading gradually to a repudiation of our historic Christian doctrines and practices, and why Bible-believing Adventists must faithfully contend for the Word. This section will likely generate interesting reactions from readers.

Section III (Chapters 7-12) offers a biblical alternative to the new approaches to Scripture. It provides answers to some specific questions that often surface in connection with discussions over the Bible, its transmission, translation, alleged internal contradictions, and interpretation. It concludes with challenges to all Bible-believing Adventists. In view of the nature of the material in Sections I and II, readers will find this section to be reassuring.

Source References. I have gathered the ideas reflected in *Receiving the Word* over a period of time from many springs of thought—including reading, interaction with students and teachers, conversations, correspondence, debates with several individuals, and observation at church and scholarly gatherings. At first, I did not always document the original sources for the ideas that I later adopted as my own. Thus, though I have tried to give proper credit for all quotations and ideas used, there are countless individuals whose thoughts I may have unconsciously echoed in the pages of this volume. If perchance I have used a quotation, sentence, thought, or expression of someone without giving due credit, I offer my heartfelt apologies—and thanks!

One final word. Occasional repetitions appear from one chapter to another, because in each place they augment new arguments. In the words of the Apostle Paul, "It is no trouble for me to write the same things to you again, and it is a safeguard for you" (Phil 3:1, NIV)!

Expectation

A critical work of any kind is hardly welcomed, even by those who advocate dialogue and objectivity in theological inquiry. Anyone who attempts to examine variant theological views critically *in the light of Scripture* is often branded divisive, strident, or unkind. This powerful intimidation factor has muffled the voices of many whose responsibility it is to uphold truth and expose error.

But is it really divisive, unkind, or unloving to challenge biblically inconsistent views?

Contrary to the assertions of today's champions of theological pluralism, the Bible forbids exchanging truth for superficial peace or unity; it prohibits substituting the popular and eloquent speech called silence for the proclamation of truth. Instead, the Bible encourages believers to "contend for the faith that was once for all entrusted to the saints" (Jude 3 NIV). It urges them to counteract false teaching and false teachers (1 Tim 1:3; 4:1, 6; Titus 1:9-11). And it calls upon Christians to uphold sound teaching (1 Tim 6:20; 2 Tim 1:13), if they are to preserve the "unity of faith" (Eph 4:13).

Thus, in epistles written *for public reading,* the apostle Paul occasionally exposed the false teachings of certain individuals (1 Tim 1:20; 2 Tim 2:17; 4:10; cf. Phil 4:2-3). John, the apostle of love, and Jude, the brother of our Lord Jesus Christ, also found it necessary to call attention to those who were departing from the teachings of the apostles (3 John 9-10; Jude). These scriptural evidences suggest to Bible-believing Christians the need to "Prove all things; [and] hold fast that which is good" (1 Thess 5:21).

The example of the Bereans is also noteworthy. They searched the Scriptures critically before accepting even the inspired theology of Paul (Acts 17:11).

When Paul commends them as noble Christians it suggests to us that "it is a praiseworthy thing to uphold God's truth and affirm those who accurately proclaim it. On the other hand, it is spiritually lethal to tolerate false doctrine and apostate teachers—and foolish not to know the difference. But the spirit of ignorant tolerance that plagues the church today often brands any attempt to scrutinize others' teaching as narrow-minded, unloving, or divisive. The flip side of tolerance of error is indifference to truth—and that is disastrous."[15]

Against this background of indifference to truth, *Receiving the Word* is being sent forth with a prayer that it will stimulate and encourage Christians to develop the Berean attitude to Scriptures—that is, to adopt only those theological methods and views which have passed the scrutiny of *biblical* investigation. Such an attitude refuses to succumb either to the flattery or the coercion of the theological spirit of our age.

At a time when scholars of theological pluralism are applauding the peaceful cohabitation of truth and error, and at a time when it has become politically expedient for church members and leaders to adopt postures of theological neutrality, Bible-believing Adventists must join Ellen G. White in insisting that *"light and darkness cannot harmonize. Between truth and error there is an irrepressible conflict. To uphold and defend the one is to attack and overthrow the other"* (*The Great Controversy*, p. 126).

Samuel Koranteng-Pipim
Berrien Springs, Michigan
October, 1996

NOTES

1. Although the term *fundamentalist* is quite elastic, today it is usually a "put-down" for Bible-believing Christians who reject the higher criticism of theological liberalism. Their "progressive" counterparts often perceive such Christians as anti-intellectual, reactionary, and authoritarian. James Barr's suggestion that the word *fundamentalism* connotes "narrowness, bigotry, obscurantism, and sectarianism" highlights this point (Barr, *Fundamentalism* [Philadelphia, Penn.: Westminster, 1977], p. 2).

2. Jim Walters, "General Conference Delegates Say NO on Women's Ordination," *Adventist Today*, July-August, 1995, p. 13, emphasis supplied. Walters is an editor of *Adventist Today*, an independent publication whose stated purpose is to follow "basic principles of ethics and canons of journalism," striving "for fairness, candor, and good taste."

3. J. David Newman, "Stuck in the Concrete," *Adventist Today*, July-August, 1995, p. 13, emphasis supplied. Newman last served as the editor of *Ministry*, "the international journal of the Seventh-day Adventist Ministerial Association."

4. The current editors of *Adventist Review* and *Ministry* have also suggested that two conflicting methods of interpretation—"principle-based approach" and "literal approach"—are operating in the church, although they do not attach undertones of cultural snobbery to their assertions. See William G. Johnsson, "The Old, the New, and the Crux," *Adventist Review*, General Conference Bulletin no. 7,

July 7, 1995, p. 3; Will Eva, "Interpreting the Bible: A Commonsense Approach," *Ministry,* March 1996, pp. 4-5; cf. Caleb Rosado, "How Culture Affects Our View of Scripture," *Spectrum,* December 1995, pp. 11-15. Rosado calls the two methods "principle/spirit approach" and "literal/letter" approach. Another author refers to the two conflicting approaches as a clash between the "contextual approach" and the "key-text approach" (Steve Case, "Thinking About Jewelry: What the Bible (Really) Says," in *Shall We Dance: Rediscovering Christ-Centered Standards,* ed. Steve Case [Riverside, Calif.: La Sierra University Press, 1996], pp. 184-193). For at least 30 years, Seventh-day Adventist scholars have been polarized into two camps—those who use the methods of higher criticism (the historical critical method) and those who remain faithful to the church's historic plain reading method of interpretation (the historical-grammatical method). Among those who have correctly articulated the issue are William H. Shea, "How Shall We Understand the Bible?" *Ministry,* March 1996, pp. 10-13; Robert K. McIver, "The Historical-Critical Method: The Adventist Debate," *Ministry,* March 1996, pp. 14-17. Thus, perceptive observers have justifiably wondered whether the recent "principle" and "literal" approaches are not new terms for an old conflict between the historical-critical method and the historical-grammatical method. Subsequent chapters in *Receiving the Word* will pursue this question further.

5.   William Johnsson, *The Fragmenting of Adventism* (Boise, Id.: Pacific Press, 1995). Johnsson discusses some ten issues that threaten Adventism with fragmentation.

6.   *Adventist Today,* January-February 1993, emphasis mine. This bimonthly publication is edited by Raymond Cottrell and James W. Walters. The phrase "A *Gathering* of Adventisms" is the cover title of this particular issue of *Adventist Today;* the emphasis is supplied by this writer to underscore the irony of how a "fragmentation" in the church (Johnsson) can be hailed as a "gathering" (Cottrell and Walters; see also their editorial comment on page 2 of this issue of *Adventist Today*).

7.   Kenneth R. Samples, "The Recent Truth About Seventh-day Adventism," *Christianity Today,* February 5, 1990, pp. 18-19.

8.   Ibid., p. 19.

9.   Robert S. Folkenberg, "When Culture Doesn't Count," *Ministry,* December 1995, p. 7, emphasis supplied.

10.   David R. Hall, *The Seven Pillories of Wisdom* (Macon, Ga.: Mercer University Press, 1990), p. vii.

11.   See note 4 above. More will be said of these in chapter 4.

12.   Those not familiar with scholarly discussions may question the legitimacy of citing and reviewing published *Adventist* works. However, references to these published materials should be seen as objective or scholarly citations, just as one would treat the works of authors like Rudolf Bultmann or Oswald Chambers, or any other theologian or minister. Taking issue with such published Adventist works is not the same as questioning the sincerity of the individuals whose works are cited; neither does it mean an expression of personal dislike for the authors whose works are being reviewed.

Readers are encouraged to consult the notes not only for the sources cited but, in some cases, also for counter views by other Adventist scholars. Although many more sources could have been cited to illustrate the cracks in our theological foundation, we have limited ourselves to a few works representative of a growing trend within the church.

13.   See notes 2 and 3. In earlier works we have addressed the spirit underlying this kind of statement. See the author's "The Triumph of Grace Over Race," *Adventists Affirm,* Fall 1995, pp. 35-49; "Racism and Christianity," *Dialogue* 7/1 (1995):12-15; "Saved By Grace and Living By Race: The Religion Called Racism," *Journal of the Adventist Theological Society* 5/2 (Autumn 1994):37-78.

14.   These are parts of the recommendations set forth in two important documents discussed by delegates at the 1995 General Conference session in Utrecht, the Netherlands. See "The Authority of Scripture," and "The Use of Scripture in the Life of the SDA Church," reproduced as Appendix A and B, respectively, in *Receiving the Word.*

15.   John MacArthur, Jr., *Our Sufficiency in Christ* (Dallas, Tex.: Word Publishing, 1991), p. 130, commenting on Acts 17:11.

Acknowledgments and Dedication

Acknowledgements

Receiving the Word distills my views on the crucial issue of biblical authority and interpretation, developed through interaction with others. I claim neither originality nor infallibility for it. It is simply an honest attempt by an inquiring Bible student to make sense of today's theological issues amid the confusing voices being echoed by some of our brightest and most articulate.

While taking full responsibility for the contents in this volume, I want to express my profound gratitude to the following individuals who in various ways have influenced my thought and temperament on fundamental issues of theology.

• To all the scholars whose views have come under review in this work. But for their critical questions, I would have taken for granted the serious efforts by our Adventist forebears in grounding our doctrines on a solid theological foundation—the Bible.

• To my teachers—especially Daniel Augsburger, Fernando Canale, Arthur Coetzee, Richard Davidson, Raoul Dederen, Hans LaRondelle, and William Shea. They modelled for me what is expected of a Seventh-day Adventist student of the Bible.

• To my friends and colleagues—Ganoune Diop, Ron du Preez, Victor Dyman, Martin Hannah, Frank Hasel, Roland Hill, Trust Ndlovu, Leslie Pollard, Denton Rhone, Elwin St. Rose, Carlos Steger, Winfried Vogel, Nathaniel Walemba, Janice Watson, and Oswald Williams (deceased). Their indomitable spirit in past debates taught me what is required in the battle of ideas.

• To my partners in evangelism—Paul Yeboah, Emmanuel Osei, and other leaders and members of the Ghanaian churches in North America and Europe. They have confirmed my belief that true Adventist theology, when proclaimed with conviction, results in revival and conversion.

• To the scores of readers of the different drafts of the book manuscript—men and women, leaders and lay members, teachers and students—for their input and helpful critiques. Special appreciation goes to those who have publicly endorsed the book; though the views of each may be expected to vary on a few specifics, they have all found this work worthy of their commendation.

• To the students, faculty, staff, and all participants in our Summer 1996 evangelistic/revival meetings on the campus of the Adventist Seminary of West

Africa (ASWA), Nigeria—whose spiritual support hastened the publication of this work.

• Finally, a word of appreciation to my family—Becky, Jessica, Ellen, and Samuel, Jr., who have demonstrated to me the meaning of the favorite Adventist phrase, "Here is the *patience* of the saints. . . ." Their spirit of sacrifice assures me that, indeed, "those who in everything make God first and last and best are the happiest people in the world" (*My Life Today,* p. 161).

Dedication

Receiving the Word is dedicated to five Seventh-day Adventists who have played significant roles in upholding God's Word, even against tremendous odds. Of these, three are resting in the hope of the resurrection, while two are still laboring for the Lord.

• The late Elder Enoch de Oliveira of Brazil last served the church as a General Conference vice-president; he represents the courageous church administrators who are faithfully guarding the Word, no matter the political cost.

• The late Dr. Gerhard F. Hasel of Germany was the dean of the Seventh-day Adventist Theological Seminary at Andrews University and the director of its Ph.D. program; he represents the faithful scholars of the church who contribute greatly to scholarship without surrendering the Word.

• Elder Paul K. Nsiah of Ghana, West Africa, is a dedicated church member who has been instrumental in the growth and leadership of the church in that part of the world; he represents the gallant laymen around the world who are fearlessly holding church leaders and scholars accountable to the Word.

• The late Larisa Petrovna Ivanisheva of Ukraine was one of the faithful believers who kept the faith alive during the difficult days of Soviet communism by preserving, secretly copying, and distributing copies of the Bible and the Spirit of Prophecy; she represents our God-fearing and devoted lay women worldwide who would rather die than dishonor the Lord and His Word.

• Elder Charles D. Brooks of the United States, a dedicated pastor and evangelist, is a field secretary of the General Conference. At a time when it has become fashionable for preachers to turn to secular psychology, entertainment, politics, rhetoric, and all the latest fads of contemporary culture, he has set an example for Christians around the world by courageously preaching the Word.

What is the nature of Adventism's crisis over biblical authority and interpretation? Why did Bible-believing Christians throughout the centuries accept the Bible as God's inspired Word? How are liberals assaulting the Bible today, and what are the foundations of contemporary higher criticism?

I. BACKGROUND OF THE CRISIS

Chapter One

Crisis Over the Word

These are exciting days for Seventh-day Adventists. Inspiring mission reports at the General Conference session. Progress in God's work worldwide. Growth of the church, even in the industrialized areas of Australia, Europe and North America. Gathering of God's people from "every nation, and kindred, and tongue, and people." Thousands everyday heeding the voice from heaven saying, "Come out of Babylon, my people."

These are, indeed, thrilling days for Adventists around the world.

But alongside revival and rapid growth come disturbing indications that many Seventh-day Adventists, at least in the industrialized world, are facing an identity crisis.[1] The church's most distinctive theological doctrines are being challenged—from within. Uncertainty prevails over the church's unique identity and mission, and its worldwide organizational unity is being defied. This is the crisis facing the church today. But why?

The "Liberal Left" and The "Independent Right"

The Seventh-day Adventist church is caught in the middle of a crossfire of attacks from the "liberal left" and the "independent right." The liberals, often educated and influential, operate within the church structure; the independents, appearing spiritual and orthodox, operate from without by establishing organizations and structures of their own.

Both groups are critical of the church because they believe that today's Adventism is not what it should be. So both attempt to "rehabilitate" the church.

In order to make Adventism "relevant" for this generation, the liberals seek to "liberate" the church from its alleged "fundamentalist" doctrines and nineteenth-century Victorian lifestyle. In their attempt to bring a "revival" to the church, the independents desire to "reform" the church from its ways of "apostasy." The liberals reinterpret Adventism's historic doctrines; the independents oppose any tampering with the Adventist pillars.

Regarding lifestyle or conduct, the liberals emphasize "love," "acceptance," and "inclusiveness." The independents stress "law," "perfectionism," and "uniqueness."

When the liberals on the left speak about the Adventist church, they often seem to see only the independents on the right; and when the independents discuss the church, one could almost believe that all members of the church are liberals.

The independent right is often perceived as siphoning off tithe from the church; the liberal left, which includes many church workers, is paid with tithe money while it often appears to be challenging, if not undermining, the beliefs and practices of the church.

The activities of both groups are often encouraged by the silence and indifference of mainstream Adventism.

Although in recent times an effort has been made to inform church members (not always accurately) about the activities of the independent right,[2] little has been done to alert unwary Adventists to the influence of the entrenched liberal left. Ellen G. White stated that "we have far more to fear from within than from without" (*Selected Messages,* 1:122). If this applies to our current situation, then the mainstream Seventh-day Adventist church, caught in the crossfire, should be more concerned about the liberals within than about the independents without.

The "crisis over the Word" is really a clash between two versions of Adventism that currently operate *within* the church: mainstream Adventism and liberal Adventism.

This book, *Receiving the Word,* is a response to liberal Adventism's challenge to the mainstream Adventist faith and lifestyle. It is this challenge, and the sophisticated manner in which it is articulated by some leading thought leaders, that is creating an identity crisis in the church.

A Crisis of Identity

Recently an Adventist professor of religion captured well the identity crisis plaguing the church. She began with this thought-provoking question: "How seriously should Adventists take apocalyptic books like Daniel, Revelation, and *The Great Controversy?*" Echoing the concerns of some church scholars and members that apocalypticists (i.e., those holding to unique doctrines about end-time events) "are embarrassing to have around," she continued, "We may even wish to revise our apocalyptic stance. Aren't we triumphalistic in seeing ourselves as the one true church? Hasn't the Sabbath/Sunday issue, so relevant when *The Great Controversy* was written, become obsolete in today's secular society? Haven't Adventists erred in focusing on the pope while neglecting to take a stand against oppressive dictators of the 20th century? Shouldn't we concentrate on the modern 'beasts' of ethnic hatred, oppression of minorities, and abuse of the ecosystem? Perhaps apocalyptic, with its sensationalism, represents an immature stage of Christianity. Perhaps we should replace it with the gospel of love, acceptance, and forgiveness."[3]

No evidence in the article suggests that its author shares the views of those raising these questions. But as we shall demonstrate in a later chapter, there are troubling signs that some within our membership do want us to *reinterpret* our distinctive doctrines to accommodate contemporary secular thought.

For example, in a book endorsed by several thought leaders of the church, a chaplain and teacher in an Adventist university urges the church to consider seriously the need to embrace the "new ecumenism" of the charismatic movement. In his opinion, Adventist "remnant" theology, which is "more firmly ingrained in the Adventist psyche because of Ellen White's powerful endorsement," leads to "ethnocentrism," "xenophobia," and "paranoia."[4]

On the basis of naturalistic interpretations of scientific data, a retired General Conference vice-president and educator recently announced his belief that animals lived *and died for millions of years* before human beings came into existence. He asserted that his new belief "is a big step for a Seventh-day Adventist when you are taught that every form of life came into existence in six days."[5]

Various Adventist authors are challenging the necessity of Christ's substitutionary death for sinners, the relevance of the sanctuary doctrine, the Spirit of Prophecy, and the belief in the nearness of Christ's second coming. Still others are embracing homosexuality, the moderate use of alcohol, the eating of unclean foods, and the wearing of jewelry as acceptable lifestyle elements for Adventists.[6] These authors and scholars suggest that the historic beliefs and practices of the Seventh-day Adventist church, indeed, its self-understanding as God's end-time remnant, represent "an immature stage of Christianity."

What has led to these conclusions?

Crisis Over the Word

It is far too simple to claim, as some do, that our varying positions on abortion, women's ordination, homosexuality, polygamy, divorce, war, and racism have arisen merely because of our different cultural or educational backgrounds.[7] Rather, the fundamental issue concerns the way we interpret the Bible.

The crisis facing contemporary Adventism is not necessarily due to a clash of two cultures—"the church of the West" and "the rest of the church." Rather, it is a crisis over *biblical hermeneutics,* the appropriate principles for interpreting the Bible. Recently this crisis has spawned much new hermeneutical terminology in our church: casebook vs. codebook, principle vs. literal approach, contextual vs. key text approach, dynamic vs. rigid approach, principle/spirit vs. literal/letter, historical-*critical* method vs. historical-*grammatical* method, and perhaps other terms as well.

In addressing the issue of Bible interpretation (hermeneutics), Seventh-day Adventists are faced with only two options: (1) the historic Adventist approach to Scripture, which recognizes that the Bible is fully inspired, trustworthy, and authoritative, and (2) the contemporary liberal approaches to the Bible, which deny the full inspiration, reliability and authority of Scriptures.

Although these two approaches are miles apart, they are both agreed in their rejection of a third approach—namely, the "proof-text" method of interpretation. It may be helpful to explain why.

Proof-Text Method of Interpretation

Simply put, a proof-text is a verse or a longer passage used to establish a point. If the passage in its context supports the point, such use is legitimate.

When we refer to a proof-text *method,* however, we mean using an isolated text *arbitrarily* to prove one's own point. Such a proof-text approach emphasizes the practical, devotional application of Scripture to the interpreter's needs. The student goes to the Bible to search for some texts to support or prove positions on which he has already made up his mind. This method is inadequate because it fails to take into account the historical and literary context of each passage of Scripture.

Some Examples. The proof-text method takes passages out of context in order to feed them into the world of one's personal preoccupations. One writer cites the example of a seminary student who, after accepting a call to start his ministry in the *North* of England, later received a more attractive offer to teach in *South* Wales. Earnestly seeking ways to withdraw from his previous commitment, he read the words of Isaiah 43:6, "I will say to the north, Give up," and concluded that God was providentially telling him to "give up" his commitment to serve in the *North* of England! Of course, if he had read the next line of that verse, he would have heard the continuation of God's "providential message." It reads: ". . . and to the south, Keep not back"!

This illustrates the old maxim that "a text without its context becomes a pretext." The proof-text method of Bible interpretation *fails to consider seriously the historical context of a given passage.* Instead of reading the entire passage in which the texts were found, the interpreter simply chooses several key phrases that coincide with his concerns.

Second, *it ignores the literary context in which a given text is found* by taking the Bible in a "literalistic" manner. Whereas a sound method of interpretation will recognize the different kinds of literature and idioms in the Bible, a proof-text method reads the Bible naively. For example, it fails to realize that since the story about the rich man and Lazarus is a parable, it cannot be taken as an event that actually happened. The proof-text method also fails to recognize that the Bible exhibits other literary features, such as poetry (e.g., Psalms, Proverbs, etc.), symbolisms (as found in apocalyptic books, e.g., Daniel, Ezekiel, Zechariah, and Revelation), and idioms, that require careful interpretation.

Third, the proof-text method *approaches biblical interpretation superficially.* Instead of engaging in a responsible and painstaking study of Scriptures, those adopting this method take the easy route, sneaking foreign meanings into a text to obtain a desired response. Often, those resorting to this method are content with studying the Bible only in a particular translation (e.g., the King James Version, Revised Standard Version, New International Version, etc.), with little desire to consult either the original languages in which the Bible was written, or other translations, or even the understanding of the text gained by other godly Christians who also have wrestled with the same kinds of issues.

The proof-text approach to Scripture *can lead to misguided conclusions.* You probably have heard the story of the man who adopted such an approach to seek the will of God in a major decision of his life. Unwilling to engage in the painstaking effort of studying the Bible in its historical and grammatical context as the basis for drawing valid applications for his situation, he decided to close his eyes, open his Bible at random, prayerfully put his finger down, and get guidance from whatever verse his finger landed on. His first try came up with "Judas went out and hanged himself" (Matt 27:5). Finding these words unhelpful, he tried again and this time got "Go, and do thou likewise" (Luke 10:37). In desperation he tried one more time. The text he found was: "That thou doest, do quickly" (John 13:27).

This story may not be true, but it aptly illustrates the dangers inherent in the proof-text method. Though this approach takes the Bible as God's inspired, trustworthy and authoritative message for all people—a foundational assumption which every Bible-believing Christian must share—yet the proof-text method fails to "rightly divide the word of truth" (2 Tim 2:15). It looks for meaning in Scripture not by probing the historical-grammatical context, but by discarding it.

Correct biblical hermeneutics seeks to discover the original meaning of Scripture in its proper context and to draw out principles for contemporary application. We must always read what is there in the text, not read into the text our own presuppositions. Bringing out from the text what is already there is called *exposition;* the technical name is *exegesis.* Reading into the text one's opinions, ideas, or assumptions is known as *imposition;* the technical term is *eisegesis.*

Not a Legitimate Approach. Because of the proof-text method's inadequacies, no serious Seventh-day Adventist Bible student accepts this method as legitimate. This is why, in the present *crisis over the Word* in the church, proponents of the two competing methods have rightly rejected the proof-text method of biblical interpretation.

These two methods to which we shall now direct our attention—mainstream Adventism's plain reading of Scripture and contemporary liberalism's historical-critical method—seek an understanding of Scripture that takes into account the historical and literary contexts of the Bible. But as we pointed out earlier, these two approaches differ in their views regarding the full inspiration, trustworthiness, and authority of the Bible.

The Cause of the Hermeneutical Crisis

To understand the cause of the hermeneutical crisis—the crisis over the principles and methods of Bible interpretation—it may be helpful to present a potential problem from Scripture and show how adherents of the two conflicting approaches (the mainstream Adventist approach and liberalism's historical-critical method) are likely to respond.

The Quail Problem. Most Christians tend to skip over the details of the "quail story" in the Bible, but those details can present a challenge to serious Bible students. Numbers 11 records how, in response to the cries of the wandering Israelites for meat, God provided so many quails to be eaten that in one month the meat would virtually come out of their nostrils and become "loathsome" to them. The quails are reported as covering territory extending a day's journey on each side of the camp—an area some forty miles across, and two cubits (about three feet) high above the ground (Num 11:4-23, 31-35).

Are the details in this quail story trustworthy? Or is the Bible simply teaching that God miraculously sustained Israel in the wilderness? Should we consider all the information recorded in the account as inspired, or are some things in the account not inspired?

Similar questions also confront Christians on other matters, such as the issue of the Genesis creation account. When the Bible says God created the world in six literal days, is the statement trustworthy? Or do the Scriptures simply seek to teach us *Who* is the ultimate Creator, not necessarily *how* He created and *how long* it took? Shall we accept the *principle* that God is the Creator but discard the *literal* six-day creation as uninspired, culturally conditioned, an un-scientific myth, or even a minor error?

Compounding the Issue. Regarding the quail, critics of the Bible often raise "troubling" issues regarding the sheer number of birds involved (Num 11:31). Assuming that one's understanding of the Bible is correct in maintaining that God caused the birds to be piled up three feet deep over an area of 1600 square miles (40 miles x 40 miles), Bible-believers are faced with two major problems.

First, since some of the birds would die from the sheer pressure of those lying on top of them, how could Israel cope with the resulting health hazards and environmental problems? Second, and more significant, is the problem of the number of quails for each Israelite to consume during the thirty days. Assuming that the birds were distributed equally to each Israelite, each person would have had to eat about 52,100 bushels during the month. This works out to approximately 578 bushels of quails per person *per meal,* three times a day for each of the thirty days! This is equivalent to eating some 742 roasted turkeys at each meal![8]

Clarifying the Issues. Assuming that we have not misread the biblical account and that our calculations are correct, are we really to believe that each Israelite ate 578 bushels of quail meat at each meal? If not, does it mean that while we may accept the fact that God provided quails for the wandering pilgrims, we cannot trust the reliability of the data? The Bible says, "And there went forth a wind from the Lord and brought quails from the sea, and let them fall by the camp, as it were a day's journey on this side, and as it were a day's journey on the other side, round about the camp, and as it were two cubits high upon the face of the earth" (Num 11:31).

Should we accept the *fact* of God's providence of quail but not the associated *details?* Is the Bible fully inspired or partially inspired—that is, did God inspire the Bible writers to record these details, even though they appear to us unrealistic?

The answers one gives to such questions determine whether one will uphold the long-standing Adventist approach to Scripture or the contemporary liberal approaches, collectively known as the historical-critical method. These two approaches to Scripture have become the focal point of Adventism's crisis over biblical authority and interpretation. Responses to the quail story, to which we will return, illustrate the two major attitudes regarding biblical authority and interpretation.

The Historic Adventist Approach: Plain Reading of Scripture

The mainstream Seventh-day Adventist church consists of millions of people around the world who have accepted Jesus as their Savior and Lord, the Bible as His inspired and solely-authoritative Word, the church as God's end-time remnant movement, and the writings of Ellen G. White as a manifestation of the true gift of prophecy. As a summary of their doctrinal beliefs, they uphold the "Fundamental Beliefs" of Seventh-day Adventists, which have been expounded in the book *Seventh-day Adventists Believe . . .: A Biblical Exposition of 27 Fundamental Beliefs.*[9]

Method: Plain Reading. Seventh-day Adventists have always adopted the approach advanced by the Protestant reformers, in which they sought the simple, plain, direct, or ordinary sense of Scripture. Technically, this method of studying Scriptures is known as the *historical-grammatical method,* a term dating to 1788.[10]

Until the eighteenth century Enlightenment, when higher criticism of the Bible led some skeptics to question the full inspiration and trustworthiness of Scriptures, the overwhelming majority of Bible-believing Christians followed this "plain sense" method of interpreting the Bible. The name "historical-grammatical method" describes the approach that focuses attention on a detailed analysis of the biblical text in accordance with the original language and historical situation.

Though the term may seem new to some readers, it represents the Adventist church's historic practice of interpreting Scripture according to its simple, literal, plain, direct, or ordinary sense. The specific details of this historical-grammatical method are spelled out in a 1986 General Conference Annual Council document called "Methods of Bible Study," published in the *Adventist Review* of January 22, 1987, and reprinted here in Appendix C. Opposite to "historical-grammatical" is "historical-critical," a relatively new term for what was long known as "higher criticism."

Assumptions About the Bible. Adventism's plain reading of Scripture (the historical-grammatical approach) recognizes that the Bible is (a) fully inspired, (b) absolutely trustworthy, (c) solely authoritative, and (d) thoroughly consistent in all its parts, since it comes ultimately from one divine mind.

Goal in Interpretation. Relying upon the Holy Spirit's illumination, believers using this method seek to ascertain the meaning of Scripture by carefully discovering the historical, literary and grammatical identity of a given biblical passage in its immediate historical context and in the wider context of the whole Bible. Having thus understood what a given passage meant in its historical context, the interpreter makes a responsible application to the contemporary situation. This method should *not* be confused with a "literalistic" approach which does not take into consideration the historical, grammatical, and literary (e.g., poetry, parable, symbol, epistle, etc.) characteristics found in the Bible.

Adventists and Quails. Regarding the "quail problem," those who adopt the historic Adventist approach insist that the Bible is fully inspired and trustworthy even in the details about the quails. Therefore, in the face of an unresolved difficulty, rather than maintaining that the Bible writer was mistaken in his figures, *we* carefully re-study the biblical account to see if we have not erred in *our* interpretation. We shall explore the quail problem more fully shortly, to show in detail how a Bible-believing student may approach it.

The Contemporary Liberal Approach: The Historical-Critical Method

Alongside historic Adventism's plain reading of Scripture are also the methods of theological liberalism, collectively known as the historical-*critical* method. At the time the Seventh-day Adventist church emerged in the nineteenth century, this approach to Scripture was already in full bloom, going by the name "higher criticism." One Adventist scholar correctly observed, "Known as 'higher criticism,' right up to the early 1970s the historical-critical method was perceived as highly suspect by almost all Adventists who were aware of it."[11] We shall use the terms interchangeably throughout this book.

Two Kinds of Liberalism. Since higher criticism is the method of liberalism, it may be helpful to note that two kinds of liberalism operate in Christian churches: (1) classical (radical) liberalism and (2) moderate (progressive) liberalism.

Classical liberalism denies God's supernatural intervention in the world; hence, it denies the virgin birth, the bodily resurrection, the penal substitutionary atonement of Christ, miracles, etc. *Because of classical liberalism's anti-supernatural assumptions, it cannot accept the Bible's claim to be divinely inspired by God.* The Bible is "inspired" in the sense that Shakespeare is inspired; it is an inspiring book that reflects the religious expressions of certain ancient people. All the miracles in the Bible are myths designed to teach truths. Because of this naturalistic outlook, liberal scholars in conservative churches *cannot* be liberals in the classical or radical sense; they choose moderate liberalism.

Unlike classical liberalism, *moderate liberalism* attracts some scholars in Bible-believing conservative churches, who present themselves as "moderates" because they perceive themselves as standing between the "extremism of the left" (classical liberalism) and "the extremism of the right" (which they label as "fundamentalism" or "ultra conservativism"). Although moderate liberals reject classical liberalism's outright denial of supernatural events in the Bible, they nevertheless *endorse liberalism's skepticism regarding the full inspiration, trustworthiness, and authority of the Bible.* In their attitude toward the Bible, the liberalisms of both the moderate and classical stripe are basically the same; they differ only in degree. Because moderate liberalism does not accept the full authority, authenticity, historicity, and reliability of the Bible, its followers rely on the methods of classical liberalism to determine which parts of the Bible are inspired and trustworthy.

Liberalism's Method. Both forms of liberalism deny the full inspiration of the Bible, choosing to approach Scripture "like any other book." In doing so, liberalism offers a number of "scientific" methods collectively called the *historical-critical method.*[12] Although the roots of contemporary higher criticism go back as far as the seventeenth century, the nineteenth-century German theologian and historian Ernst Troeltsch (1865-1923) holds the distinction of formulating the cardinal principles of the historical-critical method.[13]

The historical-critical method consists of such diverse and often conflicting approaches as "historical criticism," "literary-source criticism," "form criticism," "redaction criticism," "comparative-religion criticism," "structural criticism," etc.[14] By employing these approaches, liberalism seeks to elucidate the true meaning of the Bible.

Both classical and moderate liberalism employ today's higher criticism; they differ only in how far they go in denying explicit biblical teaching. Moderate liberalism, the kind found in conservative Bible-believing churches, believes that it can employ the methods of classical liberalism without accepting its anti-supernatural presuppositions. But moderate liberalism and classical liberalism are basically the same in their methods of approaching Scripture.

Assumptions. Unlike the traditional Adventist approach, the higher-critical methods assume that: (a) the Bible is not fully inspired (i.e., some parts of the Bible are more inspired than others[15]); (b) the Bible is not fully trustworthy (because of alleged discrepancies, contradictions, and mistakes); (c) the Bible is not absolutely authoritative in all that it teaches or touches upon (portions allegedly shaped by the personal or cultural prejudices of the writers and their times are "uninspired" and not binding on us); and (d) because of the Bible's many human writers, there is "diversity" in Scripture (i.e., pluralism or conflicting theologies in the Bible).

Goal of Interpretation. Relying upon "reason dialoging with Spirit" or "sanctified imagination," proponents of contemporary higher criticism seek to *reconstruct* the meaning of Scripture by *recreating* the real-life situations, the various socio-cultural elements that allegedly shaped the biblical text in a long evolutionary development from its earliest stages to its present form. In some cases, they may attempt to draw applications ("positive principles") for our time.

Liberals and Quail. The two kinds of liberals are likely to respond in slightly different ways to the quail story.

On the one hand, *classical* (or radical) liberalism, denying any possibility of miracle, rejects as a myth the account of God's provision of quails. At best, it will reinterpret the miracle and reconstruct the biblical account along this line: "A group of nomadic tribes of pre-historic Israel (numbering far less than the 600,000 figure given in the Bible), while wandering in the wilderness, came across a few migrating birds which had paused to rest for the night. Seeing this phenomenon for possibly the first time, the Israelites attributed it to their God and exaggerated the number of birds 'rained down' to highlight their God's omnipotence."

On the other hand, *moderate* liberals accept the miracle of God in providing quails. But because of such problems as the 578 bushels per meal per person and the environmental hazard, they may discount the accuracy of the story. They are likely to argue that Christians should not be concerned about *how* God provided the quails. The important point in the story, they would say, is that God did provide food for His people, a truth that is valid even though the details about it may not be trustworthy. The underlying assumption is that some parts of the Bible are inspired while others are not.

Although moderate liberals differ from classical liberals in their attitudes toward miracles, they both share a skeptical attitude toward the full inspiration and trustworthiness of Scripture. In order to arrive at a more "realistic," "objective" or "scientific" understanding of the quail story, they both employ liberalism's historical-critical method.

This manner of addressing the "difficulty" in the quail story finds expression also in other issues, such as the Genesis creation account, the universality of Noah's flood, the account of the Exodus, the question of God's showing a real sanctuary to Moses as the model upon which he was to construct Israel's tabernacle, the veracity of the four gospel writers in reporting the same events, etc. In short, a misunderstanding about the nature of the Bible's inspiration, trustworthiness, authority, and interpretation influences one's views about other doctrines of the Bible.

Historic Adventism and Contemporary Liberalism

Various expressions in use today disguise the conflict between liberal and historic Adventist approaches to Bible interpretation. These expressions, as we noted earlier, include: casebook vs. codebook approach; principle vs. literal approach; contextual vs. key text approach; dynamic vs. rigid approach; principle/spirit vs. literal/letter approach; Christ-centered vs. fundamentalist approach; and many more. But inasmuch as the hermeneutical crisis facing the church threatens to undermine our basic doctrines and lifestyle, Adventists must understand the real issues.

Similarities and Differences. Both the historic Adventist approach and the contemporary liberal approaches seek to understand, through a careful study of the historical setting, literary characteristics, grammar, syntax, etc., what Scripture meant to its original recipients. Both also apply Scripture's message to contemporary situations. They differ not only in *how* they accomplish their common goal of elucidating the meaning of Scripture, but more importantly, in their assumptions or presuppositions regarding the nature of Scripture itself.

One knowledgeable Adventist scholar has summarized the difference between these two approaches: "The historical-critical scholar comes to the [biblical] text with a natural bias against the historicity of the events described therein. The historico[-]grammatical scholar comes to the text with a natural bias in favor of the historicity of the events described therein. How, then, shall the matter be settled? There should be a neutral ground upon which the matters involved could be examined dispassionately and objectively. *Unfortunately, there is not.*"[16]

Yet, in spite of the fact that even some reputable non-Adventist scholars have found the use of today's higher-critical methodologies to be "an illusion,"[17] "secular and profane,"[18] and even "bankrupt,"[19] some Adventist Bible scholars believe they can reasonably use a little of the historical-critical method without adopting the naturalistic presuppositions on which the method is founded[20]—a claim to which Eta Linnemann responded bluntly: "One can no more be a *little* historical-critical than a *little* pregnant."[21] Linnemann, by the way, is unquestionably a world-class expert in, and a former advocate of, the historical-critical method.[22]

Quail Revisited. We promised to return to the quail story and look at it using the historic Adventist approach, the perspective of faith rather than of doubt. This approach rejects liberalism's skepticism regarding the full inspiration and trustworthiness of the Bible account. Heeding Mrs. White's counsel and example, its practitioners "take the Bible just as it is, as the Inspired Word," and they "believe its utterances in an entire Bible" (*Selected Messages,* 1:17). If they find difficulties they cannot immediately resolve, rather than considering them as mistakes or exaggerations by the Bible writers, they prayerfully seek guidance from the Holy Spirit to open their minds to see the divine truthfulness of the Scriptures.

Regarding the quail, the Bible simply states: "And there went forth a wind from the Lord, and brought quails from the sea, and let them fall by the camp, as it were a day's journey on this side, and as it were a day's journey on the other side, round about the camp, and as it were two cubits high upon the face of the earth" (Num 11:31). Notice that the Bible doesn't say that the quails were packed solid, or piled up two cubits (three feet) *deep,* from ground up, over a territory forty miles across. Rather, Scripture says that the birds were brought "two cubits *high* upon the face of the earth." The New International Version translates it, "Now a wind . . . brought them down all around the camp to about three feet *above the ground,* as far as a day's walk in any direction." The Bible is merely saying that instead of the birds flying so high that they were out of reach, God brought them so low—about three feet above ground level—that anyone could take as many as he wanted (note Num 11:32).

All the mathematical calculations showing that each Israelite had to eat some 578 bushels of quail meat per meal and all the worry about environmental hazards resulting from the carcasses of tons of birds are misdirected. The "troubling problems" raised about the quail story do not reside in the text but in the minds of critics who read the Bible superficially. Ellen White may have been referring to such situations when she wrote about the dangers of presenting the works of infidel authors to students of the Bible: "Scientific research becomes misleading, because its discoveries are misinterpreted and perverted. The word of God is compared with the supposed teachings of science, and is made to appear uncertain and untrustworthy. Thus the seeds of doubt are planted in the minds of the youth, and in time of temptation they spring up. *When faith in God's word is lost, the soul has no guide, no safeguard.* The youth are drawn into paths which lead away from God and from everlasting life" (*Christ's Object Lessons,* p. 41).

The simple resolution of the quail problem should encourage us always to trust the Word as God's inspired revelation, even if we face apparent difficulties. "The Bible is a book which has been refuted, demolished, overthrown, and exploded more times than any other book you ever heard of. Every little while somebody starts up and upsets this book; and it is like upsetting a solid cube of granite. It is just as big one way as the other; and when you have upset it, it is right side up, and when you overturn it again, it is right side up still. Every little while somebody blows up the Bible; but when it comes down, it always lights upon its feet, and runs faster than ever through the world."[23]

Moderate Liberalism: A Challenge to Adventism

The greatest challenge facing the Seventh-day Adventist church does not come from the *independent right* who operate from without, but rather from the *liberal left* who are working from *within*. These moderate liberals seek to redefine historic Adventist beliefs according to their new views of the Bible.

The Church's Challenge. We must be clear about it. The crisis of identity in the Seventh-day Adventist church is a crisis over Bible interpretation. It arises from the fact that some in our ranks believe they can safely use elements of the historical-critical method without adopting the naturalistic presuppositions upon which the method was founded. However, in the words of one non-Adventist scholar, the attempt to do so is "as futile and absurd an undertaking as eating ham with Jewish presuppositions."[24]

Indeed, as some of our Adventist scholars have begun using the higher critical approaches of liberal theology, the church has seen challenges to its distinctive truths: the prophetic significance of 1844, the necessity and relevance of the sanctuary doctrine, the inspiration of Ellen G. White, a literal six-day creation, the necessity of Christ's substitutionary atonement for sinners, and the self-understanding of the Seventh-day Adventist church as God's end-time remnant. At the same time, the church has been thrown into turmoil over abortion, polygamy, divorce and remarriage, women's ordination, and homosexuality.

In the coming days, the Seventh-day Adventist church will be focusing on the issues of biblical authority and interpretation. Reading the Bible through one or the other of the two basic hermeneutical lenses—Adventism's plain reading of Scripture or the higher criticism of contemporary liberalism—will result in either a clear *perception* or in a blind *deception* regarding the Bible's message. Bible-believing Adventists must look beyond the fancy labels and claims, inquiring to what extent these new approaches uphold the Bible as fully inspired, trustworthy and the sole authoritative norm for every doctrine and practice. Such a test will uncover the foundations and ultimate destinations of the new methods of biblical interpretation. It will also reveal whether the new approaches will result in either *trusting the Word* or in *doubting the Word*. Subsequent pages in this book will explore this issue in greater depth.

NOTES

1. The president of the General Conference stated this concern recently: "In many of the more developed and sophisticated areas of the world, I sense that an increasingly secular value system is negatively impacting many of our members. I sense a *growing uncertainty about why we exist as a church and what our mission is.*" See Robert S. Folkenberg, "When Culture Doesn't Count," *Ministry,* December 1995, p. 7, emphasis supplied.

2. See, for example, the North American Division's *Issues: The Seventh-day Adventist Church and Certain Private Ministries* (Silver Spring, Md.: North American Division, 1993). This work takes issue with the activities of private organizations such as Hope International, Hartland Institute, Prophecy Countdown, Inc., and Steps to Life. For a response to the above work, see Hope International's *Issues Clarified: A Clarification of Issues: The Seventh-day Adventist Church and Certain Private Ministries* (Eatonville, Wash.: Hope International, 1993); cf. Hartland Institute's *Report and Appeal of Hartland Institute to Seventh-day Adventist Leadership and Worldwide Membership* (Rapidan, Va.: Hartland Institute, 1993). Although some independent self-supporting ministries are often lumped with the independent right, readers should understand that there are many legitimate independent ministries whose goals and methods complement the work of the mainstream church.

3. Beatrice Neall, "Apocalyptic—Who Needs It?" *Spectrum* 23/1 (May 1993):46.

4. Steven G. Daily, *Adventism for a New Generation* (Portland/Clackamas, Ore.: Better Living Publishers, 1993), pp. 312-315. Because this book has received endorsement from prominent thought leaders of the church—administrators and educators—chapter 5 of *Receiving the Word* pays closer attention to this work. For a helpful corrective to the challenge to Adventism's remnant doctrine, see Clifford Goldstein's *The Remnant: Biblical Reality or Wishful Thinking?* (Boise, Id.: Pacific Press, 1994).

5. Richard Hammill, "Journey of a Progressive Believer," transcript of a talk given to an Association of Adventist Forums convention, Seattle, Washington, October 13, 1989, cited by James L. Hayward, "The Many Faces of Adventist Creationism: '80-'95," *Spectrum* 25/3 (March 1996):27-28. See also Richard Hammill's other works: "Fifty Years of Creationism: The Story of an Insider," *Spectrum* 15/2 (August 1984):32-45; "The Church and Earth Science," *Adventist Today,* September-October 1994, pp. 7, 8; *Pilgrimage: Memoirs of An Adventist Administrator* (Berrien Springs, Mich.: Andrews University Press, 1992).

6. In chapter 5 of this book we shall document some of the sophisticated ways in which the historic Adventist doctrines and practices are being undermined.

7. For example, see Jack W. Provonsha's analysis of the "Roots of the Crisis" of identity regarding Adventists' understanding of the remnant. Provonsha, *A Remnant in Crisis* (Hagerstown, Md.: Review and Herald, 1993), pp. 27-35.

8. The calculation was worked out in this manner: (a) A day's journey is about 20 miles; since the quails fell by the camp "as it were a day's journey on this side, and as it were a day's journey on the other side, round about the camp," it suggests that the quails covered a distance of 20 miles on each side of the camp, totaling 40 miles from north to south, and 40 miles from east to east; (b) An estimate of the total amount of quail rained down 3 feet deep and 40 miles across and 40 miles in width gives 133,816 *million* cubic feet (i.e. 40 miles [211,200 feet] x 40 miles [211,200 feet] x 3 feet); (c) 1 cubic foot = 0.77873 bushels, so that there were over 100 *billion* bushels (104,206,482,800, i.e., 0.77873 x 133,816,320,000); (d) There were 600,000 men (Num 11:21), so that allowing for children and women, there were about 2 million people. If we divide 104,206,482,800 bushels of quail among 2 million people, each gets about 52,000 bushels in the month. Now if each person eats three meals of quail a day, the average person will eat some 578 bushels at each meal (i.e., if we divide 52,000 by 90 meals [3 meals/day x 30 days/month = 90]); (e) Since 1 bushel = 1.28 cubic feet, if we estimate that one roasted turkey can be contained in a box measuring 1.28 ft. x 1.28 ft. x 1.28 ft., the 578 bushels of quail meat will be equivalent to 742 roasted turkeys.

9. Ministerial Association of the General Conference of Seventh-day Adventists, *Seventh-day Adventists Believe . . .: A Biblical Exposition of 27 Fundamental Beliefs* (Hagerstown, Md.: Review and Herald, 1988).

10. Evangelical scholar Walter C. Kaiser, drawing on the work of Milton S. Terry, attributed the term "grammatico-historical" to Karl A. G. Keil's Latin treatise on historical interpretation (1788) and his German textbook on New Testament hermeneutics (1810). The aim of this method of exegesis is to determine the author's intended meaning by means of the grammar of his language and by the historical and cultural circumstances. While the *historical* component is self-explanatory, according to Kaiser "The term *grammatico-,* however, is somewhat misleading since we usually mean by 'grammatical' the arrangement of words and construction of sentences. But Keil had in mind the Greek word *gramma,* and his use of the term *grammatico* approximates what we would understand by the term *literal* (to use a synonym derived from the Latin). Thus, the grammatical sense, in Keil's understanding, is the simple, direct, plain, ordinary and literal sense of the phrases, clauses and sentences" (Kaiser, *Toward An Exegetical Theology* [Grand Rapids, Mich.: Baker, 1981], pp. 87-88; cf. Terry, *Biblical Hermeneutics: A Treatise on the Interpretation of the Old and New Testaments* [New York: Phillips & Hunt, 1890; reprint ed., Grand Rapids, Mich.: Zondervan, 1964], pp. 203-242). Readers should also note that, at least in the nineteenth-century, some higher critics claimed that they were actually using the historical-*grammatical* method. For a discussion of this, see P. Gerard Damsteegt, *Foundations of the Seventh-day Adventist Message and Missions* (Grand Rapids, Mich.: Eerdmans, 1977), pp. 63-77, esp. p. 70.

11. Robert McIver, "The Historical-Critical Method: The Adventist Debate," *Ministry,* March 1996, p. 14.

12. The historical-critical method is described as "critical" because, instead of simply receiving the Word as God's inspired and trustworthy communication of His will to all humanity, this approach adopts an attitude of skepticism to the Bible, rejecting those parts of the Scriptures that are incompatible with the tenets of Enlightenment rationalism. Thus, the historical-critical method has correctly been defined as "that principle of historical reasoning . . . that reality is uniform and universal, that it is accessible to human reason and investigation, that all events historical and natural occurring within it are in principle comparable by analogy, and that man's contemporary experience of reality can provide the objective criteria by which what could or could not have happened in the past is to be determined" (R. N. Soulen, *Handbook of Biblical Criticism* [Atlanta, Ga.: John Knox, 1976], p. 78).

13. For the contribution of Troeltsch, see Robert Morgan, Introduction to *Ernst Troeltsch: Writings on Theology and Religion,* trans. and ed. Robert Morgan and Michael Pye (Atlanta, Ga.: John Knox, 1977). For the contributions of others to the historical-critical approach to Scriptures, see Gerhard Maier, *Biblical Hermeneutics* (Wheaton, Ill.: Crossway, 1994), pp. 251-255; William Larkin, *Culture and Biblical Hermeneutics* (Grand Rapids, Mich.: Baker, 1988), pp. 29-40; Clark H. Pinnock, *Tracking the Maze: Finding Our Way Through Modern Theology from an Evangelical Perspective* (San Francisco: Harper and Row, 1990), pp. 89-106.

14. For more on these, see Gerhard Hasel's *Biblical Interpretation Today: An Analysis of Modern Methods of Biblical Interpretation and Proposals for the Interpretation of the Bible as the Word of God* (Washington, D.C.: Biblical Research Institute, 1985); Hasel, *Understanding the Living Word of God* (Mountain View, Calif.: Pacific Press, 1980).

15. This is the moderate view; classical historical criticism would not speak of "inspiration" in this sense at all, since such a concept is unscientific and beyond the assumptions of history.

16. William H. Shea, "How Shall We Understand the Bible?" *Ministry,* March 1996, p. 13. Shea correctly concluded that "the subject of hermeneutics eventually comes back to the matter of presuppositions. . . . As far as the presupposition of the historico[-]grammatical method, that presupposition is ultimately one of faith. I commend that presupposition to the readers of this journal. When that presupposition is adopted, scholars are freed from their procrustean bed to examine all of the evidence that comes to bear upon the interpretation of God's Word."

17. Eta Linnemann, *Historical Criticism of the Bible: Methodology or Ideology?* Translated by Robert W. Yarbrough (Grand Rapids, Mich.: Baker, 1990), p. 123.

18. Edgar Krentz, *The Historical-Critical Method* (Philadelphia, Pa.: Fortress Press, 1975), p. 67.

19. Walter Wink, *The Bible in Human Transformation: Toward a New Paradigm for Biblical Study* (Philadelphia, Pa.: Fortress, 1973), p. 2. At the time that some Adventists scholars were hailing the historical-critical method, non-Adventist biblical scholars who had earlier used and recommended the method were abandoning it because of its failure to lead to a true understanding of the Bible. For more on this, see the summary in William J. Larkin, Jr., *Culture and Biblical Hermeneutics: Interpreting and Applying the Authoritative Word in a Relativistic Age* (Grand Rapids, Mich.: Baker, 1988), pp. 50-63; cf. Gerhard Maier, *Biblical Hermeneutics* (Wheaton, Ill.: Crossway, 1994), pp. 247-306.

20. For example, in 1981, a delegation of North American Bible scholars met at Washington, D.C. and affirmed that "Adventist scholars could indeed use the descriptive [historical-critical] method (e.g., source criticism, redaction criticism, etc.) without adopting the naturalistic presuppositions affirmed by the thorough-going practitioners of the method." See Alden Thompson, "Are Adventists Afraid of Bible Study?" *Spectrum* 16/1 (April 1985):58, 56; see also his "Theological Consultation II," *Spectrum* 12/2 (December 1981):40-52; *Inspiration: Hard Questions, Honest Answers* (Hagerstown, Md.: Review and Herald, 1991), pp. 271-272. The latter work was established on the assumptions of the historical-critical method. A detailed analysis and critique of *Inspiration* has come from the Adventist Theological Society; see *Issues in Revelation and Inspiration,* ed. Frank Holbrook and Leo Van Dolson (Berrien Springs, Mich.: Adventist Theological Society Publications, 1992).

21. Eta Linnemann, *Historical Criticism of the Bible: Methodology or Ideology?* p. 123. Linnemann is a leading Bultmannian who has turned evangelical. In this work, she argues forcefully that historical criticism is not a scientific methodology as it claims, but rather is a pagan ideology.

22. Robert W. Yarbrough, the translator of Eta Linnemann's book from German into English, writes: "Linnemann lodges a strong protest against the tendencies and methods of a discipline she knows from the inside out. She is not taking potshots from afar; she was a diligent and receptive student of some of this century's truly seminal thinkers in German New Testament scholarship: Bultmann, Fuchs, Gogarten, and Ebeling. Later, inducted into the world's most prestigious professional society for New Testament research, she was the peer of many others of like stature" (*Historical Criticism: Methodology or Ideology,* p. 7). A later chapter of *Receiving the Word* ("Testifying About the Word") presents Linnemann's own testimony about how she came to give up the historical-critical method.

23. H. L. Hastings, *Will the Old Book Stand?* (Washington, D.C.: Review and Herald, 1923), p. 11.

24. Kurt E. Marquart, *Anatomy of an Exploration: Missouri in Lutheran Perspective* (Fort Wayne, Ind.: Concordia Theological Seminary Press, 1977), p. 114.

Chapter Two

Trusting the Word

Throughout the centuries, Bible-believing Christians have received the Scriptures as the inspired, trustworthy, and authoritative Word of God. In this they have followed the example of the Berean believers, whom Paul commended as "noble" because "they received the word with all readiness of mind, and searched the Scriptures daily" (Acts 17:11). What makes the Bible unique? And why have the followers of Christ always been found *trusting the Word?*

The Book of Books

The Christian church has always prized its Book as unique. The church family has treasured this Book like an expensive jewel, even in the face of adversity and opposition from unbelievers. This Book has separated Christians from non-Christians. It has divided the church into orthodox and heretics, Protestants and Catholics, and in recent times conservatives and liberals. What exactly is this Book called the Bible?

It refers to itself as "the Scriptures" (Matt 21:42; Luke 24:25-27, 44-45), "the book of the Lord" (Isa 34:16), "the oracles of God" (Rom 3:2), "the good word of God" (Heb 6:5), and "the Word of Christ" (Col 3:16).

Scripture also compares itself to a number of things to emphasize its important function. As a *lamp* or *light* (Ps 119:105, 130; 2 Pet 1:19), it not only dispels the clouds of darkness in our world and doubt in our lives but also helps us to escape dangers and see our way clearly in life. As *bread* or *food* (Matt 4:4; Job 23:12), it feeds the hungry and provides nourishment for their spiritual growth. As a *mirror* (James 1:23-25), it makes us see ourselves as we really are so that we can be changed into the perfect mirror-image of Jesus Christ (2 Cor 3:18). As *water* (Ps 119:9; Eph 5:26; John 15:3), it has a cleansing and transforming power. As *fire* (Jer 20:9; 23:29; Ps 39:3), it can melt all the alloys of sin in our lives. As a *hammer* (Jer 23:29), it can break hardened hearts in ways that no human method can ever hope to do. As a *sword* (Eph 6:17; Heb 4:12), it can pierce the conscience, wound our pride and slay our rebellious spirit. As *seed* (Luke 8:11) it produces fruit in life. And as a "discerner of the thoughts and intents of the heart" (Heb 4:12), it teaches us not to criticize and judge the Bible, but rather to submit to its teachings.

Truly, this Book is like no other book.

A Unique Book

The Bible was written by some 40 different authors on three different continents (Africa, Asia, and Europe), in countries hundreds of miles apart, over a period of about 1500 years. It deals with matters of universal interest—history, philosophy, science, health, architecture, religion, etc. It speaks to the needs of every generation, offers solutions to life's perplexities, and even reveals the origin and future of our world. It has brought peace to troubled consciences, comfort to the sorrowful, hope to the despairing, courage to the despondent, and the assurance of reunion to the bereaved.

Originally written in Hebrew, Aramaic, and Greek, the Bible has been published in more languages than any other book in history, and yet it has not lost its original emphasis. This unique Book appeals to the young as well as the old, rich as well as poor, simple as well as wise. It advocates the rights of every individual, including the poor and defenseless, and it demonstrates a mysterious power to transform lives.

A careful reading of this unique Book reveals that: "The Bible was written by men upon every level of political and social life, from the king upon his throne down to the herdsmen, shepherds, fishermen, and petty politicians. Here are words written by princes, by poets, by philosophers, by fishermen, by statesmen, by prophets, by priests, by publicans, by physicians, by men learned in the wisdom of Egypt, by men educated in the school of Babylon, by men trained at the feet of rabbis like Gamaliel. Men of every grade and class are represented in this miraculous Volume. The circumstances under which the Book was written were sometimes most difficult and always most varying. Parts of it were written in tents, deserts, cities, palaces, and dungeons. Some of it was written in times of imminent danger and other parts in times of ecstatic joy."[1]

But the remarkable thing about the Bible is that, despite the circumstances that gave birth to the 66 different books of this Book, the contents of the Bible show a unique harmony. "It contains all kinds of writing; but what a jumble it would be if sixty-six books were written in this way by ordinary men. Suppose, for instance, that we get sixty-six medical books written by thirty or forty different doctors of various schools, . . . bind them all together, and then undertake to doctor a man according to that book! . . . Or suppose you get thirty-five ministers writing books on theology, and then see if you can find any leather strong enough to hold the books together."[2]

A Unique Preservation

But there is more; the Bible has been preserved remarkably during the process of transmission. Despite the fact that it was written on perishable material and was copied and recopied for hundreds of years before the invention of the printing press or computers, the Bible, when compared to all other ancient manuscripts, has displayed an unusual correctness in transmission. Though we will say more in Chapter Eight, a brief explanation here will illustrate this remarkable preservation.

With the exception of some sections of Ezra and half of Daniel that were written in Aramaic, the Old Testament was written originally in Hebrew. The Hebrew alphabet had many letters that looked very much alike. Observe, for example, the close resemblance between the following letters:

> *Beth* (ב) and *Kaph* (כ)
> *Daleth* (ד) and *Resh* (ר)
> *Daleth* (ד) and final *Kaph* (ך)
> *Vav* (ו) and *Yodh* (י)
> *Vav* (ו) and final *Nun* (ן)
> *Heth* (ח) and *He* (ה)
> *Heth* (ח) and *Tav* (ת)
> *Pe* (פ) and *Kaph* (כ)

Further, if the left hand perpendicular line of *He* (ה) is accidentally omitted or blurred by a copyist, we have *Daleth* (ד); so also, *Tav* (ת) and *Resh* (ר), and similarly *Pe* (פ) and *Kaph* (כ).

Up until about 700 A.D. when a group of Jewish scribes (called the Massoretes) invented a system for writing the vowels, Hebrew writing consisted only of consonants with no punctuation marks and, at times, barely any spaces between the words! It is a little like reading Genesis 1:1-3 (KJV) as:

NTHBGNNNGGDCRTDTHHVNNDTHRTHNDTHRTHWSWTHT
FRMNDVDNDDRKNSSWSPNTHFCFTHDPNDTHSPRTFGDMV
DPNTHFCFTHWTRSNDGDSDLTTHRBLGHTNDTHRWSLGHT

The remarkable accuracy with which the Massoretes wrote down the text of the Bible is due to strict rules that they followed. For example, no word or letter could be written from memory. The words or letters of each section were counted, and if these did not tally with the newly made copies, the new copy was discarded altogether and the task begun again. Bernard Ramm has described the process that led to this unique accuracy:

"In reference to the Old Testament we know that the Jews preserved it as no other manuscript has ever been preserved. With their *masora (parva, magna and finalis)* [methods of counting] they kept tabs on every letter, syllable, word and paragraph. They had special classes of men within their culture whose sole duty was to preserve and transmit these documents with practically perfect fidelity—scribes, lawyers, massoretes. Who ever counted the letters and syllables and words of Plato or Aristotle? Cicero or Seneca?"[3]

On the other hand, the New Testament was written in Koiné Greek—the common language of people in the apostolic times. Though there are no original copies of the earliest writings of the apostles, later hand-written copies have survived. These are called *manuscripts*—from the Latin words *manu scriptum,* meaning "written by hand"; the abbreviations generally used by scholars for the manuscripts are "MS" for the singular, and "MSS" for the plural.

The New Testament materials are much more recent to us than the Old Testament. But whereas well-trained Jewish copyists were extremely careful in copying every word of the Old Testament documents, factors such as the great demand for copies of New Testament to instruct new believers and the frequent interruptions in copying due to hostilities and persecutions led to hasty and sometimes careless copies of the original New Testament manuscripts. Fortunately for us, because so many New Testament manuscripts have been preserved, we can always cross-check any section whenever there is any doubt.

Because the original text of the Bible has been uniquely preserved, Christians can be absolutely certain of its essential accuracy. The late Sir Frederic Kenyon, one-time director of the British Museum and an authority on Bible manuscripts, put it this way: "The Christian can take the whole Bible in his hand and say without fear or hesitation that he holds in it the true Word of God, handed down without essential loss from generation to generation throughout the centuries."[4]

A Unique Survival

Still, of all the books ever produced, the Bible has suffered the most vicious attacks. Yet it has survived the persecution of critics and enemies. As on an anvil, "The hammers of the infidels have been pecking away at this book for ages, but the hammers are worn out, and the anvil still endures. If the book had not been the book of God, men would have destroyed it long ago. Emperors and popes, kings and priests, princes and rulers have all tried their hand at it; they die and the book still lives."[5]

Bernard Ramm asked rhetorically whether, besides the Bible, there has ever been a book on philosophy, religion, psychology, or any other subject that has been so "chopped, knifed, sifted, scrutinized, and vilified . . . with such venom and skepticism? with such thoroughness and erudition? upon every chapter, line and tenet?" Ramm concluded: "A thousand times over, the death knell of the Bible has been sounded, the funeral procession formed, the inscription cut on the tombstone, and the committal read. But somehow the corpse never stays put. . . . Considering the thorough learning of the critics and the ferocity and precision of the attacks, we would expect the Bible to have been permanently entombed in some Christian genizah.* But such is hardly the case. The Bible is still loved by millions, read by millions and studied by millions."[6]

Jesus said it best almost 2,000 years ago: "Heaven and earth shall pass away, but my words shall not pass away" (Matt 24:35). Concerning this statement, someone has written: "The empire of Caesar is gone; the legions of Rome are mouldering in the dust; the avalanches Napoleon hurled upon Europe have melted away; the pride of the Pharaohs is fallen; the pyramids they raised to be their tombs are sinking every day in the desert sands; Tyre is a rock for fishermen's nets; Sidon has scarcely a rock left behind; but the Word of God survives. All things that threatened to extinguish it have aided it, and it proves every day how transient is the noblest monument that man can build, how enduring the least word God has spoken. Tradition has dug a grave for it; intolerance has lighted for it many a fagot; many a Judas has betrayed it with a kiss; many a Peter has denied it with an oath; many a Demas has forsaken it; but the Word of God still endures."[7]

How do we account for the remarkable unity, power, survival and universal appeal of this ancient Book?

A Unique Claim: Revelation

Though produced by human writers, the Bible makes a bold claim to its divine origin. The apostle Paul wrote: "All Scripture is given by inspiration of God" (2 Tim 3:16). This text raises three questions about the Bible: (a) *How much* of Scripture is inspired? (b) *How* is "all Scripture" inspired? (c) *When* and *in what manner* was Scripture inspired?

1. How much of Scripture is inspired? The context of 2 Timothy 3:16 suggests that "all Scripture" refers to the entire Old Testament, the books that made up the Bible in the days of Jesus and the apostles. But according to other New Testament passages, "all Scripture" also includes the New Testament writ-

---

*A genizah is a synagogue storage room for worn-out Scripture manuscripts too sacred to be destroyed or discarded.

ings. For example, the apostle Peter refers to the writings of Paul on the same basis as "the other scriptures" (2 Pet 3:15, 16); and Paul in 1 Timothy 5:18 quotes the record in Luke 10:7, "The laborer is worthy of his reward," and refers to the statement as "scripture."

If "all Scripture"—consisting of both the Old and New Testaments—is inspired, this implies, contrary to the claims of critics and liberals, that the sections of the Bible which talk about miracles, history, geography, ethics, science, etc., are all inspired, just as the doctrinal sections are.

2. How is "all Scripture" inspired? 2 Timothy 3:16 makes it clear that "all Scripture is given by inspiration of God [Greek *theopneustos,* literally 'God-breathed'8]," that it to say, all the books of the Bible have a divine origin. Not only is God the fundamental source of the Bible, but Jesus Christ was also intimately connected with the production of the Scriptures. Peter wrote: "Of which salvation the prophets have enquired and searched diligently, who prophesied of the grace that should come unto you: searching what, or what manner of time the Spirit of Christ which was in them did signify, when it testified beforehand the sufferings of Christ, and the glory that should follow" (1 Pet 1:10, 11).

The apostle Peter later wrote that the Holy Spirit was also an active participant in producing the Scriptures: "Prophecy came not in old time by the will of man: but holy men of God spake as they were moved by the Holy Ghost" (2 Pet 1:21).

Thus the testimony of Scripture is that the book we call the Bible has its source in all the members of the Trinity—God the Father, God the Son, and God the Holy Spirit. Just as all three members of the Godhead cooperated in the creation of the world, so also do we find all three working together in giving to the world a unique Book, the Bible.

The Scriptures rarely discussed the method of revelation from God to the Bible writers. The inspired Word simply states: "In many and various ways God spoke of old to our fathers by the prophets; but in these last days he has spoken to us by a [His] Son" (Heb 1:1, 2). The "many and various ways God spoke" include: visions and dreams (Isa 1:1; Eze 1:1; Dan 7:1), direct appearances (theophanies) and messages from God (Ex 3:2-7; 20:1), through an angel (Dan 8:15-16; 9:21-22; Rev 1:1-4), eyewitness accounts (1 John 1:1-3; 2 Pet 1:16-18), reflection on nature and human experience (Ps 8:3, 4; Rom 2:14-15; 1 Cor 7:12; as are found, for example, in the books of Job, Psalms, Proverbs and Ecclesiastes), and historical research.

Historical research deserves some emphasis as a manner of revelation since, in the minds of some, an inspired writer is not supposed to do any borrowing or compilation in writing the Book, or even to employ secretarial or editorial assistance.

Contrary to this view, the Bible clearly indicates that inspired writers quoted or borrowed from earlier authors. All truth, wherever it is found, belongs to God. Thus, Moses records that he used material from the Book of the Wars of the Lord (Num 21:14); Joshua and Samuel mention that they borrowed some material from the book of Jasher (Josh 10:13; 2 Sam 1:18); the authors of Kings and Chronicles refer to at least eight lost books that they used as sources of information (1 Kings 11:41; 15:29; 2 Chron 9:29; 12:15; 20:34; 33:19); and Luke informs us that his work drew on historical research (Luke 1:1-4). Because the Holy Spirit guided the Bible writers in their selection and use of sources, these writings are as much the Word of God as those whose content was directly revealed to them in visions, dreams, and theophanies.

Sometimes, a prophet also employed a secretary or editorial assistant in communicating a message from God, as for example, Jeremiah employed the assistance of Baruch (Jer 36).[9]

3. When and in what manner was Scripture inspired? How did God ensure that the frailty of the Bible's human writers did not affect the trustworthiness of the Bible? The answer is found in the unique cooperation between God and His chosen human agents.

A Unique Cooperation: Inspiration

Probably the most mysterious thing about the Bible is the manner in which the Principal Authors of the Book—the members of the Holy Trinity—were able to employ fallible human beings as their instruments to write down, in a trustworthy manner, the message of God. This process is called "inspiration."

Fallible Writers, Infallible Record. Some might entertain the thought that (1) the prophetic message was the invention of the Bible writers and that (2) because the human writers were fallible, the Bible is not absolutely dependable. In response to such ideas, the apostle Peter asserts:

"For we did not follow cleverly devised myths [Greek *mythos,* a story, whatever its significance, that has no factual basis] when we made known to you the power and coming of our Lord Jesus Christ, but we were eyewitnesses of his majesty. . . . And we have the prophetic word made more sure [Greek *bebaioteron,* which has the force of "standing firm on the feet," "steadfast," "reliable," "valid"]. You will do well to pay attention to this as to a lamp shining in a dark place, until the day dawns and the morning star rises in your hearts. First of all you must understand this, that no prophecy of scripture is a matter of one's own interpretation, because no prophecy ever came by the impulse of man, but men moved [Greek *pheromenoi,* literally, "carried along"[10]] by the Holy Spirit spoke from God" (2 Pet 1:16-21).

Peter, himself a recipient of inspiration, does not deny human will or personality in the writing of Scriptures (the writers actually "spoke"); rather he underscores three important facts about the inspiration phenomenon: (1) the ultimate source of the message was not the human messengers' thoughts and impulses; (2) the human writers were divinely aided ("carried along") by the Holy Spirit to communicate their divine messages, so that (3) the product of this cooperative effort between the human and the divine was trustworthy ("more sure").

Because of the unique cooperation between God and the human writers of the Bible, both Jesus and the New Testament Christians acknowledged that while the Bible writers employed their own words and expressions, the final product (the Bible) had God's stamp of approval as being truly His Word.

This last point is very important. Some modern theologians (called Neoorthodox or Barthians, following the Swiss theologian Karl Barth) hold that the Bible *is not* the word of God but can *become* the word of God at the moment the Bible speaks to a person in a significant personal encounter. In a subtle denial of the Bible's inspiration, these theologians suggest that until the Bible "becomes" the Word of God, it is merely the word of humans, or at best a human document that *contains* the Word of God. Because this position has gained a large number of adherents, it is important to consider what the Bible itself says on whether the Bible is the word of humans or is actually the Word of God.

Truly the Word of God. Just as the Old Testament prophets warned against those who prophesy their own words rather than words that God has given them (Deut 18:18, 20; Jer 23:16), Jesus also made it clear that "he whom God has sent utters the words of God" (John 3:34). The implication is that all true messengers of God (prophets and Bible writers) communicate the message that God has given them in a trustworthy manner. Thus, Jesus could say of Himself, "the Father who sent me has himself given me commandment what to say and what to speak" (John 12:49); "the word which you hear is not mine but the Father's who sent me" (John 14:24).

The repeated assertion, "Thus saith the Lord," prefixing many messages of the Old Testament prophets testifies to the truthfulness of their messages. The New Testament writers also make it clear that all the writings of the Old Testament prophets are indeed the words of God. For example, Mark quotes Jesus as saying, "David himself, inspired by the Holy Spirit, declared. . ." (Mark 12:36). Zechariah, the father of John the Baptist, said that God spoke "by the mouth of His holy prophets from of old" (Luke 1:70). At the first recorded prayer meeting of the early church, the believers "lifted their voices together to God and said, Sovereign Lord, who . . . by the mouth of our father David, thy servant, didst say by the Holy Spirit . . ." (Acts 4:24, 25). Speaking to the Jews in Rome, Paul said, "The Holy Spirit was right in saying to your fathers through Isaiah the prophet . . ." (Acts 28:25).

Besides identifying God as the source of the words of the Old Testament writers and those of Jesus Himself, the New Testament writers also testified that their own words were authoritative because their message was of divine origin (Luke 10:16; Gal 1:8-9). Hence Peter urged his readers to remember the words "of the holy prophets and the commandment of the Lord and Savior through your apostles" (2 Pet 3:2). Paul added his voice when he said of the things which "God has revealed to us through the Spirit . . . we impart this in words not taught by human wisdom but taught by the Spirit, interpreting spiritual truths to those who possess the Spirit" (1 Cor 2:10, 13).

"That is, the Spirit of God did not mechanically whisper the text into the writer's ears, nor did the authors experience automatic writing. Instead, they experienced a *living assimilation* of the truth, so that what they had experienced in the past by way of culture, vocabulary, hardships, and the like was all taken up and assimilated into the unique product that simultaneously came from the unique personality of the writers. Just as truly, however, it came also from the Holy Spirit! And the Holy Spirit stayed with the writers not just in the conceptual or ideational stage, but all the way up through the writing and verbalizing stage of their composition of the text."[11]

The Spirit's guidance of the inspired writers in expressing their God-given thoughts and ideas in their own words is known technically as *verbal (propositional) inspiration.* This should not be confused with *mechanical (dictation) inspiration,* a mistaken theory which claims that the Holy Spirit dictated each word of Scripture.

The apostle Paul summed up the unique cooperation between God and the human Bible writers in his letter to the Christians of Thessalonica: "And we also thank God constantly for this, that when you received the word of God which you heard from us, you accepted it not as the word of men but as what it really is, the word of God, which is at work in you believers" (1 Thess 2:13). In other words, the fact that the Scriptures are inspired implies that the Bible *is* truly the Word of God.

A Unique Analogy: Human and Divine

The dual nature of the Bible as the product of both the human and the divine may be compared with Jesus Christ at His incarnation. Just as Jesus, the incarnate Word, was fully both human and divine, so also is the Bible, the written Word, fully human and fully divine. Just as Jesus had authority to speak, command and give life to those who accepted Him, so does the Bible claim the same. These claims are evident in the manner in which the New Testament writers quoted the Old Testament.

What Scripture Says, God Says. The New Testament writers often personify Scripture with the expression, "The Scripture says . . . ." This "Scripture" was in existence even at the time of Abraham (Gal 3:8) and Pharaoh (Rom 9:17); Scripture can speak (Rom 10:11), give commands (1 Tim 5:18) and foresee events some 2,000 years into the future (Gal 3:8). This startling manner of citing Old Testament passages suggests that the New Testament writers saw something superhuman about the Old Testament. The frequent use of the Greek present tense, *legei* ("it says"), to describe the action of Scripture suggests that the Old Testament "is still speaking." The New Testament speaks of the Old Testament as if God were speaking; obviously the New Testament writers had no doubts regarding the close relationship between Scripture and God. By using this kind of introductory formula, the Bible writers strongly imply the divine origin and the resulting authority of Scripture.

Paul, for example, sometimes cites Scriptures by the verb *legei* ("he/she/it says") without expressly naming the subject (God, Scripture, etc.).[12] However, a look at the context shows that God is the implied subject. Similarly, in the Old Testament passages cited, God was the subject. Another frequently used quotation formula is "God says" or "God said." For instance, in Matthew 19:5 Jesus introduced Genesis 2:24 with the phrase "and [God] said," but in the Genesis verse it was Moses—not God—who was speaking. In 2 Corinthians 6:16 Paul introduces his Old Testament quotations by saying "as God has said," thereby affirming that the message of the Old Testament is the message of God. Whether "Scripture says" or "God says" makes no difference to Paul; they all share the same authority.

The three introductory formulas we have discussed ("Scripture says," "It says," and "God says") have revealed that the Old Testament Scriptures are a divine book, speaking with authority. But the strength and constancy with which New Testament writers emphasize this fact do not prevent them from recognizing that the Scriptures have come into being through human instrumentality. We see this in another way they quote the Old Testament.

David, Isaiah, Moses, "Says." Paul has no difficulty ascribing Scripture to its human authors. In fact, he freely quotes the Old Testament by simple formulas such as, "David pronounces a blessing" (Rom 4:6-8), Isaiah "says," "predicted," "cries out" (Rom 10:16; 9:29; 9:27), and Moses "says" (Rom 10:19).

Whether Old Testament prophets wrote or spoke, their messages are quoted as Scripture, suggesting that inspiration includes oral and written communication. Also, Paul seems indifferent as to whether the words are comments of these authors or direct words of God which they recorded (Rom 10:5, cf. Lev 18:5).

We may conclude that Scripture has a double authorship—God being the primary Author through whose initiative the human writers did their work. It would be inexact to say that the Bible is a human book containing the Word of God or to assign some parts of Scripture respectively to God and man. Scripture is the Word of God given through the instrumentality of men. Just as we cannot separate the human nature of Jesus from His divine nature, so also we cannot divide Scripture, claiming some parts as human and some divine.

An Unmistakable Evidence. One unmistakable evidence that the Bible has a divine imprint is the manner in which its human writers recorded biographical accounts of its heroes and heroines when they did wrong. Noah, the survivor of the flood, got drunk and exposed his nakedness; Abraham, the friend of God, lied and doubted God; Lot, the hero of the story of Sodom and Gomorrah, got drunk and had an incestuous relationship with his daughters; Miriam, the beautiful singer and prophetess of Israel, had a racial and jealousy problem and was struck with leprosy; Rahab, the woman of faith and the ancestor of Jesus Christ, had been a prostitute; David, a man after God's own heart, was guilty of adultery and murder; Solomon, the wisest man who ever lived, lived the life of a fool; Judas, one of the most influential among the twelve disciples of Christ, was a thief and a traitor; Peter, a leading apostle of Christ, denied his Master with curses and swearing; John, the apostle of love, called for fire to destroy his enemies; and Paul, the apostle to the Gentiles, persecuted the followers of Christ.

If the biographical accounts in the Scriptures were simply human efforts to enhance the moral standing of some prominent men and women, the writers would have judiciously omitted or reconstructed the negative and embarrassing aspects of those lives. "This is the way *men* write history; but when the Lord undertakes to tell *His* story of a sinful man, He does not select a poor miserable beggar, and show him up; He does not give even the name of the thief on the cross, nor of the guilty woman to whom He said, 'Neither do I condemn thee; go, and sin no more;' but He takes King David from the throne, and sets him down in sackcloth and ashes, and wrings from his heart the cry, 'Have mercy upon me, O God, according to Thy loving-kindness: according unto the multitude of Thy tender mercies blot out my transgressions.' And then when he is pardoned, forgiven, cleansed, and made whiter than snow, the pen of inspiration writes down the whole dark, damning record of his crimes, and the king on his throne has not power, nor wealth, nor influence enough to blot the page; and it goes into history for infidels to scoff at for three thousand years. Who wrote that?"[13]

"You find a man who will tell the truth about kings, warriors, princes, and rulers today, and you may be quite sure that he has within him the power of the Holy Ghost. And a book which tells the faults of those who wrote it, and which tells you that 'there is none righteous, no, not one,' bears in it the marks of a true book; for we all know that men have faults, and failings, and sins; and among all the men whose lives are recorded in that book, each man has some defect, some blot, except one, and that is 'the man Christ Jesus.'"[14]

A Book to Trust

Inspired Word of God. On the basis of the discussion in this chapter, Bible-believing Christians throughout the ages have always received the Bible as the inspired, trustworthy, and authoritative Word of God. For this reason the apostle Paul wrote to the Thessalonian believers: "When you *received the word of God* which you heard from us, *you accepted it not as the word of men but as what it really is, the word of God,* which is at work in you believers" (1 Thess 2:13; cf. Acts 17:11).

Against those "who think to make the supposed difficulties of the Scripture plain, in measuring by their finite rule that which is inspired and that which is not inspired," Ellen White warned: "When men, in their finite judgment, find it necessary to go into an examination of scriptures to define that which is inspired and that which is not, they have stepped before Jesus to show Him a better way than He has led us (*Selected Messages,* 1:17).

She urged us to reject the attempt to discover "degrees of inspiration" in inspired writings—whether the Bible or her own writings—by ascribing some parts to the Spirit's inspiration and pronouncing others as uninspired: "When men venture to criticize the Word of God, they venture on sacred, holy ground, and had better fear and tremble and hide their wisdom as foolishness. God sets no man to pronounce judgment on His Word, selecting some things as inspired and discrediting others as uninspired. The testimonies have been treated in the same way; but God is not in this" (*Selected Messages,* 1:23).

Meets Human Needs. Because Scripture is an inspired Book, it is also a true and dependable book. "The Bible is more than a good or true book, however. Man may write a good book, a true book, even a wonderful book, but man has never produced a volume that compares with the Holy Scriptures. The Bible *lives!* Through its sacred pages God moves and speaks to human hearts. It is a Book of divine origin destined from the beginning to fill a unique need among the human family. No other volume has success-fully challenged it."[15]

"It points out to sinners a way of pardon, of peace, and of redemption. It tells us how men subject to like passions as we are, may yet be men of mighty faith, having fellowship with God, and prevailing in effectual and fervent prayer. It tells us how men who have sinned against the Most High may be cleansed from blood-guiltiness, and washed and made whiter than snow. It tells us how we, redeemed through God's mercy, may stand stainless as angels in the pres-ence of the eternal King. Are we ready to heed its instructions, and find life and peace in Christ the Lord?"[16]

Worthy of Our Trust. At a time when it is fashionable for Christians to "question some parts of revelation, and pick flaws in the apparent inconsisten-cies of this statement and that statement," it behooves us to follow Ellen White's example in *trusting the Word:* "I take the Bible just as it is, as the Inspired Word. I believe its utterances in an entire Bible. Men arise who think they find something to criticize in God's Word. They lay it bare before others as evidence of superior wisdom. These men are, many of them, smart men, learned men, they have eloquence and talent, the whole lifework [of whom] is to unsettle minds in regard to the inspiration of the Scriptures. They influence many to see as they do. And the same work is passed on from one to another, just as Satan designed it should be, until we may see the full meaning of the words of Christ, 'When the Son of man cometh, shall he find faith on the earth?' (Luke 18:8)" (*Selected Messages,* 1:17).

One perceptive church member correctly stated: "God does not give us the option of choosing which parts of His Word to accept or reject any more than He gives us the option to partially accept or reject Him. Salvation requires full acceptance of Him and thus His Word; and acceptance of Him in turn requires full surrender to Him. Nothing more is required and nothing less is acceptable to God. For it is by His Word that we know Him; and it is through this Word that He leads us. God and His Word are inseparable."[17]

As Bible-believing Christians, shall we continue *trusting the Word?* Or shall we be found *doubting the Word?*

NOTES

1. W. A. Criswell, *Why I Preach That the Bible Is Literally True* (Nashville, Tenn.: Broadman Press, 1969), p. 71.
2. H. L. Hastings, *Will the Old Book Stand?* (Washington, D.C.: Review and Herald, 1923), p. 21.

3. Bernard Ramm, *Protestant Christian Evidences* (Chicago: Moody Press, 1957), pp. 230-231.

4. Frederic Kenyon, *Our Bible and the Ancient Manuscripts* (New York: Harpers, 1940), p. 21.

5. H. L. Hastings, quoted by John W. Lea, *The Greatest Book in the World* (Philadelphia: n. pub., 1929), pp. 17-18.

6. Ramm, *Protestant Christian Evidences,* pp. 232-233.

7. Alas, I cannot remember where I found this particular citation.

8. Applied to the Bible, the Greek term *theopneustos* is used only once in the Bible (2 Tim 3:16); it may be applied to any degree of divine influence. See H. Wayne House, "Biblical Inspiration in 2 Timothy 3:16," *Bibliotheca Sacra* 137 (1980): 54-63.

9. Juan Carlos Viera, "The Dynamics of Inspiration," *Adventist Review* (special undated 1996 edition on Ellen G. White), pp. 22-26, discusses six models of inspiration: "visionary model," "witness model," "historian model," "counselor model," "epistolary model," and "literary model." An excellent theological discussion of the biblical view of revelation and inspiration is Raoul Dederen's "The Revelation-Inspiration Phenomenon According to the Bible Writers," in *Issues in Revelation and Inspiration,* ed. Frank Holbrook and Leo Van Dolson (Berrien Springs, Mich.: Adventist Theological Society Publications, 1992), pp. 9-29.

10. The Greek word used here, *phero* ("to bear" or "to carry along"), was used for a sailing ship being carried along by the wind. As Peter was himself a fisherman, his use of this word is significant. It implies that the human writers of the Bible were gently led by the Spirit in communicating the message that God had given them by revelation.

11. Walter Kaiser makes the above statement in describing the divine-human concursus (i.e., a "running together" in the realm of thought) as the Holy Spirit used human beings to communicate in a trustworthy manner the divine truths of the Bible. See chapter 2 ("The Meaning of Meaning") of Walter Kaiser and Moises Silva, *An Introduction to Biblical Hermeneutics: The Search for Meaning* (Grand Rapids, Mich.: Zondervan, 1994), pp. 40-41.

12. Rom 9:15 (cf. Ex 33:19), Rom 9:25 (cf. Hos 2:23; 1:10), Eph 4:8 (cf. Ps 68:18).

13. H. L. Hastings, *Will the Old Book Stand?* (Washington, D.C.: Review and Herald, 1923), pp. 17-18.

14. Ibid., p. 18.

15. Robert H. Pierson, *Though the Winds Blow* (Nashville, Tenn.: Southern Publishing Association, 1968), p. 53.

16. Hastings, *Will the Old Book Stand?,* p. 345.

17. Kathleen McCan to Samuel Koranteng-Pipim, correspondence dated June 7, 1996.

Chapter Three

Doubting the Word

As we have already noted, for centuries the Bible has come under vicious attack from critics outside the church. In some instances, the Bible was ridiculed, banned, and even burned. Yet not only has the Bible survived, but Christians have also been *receiving the Word* as the inspired, trustworthy, and authoritative revelation of God's will.

Today, however, an assault on the Bible is coming from people claiming to be Christians and occupying positions of responsibility in many denominations. A careful look at the contemporary theological scene will reveal that much of today's theological activity is directed towards discrediting the Bible or creating doubts over its trustworthiness and absolute reliability. Many theologians in the classrooms, many preachers in the pulpits, and many leaders in administrative positions are subtly creating doubts in the minds of their hearers by suggesting that the Bible can no longer be fully trusted on almost any issue.

Nature of the Doubts. Contrary to the claims of the Bible, these dissenting theological voices allege that fulfilled prophecies of the Bible were actually written after the events took place. The Bible's history, they say, is not historical, its science not scientific; its stories are myths, its facts are fables, its heroes were immoral, and its ethics are not practical today. All these they present as new views of the Bible that will bring about a greater "appreciation" of the "beauty" of the Bible! To make this perspective palatable to unsuspecting believers, these critics have come up with different theories to explain the *nature* of the Bible (inspiration) and the appropriate *method* for its interpretation.

These two subjects—inspiration and interpretation—have a bearing on whether the Bible is fully trustworthy, absolutely dependable, and completely reliable in all that it deals with. Questions regarding biblical inspiration and interpretation have contributed to *doubting the Word*.

Theological Divisions. This crisis over the Word has caused division in various denominations. For lack of standard terminology, I have described the three major positions in contemporary theology as: (i) the Liberal (Radical) position, (ii) the Conservative (Bible-believing) position, and (iii) the Moderate (Progressive/Accomodationist/Neo-liberal) position.

Caution in the Use of Labels. Although the terms, "liberal," "conservative," and "moderate" are now employed in theological discussions, one crucial point should be emphasized in the use of these labels: the terminology is also used in, if not borrowed from, the world of politics. Because of the political undertones of these words, and because it is very easy to assume mistakenly that the terms mean the same things in both politics and theology, it would have been preferable to avoid these labels altogether.

Besides, these terms sometimes have completely opposite meanings from their usage in the past. For example, there was a time when a Christian could proudly carry the label of a "liberal" and boast of being "warm-hearted or generous," "open-minded," or "free from narrow-minded thinking, prejudice or arbitrary authority." But today, as we shall show, when a Christian is described as a liberal, it connotes one who has betrayed the truths of the biblical religion which, if cherished, can make a person truly generous, open-minded, and free.

Similarly, in the past the term "conservative" had negative undertones. In those days a conservative Christian described a person who: blindly fastened himself to prevalent views; was cautious toward or suspicious of change or innovation; had a tendency to avoid open-minded discussions for fear of being won over to the other side.

In fact, most of Ellen G. White's usage of this term carried this negative meaning. Notice the context in which she employed the word: "But as real spiritual life declines, it has ever been the tendency to cease to advance in the knowledge of truth. Men rest satisfied with the light already received from God's word, and discourage any further investigation of the Scriptures. They become conservative, and seek to avoid discussion" (*Counsels to Writers and Editors,* p. 38; cf. *Testimonies to the Church,* 5:706, 370; *The Signs of the Times,* December 10, 1894).

Ellen G. White's uncomplimentary use of the term conservative in other citations could aptly describe today's theological liberals! For instance, she classed the "conservatives" in her day among: the "worldly" and "superficial" class; those whose influence retard the progress of God's work by putting "worldly conformity" first and God's cause second, or whose sympathies are with the enemies of God's truth;[1] those who instead of being true to biblical convictions would rather shape the scriptural message "to please the minds of the unconsecrated";[2] those who betray the cause of truth by compromises and concessions;[3] those who choose to be "self-centered," instead of "living the unselfish life of Christ";[4] and those who defer to the "traditions received from educated men, and from the writings of great men of the past," instead of seeking guidance from the "holy principles revealed in the word of God."[5]

Because the theological labels—liberal, conservative, and moderate—also describe political views, and because today the usage of these terms often varies from its use in the past, our own preference would have been the following terms: *Bible-rejecters, Bible-believers,* and *Bible-doubters.* However, we have chosen to maintain the above theological labels because, rightly or wrongly, they are the best known.

To avoid confusing the three warring factions in the Christian church's ongoing quarrel over the Word, we shall now (a) briefly describe each of the theological divisions and (b) explain why they are engaged in this family feud.

The Three Major Theological Factions

Liberals: Bible Rejecters. Theological liberals deny the full trustworthiness of the Bible. Seeking to accommodate Bible truth to modern culture or science, they deny the validity of miracles and the supernatural, adopting the methods of higher criticism as the way to restore the truthfulness of the Bible. In terms of numbers, the liberals are relatively few, but they hold prominent positions in various theological institutions and sometimes in the churches.

Their impact stems largely from their published articles, books, and commentaries on the Bible. These works are regarded as the standard criteria for scholarship, and those who do not accord with them are treated as academic misfits. Because their publications tend to be reference works, when new believers or untrained students are exposed to them their faith in the Bible and its teachings is shaken.

Conservatives: Bible Believers. Theological conservatives, as their name implies, seek to conserve or preserve the traditional view of Scripture against the newer views. This does not mean that they accept tradition uncritically or that they refuse to be open to new ideas. Rather, they aim to preserve the view of Scripture set forth in the inspired Word and which has been the consensus of Christendom from its very beginning until modern times. Bible-believing conservatives accept the full reliability and trustworthiness of the Bible in matters of salvation as well as on any other subject the Bible touches upon. Their view of the Scriptures is described in the previous chapter. Conservative scholars also reject even a moderate use of the higher critical methodologies.

As a conservative denomination, Seventh-day Adventists historically have affirmed their faith in the inspiration, unity, authenticity, and authority of the Bible as the Word of God in its totality. The very first of our Fundamental

Beliefs reads: "The Holy Scriptures, Old and New Testaments, are the written Word of God, given by divine inspiration through holy men of God who spoke and wrote as they were moved by the Holy Spirit. In this Word, God has committed to man the knowledge necessary for salvation. The Holy Scriptures are the infallible revelation of His will. They are the standard of character, the test of experience, the authoritative revealer of doctrines, and the trustworthy record of God's acts in history."[6] The conservative implications of this fundamental belief are reflected in the 1986 "Methods of Bible Study Report" voted by church leaders in Rio de Janeiro, Brazil (see Appendix C).

Generally, a large majority of church members tend to be conservative Bible-believing Christians. Recognizing the power of Christ in their own lives, they submit to the authority of their Savior and His written Word. In their search to know Christ and His Word better, these Christian believers sometimes find themselves confused and shaken by the discordant notes of liberals and moderates in the church.

Moderates or Accommodationists: Bible-Doubters. Theological moderates give the appearance of being conservatives, and yet they hold onto a liberal agenda. Because they accommodate conservative beliefs to liberal thought, moderates can very well be described as "accommodationists." Unlike liberals, moderates accept *some* or even *all* of the Bible's miracles and supernatural events, but they maintain that the Bible is not fully reliable in everything it says since it contains some minor "mistakes," "discrepancies," "inconsistences," "inaccuracies" or even "errors."

By "errors" they do not simply refer to the ones that apparently crept into the text during the process of copying the manuscripts (e.g., occasional discrepancies due to copyist glosses, slips, misspellings, etc.) and which can be ascertained and corrected by comparing the various available manuscripts.[7] When moderates/accommodationists speak of errors or discrepancies, they are referring to mistakes that are purported to have originated with the Bible writers themselves. These alleged errors include statements in the Bible that deal with chronology, numbers, genealogy, history, geography, and science, which the scholars insist are inaccurate.

Moderates, however, argue that these "inaccuracies" are few and largely trivial factual mistakes. They also add that in the areas of religion and ethics, and especially in the central teachings regarding God, Christ, and salvation, the Bible is most dependable. Those in this group generally believe that it is possible to make a moderate use of the critical methodologies.[8]

Although the moderates do not come out as strongly as the radical liberals, yet in subtle ways they present modified and popular versions of liberalism to unsuspecting believers. Moderates tend to occupy high positions in the church where their neo-liberal influence is felt in the classrooms, in the pulpits, and in administrative decision-making positions. Therefore, when many church members speak of "liberals," they are actually referring to these "accommodationists" in their churches.

The Issue Dividing the Factions

All the three factions—theological liberals, moderates/accommodationists, and conservatives—claim to take the Bible very seriously. The quarrel over the Word started when some confronted seemingly unresolvable difficulties in Scripture. While the three groups all claimed that in the face of difficulties they would allow the Bible to speak for itself, it became apparent that letting the Bible "speak for itself" meant different things to liberals and accommodationists on the one hand and to Bible-believing conservatives on the other.

Unlike conservatives who take very seriously the claims of the Bible to be truthful, liberals and accommodationists who come across difficulties in the Bible do three things. (1) They declare these problems as inaccuracies, contradictions, or errors. (2) Then, to account for these alleged errors or contradictions in the Bible, they redefine the meaning of inspiration or the nature of the Bible to allow for the possibility of mistakes or inaccuracies in the Bible. (3) They adopt different versions of the higher-critical methodology as appropriate in resolving the scriptural difficulties. This situation has led to doubting the Word.

In order to appreciate fully how both kinds of liberalism—classical and moderate/accommodationist—are sowing seeds of skepticism regarding Scripture's inspiration, trustworthiness, and authority, we must briefly summarize what both camps of liberalism are saying about the Bible and its message.

Classical Liberalism's View of the Bible

The crisis of identity we face in the Seventh-day Adventist church arises from the fact that some in our midst want us to use liberalism's method of biblical interpretation. In this effort they have questioned not only the Bible's own inspiration, trustworthiness, and authority, but also other fundamental beliefs that are established on the Bible. Before we discuss the assumptions of liberalism's historical-critical method of interpretation, it may be helpful to examine portions of an important essay by the German New Testament professor, Rudolf Bultmann (1884-1976), one of the twentieth century's foremost liberal scholars.

In an influential 1941 article entitled "New Testament and Mythology," Bultmann argued that much of the New Testament is myth that has come down to us from a "pre-scientific" age. He maintained that the New Testament contains both the true gospel of Jesus Christ (called "kerygma") and some statements that employ fanciful mythological images typical of ancient pre-scientific ways of thinking.

According to Bultmann, since much of the New Testament contains these outdated myths, the only way to make the Bible appealing to modern twentieth-century culture is to *de-mythologize* it. Using higher criticism (generally termed "historical-critical method"), this approach denies miracles and the essentials of the Christian faith—the virgin birth, atonement, resurrection, and second coming of Christ.

A Classical Liberal's View. The following is a sampling of Rudolf Bultmann's article in which he argued for the necessity of "demythologization":

"Modern thought as we have inherited it provides us with a motive for criticizing the New Testament view of the world.

"Man's knowledge and mastery of the world have advanced to such an extent through science and technology that it is no longer possible for anyone seriously to hold the New Testament view of the world—in fact, there is hardly anyone who does. . . . No one who is old enough to think for himself supposes that God lives in a local heaven. There is no longer any heaven in the traditional sense of the word. . . . We can no longer look for the return of the Son of Man on the clouds of heaven or hope that the faithful will meet him in the air (1 Thess. 4:15ff).

"Now that the forces and laws of nature have been discovered, we can no longer believe in spirits, whether good or evil. . . . Sickness and the cure of disease are likewise attributable to natural causation; they are not the result of demonic activity or of evil spells. The miracles of the New Testament have ceased to be miraculous. . . .

"It is impossible to use electric light and the wireless and to avail ourselves of modern medical and surgical discoveries, and at the same time to believe in the New Testament world of daemons and spirits. . . .

"The mythical eschatology [view of last day events] is untenable for the simple reason that the parousia [appearance] of Christ never took place as the New Testament expected. History did not come to an end, and, as every schoolboy knows, it will continue to run its course. Even if we believe that the world as we know it will come to an end in time, we expect the end to take the form of a natural catastrophe, not of a mythical event such as the New Testament expects. . . .

"Again, the biblical doctrine that death is the punishment of sin is equally abhorrent to naturalism and idealism, since they both regard death as a simple and necessary process of nature. . . . Human beings are subject to death even before they have committed any sin. And to attribute human mortality to the fall of Adam is sheer nonsense, for guilt implies personal responsibility, and the idea of original sin as an inherited infection is sub-ethical, irrational, and absurd.

"The same objections apply to the doctrine of the atonement. How can the guilt of one man be expiated by the death of another who is sinless—if indeed one may speak of a sinless man at all. What primitive notions of guilt and righteousness does this imply? And what primitive idea of God? The rationale of sacrifice in general may of course throw some light on the theory of the atonement, but even so, what a primitive mythology it is, that a divine Being should become incarnate, and atone for the sins of men through his own blood!

"The resurrection of Jesus is just as difficult, if it means an event whereby a supernatural power is released which can henceforth be appropriated through the sacraments. To the biologist such language is meaningless, for he does not regard death as a problem at all. The idealist would not object to the idea of a life immune from death, but he could not believe that such of a life is made available by the resuscitation of a corpse. . . .

"And as for the preexistence of Christ, with its corollary of man's translation into a celestial realm of light, and the clothing of the human personality in heavenly robes and a spiritual body—all this is not only irrational but utterly meaningless. Why should salvation take this particular form? Why should this be the fulfillment of human life and the realization of man's true being?"[9]

The reason why Bultmann rejects many biblical truths is that those truths are either not in harmony with today's scientific discoveries or they are offensive to the modern person's sensitivities. Because of this naturalistic, anti-supernatural assumption, when liberal scholars approach the Scriptures they adopt the historical-critical method of interpretation to explain away the supernatural activities recorded—the creation account, the worldwide flood, the crossing of the Red Sea by a large number of people, the shekinah that represented God's visible presence in the sanctuary, the fall of Jericho, prophecies about the future, the virgin birth, miracles of Jesus, Christ's *bodily* resurrection, a literal second coming, etc.

Consequently, the various approaches of the historical-critical method assume that the Bible is not inspired, trustworthy, or authoritative. *Classical liberalism's naturalistic assumption* that denies supernatural occurrences *became the basis of a plethora of methods to interpret the Bible.* Collectively, these are called the historical-critical method.

Naturalistic Foundations of the Historical-Critical Method

The various approaches included within contemporary higher criticism are all built on the following three naturalistic (anti-supernaturalistic) assumptions, all of which contribute to doubting the Word. These cardinal principles, without which there can be no historical-critical method, find classical expression in the works of the nineteenth-century German theologian and historian Ernst Troeltsch (1865-1923).[10]

The Principle of Correlation. *Every Effect Has a Natural Cause.* This principle states that every event must be explained solely by natural causes, that is, by cause and effect in the natural world. This means that there can be no miracles or supernatural occurrences; therefore, wherever miracles occur in the Bible, we must either reject those sections or give the miracles a naturalistic explanation. On the basis of this principle, such events as the six-day creation, the exodus of the Israelites from Egypt, the provision of manna in the wilderness, etc., are all rejected or considered as theological statements—not scientific or historically accurate accounts, but rather, history-*like* statements.

How does this principle explain the miracle of Christ's resurrection, for example? Since classical liberals maintain that there cannot be miracles, if Jesus was really seen on Easter Sunday as the Bible says, then either Jesus never really died on Friday (He may have been unconscious or in a coma), or those who claimed to have seen Him may have been hallucinating.

The Principle of Analogy. *The Present is the Key to the Past.* This principle holds that past events must be explained on the basis of present occurrences.

For instance, to the question: "Could Jesus have been resurrected bodily from the grave?" classical liberalism replies that the key to this past event is found in the present. Therefore, a person must go to the cemetery and find out how many dead people are *currently* rising from the grave. If one does not find dead people rising out of their graves, it means the Gospels' accounts of Jesus' resurrection could not have been true. Consequently, the doctrine of a future resurrection of believers at the second coming must be rejected or re-interpreted (as, perhaps, a coming of Jesus in your heart).

The Principle of Criticism. *Don't Believe Everything You Hear or Read.* According to this principle, whenever you read any account in the Bible, instead of accepting it as truth, treat it with a level of skepticism or accept it only tentatively, with the possibility of revision. In today's terms, it's cool to be skeptical, naive to be trusting. After all, the Watergate and the Iran-Contra cover-ups by past presidents of the United States have taught us that one should not trust something until it can be fully checked out with scientific or investigative scrutiny. Skepticism is the key to establishing truth. Therefore, as one approaches the Bible, one must begin with suspicion rather than trust.

How does this principle relate to the account of Christ's resurrection found in the New Testament? For classical liberals, it means being suspicious of the intentions of the Bible writers who recorded this event. They argue, among other things, that the resurrection accounts could have been designed to explain away the fact that the followers of Christ were misguided in the first place in believing that He was the Messiah.

Method Denies Full Inspiration and Trustworthiness. The above three naturalistic assumptions became the basis of the classical formulation of the historical-critical method. If the Bible accounts cannot be accepted as trustworthy until they have been "checked out" by the critic, one must determine *how* to arrive at "the truth" about what is recorded in the Bible. Therefore, using the above three naturalistic assumptions, classical liberalism came up with various, often inconsistent and conflicting, methods of interpreting the Bible, all of which are bracketed together under the label "historical-critical method."

The method is based on the above presuppositions. There cannot be a historical-critical method without an *a priori* denial of the full inspiration, trustworthiness, and authority of Scripture. *Take away the naturalistic assumptions, and the historical-critical method ceases to exist.*

Liberalism's Methods of Biblical Interpretation

Since liberal scholars hold that the Bible is essentially a human document and that the reports recorded in the Bible may not be reliable or accurate accounts of what actually happened, liberals have put forward several approaches (they term these methods "scientific," "historic," or "objective" paradigms) of Bible interpretation.

Examples of contemporary higher-critical methods include:

(1) *literary-source criticism,* which attempts to determine the various literary sources presumed to lie behind the present record in the Bible;

(2) *form or tradition criticism,* which seeks to get behind the written sources of the Bible to the period of oral tradition and isolate the oral forms and traditions alleged to have gone into the written sources;

(3) *redaction criticism,* which tries to study the activity of the "editors" of the Bible as they allegedly shaped, modified and even created the final product;

(4) *comparative-religion criticism,* which assumes that the Bible writers borrowed from the neighboring polytheistic cultures and which seeks to study the evolutionary development of the biblical faith from its assumed polytheistic or primitive forms to its present monotheistic or matured form;

(5) *historical criticism,* which employs all of the above and, in addition, draws upon archeology and secular historical sources; it seeks to determine authorship, date of writing, and what actually led to the writing of the biblical books; and

(6) *structural criticism,* which attempts to investigate the relationship between the surface structure of the writing and the deeper implicit structures that belong to literature as such.[11]

Theology as taught in most seminaries and universities today is based on liberalism's historical-critical method. This method forms the basis of many scholarly commentaries, articles, and books and also filters down to the pulpits. Unfortunately, those who are most affected by it are not acutely conscious of it. And herein lies the danger. *Scholars belonging to Bible-believing conservative churches and seeking to be considered "scholars" by the liberal academic community may think that they can successfully use liberalism's methods*—literary-source criticism, form or tradition criticism, redaction criticism, comparative-religion criticism, historical criticism, etc.—*without adopting the naturalistic foundation upon which old-fashioned classical liberalism established the methods!*

This theological experiment has given birth to "accommodationism" or "moderate liberalism" in conservative churches. Scholars give the appearance of being Bible-believing conservatives, but because they accept the use of the historical-critical method they are actually neo-liberals. For in order to use the methods of the historical-critical approach, a scholar belonging to a Bible-believing church such as our own would ultimately be forced by the liberal methodology to teach that inspired writings (the Bible and Ellen White) are *not fully* inspired, trustworthy, authoritative. In other words, the use of the historical-critical method leads to *doubting the Word.*

Moderate Liberalism's View of the Bible

Anglican scholar David L. Edwards, provost of Southwark Cathedral in London, is an articulate moderate liberal. He stated his views regarding the nature and purpose of the Bible in a dialogue with John Stott, an internationally respected Bible-believing evangelical scholar.[12] Although Edwards identifies himself as liberal, he is a church-oriented liberal. His position therefore is a true reflection of the "accommodationist" viewpoint—the kind gaining currency in the Seventh-day Adventist church. In Chapter Ten of this book we shall respond to such views on Scripture.

A Moderate Liberal's View. For now, however, we wish only to acquaint readers with moderate liberalism's subtle skepticism towards the Bible's inspiration and reliability. In the paragraphs that follow, Edwards states briefly what he understands to be the saving truth which the Bible affirms. He also mentions a few things which, though found in the Bible, he considers not inspired. He writes:

"God's purpose in inspiring the composition of the Bible which Christians hold in their hands today was 'severely practical.' . . . It was to tell us that we and the rest of the universe are wonderfully his creation—not to propose that science is corrected by either Genesis 1 or Genesis 2 (the myths in these two chapters, which come from different sources and dates, contradict each other in some details). It was to tell us that we are sinners—not to instruct us how the serpent who was already wicked could speak to Eve or how the murderous Cain, so primitive that he was Adam's firstborn son, found a woman to be a farmer's wife or how a flood covered the earth (including the mountains) without leaving any worldwide traces. It was to assure us that, although we are sinners, we are loved and delivered by God—not to inform us that the children of Israel included no fewer that 603,550 adult males plus families during the journey to Canaan (Numbers 1:46). It was to command us to live as God's children—not to persuade us that he dictated the law of Moses 430 years after his promise to Abraham (Galatians 3:17) although the time spent by the people of Israel in Egypt before the exodus had also been 430 years (Exodus 12:40). It was to tell us how he used a unique people, Israel, 'people who live apart and do not consider themselves one of the nations'—not to inform us that Balaam prophesied this having held conversations with a donkey and an angel (Numbers 22:21-35). It was to teach us, through his self revelation to the Israelites, that we must worship God alone—not to complain that the genocide of the Canaanites was incomplete. . . . It was to show that the holy God demands holiness—not to tell us that the number of wicked Israelites killed off by the plague in Shittim was twenty-four thousand (Numbers 25:9) or twenty-three thousand (1 Cor. 10:8). It was to reveal his holy love through Israel's great prophets—not to provide fully accurate predictions of coming events. It was to proclaim his demand for justice—not to give us a completely coherent account of the origins of the Israelite monarchy. It was to reveal himself in the whole bitter-sweet history of Israel—not to recount that history with complete accuracy (somehow reconciling the books of Samuel and the Kings with the later Chronicles). It was to show how when swallowed up into victorious empires amid the storms of history, when exiled and deprived of all political identity, the Jews reached a better understanding of God's holiness and mercy—not to tell us how a whale could swallow and regurgitate Dove (in Hebrew *Jonah*). . . .

It was to give us spiritual light—not to affirm that the sun once halted its journey across the sky for 'about a full day' (Joshua 10:13) or went backwards (Isaiah 38:8).

"God's purpose was to proclaim that Jesus is 'a light for revelation to the Gentiles and for glory to your people Israel'—not to tell us whether Joseph's father was called Jacob (Matthew 1:16) or Eli (Luke 3:23). It was to say that the love of God was embodied in the carpenter of Nazareth—not to argue with the historians about the dates when Quirinius took a census in Judea (Luke 2:2) and when Judas and Theudas led their rebellions (Acts 5:36-37). . . . It was to tell us that Jesus died for us (whether he died on the day of the Passover feast, as in three of the gospels, or on the day before as related by John) and was raised from the dead (whatever may have been the details of his resurrection, which the gospels report differently). . . . It was to speak with converting and sustaining power about ourselves and our salvation. 'For the word of God is living and active. Sharper than any double-edged sword, it penetrates even to dividing soul and spirit, joints and marrow; it judges the thoughts and attitudes of the heart' (Hebrews 4:12)."

"Magnificent Demolition Job." Edwards' assertions may sound familiar to you; his address is the kind heard from many pulpits and in many seminary lecture rooms today. Not a few Bible-believers sense that something is wrong with this view of Scripture, and yet they do not know what it is. They could readily discount the outright denials of miracles by radical (old-fashioned) liberals like Bultmann; but they cannot do so as easily with this "fascinating" view of Scripture—even though, ultimately, radical liberals and moderate liberals say the same things. Others, after reading this "magnificent demolition job" on the Bible by Edwards, feel like John Stott, who pictured himself as a peanut, lying "bruised, battered and broken beneath the Mighty Liberal Steamroller!"[13]

Readers who closely follow developments among Seventh-day Adventists will notice that the view of biblical inspiration presented above has been popularized in the church. Regrettably, some have hailed this kind of doubt regarding Scripture's inspiration and trustworthiness as "provocative, challenging, and extremely helpful in answering questions on inspiration"; others think it is "faith-building."[14] In subsequent chapters of *Receiving the Word* we shall highlight the implications of such a view of Scripture for Adventist doctrine and mission, and we shall also address some of the questions the "magnificent demolition job" raised.

Channel of Darkness. Ellen White wrote, "The plain, authoritative 'Thus saith the Lord,' is refused for some winding sophistry of errors. Infidelity has increased in proportion as men have questioned the Word and requirements of their Maker. They have taken up the work of cheapening character, and lessening faith in the inspiration of the Bible. Men claiming great wisdom have presumed to criticize and cut and cull the words of the living God, and have started questions to make shipwreck of the happiness of their fellow men and to ruin their hopes of heaven. This is a work that is pleasing to the enemy of all righteousness. The arguments that men bring against the Bible are the result of the counsels of the evil one. The door of their minds was opened to his suggestions; and the more they drifted into error, the greater grew their desire to draw other souls into the same channel of darkness. Many claim to believe the Bible, and their names are enrolled on the church records, who are among the most influential agents of Satan. . . . The only safety is in rejecting instantly every suggestion of unbelief. Do not open your mind to entertain doubts, even for an instant; bid them a decided refusal as they come to you for admission. Fasten the mind on the promises of God. Talk of them, rejoice in them; and the peace of God will rule in your hearts" (*Advent Review and Sabbath Herald,* September 22, 1910).

Moderate Liberalism: A Challenge to Adventism

The crisis of identity in the Seventh-day Adventist church stems from moderate liberals' efforts to redefine historic Adventist beliefs according to their new views of the Bible's inspiration, trustworthiness, and authority. Some in our ranks believe that they can legitimately employ the historical-critical method without adopting its underlying presuppositions. But is this really possible?

It is like saying that one can be a good Christian without accepting Christ as Savior and Lord. As we noted in Chapter One, trying to use the historical-critical method without accepting its naturalistic presuppositions is, in the words of one non-Adventist scholar, "as futile and absurd an undertaking as eating ham with Jewish presuppositions."[15]

Where the Issue Lies. We must emphasize it again: The on-going theological debates in our midst result largely from the cracks created in our theological foundation as some scholars have attempted to marry Adventism's high view of Scripture with the "moderate" use of liberalism's historical-critical method. As we shall show in a later chapter, this attempt inevitably leads people to join the critics' subtle campaign of attacking the Bible's credibility and message.

Doubting the Word is not new. "Because of its essential goodness evil men have always hated this Book. Because it champions the cause of the poor and needy it has always been derided by callous exploiters of labor. Because it advocates the rights of the individual, claiming that the humblest of human beings is of utmost value in the sight of God, it has always been a thorn in the flesh of tyrants and dictators. Time and again down the centuries deliberate efforts have been made to get rid of this Book, but always in vain. No persecution, however severe, no subtle attacks, however cunning, have been able to destroy it or diminish its influence for good."[16]

Indeed, after hundreds of years of "skeptical assault the book still remains, and the men who are now laboring to destroy it may as well undertake to demolish the pyramids of Egypt with a tack hammer. Infidels die, but this book still lives. Scoffers fade like the flowers and wither like the grass, but above their graves this book marches triumphantly on, and on its pages we read in characters of light, 'The grass withereth, the flower fadeth, but THE WORD OF OUR GOD SHALL STAND FOREVER'."[17]

The Choice We Face. The challenge before the Seventh-day Adventist church is whether it will continue *trusting the Word* or whether it will join moderate liberalism in *doubting the Word*. This crucial question lies at the heart of the theological conflicts in the church. Until recently, when liberalism's winds of historical criticism started blowing in the church, Adventists, by and large, trusted the Word. And there was good reason for doing so:

"Born in the East and clothed in Oriental form and imagery, the Bible walks the ways of all the world with familiar feet and enters land after land to find its own everywhere. It has learned to speak in hundreds of languages to the heart of man. It comes into the palace to tell the monarch that he is a servant of the Most High, and into the cottage to assure the peasant that he is a son of God. Children listen to its stories with wonder and delight, and wise men ponder them as parables of life. It has a word of peace for the time of peril, a word of comfort for the day of calamity, a word of light for the hour of darkness. Its oracles are repeated in the assembly of the people, and its counsels whispered in the ear of the lonely. The wicked and the proud tremble at its warning, but to the wounded and the penitent it has a mother's voice. The wilderness and the solitary place have been made glad by it, and the fire on the hearth has lit the reading of its well-worn page. It has woven itself into our deepest affections and colored our dearest dreams; so that love and friendship, sympathy and devotion, memory and hope, put on the beautiful garments of its treasured speech, breathing frankincense and myrrh. . . .

"No man is poor or desolate who has this treasure for his own. When the landscape darkens and the trembling pilgrim comes to the valley named 'of the shadow,' he is not afraid to enter: he takes the rod and staff of Scripture in his hand; he says to friend and comrade, 'Good-by; we shall meet again;' and comforted by that support, he goes toward the lonely pass as one who walks through darkness into light."[18]

But while the Bible has always shone brightly as a "lamp unto our feet and a light unto our path" (Ps 119:105), today some are attempting to obscure this divine light. The result is uncertainty regarding most of our essential doctrinal beliefs and practices. Before we illustrate how historical-critical assumptions are shaping theological views, however, we must acquaint the reader with the recent interpretational (hermeneutical) civil war among Seventh-day Adventists. This is the focus of the next chapter—how Adventists are *quarreling over the Word.*

NOTES

1. *Christian Service,* p. 158; cf. *Testimonies for the Church,* 3:312; 5:463.

2. *Testimonies for the Church,* 5:263; cf. *Christian Leadership,* p. 73; *Review and Herald,* May 21, 1914.

3. *Selected Messages,* 3:397; cf. *The Signs of the Times,* January 3, 1884; *Testimonies for the Church,* 3:165.

4. *Review and Herald,* May 30, 1899.

5. *Review and Herald,* February 7, 1893; cf. *Medical Ministry,* p. 99.

6. See *Seventh-day Adventists Believe . . . . : A Biblical Exposition of 27 Fundamental Doctrines* (Hagerstown, Md.: Review and Herald, 1988), p. 4.

7. A detailed discussion of these transmission errors is found in chapter 8 of this book.

8. See for example, Stephen T. Davis, *The Debate About the Bible* (Philadelphia: Westminster Press, 1977), pp. 94-113; Dewey M. Beegle, *Scripture, Tradition and Infallibility* (Grand Rapids: Eerdmans, 1973), pp. 175-197.

9. Rudolf Bultmann, "New Testament and Mythology," in *Kerygma and Myth,* ed. Hans-Werner Bartsch, trans. R. H. Fuller (London: S. P. C. K., 1961), I, pp. 1-11.

10. Troeltsch holds the distinction of formulating the three cardinal principles of the historical-critical method. For the contribution of Ernst Troeltsch, see Robert Morgan, Introduction to *Ernst Troeltsch: Writings on Theology and Religion,* trans. and ed. Robert Morgan and Michael Pye (Atlanta, Ga.: John Knox, 1977). However, among the significant luminaries of the historical-critical method, we must mention Richard Simon (1638-1712), René Descartes (1596-1650), John Locke (1632-1704), David Hume (1711-1776), Gotthold Lessing (1729-1781), Immanuel Kant (1724-1804), Johann Salomo Semler (1725-1791), Johann Philip Gabler (1753-1826), Friedrich Schleiermacher (1768-1834), and G. W. F. Hegel (1770-1831). For the contributions of these individuals to the historical-critical approach to Scriptures, see Gerhard Maier, *Biblical Hermeneutics* (Wheaton, Ill.: Crossway, 1994), pp. 251-255; William Larkin, *Culture and Biblical Hermeneutics* (Grand Rapids, Mich.: Baker, 1988), pp. 29-40; Clark H. Pinnock, *Tracking the Maze: Finding Our Way Through Modern Theology from an Evangelical Perspective* (San Francisco: Harper and Row, 1990), pp. 89-106.

11. Millard J. Erickson, *Christian Theology,* one-volume edition (Grand Rapids: Baker, 1983-85), pp. 81-104. For more on these see Gerhard F. Hasel's *Biblical Interpretation Today: An Analysis of Modern Methods of Biblical Interpretation and Proposals for the Interpretation of the Bible as the Word of God* (Washington, D.C.: Biblical Research Institute, 1985); Hasel, *Understanding the Living Word of God* (Mountain View, Calif.: Pacific Press, 1980).

12. David L. Edwards and John Stott, *Evangelical Essentials: A Liberal-Evangelical Dialogue* (Downers Grove, Ill.: InterVarsity Press, 1988), pp. 79-82.

13. Ibid., p. 83.

14. See the comments by J. David Newman and Ralph Neall on the back jacket of Alden Thompson's *Inspiration: Hard Questions, Honest Answers* (Hagerstown, Md.: Review and Herald, 1991); cf. Gosnell L. O. R. Yorke's recommendation of the book in his review article in *Ministry*, December 1991, p. 28; Gerhard van Wyk, "A Practical Theological Perspective on Adventist Theology and Contextualisation," *Journal of Adventist Thought in Africa* 1/1 (November 1995):132-149. Because Thompson's book has been acclaimed and promoted as possibly "the most significant book published by an Adventist press in this decade" (see Newman's comment on the book's back jacket), in later chapters of our present work we shall set forth some crucial questions that it raises.

15. Kurt E. Marquart, *Anatomy of an Exploration: Missouri in Lutheran Perspective* (Fort Wayne, Ind.: Concordia Theological Seminary Press, 1977), p. 114.

16. Arthur S. Maxwell, *Your Bible and You* (Washington, D.C.: Review and Herald, n.d.), pp. 45-46 (found in the first two pages of the chapter titled, "Evidences of Inspiration").

17. H. L. Hastings, *Will the Old Book Stand?* (Washington, D.C.: Review and Herald, 1923), p. 349.

18. Henry van Dyke, quoted in John D. Snider's *I Love Books: Why, What, How, and When We Should Read,* revised edition (Washington, D.C.: Review and Herald, 1944), pp. 228-230.

What is the background of recent theological conflicts within the Seventh-day Adventist church? Why and how are our doctrinal beliefs and lifestyle being re-interpreted? What are the dangers we face and what are we to do about them?

II. NATURE OF THE CRISIS

Chapter Four

Quarreling Over the Word

In 1971, an insightful *Newsweek* article opened with these favorable words about Seventh-day Adventists: "In an age when more and more American youths are using religion to express their countercultural discontent, what could be more appealing to them than a religion that forbids members to fight in wars, promotes teamwork rather than competitive athletics, strongly advocates health foods, treats body, mind and spirit with equal reverence, appeals as much to blacks as whites, opposes conventional Sunday worship, stoutly defends the radical freedom of all religions and is firmly convinced that the millennium is just around the corner?"[1]

Strategy to Change Adventism. But the article also proceeded to mention a startling development in the church. The magazine highlighted the efforts by "liberals in the SDA church, who would like to recover the early Adventist tradition of dissent." According to the liberals "you will find few seminary professors who admit to the 6,000 year theory, and many Adventists no longer believe that the days of Creation were each 24 hours long." The liberals also charge that "Adventists traditionally have placed too literal an interpretation on the second coming—thinking it was just around the corner—and failed to recognize the power of that doctrine to motivate Christians to change the world around them." And at a time when Adventists were expected to show great interest in end-time events (known technically as apocalyptic eschatology), in the opinion of the liberal Adventist scholars the church was "fatally afflicted with eschatological paranoia."[2]

Significantly, the *Newsweek* article also stated the strategy of liberal Adventism to reinterpret the church's historic doctrines on creation, the second-coming, and last day events: "As a first step toward recovering the dissenting spirit of the past, liberal Adventists contend, the church *ought to rid itself of dependence upon an exaggerated Biblical literalism.*"[3]

So as early as 1971, the crisis over biblical interpretation was already perceptible—even to non-Adventists. The only way the liberals could change the church's traditional doctrines was by getting rid of the alleged "exaggerated Biblical literalism" of Adventism.

Was the church aware of this *crisis over the Word?* How did it respond? And what has happened since the 1970s? This chapter takes up these questions.

Adventist Awareness. Seventh-day Adventists have not overlooked the importance of the twin issues of biblical authority and interpretation. They have always understood that the interpretational or hermeneutical lens through which a person reads the Bible can result in either a clear *perception* or a blind *deception* regarding its message, leading the reader either to receive the message or depart from it. Three factors contribute to this awareness.

First, the *identity* of Seventh-day Adventists as God's "remnant church" depends upon their understanding clearly the nature and meaning of the Bible. Second, because of their urgent *mission* to proclaim a distinctive message at a special time, Adventists have a keen sense of the signs of the times which remind them that their Lord is coming soon. This understanding of their mission and their times has made them conscious of developments around them, including the questions that others are raising about the Bible. Finally, discussions over the inspiration and interpretation of Scripture inevitably raise similar questions about the *writings of Ellen G. White,* who Adventists believe received the biblical gift of prophecy.

As we mentioned in Chapter One, far greater than the threat of the *independent right* is that launched within the church by the *liberal left.* The current crisis of identity can be traced to the conflicting methods of Bible interpretation currently operating within the church. The methods are: (1) mainstream Adventism's plain reading of Scripture (the historical-*grammatical* method), and (2) liberal Adventism's higher criticism (the historical-*critical* method).

The rise of liberal methods among Seventh-day Adventists should come as no surprise, since in the larger scholarly community anyone who does not employ the liberal academic methodology is often perceived as "hopelessly uninformed," "blinded by a combination of ego needs and naivete," "narrow-minded," "anti-intellectual," "pre-scientific," and even "fundamentalistic."[4] This may explain why some Adventist scholars are calling for a modified use of the historical-critical method. But the Adventist church was not caught unawares. The church's firm stand against the historical-critical method and reactions against the church's position have led to *quarreling over the Word.*

The Quarrel: What It Is and What It Is Not

Throughout their history, Seventh-day Adventists have had disputes over a number of issues. But even in their disagreements, they have always insisted on the Bible as the only infallible norm by which all views are to be judged.

Thus, our early Adventist pioneers debated such issues as the identity of "the king of the North" in Daniel 11, Armageddon, the time to begin the Sabbath, the law in the book of Galatians, etc. In our own day, Bible-believing conservatives disagree on some details of specific doctrines (e.g., the nature of Christ's humanity, justification and sanctification, etc.). These disagreements often stem from an inconsistency in using the historic Adventist method of interpretation (the plain reading of Scripture) and an unwillingness to acknowledge that one may have been wrong.

Today, however, the key issue is different. Simply stated, it boils down to this: *In the face of theological disagreements, should Seventh-day Adventists still retain the Bible as fully inspired, trustworthy, and the sole norm for Christian belief and practice?* Bible-believing Adventists say Yes; others who have been influenced by the higher criticism of liberal theology say No. The conflicting responses to this question lie at the heart of the conflict over biblical authority and interpretation.

Two Kinds of Defects. Another way of highlighting the present hermeneutical quarrel in our church is by pointing out two major defects in Bible interpretations: (1) using a *wrong* methodology, and (b) an inconsistency in using a *right* methodology. The present disagreement is *not* due to an inconsistent use of a right methodology, but rather to the use of a wrong methodology—namely, the historical-critical method.[5]

Bible-believing Christians should avoid both kinds of defects. But if Seventh-day Adventists are ever to be criticized, it should not result from using wrong methodology but from inconsistently applying proper methodology. Unfortunately, this distinction is not always recognized.

The present quarrel over the Word has to do with the attempts by some to employ a wrong methodology (higher criticism) in interpreting the Scriptures. In the next chapter we shall show how such interpretation undermines historic Adventist teachings. Right now, we will only concentrate on the *who, why,* and *how* of this quarrel during the past twenty to thirty years.

This chapter may be uninteresting to some readers. But those who endure and understand this important historical overview will have a better grasp of the theological developments that have taken place in the church in recent times.

Key Players in the Quarrel: Leaders and Scholars

The major players in the quarrel over the Word have been the church's *leaders,* including pastors and administrators, whether elected or appointed, and *scholars,* such as professors of religion and theology, editors, publishers and institutional heads. As in other Christian denominations, these leaders and scholars greatly influence the thinking of church members, students, readers of church publications, etc., regarding the nature of biblical authority and interpretation. Courage of convictions regarding the Bible, or lack of it, by both leaders and scholars sets the tone for the theological direction of the church.[6]

The roles of these key players in the crisis over biblical authority and interpretation do complement each other. Church leaders play a vital role in that they hire and retain scholars in our institutions; their pronouncements, actions, or inaction set the trend for scholars to follow or at least give tacit encouragement. Scholars, on the other hand, through their influence in the classrooms and committees and through published books, articles, editorials, and seminars, educate the present and future leaders of the church—the very people who later dictate the theological direction of church.

One must not ignore the symbiotic relationship between leaders and scholars in shaping attitudes about the Bible. Ultimately, these major groups of people are responsible for the kinds of teaching offered in our schools, the kinds of sermons preached in our pulpits, and the kinds of materials coming out of our publishing houses and our publications.

For this reason, it is crucial to understand how church leaders and scholars have responded to the use of higher criticism in the ongoing quarrel over the Word. This chapter will reveal that whereas church leaders in the past have taken an uncompromising stand against the historical-critical method, at least in their official pronouncements, the same cannot be said of the church's scholars—the professors of religion and theology, editors, publishers and institutional heads.

Church Rejects the Liberal Approach

Symposium on Biblical Hermeneutics, 1974. In the face of a growing awareness of historical-critical challenges already bearing fruit in the church, a major effort to address the dual issues of biblical inspiration and interpretation occurred in 1974. The Biblical Research Institute (BRI) of the General Conference organized Bible conferences at Andrews University, Pacific Union College, and Southern College. These conferences examined the methods of biblical interpretation—specifically the legitimacy of liberalism's historical-critical method.

Taking a high view of Scripture as fully inspired and trustworthy, the presenters at the Bible conferences steered away from the shaky foundations of higher criticism's methodologies and emphasized principles of Bible interpretation consistent with the internal testimony of both Scripture and the writings of Ellen G. White. The BRI published the results in the definitive book, *A Symposium on Biblical Hermeneutics,*[7] which rejected the use of the historical-critical method.

The Rio Document, 1986. The BRI's rejection of the historical-critical approach to Bible study found reaffirmation in 1986 at the General Conference Annual Council meeting in Rio de Janeiro, Brazil. In a document entitled, "Methods of Bible Study," leaders representing all the world fields urged Bible students to avoid the use of historical criticism in the two forms in which liberal scholars were employing it: (a) "as *classically formulated,*" based on presuppositions that deny the miracles and supernatural events recorded in the Bible; and (b) "a *modified use* of this method" which retains the principle of criticism which subordinates the Bible to human reason.

Church leaders affirmed: "The historical-critical method minimizes the need for faith in God and obedience to His commandments. In addition, . . . such a method de-emphasizes the divine element in the Bible as an inspired book (including its resulting unity) and depreciates or misunderstands apocalyptic prophecy and the eschatological portions of the Bible." Because the historical-critical method undermines faith in God, obedience to Him, and the full inspiration and unity of the Bible, Adventist Bible students were urged "to avoid relying on the use of the presuppositions and the resultant deductions associated with the historical-critical method."

The Rio document (as "Methods of Bible Study" is also called) explicitly stated that "even a modified use . . . of the historical-critical method that retains the principle of criticism which subordinates the Bible to human reason is unacceptable to Adventists" (see Appendix C of this book).

Not surprisingly, the reaction of Adventist Bible scholars to the Rio document was mixed—a fact that has contributed to the quarrel over the Word.

The Quarrel Begins. Generally, scholars with high views of Scripture and the Spirit of Prophecy embraced the document as reflecting what Adventism stands for. But other Adventist scholars found it to obstruct their agenda or threaten their standing in the larger liberal academic community. These scholars ignored, rejected, faulted or fought against the document's categorical rejection of the historical-critical method. They believed that they could use contemporary higher criticism without adopting its anti-supernaturalistic assumptions (the classical formulation)[8] and overlooked the fact that even "a modified use of this method" indeed subjects the Bible to the criticism of human reason. These scholars saw "Methods of Bible Study" as representing a "myopic position," "altogether unacceptable."[9]

Many church members may not know, however, that the theological crises the church faced in the 1970s and 1980s—over the inspiration of Ellen White, the prophetic significance of 1844, the controversy over the Sanctuary, Desmond Ford's challenges, etc.—were due to a crisis already in progress over the interpretation of inspired writings.[10]

While Bible-believing Adventists discerned that the historical-critical method was the root cause of the theological upheaval, the method's proponents maintained that the trouble stemmed from the church's failure fully to recognize that one could use the method in historical, grammatical, and literary analysis of the Bible without adopting its classical presuppositions of anti-supernaturalism.

One such proponent wrote: "Most if not all the doctrinal differences and debates in the church over the past fifty years [1930s-1980s] have arisen between those faithful to the principles and procedures of the historical-critical method, on one hand, and those loyal to the prooftext subjectivity and presuppositions on the other."[11] "Prooftext subjectivity" is a prejudiced reference to the historic Adventist approach.

Likewise, in the current debate over such issues as creation, the substitutionary atonement of Christ, abortion, women's ordination, homosexuality, polygamy, etc., the issue is really over how to interpret the Bible. Thus, whether they are aware of it or not, church members may have shaped their views on the above issues at least in part by their alignment in the ongoing battle of interpretive approaches between the two opposing factions of Adventist scholarship—those who read Scripture through the lenses of liberalism's historical-critical method and those who reject this methodology.

Use of the Liberal Approach

Liberals Are Not Bad People. The interpreters who adopt liberalism's historical-critical method are not bad people. They are individuals experiencing what a former university president rightly identified as "shifts" in theological orientation.[12] Another church leader wrote: "They are committed believers. Many of them exhibit the beauty of Christian virtues in their lives. Most of them love the church. They would like to share the faith and certainties of our forefathers, but in the honesty of their hearts, they do not have them. They are unable to see the uniqueness of our message, the distinctiveness of our identity, the eschatological dimension of our hope, or the urgency of our mission. Representing a wide spectrum of religious thought, they attempt to reinterpret traditional theological Seventh-day Adventist thinking by dressing some of our old doctrines in what appear to them to be new and attractive semantic garments."[13]

But in order to *reinterpret* Adventism and make it "relevant," they employ a new approach to Scripture: the historical-critical method, which for some is the hallmark of a biblical scholar.

Liberal Approach in Adventist Scholarship. Contrary to the recent assertions that "No Adventist Bible scholar subscribes to that [historical-critical] method, or to its presuppositions or conclusions,"[14] the evidence points in a different direction. Even before 1974 and 1986, the years in which the Biblical Research Institute of the General Conference and the world field leaders at Annual Council spoke out against this approach, some Adventist Bible scholars were already using versions of the historical-critical method and recommending it to others.

In fact, the author of the above denial had himself, eight years earlier, asserted: "During the late 1930s Seventh-day Adventist Bible scholars began using these historical-critical principles and procedures in their study; and today [1987], half a century later, all but a few do so routinely."[15] The suggestion that no Adventist Bible scholar follows the historical-critical method is, therefore, an overstatement, or perhaps an unintentional misrepresentation of the facts.

Further, since the 1970s, *Spectrum,* an independent journal of the Association of Adventist Forums, has been the publication to foster and advocate historical-critical views within Adventism.[16] It "provided a previously unavailable outlet for critical analysis of traditional Adventist views."[17]

For example, the December 1982 issue of the journal carries an article by a New Testament professor whose historical-critical method analysis of a parable of Jesus begins with the question: "Can this approach—often called the 'historical-critical method'—be used by Bible students who hold a conservative view of scriptural inspiration?" The professor's answer is Yes. His concluding paragraph states: "Indeed, *virtually all Adventist exegetes* [sic] of Scripture do use historical-critical methodology, *even if they are not willing to use the term.* The historical-critical method *deserves a place* in the armamentarium of Adventists who are serious about understanding their Bibles."[18]

Notice the subtle implications in the above statement. Since "virtually all" Adventist exegetes use the higher critical method, those who refuse to use the historical-critical method must be an insignificant minority, if not a "fringe" group. Also, if Adventists "who are serious about understanding their Bibles" should be utilizing the historical-critical method, then one cannot be a "serious" scholar without adopting the method. In the same issue of *Spectrum,* an Old Testament scholar begins his article, "Genesis One in Historical-Critical Perspective," with the assertion: "The 'historical-critical' method of Bible study, used properly, *can be a valid and powerful tool* for Seventh-day Adventists."[19]

The descriptive phrase, "virtually all," aptly captures the direction in which many North American Adventist scholars were leaning regarding the use of the historical-critical method. Although most Seventh-day Adventist scholars who employ the method "are not willing to use the term," they insist that the historical-critical method "deserves a place" or "can be a valid and powerful tool" in the study of the Bible. Thus, one scholar wrote in 1981: "The clear majority of

Adventist biblical scholars . . . favor the use of such descriptive methodologies [of the historical-critical method—source criticism, redaction criticism, form criticism, and tradition criticism]."[20]

Editors of Publishing Institutions. Not only academics in the classroom, but key editors of our church publications also believed that using the historical-critical method did not require adopting the naturalistic presuppositions. We might well expect this, since editors tend to be selected from among the leading scholars, "virtually all" of whom were using the liberal methodology.

Thus, a book editor of a major church publishing house likened the historical-critical method to a valuable scientific tool: its utility or harm depends on the user.[21] Similarly, the editor of a church publication stated that "the question must not be *whether* we will employ historical[-critical] methods (because we already do to some extent) but *how far* we rely upon them."[22]

The question remains: Can a Seventh-day Adventist reasonably use a little of the historical-critical method without adopting its underlying presuppositions? Whereas a world-class expert in the method and a former advocate of it has responded, "One can no more be a *little* historical-critical than a *little* pregnant,"[23] some academics and editors within our ranks think otherwise. As we shall see in the next chapter, the problem with contemporary higher criticism lies not merely in its naturalistic presuppositions, but also in the unbiblical presuppositions of the method which deny the full inspiration, trustworthiness, and normative authority of the Bible. In any case, the favorable disposition of our church scholars towards the use of the historical-critical method may help to explain why some Adventist publications contain the materials they do.

Liberal Approach Popularized. In 1991 a leading publishing house of the church released *Inspiration: Hard Questions, Honest Answers*, a controversial book based on the historical-critical method.[24] The author, an Old Testament professor, candidly admitted: "To a large extent, this book simply describes the approach to Christian living that Adventists have always practiced but simply *have been reluctant to admit in print.* If anything is unusual, then, it is the candor with which the 'illustrations' are laid."[25]

This statement alludes discreetly to the historical-critical method which, as the New Testament professor asserted almost a decade earlier, "virtually all" Adventist biblical scholars employ in their interpretation—"even if they are not willing to use the term." It is therefore not surprising that one biblical scholar recently noted that while *"Inspiration* is about the more theological topic of inspiration of the Scriptures, at times it does deal with issues of methodology and approach, and on occasion specifically with the historical-critical method.

Some involved in the hermeneutical debate have perceived this book as the archetypical product of historical-critical methodology."[26]

Indeed, the contents of *Inspiration,* as we shall later demonstrate, betray its historical-critical foundations.[27]

For Seventh-day Adventists, the significance of the book *Inspiration* lies in the fact that, contrary to the General Conference Annual Council "Methods of Bible Study" position, a church-owned publishing house chose to publish a book that employed the historical-critical method.

More importantly, it was the boldest attempt yet by an Adventist scholar to popularize higher criticism for consumption by lay-members and students.[28] In the words of one perceptive observer, "The historical-critical method had come out of the academic closet into mainstream Adventism"! From that time on, things would not be the same again in mainstream Adventist publications.

A recent attempt further to domesticate higher criticism for Adventists is the publication of the pro-ordination book, *The Welcome Table: Setting a Place for Ordained Women.*[29] Although it was not from a church-owned publishing house, it has been widely promoted in the church as "a definitive collection of essays for our time from respected church leaders—both women and men. Informed, balanced, mission-oriented, and thoroughly Adventist, this book—like Esther of old—has 'come to the kin-dom [*sic*] for such a time as this."[30] Coming just four years after *Inspiration,* this widely publicized book also evidences the flourishing of the historical-critical method in the church—a fact already noted by knowledgeable scholars,[31] and which will become clearer in the next chapter of this book.

Opposition to the Liberal Approach

Liberal Approach Opposed by Scholars. To counter the inroads of higher criticism within Adventism, the Adventist Theological Society (ATS) was formally organized in 1988 by a group of conservative scholars, leaders, and members. According to the ATS Information Brochure, "The Society's theological position is based on a literal understanding of Scripture and also holds to the 'Fundamental Beliefs of the Seventh-day Adventist Church' as voted in 1980, and the 'Methods of Bible Study Committee Report' as published in the *Adventist Review,* Jan. 22, 1987. In simple terms, members of the ATS feel it necessary to say that they continue to uphold the Bible, that Jesus died for their sins, that Ellen G. White has theological as well as pastoral authority, and the Seventh-day Adventist Church has been called on the world scene as the remnant for such a time as this."

ATS Annual Reaffirmations. To prevent the Adventist Theological Society from going the way the historical-critical scholars wanted to lead the church, the ATS required its members annually to sign seven "reaffirmations"—all of which were being challenged by liberals in the church. The reaffirmations included a commitment to continued belief in:

(1) the substitutionary atonement of Christ—i.e., His death in our place pays the penalty for sin, provides forgiveness, and creates saving faith;

(2) the Bible as the Word of God—"the inspired, infallible revelation of propositional truth. The Bible is its own interpreter, provides the foundation and context for scholarship and the totality of life, and is the unerring standard for doctrine";

(3) the use of the time-honored Adventist method of biblical interpretation (the plain reading of Scripture), the necessity of relying on the Holy Spirit in this effort, and a rejection of the use of "any form of the 'historical-critical' method in Bible study";

(4) Ellen G. White as possessing more than pastoral authority, and that her writings "are an invaluable tool for illuminating Scripture and confirming church doctrines";

(5) the "literal reading and meaning of Genesis 1-11 as an objective, factual account of earth's origin and early history; that the world was created in six literal, consecutive 24-hour days; that the entire earth was subsequently devastated by a literal world-wide flood, and that since creation week the age of our world is 'about 6000 years'";

(6) a literal sanctuary in heaven, the pre-advent judgment beginning in 1844, and the identification of the Seventh-day Adventist church as the remnant movement called to proclaim the three angels' messages which prepare the world for Christ's second coming; and

(7) faithfulness to the Seventh-day Adventist church, supporting it through tithes, offerings, personal effort and influence.

The average Adventist church member takes these affirmations for granted. But these very things were being challenged by Adventist thought-leaders who were using the historical-critical method. Although the membership criteria safeguarded the ATS from deviating from its stated purposes and goals, some Adventist academics—particularly those favoring the historical-critical method—took offense at the Society's insistence on these seven reaffirmations as criteria for membership.[32]

Nevertheless, through the *Journal of the Adventist Theological Society* and through seminars and other works published by members, the ATS offered scholarly biblical defenses of the historic Adventist doctrines challenged by their historical-critical counterparts. In 1992, the Adventist Theological Society published an important book, *Issues in Revelation and Inspiration*, which is a direct rebuttal of the historical-critical assumptions underlying the book *Inspiration*.[33]

Liberal Approach Opposed at Popular Level. In 1987, one year before the Adventist Theological Society (ATS) was formally organized, another independent publication, *Adventists Affirm,* was started by "a group of scholars and other interested people" to address the liberalizing influences in the church. Believing that "a conservative approach to issues facing the Seventh-day Adventist church is not only needed but welcome," the publishers of *Adventists Affirm* indicated in their "Statement of Mission" that the publication "is dedicated to upholding the fundamental beliefs of the Seventh-day Adventist church and supporting its leadership in upholding those beliefs" against "the impact of liberalizing trends eroding confidence in the authority of the Bible for defining belief and practice."

The "Statement of Mission" expresses the goal of *Adventists Affirm* as follows: "The purpose of *Adventists Affirm* is to address issues involving doctrine and practice faced by the church, and to do so on the basis of the Bible and the writings of Ellen White. The intent is to affirm the fundamental beliefs of our church as confessed in the 'Fundamental Beliefs of Seventh-day Adventists,' affirm the Bible as the inspired Word of God, affirm the Spirit of Prophecy writings as inspired counsel and illumination on the Bible, affirm the Bible-based lifestyle and piety of Seventh-day Adventists, and affirm the leadership of the church as appointed servants of the Lord."

Similarities and Differences. Both *Adventists Affirm* and the Adventist Theological Society seek to preserve the beliefs and practices of the church from liberal attacks. Both are mainstream conservative organizations operating within the church. And prominent individuals who have been associated with *Adventists Affirm* have also played leading roles in the ATS.[34]

Because of the converging interests of the two groups, and because some participants in *Adventists Affirm* are also well-known ATS members, the two groups are sometimes confused. But there are two major differences between them.

For one, the ATS publications are written for a more scholarly readership, while *Adventists Affirm* is oriented to a wide readership—both scholars and non-scholars. Recently, though, the ATS launched a popular journal called *Perspective Digest.*

In addition, *Adventists Affirm* took a stand against the ordination of women as elders and pastors, maintaining that ordaining women to these headship roles is contrary to Scripture and historic Adventist teaching and practice.[35] A significant part of this effort was the publication of the book, *The Tip of An Iceberg,* showing how historical-critical assumptions underlie much of the argumentation and conclusions of many who advocate women's ordination.[36]

An Important Distinction. At this point, we must make it absolutely clear that there are Bible-believing Adventists who, while favoring the ordination of women, are also opposed to the use of the historical-critical method. The disagreement between conservative *proponents* and conservative *opponents* of women's ordination is not about the use of a wrong methodology (the kind used by historical-critical proponents) but has to do with *inconsistency in the use of a right methodology,* the traditional Adventist method of interpreting Scripture.[37]

With time, earnest prayer, and serious study, disagreements among conservatives are more easily resolved than with liberals, since conservative Bible students are already united in their acceptance of Scripture as fully inspired, trustworthy and the sole authoritative norm for doctrine and lifestyle. Without such common ground, it is almost impossible for liberals and conservatives to breach their differences.

This fact, though, is often overlooked in attempts to explain the nature of Adventism's crisis over Bible interpretation. Thus, some have oversimplified the 1995 General Conference arguments advanced by two leading conservative scholars regarding the ordination of women, citing them as evidence that the decades-long hermeneutical quarrel between liberals and conservatives in the church is actually a quarrel among conservatives over what some describe as "principle" and "literal" approaches.[38]

The result of this mistaken analysis, perhaps unintended, is that: (1) Bible-believing conservatives are often made to appear as supporting the liberal agenda; and (2) scholars subscribing to liberalism's historical-critical method are mistaken for Bible-believing conservatives. In this confusion, it is not always easy for ordinary church members to realize that the real quarrel in the church is between Adventists who uphold the plain reading of Scripture and those who employ higher criticism.

In any case, the continued impact of the Adventist Theological Society's efforts in exposing the inroads of liberal thought (especially through its journal and its book *Issues in Revelation and Inspiration*) combined with the work of *Adventists Affirm* (notably the book *The Tip of An Iceberg*) in unmasking the historical-critical assumptions in much of the agitation for women's ordination, may together have prompted a subtle repackaging of higher criticism for the general Adventist audience.

Repackaging the Liberal Approach

In the effort to make the historical-critical approaches user-friendly to unsuspecting church members, leaders, and students, proponents of the method have adopted several strategies.

1. A Human Face on the Liberal Approach. Historical-critical scholars put a human face on their method by giving the impression that they alone are the champions of human "liberation." Here the agenda of the historical-critical method has intersected with the goals of the different forms of *liberation theology*—a theological orientation which seeks to "liberate" the poor, the oppressed, the underclass, the marginalized, women, ethnic minorities, and "sexual minorities."

While the cause of human liberation is legitimate biblically, any agenda that leads to narrowing the Bible's scope of authority to a few sections that support the causes being promoted deserves rejection by Bible-believing Christians. And yet, some proponents of the different liberal theologies (liberation theology, feminist theology, cultural theologies, social gospel, etc.) have attempted to win Adventist support to their causes in this way, as we shall show in Chapter Eleven.

It is no passing coincidence that since the 1970s, when an increasing number of the church's Bible scholars began adopting the higher critical methods of liberal theology, the Adventist church has also been thrown into much turmoil over such "hot" issues of social ethics as abortion, polygamy, divorce and remarriage, women's ordination, homosexuality, and racism.

In the debate over these issues, advocates of the higher-critical method have harnessed the ethical sensitivities and sympathies of many good-willed Christians who are concerned about issues of injustice (whether of race, gender, or class) into supporting the liberal agenda. Thus, those in the church who are justifiably standing up against any form of injustice, unfairness, and discrimination are led to believe that in order to fight racism, gender injustice, oppression of minorities, etc., one must don the robes of liberalism. However, one can address such issues without resorting to the use of the historical-critical method—an approach that leads to diminishing the Bible's authority.[39]

2. Confusing an Illegitimate Method with an Inconsistent One. As noted earlier, two major kinds of defects in Bible interpretation affect many scholarly attempts to explain the meaning of Scriptures: (1) the use of a wrong methodology, and (2) inconsistency with a right methodology. Unfortunately, because these two defects are often confused, the misunderstanding has furthered the aims of those who espouse the liberal approach to interpreting Scripture.

Thus, the current quarrel between conservatives and liberals is made to appear as a debate among fellow conservatives. Those who employ liberalism's higher criticism give the impression that they are also Bible-believing conservatives who happen to hold different views on some subjects.

To give legitimacy to their claim, proponents of higher criticism point to disagreements among the Bible-believing Adventist pioneers, and also differences of opinion among today's Bible-believing conservatives, as no different from their own cases. However, the truth is that while the Adventist pioneers and today's conservatives are united in accepting the Bible's full inspiration, trustworthiness, and sole authority, higher-critical scholars do not accept this position. This point will become clearer in the next chapter.

3. Discrediting the Traditional Adventist Approach. A third strategy is to discredit traditional Adventism's method by insinuating that it is defective. Sometimes the impression is given that until the scholars of contemporary higher criticism came on the scene in the mid-twentieth century, Adventists did not have sound hermeneutics. Proponents imply that because our pioneers had not formally studied Hebrew, Greek, philosophy, and theology from established seminaries, they could not have done serious biblical interpretation or exegesis.

Historical-critical advocates express this unjustified disdain for the Seventh-day Adventist pioneers in several ways. In the past some have commented that "the pioneers did theology, not exegesis"; "they employed allegorical (Alexandrian) method, not historical-grammatical (Antiochian) method"; "they did practical or devotional theology, not a seriously thought-out system of beliefs."

Thus, one group of authors writing as "evangelical Adventists" maintains: "While early Adventists were clearly committed to scripture they did not understand how to interpret it. They often used a proof-text method of biblical interpretation to defend their distinctive beliefs and consequently missed the overall, uniting purpose of scripture as a revelation of God's salvation."[40] Another author writes that "the Seventh-day Adventist church has never fully outgrown the Fundamentalist view of Inspiration that it grew up with in the nineteenth century"—a view of inspiration he characterizes as "a literal, rigid, propositional, or 'proof text' interpretation of Scripture."[41]

A more nuanced, subtle discrediting of the works of those following the footsteps of the pioneers characterizes their position as the "key-text" method, over against the "contextual method."[42]

Some dismiss anyone who does not operate on historical-critical assumptions as employing an obscurantist "proof-text" method. We have already noted how one author describes the well-crafted 1986 "Methods of Bible Study" document's stance as a "myopic position,"[43] symptomatic of a "proof-text method." "In essence, the historical-grammatical method does scholarly investigation of the Bible under the control of fundamentalist proof-text principles and presuppositions, and appears to confirm proof-text conclusions by scholarly procedures."[44]

Those who are familiar with the key issues of hermeneutics reject such an assessment as a misunderstanding of the Adventist approach. In fact, a quick reference to the "Methods of Bible Study" document, reproduced in Appendix C of this book, will challenge the contention that the historic Adventist approach is a "proof-text" method.

4. Point to the "Clear Majority" of Historical-Critical Scholars. A fourth strategy for domesticating the historical-critical method in the Adventist church is to suggest that since many Adventist scholars in the industrialized world are traveling the "wide and broad way" of liberal scholarship, the path being trodden by the "majority" must be right. This strategy can be very tempting to those who crave the applause of "progressive," "open-minded" and "enlightened" scholarship.

Statements like, "*virtually all* Adventist exegetes of Scripture do use historical critical methodology"[45] and "*the clear majority* of Adventist biblical scholars . . . favor the use of such descriptive [historical-critical] methodologies"[46] can have a powerful psychological impact. Who wants to go against a position that is backed by an "overwhelming majority of our Bible teachers and theologians"? Which church member, student, administrator, even Bible teacher would want to be scorned as belonging to an uneducated, uninformed, "out-of-touch," "ultra-conservative," "extremist," or "fundamentalist" group of Adventist scholars?

Notice how the alleged "clear majority" often dismisses scholars who are traveling "the strait and narrow way" of traditional Seventh-day Adventism. Even though the approach of mainstream Adventism is consistent with the *sola scriptura* of the sixteenth-century Reformers, William Miller, and Ellen G. White, and even though their plain reading of Scripture (the historical-grammatical method) is shared by a majority of church members around the world, observe how a historical-critical author refers to the traditional Adventist approach: "the historical-grammatical method has gained [should have read "has retained"] *only limited* acceptance among Adventist scholars."[47]

The subtle implication is that the historic Adventist approach is defective because it is not embraced by historical critical scholars! Some have wondered how Joshua and Caleb would view this approach (Num 13 & 14).

5. Dress the Historical-Critical Method in a New Garment. As the faithful phalanx of Adventist scholars, represented by such groups as the Adventist Theological Society and *Adventists Affirm,* continues to expose the bankruptcy of the historical-critical method, one author has suggested that the term "historical-critical method" be dropped altogether, ostensibly because it is so loaded and so often misunderstood.[48] He seems to assume that if the expression is not employed, the method will cease to be identified as historical-critical.

Others have also simply dropped the word "critical" in the phrase "historical-critical method." Thus one author, who in earlier years had praised the historical-critical method, now insists that "*no* real Adventist scholar follows this [historical-critical] method."[49] What method, then, do "real" Adventist scholars follow? He answers: "The majority of Seventh-day Adventist Bible scholars correctly follow the *historical method* of research-level Bible study"![50]

Other Bible teachers prefer to disguise the historical-critical method as "historical analysis," "serious exegesis," "boldly studying the Bible," etc.

6. Suggest User-Friendly Labels. At the same time that the traditional Adventist approach is being frowned upon as a pre-scientific "proof-text," "fundamentalist," "key-text" method, several new labels have surfaced for the more "progressive" methods. Among these are: "principle approach," "contextual approach," "matured approach," "developmental approach," "progressive approach," "dynamic approach," "commonsense approach," "casebook approach," etc.

Regrettably, those who use these new labels fail to show how these new approaches differ from the historical-critical method favored by many North American Bible scholars. Neither do they explain whether these methods accept the Bible as fully inspired, trustworthy, and the solely authoritative norm for Adventist doctrine and practice—*the key test for evaluating the biblical legitimacy of hermeneutical methods.*

Although the immediate context for many of these new attempts to introduce new approaches into the Adventist church has been the debate over such issues as the Genesis creation account, racism, polygamy, abortion, war, divorce and remarriage, homosexuality, and women's ordination, it is the question of women's ordination more than any other which has popularized the expression, "principle approach."

This approach is said to be favored in the "matured" regions of the worldwide Adventist church. Adventists who live outside the "matured" regions of the world church allegedly follow a "literal approach."

"Principle-Based Approach": A Mature Approach?

Startling Comments. As we pointed out in "To the Reader," one Adventist professor commented shortly after the 1995 General Conference session in Utrecht, the Netherlands, that the vote refusing the North American Division's requesting the ordination of women was due to the use of "*scriptural literalism,* a view largely held in the developing world—Africa and much of South America and Inter-America." He contrasted this with a "*principle-based approach* to Scripture" followed in areas where the church "has matured for a century and a half" (i.e., North America, Europe, and perhaps Australia).[51]

Again, as we noted, a former editor suggests that those who do not subscribe to the so-called "principle-based approach" cannot think. Thus, while applauding the "principle-based approach" as one which requires a "high level of abstract thinking," he intimates that those who employ the "literal approach" are immature.

According to this former editor, "Most people have not learned to reason abstractly. This is why the *literal approach* is so appealing. Children begin with concrete and literal understandings of life. It is not until around 10 years and older that they can begin to conceptualize and reason in the abstract. If people learn only the *proof-text method* of Bible study they will never develop a principle-based approach and will always remain children in their understanding. The method that rules in the coming years will determine whether the Adventist church will continue to grow and mature or whether it will always remain in an infantile state."[52]

Legitimate Questions. We may ask: If following the Bible's teaching on role differentiation in both the home and the church will make Bible-believers "always remain children in their understanding" and leave them "in an infantile state," does not their attitude commend them to our Lord and Savior Jesus Christ? He Himself declared: "Verily I say unto you, Except ye be converted, and become as little children, ye shall not enter into the kingdom of heaven. Whosoever therefore shall humble himself as this little child, the same is greatest in the kingdom of heaven" (Matt 18:3,4). Could it be that the ultimate issue in the hermeneutical debate has nothing to do with scholarly enlightenment (the so-called "abstract thinking") but everything to do with *conversion* and *humility* of heart as one approaches God's sacred Word?

How can we harmonize the undertones of cultural conceit (some would say "veiled racism") in the above statements with the self-proclaimed "ethical sensitivity" of other proponents of a "principle-based approach," who decry the "terrible thing" that happened in Utrecht? "*We who have grown and progressed in our faith development* to understand and value racial and gender equality and justice are hurt by the lack of understanding, intolerance and animosity that was displayed at Utrecht. . . . The ministry of *sensitive and caring* men and women who voted to support this action [for women's ordination] feel hurt by the abuse that was so forcefully and overwhelmingly hurled at them here in Utrecht."[53]

Not all will agree with the statement's characterization of what happened at Utrecht. But our concern here is to note the words such as "progress," "growth," "maturity," etc., in the language of proponents of the "principle-based approach." In the next chapter, we shall explore the possible evolutionary assumptions undergirding this language.

Readers may want to know to what extent this "principle approach" is related to the historical-critical method followed by the alleged "clear majority" of North American Adventist scholars. Also, to what extent is the "literal approach," the so-called "proof-text method" of Bible study in the "developing world," related to the traditional Adventist plain reading of Scripture (the historical-grammatical method) that higher critical scholars dismiss also as a "proof-text" method?

The Crucial Issues in the Debate

No matter how one defines "growth," "progress," "maturity," "sensitive," "infantile," "principle," "literal," and "proof-text" in the above statements, there is no doubt that, indeed, "the method that rules in the coming years will determine whether the Adventist church will continue to grow and mature or whether it will always remain in an infantile state."[54] What is really at stake in this crisis over biblical interpretation is the identity, message, and mission of the Seventh-day Adventist movement.

The crucial issues are these: *Is the Bible fully inspired, trustworthy, and the sole authority for the Christian believer? Are the new approaches viable alternatives to the historic Adventist method?* The questions, then, have to do with the inspiration and interpretation of Scripture.

What the Church Did. In addressing these crucial issues, we need to be reminded again of key events in our recent history. Since the 1950s, as more of the church's scholars began using the higher critical approaches of liberal theology, the church has seen increasing challenges to its distinctive truths—the prophetic significance of 1844, the necessity and relevance of the Sanctuary doctrine, the inspiration of Ellen G. White, etc. And beginning in the 1970s, the church has experienced turmoil over such contemporary issues as abortion, polygamy, divorce and remarriage, women's ordination, homosexuality, etc.

What did the church do when it discovered that its theological house was crumbling? Rather than simply offering some cosmetic changes to embellish the crumbling walls, the church chose to identify the cause of the problem and attempted to repair the theological damage.

Thus in 1974, the church leaders and scholars—the key players in the quarrel over the Word—traced the problem to the church's theological foundation: the inspiration, trustworthiness, and sole authority of the Bible. At the Bible Conferences that year, they *took an uncompromising stand against the historical-critical method.* Given the influence of the historical-critical scholars, this decision required the courage of biblical convictions. But they rose to the occasion, publishing a book, *A Symposium on Biblical Hermeneutics,* which laid the groundwork for the 1986 Annual Council document, "Methods of Bible Study."

The Result of an Unwavering Decision. As a result of the church's unwavering decision, some individuals who had earlier believed in the higher critical methodology experienced conversion and abandoned it.

One such scholar is the current chairman of the Old Testament department of the Seventh-day Adventist Theological Seminary. He recounted something of his pilgrimage from using the historical-critical method to giving it up as a result of the 1974 Bible Conference:

"While attending that conference, I awoke as from a dream. I came to realize that my approach to the Scriptures had been much like Eve's approach to God's spoken word. She was exhilarated by the experience of exercising autonomy over the word of God, deciding what to believe and what to discard. She exalted her human reason over divine revelation. When she did so, she opened the floodgates of woe upon the world. Like Eve, I had felt the heady ecstasy of setting myself up as the final norm, as one who could judge the divine Word by my rational criteria. Instead of the Word judging me, I judged the Word." He concluded: "I am now convinced that the issue of the authority of Scripture is basic to all other issues in the church. The destiny of our church depends on how its members regard the authority of the Bible."[55]

Implications for the Future. Indeed, *the destiny of our church depends on how its members regard the authority of the Bible.* Therefore, to understand how skepticism over Scripture's full inspiration, trustworthiness, and normative authority is impacting upon the identity and mission of the Seventh-day Adventist movement, it will be important for us to show from published works how attitudes toward Scripture are shaping the theological quarrels in the church. Only then can we fully appreciate how liberal presuppositions are contributing to a *departing from the Word.*

NOTES

1. "The Day of the Adventists," *Newsweek,* June 7, 1971, p. 65.

2. Ibid., p. 66. For a Seventh-day Adventist response to this article, see Kenneth H. Wood, "The *Newsweek* Story," *Review and Herald,* July 1, 1971, p. 2.

3. "The Day of the Adventists," *Newsweek,* June 7, 1971, p. 66.

4. John Shelby Spong, *Rescuing the Bible from Fundamentalism: A Bishop Rethinks the Meaning of Scripture* (San Francisco: Harper, 1991), pp. 13-36.

5. These two defects of interpretation plague Bible students. The first defect is *the use of a wrong methodology.* This is the case with those who employ the various aspects of historical-critical methodology. Inasmuch as this approach to Scripture denies the full inspiration, trustworthiness, and sole authority of the Bible, Seventh-day Adventists cannot legitimately employ this method in any of its forms. Those who do so will acknowledge, for example, that the Bible really teaches a literal six-day creation, a worldwide flood in Noah's day, the virgin birth, resurrection and second coming of Christ. But they may refuse to accept the truthfulness of these events, choosing instead to *reconstruct* their own version of these events. The problem with this approach is that it is established on a theological

foundation of distrust in the reliability of the Bible. Therefore, anyone who attempts to explain the Scriptures with this methodology is building a theological house on sand. No matter how beautiful or impressive the outside structure appears, such a theological house cannot stand the storm.

The second kind of defect in biblical interpretation is *the failure to live up to the demands of a right method,* such as applying a right method inconsistently. For example, a Sunday-keeping Christian who believes in the eternal validity of the Ten Commandments and yet chooses to ignore the *seventh-day* Sabbath is inconsistent. A person who believes in the resurrection of the dead at the second-coming of Christ and yet holds to a doctrine that when people die they go straight to heaven or hell is inconsistent. An Adventist who keeps the seventh-day Sabbath as a memorial of creation and yet denies that God actually created the world in six literal days is inconsistent. The Christian who be-lieves that all Scripture is inspired by the Holy Spirit and yet maintains that some parts of the Bible are human opinion or culturally conditioned is inconsistent. At times, such inconsistencies may stem from wrong practices in the interpreter's lifestyle. See P. Gerard Damsteegt, "Ellen White, Lifestyle, and Scripture Interpretation," in a forthcoming issue of *Journal of the Adventist Theological Society.*

Unlike the defect of the first kind in which an interpreter builds on a wrong methodological foundation, in the second kind of defect the foundation is sound, but the structure itself is not stable. Therefore, a person who adopts the second kind of approach is like one who constructs a theological house using straw instead of bricks. In times of storm, the foundation may survive but the straw structure itself will be swept away.

6. For an insightful account of how the theological views of leaders and scholars recently con-tributed to the split in the Worldwide Church of God (the publishers of *The Plain Truth* magazine), see Samuele Bacchiocchi, "A Church in Crisis: Causes and Lessons," *Adventists Affirm* 9/2 (Fall 1995):49-55, also published as "Lessons from a Church Meltdown," *Adventist Review,* April 18, 1996, pp. 25-28. In an earlier work, we have briefly discussed how "communicators" shape the worldview of any group of people. See the author's "Contemporary Culture and Christian Lifestyle: A Clash of Worldviews," *Journal of the Adventist Theological Society* 4/1 (Spring 1993):129-150.

7. *A Symposium on Biblical Hermeneutics,* edited by Gordon M. Hyde (Washington, D.C.: Bib-lical Research Institute of the General Conference, 1974).

8. For example, in 1981, a delegation of North American Bible scholars met in Washington, D.C. and affirmed that "Adventist scholars could indeed use the descriptive [aspects of the historical-critical] method (e.g., source criticism, redaction criticism, etc.) without adopting the naturalistic presuppositions affirmed by the thorough-going practitioners of the method." See Alden Thompson, "Are Adventists Afraid of Bible Study?" *Spectrum* 16/1 (April 1985): 58, 56; see also his "Theologi-cal Consultation II," *Spectrum* 12/2 (December 1981):40-52; *Inspiration: Hard Questions, Honest Answers* (Hagerstown, Md.: Review and Herald, 1991), pp. 271-272.

9. Raymond F. Cottrell, "Blame it on Rio: The Annual Council Statement on Methods of Bible Study," *Adventist Currents,* March 1987, p. 33; cf. Jerry Gladson, "Taming Historical Criticism: Adventist Biblical Scholarship in the Land of Giants," *Spectrum* 18/4 (April 1988):19-34. In Cottrell's opinion, "The majority of Adventist Bible scholars—who now follow the historical-critical method and who aspire to be as objective as possible—enter upon their study with presuppositions that affirm the inspiration and authority of the Bible; and as a result their use of the method not only leads to a more accurate understanding of it, but contrary to the Annual Council statement, honors the divine element of Scripture, fortifies faith, and calls for obedience" ("Blame It on Rio," 33; cf. his "1844 Revisionists Not New: President Indicts the Church's Scholars," *Adventist Today,* January-February 1995, p. 16). Later in this book, as we set forth the evidence, readers will be in a better position to judge whether, indeed, the historical-critical method upholds *full* inspiration and *full* authority of the Bible and whether it leads to faith and obedience, as Cottrell suggests.

10. When in 1979 Desmond Ford raised questions about the church's sanctuary doctrine, it became apparent that three critical issues were involved in his challenge: (1) Were Ford's views merely doctrinal in nature, (2) were they dictated by his theological methodology (including his view of revelation, inspi-ration, and interpretation) or (3) both? At Consultation I, a meeting between the church's scholars and the denominational leaders at Glacier View, Colorado, in 1980, the doctrinal issue was discussed. The meth-

odological issue as it related to inspiration was the focus of Consultation II, the meeting between the scholars and the denominational leaders in Washington, D.C., from September 30 to October 3, 1981.

At this second meeting the church's biblical scholars came up with a "consensus" statement to the effect that "the descriptive aspects of the so-called historical critical method could indeed be separated from naturalistic presuppositions and thus could be used by Adventist scholars" (see Alden Thompson, *Inspiration: Hard Questions, Honest Answers* [Hagerstown, Md.: Review and Herald, 1991], pp. 271-272; cf. "Theological Consultation II," *Spectrum* 12/2 [December 1981]:40-52.). Note that the "consensus" statement was "framed largely by proponents of the historical-critical method among Seventh-day Adventist biblical scholars" (see Richard M. Davidson, "Revelation/Inspiration In the Old Testament: A Critique of Alden Thompson's 'Incarnational' Model," *Issues in Revelation and Inspiration,* ed. Frank Holbrook and Leo Van Dolson [Berrien Springs, Mich.: Adventist Theological Society Publications, 1992], p. 106).

The 1986 Rio Document ("Methods of Bible Study") was the church's definitive statement on the methodological issue arising from the theological crises of the 1970s and 1980s.

11. Raymond F. Cottrell, "Blame It On Rio: Annual Council Statement on Methods of Bible Study," p. 33. He notes that "during the late 1930s Seventh-day Adventist Bible scholars began using these historical critical principles and procedures in their study; and today, half a century later, all but a very few do so routinely" (ibid.).

12. Richard Hammill, *Pilgrimage: Memoirs of An Adventist Administrator* (Berrien Springs, Mich.: Andrews University Press, 1992), pp. 227-236.

13. Enoch de Oliveira, "A Trojan Horse Within the Church," *Journal of the Adventist Theological Society* 2/1 (Spring 1991):7, reproduced in chapter 6 of *Receiving the Word.*

14. Raymond F. Cottrell, "A Guide to Reliable Interpretation: Determining the Meaning of Scripture," in *The Welcome Table: Setting A Place for Ordained Women,* ed. Patricia A. Habada and Rebecca Frost Brillhart (Langley Park, Md.: TEAMPress, 1995), p. 84. He repeats: "*No* real Adventist scholar follows this [historical-critical] method" (ibid., p. 80; emphasis his).

15. Cottrell, "Blame It On Rio," p. 33. Since at least 1977 Cottrell has employed the euphemism "historical method," to refer to the historical-critical method. He argues that it is a method employed by conservatives, liberals, and Ellen White (see Cottrell, "Smoothing the Way to Consensus," *Review and Herald,* March 31, 1977, p. 18; "The Historical Method of Interpretation," *Review and Herald,* April 7, 1977, pp. 17-18; "A Subtle Danger in the Historical Method," *Review and Herald,* April 14, 1977, p. 12). His recent article uses the terms "historical method of research" or "historical method" to describe his historical-critical approach (see Cottrell, "A Guide to Reliable Interpretation," *The Welcome Table,* pp. 80, 84). Jerry Gladson correctly observed that Cottrell's "historical" method, which is essentially the same as his own, is actually a modified use of the historical-critical method. See Jerry Gladson, "Taming Historical Criticism: Adventist Biblical Scholarship in the Land of Giants," *Spectrum* 18/4 (April 1988):34, note 65.

16. In a well-documented study, Alberto R. Timm, a scholar in Adventist studies, noted that the Association of Adventist Forums and its *Spectrum* magazine became the main forum for those who assumed a "revisionist-critical stand" on the church's understanding of the inspiration of Bible writers and Ellen White: "Several articles advocating encounter revelation and the use of the historical-critical method came out in *Spectrum,* setting the agenda for many discussions on inspiration during the period under consideration (1970-1994)." He backed this up by citing all the articles published in this magazine that had historical-critical assumptions. See Alberto R. Timm, "History of Inspiration in the Seventh-day Adventist Church (1844-1994)," a paper read at the 1993 Scholars' Convention of the Adventist Theological Society, Silver Spring, Md., November 19, 1993, pp. 57-58. An extended bibliography of such historical-critical works is found in footnotes that fill pages 63-67. For a history of inspiration in the Adventist church from 1844-1915, see Timm's "History of Inspiration in the Adventist Church," *Journal of the Adventist Theological Society* 5/1 (Spring 1994):180-195. The Seventh-day Adventist church's position dissociating itself from *Spectrum* is found in Neal C. Wilson's statement at the 1984 Annual Council. See Myron K. Widmer, "1984 Annual Council—Part III," *Adventist Review,* November 15, 1984, pp. 4-5; cf. "Annual Council—1984," *Ministry,* December 1984, pp. 23-24.

17. Gary Land, "Coping with Change: 1961-1980," in *Adventism in America,* ed. Gary Land (Grand Rapids, Mich.: Eerdmans, 1986), p. 226.

18. John C. Brunt, "A Parable of Jesus as a Clue to Biblical Interpretation," *Spectrum* 13/2 (December 1982):42, emphasis supplied.

19. Larry G. Herr, "Genesis One in Historical-Critical Perspective," *Spectrum* 13/2 (December 1982):51, emphasis supplied.

20. Alden Thompson, "Theological Consultation II," *Spectrum* 12/2 (December 1981):45. Note that the article was written to throw a favorable light on the historical-critical method. Nevertheless, the article is useful in showing where North American Adventist Bible scholars stood in the 1980s on the use of the historical-critical method in the interpretation of the Bible.

21. Richard W. Coffen, "Taboo on Tools?" *Ministry,* September 1975, pp. 7-8. Coffen concluded his article with this paragraph: "Man, as a tool builder, has invented many valuable tools. As the inventor he controls his inventions—or should. Never must he allow his tools to enslave and dominate him. In the same way, the tools [historical-critical methodologies] that have been developed to help us understand the humanity of both the living Word and the written word must never tyrannize their Christian user. Instead the Christian recognizes that, as with all tools, they can prove dangerous. Hence, he utilizes them carefully—with his eye of flesh on the humanity of Christ and Scripture, and with his eye of faith on their divinity" (ibid., p. 8). Cf. Raymond F. Cottrell, "The Historical Method of Interpretation," *Review and Herald,* April 7, 1977, pp. 17-18.

22. William G. Johnsson, "SDA Presuppositions to Biblical Studies," paper presented to SDA members attending the American Academy of Religion/Society of Biblical Literature Convention, Chicago, Ill., October 29, 1975, pp. 44, 45, cited by Jerry Gladson, "Taming Historical Criticism: Adventist Biblical Scholarship in the Land of Giants," *Spectrum* 18/4 (April 1988):29-30. Gladson's article offers a detailed discussion of how Adventist scholars and editors related to the "Methods of Bible Study" document (ibid., pp. 19-34).

23. Eta Linnemann, *Historical Criticism of the Bible: Methodology or Ideology?* translated by Robert W. Yarbrough (Grand Rapids: Baker, 1990), p. 123.

24. Alden Thompson, *Inspiration: Hard Questions, Honest Answers* (Hagerstown, Md.: Review and Herald, 1991).

25. Thompson, *Inspiration,* p. 143, emphasis supplied.

26. Robert K. McIver, "The Historical-Critical Method: The Adventist Debate," *Ministry,* March 1996, p. 15, emphasis supplied.

27. See Appendix A of *Inspiration,* pp. 267-272, where the author purports to survey a history of Seventh-day Adventist discussion of inspiration, but climaxes it in the 1981 "consensus" statement framed largely by proponents of the historical-critical method among Adventist scholars. For obvious reasons, the author of this 1991 book failed to mention the 1986 Annual Council in Rio de Janeiro, which explicitly rejected any use of the historical-critical method. For scholarly responses to *Inspiration,* see the series of essays edited by Frank Holbrook and Leo Van Dolson, *Issues in Revelation and Inspiration* (Berrien Springs, Mich.: Adventist Theological Society Publications, 1992).

28. Unlike the publishers of *Inspiration,* who failed to alert readers to the book's historical-critical orientation, the publishers of *Luke, A Plagiarist?* (1983) judiciously included a disclaimer: "The purpose of this book is to investigate a concept of inspiration not generally held by most Seventh-day Adventists. . . . This book does not represent an official pronouncement of the Seventh-day Adventist Church nor does it necessarily reflect the editorial opinion of the Pacific Press Publishing Association." See George Rice, *Luke, A Plagiarist?* (Mountain View, Calif.: Pacific Press, 1983), p. 4.

29. In attempting to provide a theological justification for the ordination of women *as elders and pastors,* an influential group of 14 pro-ordination authors contributed essays to the book, *The Welcome Table: Setting A Place for Ordained Women,* edited by Patricia A. Habada and Rebecca Frost Brillhart (Langley Park, Md.: TEAMPress, 1995).

30. The above statement is Lawrence T. Geraty's comment at the back of the book. The "fourteen prominent SDA historians, theologians, and professionals" who contributed essays to the book are: Bert Haloviak, Kit Watts, Raymond F. Cottrell, Donna Jeane Haerich, David R. Larson, Fritz Guy,

Edwin Zackrison, Halcyon Westphal Wilson, Sheryll Prinz-McMillan, Joyce Hanscom Lorntz, V. Norskov Olsen, Ralph Neall, Ginger Hanks Harwood, and Iris M. Yob.

31. Although the introduction and recommendations of the book given on the back cover state that *The Welcome Table* comprises "carefully thought-through expositions by some of our most competent writers" and "is a definitive collection of essays for our time from respected church leaders," others have observed that, regarding the key hermeneutical issues of women's ordination, this volume is more noteworthy for its breadth than for its depth. For example, Keith A. Burton, an Adventist New Testament scholar, has exposed the historical-critical assumptions underlying some of the essays in *The Welcome Table*. He concludes his insightful critique of this pro-ordination book: "The table around which we are warmly invited to sit is one that already accommodates those who have attacked the relevance of biblical authority; those who wish to pretend that the gnostic image of the primeval and eschatological androgyne is the one toward which Adventists should be moving; those whose interest is on the acquisition of corporate power rather than the evangelization of a dying world; and finally, those who confuse the undiscriminating limitation of the familial and ecclesiastical roles that have been defined by the same Spirit." See Burton, "The Welcome Table: A Critical Evaluation," (an unpublished manuscript, 1995), available at the Adventist Heritage Center, James White Library, Andrews University. In the next chapter of *Receiving the Word*, we shall spotlight a few of the troubling aspects of *The Welcome Table*.

32. Apparently in rebuttal of criticisms and misinformation from liberal Adventists, the ATS issued a detailed clarification about its name, goals, criteria of membership, and its relationship to the church. See C. Raymond Holmes, "The President's Address," *Journal of the Adventist Theological Society* 4/2 (1993):1-11; cf., idem., "The President's Page," *Journal of the Adventist Theological Society* 4/1 (1993):1-2.

33. Frank Holbrook and Leo Van Dolson, eds., *Issues in Revelation and Inspiration* (Berrien Springs, Mich.: Adventist Theological Society Publications, 1992). In all, eight scholars from different fields of expertise responded to different aspects of the book *Inspiration;* the scholars are Raoul Dederen, Samuel Koranteng-Pipim, Norman R. Gulley, Richard M. Davidson, Gerhard F. Hasel, Randall W. Younker, Frank M. Hasel, and Miroslav M. Kis.

34. A number of scholars have had articles published by both *Adventists Affirm* and ATS, but for some the involvement goes beyond merely writing. C. Raymond Holmes (past president of the ATS) has been associated with the publication and distribution of *Adventists Affirm* from its beginning, as has C. Mervyn Maxwell (former associate editor of *Journal of the Adventist Theological Society* [*JATS*] and currently an associate editor [advisory] of ATS's *Perspective Digest*); both serve on the editorial board of *Adventists Affirm*. Also on *Adventists Affirm*'s editorial board are Samuele Bacchiocchi and Laurel Damsteegt, who also serve on the editorial resource board of *JATS*. William Fagal, *Adventists Affirm*'s editor, is an advisory board member of ATS. Other ATS appointees who have written for *Adventists Affirm* include Gerhard F. Hasel (past president of the ATS), George W. Reid (associate editor of *JATS*), P. Gerard Damsteegt, John Fowler, Jacob Nortey, and Francis W. Wernick.

35. The very first publication of *Adventists Affirm* set forth its theological reasons for rejecting ordination of women (see *Affirm* 1/1 [Spring 1987]). The ATS position on women's ordination is stated in its recent brochure, "Your Invitation to Join": "ATS is focused primarily on upholding and affirming the fundamental beliefs of Seventh-day Adventists. Because a position on women's ordination is not a doctrinal tenet of the church, discussion of that question has been outside the focus of the Society. Of course, as in the church at large, strong opinions on both sides can be found among ATS members; but that subject has not been addressed by the Society." In chapter 5 part ii of this book, we shall look at some of the hermeneutical issues raised by the ordination of women as elders/pastors.

36. C. Raymond Holmes, *The Tip of An Iceberg: Biblical Authority, Biblical Interpretation, and the Ordination of Women in Ministry* (Berrien Springs, Mich.: Adventists Affirm; Wakefield, Mich.: Pointer Publications, 1994); cf. Samuel Koranteng-Pipim, *Searching the Scriptures: Women's Ordination and the Call to Biblical Fidelity* (Berrien Springs, Mich.: Adventists Affirm, 1995).

37. For an insightful analysis of the key New Testament texts bearing on the women's ordination issue, and for crucial methodological issues involved, see Gerhard F. Hasel, "Hermeneutical Issues

he Ordination of Women: Methodological Reflections on Key Passages," an unpublished ocument, May 23, 1994, available at the Adventist Heritage Center, James White Library, University. This penetrating study will challenge *conservative* proponents of women's ordination seriously to reconsider their position.

38. Even though the crisis of biblical interpretation in the church concerns the legitimacy of the historical-critical method, since the 1995 General Conference session some have cast the conflict as between the "principle approach" and "literal approach"—believed to have been illustrated by the two conservatives who spoke on opposing ends of the issue of women's ordination. See, for instance, Will Eva, "Interpreting the Bible: A Commonsense Approach," *Ministry,* March 1996, pp. 4-5; William G. Johnsson, "The Old, the New, and the Crux," *Adventist Review,* General Conference Bulletin no. 7 (July 7, 1995), p. 3; cf. Caleb Rosado, "How Culture Affects Our View of Scripture," *Spectrum,* December 1995, pp. 11-15. Another author refers to the two conflicting approaches as a clash between the "contextual approach" and the "key-text approach" (Steve Case, "Thinking About Jewelry: What the Bible (Really) Says," in *Shall We Dance: Rediscovering Christ-Centered Standards,* ed. Steve Case [Riverside, Calif.: La Sierra University Press, 1996], pp. 184-193). Notice, however, that others have correctly identified the hermeneutical conflict. See, for example, William H. Shea, "How Shall We Understand the Bible?" *Ministry,* March 1996, pp. 10-13; Robert K. McIver, "The Historical-Critical Method: The Adventist Debate," *Ministry,* March 1996, pp. 14-17.

39. See for example, Samuel Koranteng-Pipim, "Saved by Grace and Living by Race: The Religion Called Racism," in *Journal of the Adventist Theological Society* 5/2 (Autumn 1994):37-78; see also the following works by the same author: "Racism and Christianity," *Dialogue* 7/1 (1995):12-15; "The Triumph of Grace Over Race," *Adventists Affirm,* Fall 1995, pp. 35-49.

40. M. Rader, D. van Denburgh, and L. Christoffel, "Evangelical Adventism: Clinging to the Cross," *Adventist Today,* January/February, 1994, p. 16. The origin of evangelical Adventism goes back to the crisis occasioned by Desmond Ford and the periodical *Evangelica,* which was published in the years after the Glacier View Conference in 1980.

41. Steven G. Daily, "Towards An Adventist Theology of Liberation," a paper presented to the Association of Adventist Women and the Association of Adventist Forums in Loma Linda, Calif., March 18, 1984, and reproduced as appendix B in his "The Irony of Adventism: The Role of Ellen White and Other Adventist Women in Nineteenth Century America (D.Min. project, School of Theology at Claremont, 1985), pp. 327, 317.

42. Steve Case, "Thinking About Jewelry: What the Bible (Really) Says," *Shall We Dance: Rediscovering Christ-Centered Standards,* ed. Steve Case (Riverside, Calif.: La Sierra University Press, 1996), pp. 193, 182. According to Case, Adventists who obtained their theological training before 1970 employed the "key-text" method; but those who studied after 1970 use the "contextual method."

43. Cottrell, "Blame It On Rio," p. 33.

44. Cottrell, "A Guide to Reliable Interpretation," in *The Welcome Table* (see note 14 above), p. 83.

45. John C. Brunt, "A Parable of Jesus as a Clue to Biblical Interpretation," *Spectrum* 13/2 (December 1982):42, emphasis supplied.

46. See Alden Thompson, "Theological Consultation II," *Spectrum* 12/2 (December 1981):45, emphasis supplied.

47. Raymond F. Cottrell, "A Guide to Reliable Interpretation," in *The Welcome Table* (see note 14 above), p. 83, emphasis supplied.

48. Robert K. McIver, "The Historical-Critical Method: The Adventist Debate," *Ministry,* March 1996, p. 16.

49. Cottrell, "A Guide to Reliable Interpretation," in *The Welcome Table* (see note 29 above), pp. 80, 84. Cf. Cottrell, "Blame It On Rio," p. 33, where, after dismissing the "prooftext subjectivity" of the historical-grammatical method, he writes: "During the late 1930s Seventh-day Adventist Bible scholars began using these historical critical principles and procedures in their study; and today, half a century later, all but a very few do so routinely."

50. Cottrell, "A Guide to Reliable Interpretation," in *The Welcome Table* (see note 14 above), p. 79. Elsewhere he writes: "As a matter of fact, those who favor [women's] ordination do so on the basis of the *historical method*" (ibid., p. 84). According to Cottrell, "both conservative and liberal Bible scholars employ the historical method" ("The Historical Method of Interpretation," *Review and Herald,* April 7, 1977, pp. 17-18). Jerry Gladson correctly noted that the method Cottrell describes as the "historical method" is actually the modified use of the historical-critical method which many Adventist scholars, including Gladson, accept as legitimate. See Jerry Gladson, "Taming Historical Criticism: Adventist Biblical Scholarship in the Land of the Giants," *Spectrum* 18/4 (April 1988):19-34 (see p. 34, note 65).

51. Jim Walters, "General Conference Delegates Say NO on Women's Ordination," *Adventist Today,* July-August, 1995, p. 13, emphasis supplied.

52. J. David Newman, "Stuck in the Concrete," *Adventist Today,* July-August, 1995, p. 13, emphasis supplied.

53. Penny Miller (chairperson of the Gender Inclusiveness Commission of the Southeastern California Conference), "Women Denied Equal Rights at 56th GC Session in Utrecht," *Dialogue* [Loma Linda University Church Paper] 6/8 (August 1995), p. 1, emphasis supplied.

54. Newman, "Stuck in the Concrete," p. 13.

55. Richard M. Davidson, "The Authority of Scripture: A Personal Pilgrimage," *Journal of the Adventist Theological Society* 1/1 (1990):41. More such testimonies will be found in chapter 11 below.

Chapter Five

Departing from the Word

Historically, Bible-believing Seventh-day Adventists have accepted the sixty-six books of the Old and New Testament Scriptures as the normative governing authority for all issues of faith and practice. On this foundation they have developed a unique system of beliefs, among which are the following distinctive S's:

(1) Scripture's inspiration, trustworthiness, and sole authority, (2) the Substitutionary atonement of Christ, (3) Salvation by grace alone through faith in Jesus Christ, (4) the Sanctuary message, (5) the imminent Second Coming of Christ, (6) the Sabbath of the fourth commandment, (7) the State of the dead, (8) the Spirit of Prophecy, (9) Stewardship, and (10) Standards regarding food, drink, dress, entertainment, relationships, etc.

But today, under the impact of higher criticism, some are challenging the Bible's authenticity, distrusting its credibility, and questioning its essential and sole authority as a sufficient guide in today's complex and sophisticated world.

Such *departing from the Word* has led a number of Adventist Bible teachers and theologians to challenge the following teachings: the historicity of Genesis 1-11, the literal six-day creation, the inspiration of the Bible, the prophetic guidance of the Spirit of Prophecy, the belief that the Seventh-day Adventist church is the remnant of Bible prophecy, the sanctuary doctrine, the binding claims of the Ten Commandments, the substitutionary death of Christ in our behalf, and the possibility of victorious Christian living. In the same vein, some of these thought leaders see no biblical objection to polygamy, women as elders or pastors, homosexuality, eating unclean foods, drinking alcohol, wearing of jewelry, divorce and remarriage, etc.[1]

Gradual Departure. As in other Christian churches, this departure from our distinctive doctrines has not happened overnight. One writer noted: "People don't often go heretical all at once. It is gradual. And they do not do so intentionally most of the time. They slip into it through shoddiness and laziness in handling the word of truth. . . . All it takes to start the road to heresy is a craving for something new and different, a flashy new idea, along with a little laziness or carelessness or lack of precision in handling the truth of God. All around us today are startling reminders of doctrinal slippage and outright failure. In case after case someone who should have known the truth of God better failed in upholding that truth."[2]

Objective of Chapter. In this chapter, we shall illustrate how *departing from the Word* has led to a challenge to our historic teachings. The underlying goal is to explore the extent to which even the moderate use of the historical-critical method leads to skepticism toward the Bible and its teachings. This effort can enable readers to evaluate the claim by some that Seventh-day Adventist scholars can legitimately use liberalism's higher criticism without adopting its naturalistic presuppositions.

This line of investigation is also crucial for other reasons. First, it enables readers to understand fully where the debate really lies over the appropriateness of the higher-critical methodology. Second, at a time when hermeneutical jargon is flowering in the church,[3] this chapter will encourage readers not to settle for fancy, nice-sounding labels or claims without first asking whether those approaches uphold the full inspiration, trustworthiness and sole authority of Scripture. Third, it allows readers to assess how much they themselves may have been influenced by the assumptions of the historical-critical method, even though they may not be crusading advocates of the method.

Organization. The chapter has six parts, each of which (1) raises a critical issue dealing with basic assumptions about the Scriptures, (2) sets forth the mainstream Seventh-day Adventist position, (3) presents evidence of a departure from the historic Adventist position, (4) offers a Bible-believing Seventh-day Adventist response, and (5) provides references showing the sources cited and in some cases pointing readers to materials dealing with similar concerns or offering views counter to those expressed in the cited sources.[4]

A Word of Explanation. The illustrations employed in this chapter are not chosen to cast doubt on the sincerity of those expressing these views or to suggest that the writers cited are the only ones disseminating such views. Neither do we suggest that everything they have written on a particular subject is necessarily wrong.

We wish merely to examine the soundness and implications of the methodology being used. By engaging in this line of investigation, we are simply heeding the judicious counsel of an Adventist scholar who recently argued that in developing a wholesome hermeneutic, Adventists who hold a "high view" of the Bible must "examine the full consequences of our theological method lest we prove more than we intend."[5]

Subjecting the published views of popular and influential thought leaders to the scrutiny of biblical investigation is not always appreciated. Factors that discourage Adventists from examining the soundness of discordant ideas include: (1) the fear of being branded as divisive, dogmatic, or intolerant; (2) the risk of being perceived as opposing academic freedom or as supporting an alleged "inquisition" by "reactionary" church administrators; and (3) concern over being dismissed as cherishing "authoritarian" tendencies, especially if one happens to come from regions outside the "democratic" areas of the world.[6]

But are intimidating psychological factors reason enough to keep silent on crucial hermeneutical issues?

An African proverb says: "The threatening eyes of the crocodile do not prevent the thirsty frog from drinking from the pond." Fear or intimidation must never prevent us from doing the right thing. Subjecting the theological views of fellow Christians to the searching light of Scripture is not only an honorable thing to do (Acts 17:11), but it is also a Christian obligation (1 Thess 5:21). This is why the following pages explore how higher-critical assumptions are leading some within our ranks to depart from the Word.

Beyond the predictable reactions from those who hold the kinds of views being examined, this chapter may also be disturbing to those who have been unaware of the sophisticated internal challenge to our doctrine and lifestyle.[7] Yet we encourage all to read carefully, thoughtfully, and critically (in the best sense of the word).

This book's readers, no less than its author, are accountable to God for how they relate to the truths of His inspired Word. Therefore we urge all to read prayerfully, with an honest desire to know the will of God and with a single-minded commitment to act upon it. The Lord Himself has promised: "If anyone wants to do His will, he shall know concerning the doctrine, whether it is from God or whether I speak on My own authority" (John 7:17).

NOTES

1. Church historian C. Mervyn Maxwell, "Response to NAD President's Request to Annual Council," *Adventists Affirm* 9/1 (Spring 1995):34, recently called attention to this fact. This chapter of *Receiving the Word* documents some of his observations.

2. Robert Thomas, "Precision as God's Will for My Life," pamphlet (Panorama City, Calif.: The Master's Seminary, 1989); quoted in John MacArthur, Jr. *Our Sufficiency in Christ* (Dallas, Texas: Word Publishing, 1991), p. 128.

3. Note the following loaded contrasts: casebook/codebook approach; principle/literal approach; contextual/key-text approach; commonsense/proof-text approach; matured/infantile approach; progressive/obscurantist approach, historical/fundamentalist; dynamic/rigid approach; etc.

4. Though we could have cited additional sources from Seventh-day Adventist publications like *Adventist Review, Ministry, Signs of the Times, Insight,* etc., to illustrate our points further, we have

chosen to limit the citations. But the thinking referenced here typifies a growing trend in our pulpits, classrooms, committee meetings, and publications.

5. George R. Knight, "Proving More Than Intended," *Ministry*, March 1996, p. 28. Though informed readers may justly challenge his oversimplified analysis of the hermeneutical issues regarding jewelry and women's ordination (the two illustrations he uses in his article), yet all serious Adventists can agree with his admonition that in developing a wholesome hermeneutic, "we should extend our methodology to its logical conclusions" (ibid., p. 26).

6. For example, Alden Thompson's *Inspiration: Hard Questions, Honest Answers* (Hagerstown, Md.: Review and Herald, 1991), pp. 90-95, 97, dismisses those who do not agree with his "incarnational model" of Scripture as individuals with "authoritarian" tendencies. For a brief response, see our "An Analysis and Evaluation of Alden Thompson's Casebook/Codebook Approach to the Bible" in Frank Holbrook and Leo Van Dolson, ed., *Issues in Revelation and Inspiration* (Berrien Springs, Mich.: Adventist Theological Society Publications, 1992), pp. 40-42, 62.

7. Paul Yeboah has spoken eloquently on the predictable reactions from proponents and adherents of the views spotlighted and challenged (see his Foreword to this book).

DEPARTING FROM THE WORD

PART I

The Bible—
Sole or Primary Authority?

Objective. This section explores the extent to which higher-critical assumptions are influencing Seventh-day Adventist views on the use of alcohol, the morality of homosexuality and lesbianism, and the belief in a literal six-day creation.

Key issue. Is the Bible the sole authority for Christian belief and practice or is it only the primary authority?

Traditional Adventist Belief. Seventh-day Adventists generally have always upheld the *sole authority* of Scripture. Believing that the sixty-six books of the Old and New Testaments are the clear, trustworthy revelation of God's will and His salvation, Adventists hold that the Scriptures alone constitute the standard on which all teachings and practices are to be grounded and by which they are to be tested (2 Tim 3:15-17; Ps 119:105; Prov 30:5, 6; Isa 8:20; John 17:17; 2 Thess 3:14; Heb 4:12).

The first article of the Seventh-day Adventist "Fundamental Beliefs" states: "The Holy Scriptures are the infallible revelation of His [God's] will. They are the standard of character, the test of experience, the authoritative revealer of doctrines, and the trustworthy record of God's acts in history."

Ellen G. White wrote, "The Word of God is the great detector of error; to it we believe everything must be brought. The Bible must be our standard for every doctrine and practice. We must study it reverentially. We are to receive no one's opinion without comparing it with the Scriptures. Here is divine authority which is supreme in matters of faith. It is the Word of the living God that is to decide all controversies" (*The Ellen G. White 1888 Materials,* pp. 44, 45; cf. *The Great Controversy,* p. 595).

But under the impact of higher-critical assumptions the Bible's role as the *sole* source of authority for Christian faith and lifestyle is being challenged.

Effect of the Liberal Approach

Influenced by the historical-critical method, some now assert that the Bible is "silent," "inadequate," or "irrelevant" on several contemporary issues, implying that the Bible cannot remain the *sole* source of authority on issues of doctrine and lifestyle. We must supplement the authority of the Bible with experience and empirical data. A New Testament scholar voiced this new view in relation to the abortion question: "Respect for the Bible's agenda means honestly balancing biblical evidence with other relevant data. *The Bible is not our only source of evidence*, even if it is the central controlling norm. Obviously *our experience and empirical data* will condition our views, and this must be admitted."[1]

According to this view, the Bible is not the sole source of authority; it only holds a *priority* ("the central controlling norm") over other sources—experience and empirical data. Similarly, another author argues that "doctrines arise, *not from the Bible alone,* but from the dynamic interplay between the Bible and the living experience of the church." For him, the Bible is only the "central authority for Christian belief," sharing a place alongside Christian experience and tradition.[2] The Bible is the primary source of authority, not the sole source.

This shift of religious authority from *sola scriptura* (the Bible's sole authority) to other sources—empirical data, experience, and tradition—is shaping Adventist discussions on the use of alcohol, the moral legitimacy of homosexuality, and the question of life origins.

Use of Alcohol. Does the Bible condemn the *use* of alcohol, or is it only against alcohol's *abuse?* In other words, should Seventh-day Adventists just say "No" to alcohol, or should they simply say "No more" (i.e., "no more" than, say, two bottles of beer)?

The editor of a recent book, *Shall We Dance,* devotes two chapters to this issue. The first closes with the assertion that a person's "bias" influences his conclusions regarding the use or abuse of alcohol: "Those with a bias for moderate use of alcohol receive supportive evidence from both Scripture and modern science. But there is ample support [for] abstinence, too."[3]

How then does this author conclude his "biblical principles *that relate to moderate use [of] alcohol"*?[4]

While he makes a "recommendation" to the Seventh-day Adventist church to hold "an abstinence position on alcohol and seek to correct *the negative results of alcohol abuse* throughout our society," he attempts to resolve the question with a carefully nuanced position: "Rather than being satisfied with the support of either position [the use or abuse of alcohol], this chapter attempts to *look beyond the obvious 'wine texts' in the Bible* and consider other Scriptural principles that would have a bearing on the moderate use of alcohol today, especially in North America."[5]

Does moving "beyond" the wine-texts in the Bible for "Scriptural principles" include going to extra-biblical sources? He answers: *"For Christians, sometimes it's useful to temporarily put aside biblical passages and simply consider what those speaking outside the church have to say on a given matter. Listening to a different voice can give a new perspective of Scripture.* For this reason we will now turn to what people outside the community of faith say about alcohol. While some may be Christians, they do not speak for Christians."[6]

The subtle message in this carefully worded statement is that the Bible is not a sufficient guide or the sole authority to address this issue. We have to allow extra-biblical sources to "give a new perspective of Scripture."

In the second of his two chapters devoted to the subject, the author discusses the "new perspective" that we gain when we listen to different voices: (1) "Abstention is acceptable in all circumstances" (it is not necessarily mandatory); (2) "Alcohol in high-risk settings is discouraged" (but apparently okay in non-risk settings); (3) "Heavy consumption is discouraged" (implying that lighter consumption may be all right); (4) "Moderate consumption in low risk situations is acceptable." Indeed, some research findings on the "medical benefits" of alcohol use suggest that "2-3 drinks per day is okay. In fact, it may be healthier than a nonalcoholic diet."[7]

The critical hermeneutical question illustrated by the above example is this: Should we decide on the use/abuse of alcohol solely on the basis of Scripture, or must we also look outside of Scripture (research findings, experience, culture, etc.) for answers? Similar questions are also shaping the discussion on homosexuality and lesbianism.

Morality of Homosexuality. An increasing number of Adventist Bible scholars are arguing that the teaching of Scripture on the subject of homosexuality is not sufficiently clear to settle the question of the morality of homosexual acts or relationships in our world.[8] If the Bible cannot settle this question, where does the Christian go for dependable answers?

The argument of one theologian was summarized thus: "Moral norms, he asserted, should be determined by scripture, *but there is also need for empirical evidence about what is. Norms are useless in a vacuum.*"[9] The empirical evidence alluded to is the "finding" that people are born gay. But what happens if the evidence conflicts with Scripture?

If one accepts the Bible as the sole authority for Christian belief and practice, one cannot accept homosexuality as biblically legitimate. However, a Kinsey Institute study of homosexuals in California's San Francisco Bay Area maintained that gays involved in reciprocal, permanent, and sexually exclusive relationships tend to be the happiest, healthiest, and best-adjusted people of the entire group being analyzed. Based on this highly questionable source,[10] an

Adventist professor of ethics concluded: "Christians therefore have every reason to encourage homosexuals who are honestly convinced that they should neither attempt to function heterosexually nor remain celibate to form Closed-Couple homosexual unions."[11]

The reason given for endorsing closed couple homosexual unions is not biblical revelation, but rather an empirical finding about the subjective experience of homosexuals.[12]

Morality of Lesbianism. This new way of knowing truth (what scholars refer to as epistemology) is echoed in the Adventist Women's Institute's book, *In Our Own Words*. This work carries the testimony of a lesbian, who identifies herself as an "Adventist-connected" theologian, Bible instructor/academy teacher-turned-minister. Observe how she came to the conclusion that her lesbianism was "an unusual calling" from the Lord and why her lesbian partner also believes that their lesbian relationship was "God's gift for her conversion."

She speaks about her naivete in blindly following the teaching of the Seventh-day Adventist church that "told me that my own nature was sinful, so *looking to myself* would be my downfall. . . . It did not tell me *to look at the rest of the natural world* and discover that same-gender nesting occurs in many species." She explains, however, that following her "unusual calling" or "Martin Luther experience" (the "ecstasy and torment" of her lesbian encounter), she came to value the importance of "inner knowing"—listening to "the voice of God within me."[13]

Scripture, according to this writer, is not the sole authority. We need "to look at the rest of the natural world" (empirical data) and also listen to "the voice of God within me"—an "inner knowing" (experience). For her, subjective human experience was trustworthy because she did not believe that her "own nature was sinful."

The above examples illustrate an increasing departure from biblical revelation toward empirical experience as the authority base for religious and ethical issues. This trend raises questions for Bible-believing Christians regarding the starting point for discussions on theological issues: Should it be *observation, introspection,* or biblical *revelation?*[14] One's response has consequences beyond the issue of homosexuality or lesbianism. It determines whether the Bible or the hypothesis of naturalistic evolution will provide the grounds for ascertaining, for example, whether or not Genesis 1 and 2 teach a literal-day creation—an issue that affects the validity of the seventh-day Sabbath.

The Question of Origins. Based on naturalistic interpretations of scientific data, some Adventist scholars now hold: (a) a long rather than short chronology for the age of our earth (i.e., millions instead of thousands of years); (b) gradual, uniformitarian deposit of the geologic column, instead of catastrophism (i.e., Noah's flood); (c) views that reinterpret the days of creation to represent millions of years, instead of the six literal days taught by the Bible.[15]

The shift from the sole authority of Scripture to empirical data is remarkably illustrated in the case of a former Adventist university president and General Conference vice president. After reviewing theories of continental drift, fossil records, and radioactive isotope dating, he concluded that: *"animals [were] living in the earth . . . millions of years* before these [continental] plates separated. And, moreover, as I got to looking into the geologic column, I had to recognize . . . that the geologic column is valid, that *some forms of life were extinct before other forms of life came into existence.* I had to recognize that the forms of life that we are acquainted with mostly, like the ungulate hoof animals, the primates, *man himself,* exist only in the very top little layer of the Holocene, and that *many forms of life were extinct before these ever came in,* which, of course, is a big step for a Seventh-day Adventist when you are taught that every form of life came into existence in six days. . . . I had felt it for many, many years, but finally there in about 1983 I had to say to myself, That's right. *The steadily accumulating evidence in the natural world has forced a reevaluation in the way that I look at and understand and interpret parts of the Bible."*[16]

Such conclusions have implications. First, denying a literal six-day creation implies that: (i) if Adventists continue keeping the seventh-day Sabbath, they must reinterpret its origin and significance; (ii) if Sabbath observance is retained, there would be no solid basis for *seventh-day* worship, setting the stage for the end-time recognition of Sunday sacredness in place of the true Sabbath; (iii) if the Bible's authoritative record of creation, which Jesus Christ confirmed (Matt 19:4-6; Mark 2:27-28), can be so easily set aside, we can also ignore its authority in other areas (e.g. morality and lifestyle).

Second, if animals were dying millions of years before the existence of human beings, then death (even of animals) is not the result of human sin. But the Bible says that "the wages of sin is death" (Rom 6:23), and that because of sin "the whole creation groaneth and travaileth in pain together until now" (Rom 8:22). Also, if death came before sin, Paul's statement that "by one man sin entered into the world, and death by sin" (Rom 5:12; cf. 8:22) is not trustworthy; neither can we believe that "as by the offence of one [Adam] judgment came upon all men to condemnation; even so by the righteousness of one [Christ] the free gift came upon all men unto justification of life" (Rom 5:18). Pursuing this argument to its logical end raises serious doubts about the necessity and efficacy of Christ's death for our sins, the possibility of human redemption, and the likelihood of Christ's second coming and a new creation (see 2 Pet 3:1-

15).[17] Thus, giving up the Bible's teaching on origins may lead to theological skepticism or agnosticism.

Agnosticism, the End-Result. The experience of a former Adventist, a grandson of a General Conference president, illustrates this danger. In the introduction to his book *The Creationists*, he explains how he gave up his Adventist views on a literal creation and became an agnostic: *"Having thus decided to follow science rather than Scripture on the subject of origins,* I quickly, though not painlessly, slid down the proverbial slippery slope toward unbelief. . . . [In a 1982 Louisiana creation-evolution trial, he elected to serve as an expert witness for the evolution cause, against the creationist lawyer, Wendell R. Bird. At that trial, he continues,] Bird publicly labeled me an 'Agnostic.' The tag still feels foreign and uncomfortable, but it accurately reflects my theological uncertainty."[18]

In summary, the slide into the abyss of theological uncertainty begins with a departure from the Bible as the Christian's sole norm of authority. Then follows a reinterpretation of the Scriptures according to the extra-biblical knowledge, whether from science, experience, tradition, psychology, or other sources. As the retired General Conference administrator himself said: "The steadily accumulating evidence in the natural world has forced a reevaluation in the way that I look at and understand and interpret parts of the Bible."[19]

A Bible-Believing Adventist Response

While upholding the sole authority of Scripture, Bible-believing Christians do not totally reject the value of extra-biblical data and experience in informing their understanding of inspired writ. The Bible itself teaches that God has revealed Himself in nature, history and human experience (Ps 19; Rom 1 & 2; Heb 1:1-2). Adventists may indeed learn from extra-biblical sources such as science, history, tradition, psychology, and archaeology.[20]

However, *because of the impact of sin* on all of God's creation, including nature and human experience, the knowledge obtained from data outside Scripture (and scholars' interpretation of such knowledge) may sometimes be flawed. To correct such distortions, God has given the Holy Scriptures as the objective basis to evaluate extra-biblical data.

Experience is important in the Christian religion (1 John 1:1-3). But experience is not necessarily a reliable source of truth. To avoid equating subjective religious experience with "the Holy Spirit's leading," believers need the corrective norm of the Holy Scriptures, which are "more sure" than any experience. The apostle Peter's manner of addressing this issue is significant. In 2 Peter 1:16-18 he rejects the charge that the Christian message is a myth with no objective basis in a factual historical event. For proof he appeals to the apostles' first-hand experience: "We were eyewitnesses . . . we heard . . . we were with Him." However, in verse 19 he appeals to something "more sure" than experience—namely, the prophetic word, the divinely inspired, authoritative Scriptures (cf. verses 20-21). Peter's approach is the very opposite of our pluralistic generation's, which accepts the Bible because it confirms our experience—the experience is the norm. But the apostle argues that his sanctified experience is trustworthy because it is confirmed by the Scriptures!

Likewise Jesus, in explaining His death and resurrection (Luke 24:25-27), could have appealed to real experiences—resurrected saints, angels appearing at the tomb, etc. Instead, He pointed them to "Moses and all the prophets," something "more sure" than experience. The men from Emmaus later testified that what caused their hearts to "burn within" them (v. 32) was Jesus' opening of the Scriptures to them.

Scripture must always be the *sole authoritative source* of human knowledge—above knowledge from nature (science), human experience (psychology), human history, church tradition, etc. Recognizing that God has revealed Himself in nature, history, and human experience should not lead us to overlook the impact of sin on these sources of revelation or to ignore sin's impact on the human reason employed to interpret these data. Without recognizing these limitations, admitting experience and empirical data as *rival sources* of truth will soon lead us to treat them as *equal partners* with, and finally as *judge* over, Scripture.

For the crucial issue, "The Bible, Sole Authority or Primary Authority?" the Bible's response is: "Trust in the Lord with all your heart, And lean not on your own understanding; In all your ways acknowledge Him, And He shall direct your paths" (Prov 3:5-6). If data from extra-biblical sources accord with the teaching of the Bible, they should be accepted; otherwise they should be rejected. Experience, reason, tradition, public opinion, verdicts of scholars, leaders, or other sources cannot be our authority; the Bible, and the Bible only (*sola Scriptura*), must be the sole authority over extra-biblical data.

NOTES

1. John C. Brunt, "Adventists, Abortion and the Bible," in *Abortion: Ethical Issues & Options*, ed. David R. Larson (Loma Linda, Calif.: Loma Linda University Center for Christian Bioethics, 1992), p. 38, emphasis supplied.

2. Richard Rice, *Reason and the Contours of Faith* (Riverside, Calif.: La Sierra University Press, 1991), pp. 90, 91, emphasis supplied.

3. Steve Case, "Mixing Alcohol, Abstinence, and the Bible," *Shall We Dance: Rediscovering Christ-Centered Standards* (Riverside, Calif.: La Sierra University Press, 1996), p. 313. This book is a *Project Affirmation* publication, coordinated with Hancock Center for Youth Ministry at La Sierra

University, North American Division Joint Boards of Education, La Sierra University Press, and Piece of the Pie Ministries (ibid., pp. 1, 4).

4.   Ibid., p. 303, emphasis supplied.

5.   Ibid., p. 313, emphasis supplied.

6.   Ibid., emphasis supplied.

7.   Steve Case, "What Those Outside the Church Say," *Shall We Dance*, pp. 316-317.

8.   This was the conclusion of six Bible scholars and pastors who, in August 1980, were commissioned by the church to attend a meeting organized by Kinship, a group which describes itself as "An Organization for Gay Seventh-day Adventists and Their Friends." The six consisted of three biblical and theological scholars (James J. C. Cox, Lawrence Geraty and Fritz Guy), two representing pastoral concerns (James Londis and Josephine Benton) and one who claimed to have given up his homosexual lifestyle (Colin Cook). For a summary of the meeting, see Elvin Benton, "Adventists Face Homosexuality," *Spectrum* 12/3 (April 1982):32-38. A recent presentation of this view of homosexuality appeared in *Insight*, December 5 1992, a special issue devoted to the subject. The questions raised by this issue of *Insight* still await a detailed theological analysis and evaluation. In the meantime, those seeking a brief treatment of the Bible's position may benefit from Raoul Dederen's "Homosexuality: A Biblical Perspective," *Ministry*, September 1981, pp. 14-16; and Ronald M. Springett, *Homosexuality in History and the Scriptures* (Washington, D.C.: Biblical Research Institute, 1988).

9.   This argument is attributed to Fritz Guy; see Elvin Benton, "Adventists Face Homosexuality," p. 35, emphasis supplied.

10.   For a detailed challenge to the dubious research of Kinsey, see, for example, Judith Reisman and Edward W. Eichel, *Kinsey, Sex, and Fraud: The Indoctrination of a People* (Lafayette, La.: Lochinvar-Huntington House, 1990).

11.   David Larson, "Sexuality and Christian Ethics," *Spectrum* 15/1 (May 1984):16.

12.   Perceptive readers will notice that David Larson's view on homosexuality is consistent with his view and approach to Scripture. Instead of the sole authority of Scripture, he recently recommended to the Adventist church four sources of religious authority: Scripture, tradition, reason, and experience. See his article, "Beyond Fundamentalism and Relativism: The Wesleyan Quadrilateral and Development of Adventist Theology," paper presented at the meeting of the Adventist Society of Religious Studies (Philadelphia, Pa., November 1995). A modified version is published in *Adventist Today*, January/February, 1996.

13.   Lin Ennis, "Seeker of Truth, Finder of Reality," in Iris M. Yob and Patti Hansen Tompkins, eds., *In Our Own Words: Women Tell of Their Lives and Faith* (Santa Ana, Calif.: Adventist Women's Institute, 1993), pp. 239, 232, 237, 238, 230-235, emphasis supplied. She explains: "I was so naive about God, so blind to the real needs of human beings, so willing to be led as a sheep, mindlessly following, not thinking for myself, except just enough to afford me the illusion of independence of thought. Far more than I cared to admit, I did what the church said, what the *Church Manual* said, what the ministers and evangelists I had worked with said" (ibid., p. 234).

14.   For an analysis and critique of how the new ways of thinking are shaping Adventist views in ethics, see Ronald A. G. du Preez, "Thinking About Thinking: An Assessment of Certain Presuppositions Underlying Some Adventist Lifestyle Issues," *Journal of the Adventist Theological Society* 4/1 (Spring 1993):114-128; cf. Samuel Koranteng-Pipim, "Contemporary Culture and Christian Lifestyle: A Clash of Worldviews," *Journal of the Adventist Theological Society* 4/1 (Spring 1993):129-150.

15.   For a helpful summary of Adventist views, see James L. Hayward, "The Many Faces of Adventist Creationism: '80-'95," *Spectrum* 25/3 (March 1996):16-34. He concludes his documented survey thus: "By the end of 1995, Adventist creationism stood at an important crossroad. Earlier voices were fading. A larger and more diverse generation of scientists and theologians was setting the terms of conversation now than in 1980" (ibid., p. 31). Generally speaking, while most of the "revised" views regarding creation and origins are found in *Adventist Today* and *Spectrum*, the positions that uphold the traditional Adventist views are found in *Journal of the Adventist Theological Society*, *Adventist Perspectives*, *Dialogue*, *Origins*, and *Adventists Affirm*.

16. Richard Hammill, "Journey of a Progressive Believer," transcript of a talk given to an Association of Adventist Forums convention, Seattle, Washington, October 13, 1989, cited by Hayward, "The Many Faces of Adventist Creationism: '80-'95," *Spectrum* 25/3 (March 1996):27-28, emphasis supplied. See also Richard Hammill's other works: "Fifty Years of Creationism: The Story of an Insider," *Spectrum* 15/2 (August 1984):32-45; "The Church and Earth Science," *Adventist Today*, September-October 1994, pp. 7, 8; *Pilgrimage: Memoirs of An Adventist Administrator* (Berrien Springs, Mich.: Andrews University Press, 1992).

17. For more on this, see John T. Baldwin, "Progressive Creationism and Biblical Revelation: Some Theological Implications," *Journal of the Adventist Theological Society* 3/1 (1992):105-119; Marco T. Terreros, "Death Before the Sin of Adam: A Fundamental Concept in Theistic Evolution and Its Implications for Evangelical Theology" (Ph.D. dissertation, Andrews University, 1994); idem., "The Adventist Message and the Challenge of Evolution," *Dialogue* 8/2 (1996):11-13; Richard M. Davidson, "In the Beginning: How to Interpret Genesis 1," *Dialogue* 6/3 (1994):9-12. See also the insightful articles by Frank L. Marsh, "Evolution and the Bible," *Adventist Review*, January 16, 1992, pp. 8-9; "The Conflict Over Origins," *Adventist Review*, January 23, 1992, pp. 16-17; "Variety—The Species of Life," *Ministry*, February 1981, pp. 24-25.

18. Ronald L. Numbers, *The Creationists* (New York: Alfred Knopf Inc., 1992), p. xvi, emphasis supplied.

19. Richard Hammill, "Journey of a Progressive Believer," cited in *Spectrum* 25/3 (March 1996):28.

20. A detailed discussion of this is found in Martin F. Hanna's "Science and Theology: Focusing the Complementary Lights of Jesus, Scripture and Nature," *Journal of the Adventist Theological Society* 6/2 (1995):6-51.

PART II

The Bible—
Fully or Partially Inspired?

Objective. In this section we will investigate to what extent higher-critical assumptions are influencing Seventh-day Adventist discussions on biblical inspiration, dress and adornment, the role of women in the home, ordaining women as elders or pastors, and the nature and relevance of Ellen G. White's prophetic gift.

Key issue. Is the Bible fully inspired or partially inspired?

Traditional Adventist Belief. Adventists believe that "*all* Scripture is given by inspiration of God, and is profitable for doctrine, for reproof, for correction, for instruction in righteousness" (2 Tim 3:16). When the Bible teaches that "in many and various ways, God spoke . . ." (Heb 1:1), it suggests that God varied His methods of disclosing His will to us. These methods included dreams, visions, historical research, personal reflection, etc.[1] But none of the sources of the Bible writers' messages renders their writing as "uninspired" or culturally conditioned (2 Tim 3:16, 17; 1 Cor 10:6, 11).

The Bible identifies the processes involved in revelation and inspiration: "Knowing this first, that no prophecy of the scripture is of any private interpretation. For the prophecy *came not in old time by the will of man: but holy men of God spake as they were moved by the Holy Ghost*" (2 Pet 1:20-21). The apostle Paul wrote: "For this reason we also thank God without ceasing, because when you received the word of God which you heard from us, *you welcomed it not as the word of men, but as it is in truth, the word of God,* which also effectively works in you who believe" (1 Thess 2:13).

In the light of these passages, Adventists hold that the Bible is not culturally conditioned. Rather, as a *divinely conditioned* but *historically constituted* document, it is fully inspired and therefore binding upon all people in all ages and in all places.

Cultural Conditioning. In an effort to show that some parts of the Bible are not fully inspired, proponents of contemporary higher criticism often argue that the Bible is historically or culturally conditioned. *By this expression they mean that the Bible mirrors the prejudices or limitations of the inspired writers' culture and times.* For instance, many such proponents in various denominations dismiss the Bible's condemnation of pre-marital and extra-marital sex as culturally conditioned. They claim that in contrast with our enlightened age, the Bible writers lived in a "pre-scientific" era with no antibiotics for venereal diseases, and no condoms and contraceptives to prevent pregnancies; their views were consistent with the conditions of their times. But, they continue, if the Bible writers had lived in our day, they would have viewed pre-/extra-marital sex differently.

On a related issue, is the denunciation of homosexuality culturally conditioned, stemming from Moses and Paul's lack of knowledge about psychological and genetic factors that may contribute to homosexuality? When Christians read the condemnations of homosexuality in the Bible, should they understand the Bible writers not as condemning the *offense* of homosexuality but an *offensive kind* of homosexuality (e.g., homosexual rape and promiscuity, or those associated with pagan practices)? Are other practices of Adventist lifestyle—such as abstaining from unclean meats, alcoholic drinks, and from wearing jewelry—culturally conditioned to the pre-scientific Bible times or, perhaps, to the nineteenth-century Victorian age of Ellen White?[2]

The cultural-conditioning argument implies that in some cases the Bible writers wrote from ignorance or a distorted view of reality. In effect, today's historical-critical interpreters believe they can decide which parts of the Bible are inspired and valid and which are not—the latter being the alleged culturally-conditioned sections of the Bible, not fully binding on all people in all ages. But they fail to show by what criteria they are able to sort out those parts tainted by the inspired writers' so-called prejudices, ignorance, or culture.

Basis for Cultural Conditioning Argument. The cultural conditioning argument assumes erroneously that because the people who lived in Bible times did not have the benefit of modern education, technology, and scientific laboratories, they were "primitive"—a view stemming from the myth of evolutionism. Evolution*ism* is not the same as the scientific theory of evolution. It is the philosophical theory that ideas and thought are continually progressing, so that the ideas of today are necessarily better than the ideas of yesterday. The English liberal scholar Dennis E. Nineham expresses such a view when he describes the Bible as "the expression, or at any rate an outcrop, of the meaning-system of a relatively primitive cultural group."[3]

Moderate proponents of higher criticism argue that since the Bible is both divine and human, the divine part may be fully trustworthy but not the human part. They maintain that such a view of Scripture is the best way to understand the incarnational analogy between Christ and the Bible—for both are fully human and divine. However, they fail to realize that a true incarnation model of Scripture does not permit finite human beings to separate the mysterious union of divine and human or to suggest that one part of Scripture (the human) is not fully inspired (see *Testimonies for the Church,* 5:747; cf. *The Great Controversy,* p. vi).[4]

One perceptive Adventist scholar captured the true biblical understanding of the divine and human in Scripture: "Jesus Christ became a man in time and space. Yet, this fact did not eliminate his divinity nor did it make him historically relative. In the same way, God's written Word, the Bible, also was given in time and space. But rather than being historically conditioned by immanent cause and effect relations, and thereby being rendered relative and not universally binding, God's Word is divinely conditioned and *historically constituted.* Thus it remains binding upon all men at all ages and in all places. It is *God's* Word, revealed to man and written by man under divine guidance and under the supervision of the Holy Spirit."[5]

How are the two higher-critical assumptions—the cultural-conditioning argument and doubts about the alleged "human" elements in Scripture—shaping Adventist views on the Bible's full inspiration?

Effect of the Liberal Approach

Bible-believing Adventists hold that God accommodated His message— i.e., He expressed His message in terms that could be understood by the messengers and their audience—*without compromising the truth in the process.* The new views of inspiration, on the other hand, allow for the truth to have been distorted.

New Views. For example, the author of *Inspiration: Hard Questions, Honest Answers* suggests that in divine accommodation God adapts Himself to the opinions of "surrounding culture"—even opinions that are false.[6] Because he believes that "revelation is adapted to the conditions of fallen humanity, [and thus] it partakes of the imperfections of that humanity," the author of *Inspiration* considers the Scriptures to have "a generous sprinkling of human 'imperfections' in the text," so that he finds "the quality" of the Bible's contents and mechanics sometimes falling to a mere C- passing level on his grading scale.[7]

For this scholar, the fact that the Bible is both divine and human suggests that while the divine portions of Scripture are infallible or trustworthy, the human aspects are not always reliable. He apparently did not consider that just as we cannot discern precisely where in Christ the divine part starts and the human ends, so also, in the case of Scripture, we cannot separate the "eternal" divine aspect of Scripture from the human aspect.[8] In the opinion of this Old Testament professor, the various "strange" laws in the Old Testament (such as capital punishment, the command to destroy the Canaanites) were culturally conditioned, in the sense that God simply treated Israel according to the cultural norms of justice of their times.[9]

Another who espouses what he styles "a structural view of inspiration" has written: "Personally, I believe there are demonstrable errors of fact in inspired writings." He explains that the "distortions" he claims to have found in Scripture arise from the fact that "perhaps the prophet did not fully understand the message, perhaps because the prophet's prejudices or ignorance distorted the message."[10] Did, for example, the ignorance and prejudices of Moses and Paul lead them to denounce homosexuality as morally wrong? If they had lived in our enlightened age, would they still have condemned homosexuality or fornication?

The "culturally conditioned" view also surfaces in the heated debates on dress and adornment, women's ordination, and the inspiration and relevance of Ellen White's writings. A few examples will illustrate.

Dress and Adornment. Is the Seventh-day Adventist teaching on dress and adornment culturally conditioned to nineteenth-century America? Extricating the Adventist practice from its biblical foundations, a professor of history argues that Adventists inherited the "plain dress" tradition from colonial American culture. He explains that although the Puritans and Quakers established this tradition in America, Adventists, under the dominant role of Ellen White, borrowed their practice from Methodism.[11]

Putting a feminist spin on this issue, one New Testament professor maintains that the rules governing female dress are yet another example of male oppression of women. In her opinion, the Old Testament "never prohibited adornment itself." As far as the New Testament is concerned, even though the practice was proscribed, only "lavish" adornment was disallowed because of the conditions at that time. She asserts: "Such conditions do not exist in American culture today. . . . Furthermore, ours is a democratic society that inculcated the equality of women and men; we must be careful not to teach inequality by prohibiting adornment for women while we permit it for men."[12]

The implication of this argument is that contemporary culture is the norm for Christian lifestyle. A person who accepts this view of bodily adornment will logically have to accept as morally appropriate the current practice even in Western societies of men piercing their ears and noses in order to be "equal" with women.

Role of Women *in the Home.* The relationship of men and women *in the home* is another issue that has felt the impact of higher criticism's assumptions. Are Paul's counsels on male headship and female submission (Eph 5:22-33; Col 3:18-19; 1 Cor 11:3, 11-12; cf. 1 Pet 3:1-7) to be lightly dismissed as culturally conditioned, so that in our day the man is no longer to be the head of the home? Or should Christians continue to uphold the Bible's teaching of *headship*—a theological concept which means that *within the loving relationship of male-female equality and complementarity, God calls upon men to be heads of their families and He holds them accountable if they refuse to shoulder leadership responsibilities?*[13]

The widely distributed book *Seventh-day Adventists Believe . . . ,* a volume described by the Ministerial Association of the General Conference as "an authentic exposition of Adventist beliefs," rightly affirms the contemporary validity of male headship responsibility.[14] But historical-critical scholarship is challenging this biblical doctrine.

Reasoning along cultural-conditioning lines, one contributor to the book, *The Welcome Table: Setting A Place for Ordained Women,* claims that Paul's statements defining the role relationships between male and female in the home derive from the Greco-Roman "household codes." Thus, Paul's statement in Ephesians 5 ("Submit to one another out of reverence for Christ. Wives, submit to your husbands as to the Lord. For the husband is the head of the wife . . .") is culturally conditioned and therefore not applicable to our situation today.

She maintains: "Paul was a man of his own time, and utilized familiar forms to help the people understand ways to live together, forms commonly known as the 'household codes' that are found in [Eph 5] verses 21 through 33. . . . It seems that Paul dealt with the political situation of his day in a way that was most conducive to the spread of the gospel. . . . Even as we struggle with such issues in our culture, Paul worked to find new ways to live the gospel in his. Though he occasionally glimpsed the ideal that Jesus established during His time on earth, he nonetheless fell into old patterns [the Greco-Roman 'household codes'] of coping during times of crisis." She therefore concludes that in our effort to arrive at "the gospel ideal," *"Paul's own cultural upbringing does not establish the pattern for today."*[15]

The implications are shocking for Bible-believers: we are to take these verses of instruction and counsel in Ephesians 5 not as expression of God's will but of "Paul's own cultural upbringing." The apostle did not write this under inspiration; he "fell into old patterns of coping during times of crisis," only "occasionally" glimpsing Christ's ideal. What leads this writer to think that she understands Christ's "ideal" for the home better than the apostle Paul did? And when she suggests that "Paul's own cultural upbringing does not establish the pattern for today," what contemporary pattern is she referring to? Is the "pattern for today" better than the Bible's role-differentiation that assumes an equal and complementary relationship between male and female?

Ordaining Women *as Elders/Pastors.* The discussion of the role of men and women *in ministry* also raises the question of cultural conditioning. As one proponent correctly observed, the issue of women's ordination is "a topic that has shaken the church to its foundations."[16] It has also afforded some scholars the opportunity both to reinterpret early Seventh-day Adventist history and to domesticate the historical-critical method in the Adventist church. One evidence of this is the independently published book, *The Welcome Table,* a pro-ordination volume widely promoted in some church publications and Adventist Book Centers.[17] For this reason the issue of women's ordination warrants a little more attention.

A Brief Background. The debate in the church over the ordination of women as elders/pastors arises because, in the face of calls for it from some quarters today, (1) there is no biblical *precedent* in either the Old or New Testament for women being ordained to serve in the roles of priest, apostle, and elder/pastor;[18] and (2) some explicit biblical *prohibitions* seem to militate against the practice (1 Tim 3:2; Titus 1:6; 1 Tim 2:11 ff.; 1 Cor 14:34, 35).[19]

Areas of Agreement. Both sides of the women's ordination question agree that: (1) Men and women are equal, equally created by God in His image and equally saved by Christ's precious blood (Gen 1:26, 27; Gal 3:28; 1 Pet 1:19); (2) Both men and women have been called to soul-winning ministry, to utilize their skills and spiritual gifts (Joel 2:28, 29; 1 Cor 12);[20] (3) God has called women to public service in Seventh-day Adventist history as in Bible times;[21] (4) Men and women should receive equal pay for equal work; (5) Ordination is the act of the church in choosing, appointing, and setting apart certain individuals (male and female) for assigned services through the laying on of hands.[22]

Points of Disagreement. The issue that divides them is this: "Since both male and female, through an act of dedication ("the laying on of hands"), can be commissioned *to perform certain specific functions,* the debate over women's ordination is not whether women can or cannot be ordained in this sense; the Bible and the Spirit of Prophecy suggest that both men and women may be commissioned to do certain assigned tasks on behalf of the church. The key issue to be addressed is whether, among the varied ministries of the church, women may legitimately be commissioned through ordination to perform the *headship functions of elders or pastors."*[23] The issue is not ordination *per se,* but ordination *to what function?*

In other words, the two sides on the women's ordination question disagree over: (1) whether the Bible *permits* women to be "appointed and commissioned" *as elders/pastors* or whether the Bible *prohibits* it; and (2) whether the matter is *merely cultural and administrative* and can be settled by vote, or whether it is a *biblical and theological* issue, on which God calls us to obedience. The disagreement is not over whether women *can* serve as elders/pastors, but whether God *permits* them to.

The Heart of the Disagreement. Four issues lie at the heart of the disagreement:

(1) The headship principle, which asserts that within the loving relationship of male-female equality and complementarity, God calls upon men to exercise Christ-like leadership in both the home and the church. Is this theological principle culturally conditioned to the days and culture of the Bible writers or is it still valid today?

(2) The relationship between the roles of elder/pastor and prophet: If God can call women to serve as prophets, what prevents them from serving as elders or pastors?

(3) The position of the early Adventist pioneers on the above two issues: How did the pioneers understand the headship principle? How did they relate the office of elder/pastor to that of prophet?

(4) Did the early Adventists ordain women as elders or pastors? Was Ellen G. White ordained?

1. Biblical Headship. The lack of biblical precedent for ordaining women to the headship role in the church, combined with the Bible's prohibitions of the practice, raises some questions. Were the Old Testament writers, Jesus Christ, and Paul male chauvinists? Should we explain away the male headship role as an accommodation to the Bible writers' culture and times? If so, how can we account for the fact that at the same time, the Bible also noted the significant role of women in ministry, including prophesying, praying, teaching, etc.? Could it be that women's exclusion from the Old Testament priesthood and from the New Testament roles of apostle and elder/pastor stems not from mere sociological or cultural factors but rather from God's divine arrangement established at creation?

Those favoring women's ordination argue that the patterns of ordination in the Bible (i.e., ordination of males as priests, apostles, and elders/pastors) and the specific biblical prohibitions (1 Tim 2:11 ff.; 1 Cor 14:34, 35; 1 Tim 3:2; Titus 1:6) are *culturally conditioned* to the Bible writers' time. They argue that the headship principle was introduced *after* the Fall and reversed by Christ in His life and work.[24] Some maintain that the headship principle is still valid in the *home,* but not in the church.

On the other side, those opposing women's ordination maintain that the patterns of ordination in the Bible confirm the *contemporary validity* of the headship principle of male headship and corresponding female cooperation. They argue that God instituted headship *at creation* by assigning men and women differing roles; this was *reiterated* after the Fall. Christ's work of redemption did not abolish gender-based roles; rather, it ensures that, even in this sinful world, men and women can realize "in the Lord" the true harmony that results from living in accordance with God's ideal of complementarity.[25]

Before looking at key hermeneutical questions raised by the headship principle,[26] we must first clarify the relationship between the roles of elder/pastor and prophet. We must also consider how the Seventh-day Adventist pioneers understood the headship principle and whether they ordained women (including Ellen G. White) as elders or pastors.

2. Elder/Pastor Not the Same as Prophet. The issue of women exercising the leadership authority of *elders* or *pastors* should not be confused with the legitimacy of women filling the messenger role of *prophets*. The role of the prophetic office is not the same as that of the elected office of elder or pastor. God Himself chooses and authoritatively commissions (ordains) prophets as His mouthpiece; they are not elected by the people as leaders to exercise administrative or executive authority. In both the Old and New Testaments, God chose and commissioned (ordained) prophets without regard to gender (e.g., Miriam, Deborah, Huldah).

On the other hand, the Bible teaches that elders and pastors are to be chosen and commissioned (ordained) by the church within guidelines stipulated in Scripture. One such criterion for the office of elder or pastor is that the one chosen must be "the husband of one wife" (1 Tim 3:2; Titus 1:6), an expression whose Greek construction emphasizes that the elder or pastor must be the kind of man who loves only one woman as his wife.[27]

Elders and pastors (the Bible makes no distinction in their office) are subject to the authority of God's messages coming through His chosen prophets.[28] As leaders of the church, elders and pastors are given administrative/leadership responsibility and authority that prophets are not. Church leaders are responsible to God for their reception of the prophetic message, but they are not under the administrative authority of the prophets.

We may see this difference clearly both in Scripture and in the experience of Ellen G. White. Elijah could give King Ahab God's message, but he did not have executive authority to make the king obey or to countermand his orders to have Elijah arrested (1 Kings 17:1-3, 18:7-10). Jeremiah proclaimed God's judgments with divine authority, for which he was imprisoned by priest, princes, and king (Jer 20:1, 2; 37:11-38:10). They had authority different from his.

In the early 1870s, Mrs. White had authority to give God's plan for Seventh-day Adventist education, but she did not have authority to make the leaders follow it in founding Battle Creek College. Prophetic authority is not the same thing as leadership/administrative responsibility. She herself refused to be called the leader of the Seventh-day Adventist church, referring to herself as "a messenger with a message": "No one has ever heard me claim the position of leader of the denomination. . . . I am not to appear before the people as holding any other position than that of a messenger with a message" (*Testimonies for the Church,* 8:236-237).

3. *The Adventist Pioneers and Headship Responsibility.* The Seventh-day Adventist pioneers recognized clearly that while women were prohibited from exercising the headship role of elder or pastor, Paul's instructions (cf. 1 Tim 2:11 ff.; 1 Cor 14:34) did not preclude women from the office of prophet. Though some contemporary scholars overlook the above distinction, our pioneers understood the difference.[29]

For example, in 1878, an editorial in *The Signs of the Times* summarized the understanding of the Adventist pioneers on the headship responsibility of the man in both the home and the church: "The divine arrangement, even from the beginning, is this, that the man is the head of the woman. Every relation is disregarded or abused in this lawless age. But Scriptures always maintain this order in the family relation. 'For the husband is the head of the wife, even as Christ is the head of the church.' Eph. 5:23. Man is entitled to certain privileges which are not given to woman; and he is subjected to some duties and burdens from which the woman is exempt. A woman may pray, prophesy, exhort, and comfort the church, but she cannot occupy the position of a pastor or a ruling elder. This would be looked upon as usurping authority over the man, which is here [1 Tim 2:12] prohibited."[30]

The editorial concluded: "Neither do the words of Paul confine the labors of women to the act of prophesying alone. He refers to prayers, and also speaks of women who 'labored in the Lord,' an expression which could only refer to the work of the gospel. He also, in remarking on the work of prophets, speaks of edification, exhortation, and comfort. This 'labour in the Lord,' with prayer, comprises all the duties of public worship. Not all the duties of *business meetings,* which were probably conducted by men, or all the duties of *ruling elders,* and *pastors,* compare 1 Tim. 5:17, with 2:12, but all that pertain to exercises purely religious. We sincerely believe that, according to the Scriptures, women, as a right may, and as a duty ought to, engage in these exercises."[31]

We must, therefore, summarize the views of the Seventh-day Adventist pioneers. Recognizing that no part of the Bible is culturally-conditioned, our pioneers clearly understood that: (1) there is a critical distinction between the authority of prophets and that of elders or pastors; (2) women have significant roles to play in soul-winning ministry (including teaching, preaching, etc.):[32] and (3) some explicit biblical statements forbid women to exercise authority over men in the home and the church (1 Tim 2:11-14, 1 Cor 14:34-35; cf. 1 Tim 3:2, Titus 1:6).[33]

Based on the above *theological* positions, our Adventist pioneers did four things: (a) they accepted the prophetic authority of Ellen G. White; (b) they encouraged women in different aspects of the work of soul-winning ministry;[34] (c) they refused to ordain women as elders/pastors, even when such a resolution came up for debate at the 1881 General Conference session;[35] (d) they issued ministerial *licenses* to a number of full-time women workers of the church, the same as were issued to non-ordained male pastors. These licenses are to be distinguished from ministerial *credentials,* the church's highest authorization, given to its ordained ministers. Ellen G. White, though not ordained, was the only woman known to have been issued ministerial *credentials,* apparently because the church had no way to commission a prophet.[36]

4. Women as Ordained Elders/Pastors? In early Seventh-day Adventist history women played major roles in the publishing and editorial work, home missionary work, the work of Sabbath schools, church finances and administration, frontier missions and evangelism, and medical and educational work.[37] As we noted earlier, those women who labored as full-time workers were issued the denomination's ministerial *license* rather than the ministerial *credentials* reserved for ordained ministers—indicating that they were not authorized to perform the distinctive functions of the ordained ministers.

Recently, however, some have mistakenly asserted that because early Adventist women labored faithfully and successfully in the soul-winning ministry, and because they were issued ministerial licenses, these women also performed the functions of the *ordained* ministry. On this inaccurate assumption, it is often argued that today the "ordination of women to full gospel ministry is called for by both the historical heritage of the Seventh-day Adventist Church and by the guidance of God through the ministry of Ellen G. White."[38]

Contrary to such creative reinterpretation, the Adventist women of the past understood that while they had been called to do the work of soul-winning, and while it was biblically legitimate for them to preach, teach, counsel, minister to the needy, do missionary work, serve as Bible workers, etc., the Scriptures prohibited them from exercising the headship responsibility of elder or pastor. These dedicated Adventist women of the past did not view their non-ordination as a quenching of their spiritual gifts or as an arbitrary restriction on the countless functions they could perform in gospel ministry. As they labored faithfully within the biblical guidelines of what is appropriate for men and women, the dedicated women of old discovered the joy in God's ideal for complementary male-female roles in the church.[39]

It is equally incorrect to suggest that the "guidance of God through the ministry of Ellen G. White" allows for women's ordination. Contrary to the suggestion in a recent issue of *Elder's Digest,* Mrs. White never called for the ordination of women as elders or pastors.[40] And as we already observed, although Ellen G. White was the only woman known to have been issued Seventh-day Adventist ministerial *credentials,* she was never ordained.

Mrs. White herself makes it clear that she was never ordained. In 1909, six years before her death, she personally filled out a "Biographical Information Blank" for the General Conference records. In response to the request on Item 26, which asks, "If remarried, give date, and to whom," she wrote an "X," indicating that she had never remarried. Earlier, Item 19 had asked, "If ordained, state when, where, and by whom." Here she also wrote an "X," meaning that she had never been ordained. She was not denying that God had chosen her and commissioned her as a prophet, but she was responding to the obvious intent of the question, indicating that there had never been an ordination ceremony carried out for her.[41]

During her later years, Mrs. White was known mostly as "Sister White" and affectionately as "Mother White." She was never known as "Elder White" or "Pastor Ellen." Every church member knew that "Elder White" was either her husband, James, or her son, W. C. White.[42]

Thus, for more than 100 years the Adventist position on the ordained ministry claimed the support of Scripture, as expressed in the teaching and practice of the Adventist pioneers, including Ellen G. White. By the 1970s, however, this established position began to be reversed in favor of ordaining women as elders and pastors, a situation that has created a theological and ecclesiological dilemma for Seventh-day Adventists.

5. *Our Contemporary Dilemma.* The major impetus for redefining the Adventist understanding and practice of ministry (and hence, for women's ordination) was the desire by church administrators to permit full-time *non-ordained* gospel workers (i.e. men and women holding ministerial *licenses*) in the United States to enjoy tax benefits reserved by their government for those "invested with the status and authority of an ordained minister." Whereas Adventists historically have insisted that their practice must always be brought into line with the inspired Word, on the issue of women's ordination it was the reverse. Tax-benefit considerations provided the critical *motivation* for the church to effect a series of Annual Council policy revisions and *Church Manual* alterations, allowing for a change in the church's long-standing policy regarding the ministry of ordained elders and pastors.[43]

Having thus allowed tax considerations to redefine the Adventist theology of ordination, the church has since faced this dilemma: (1) Should the church humbly admit that it was wrong in allowing financial interests to dictate its theology and proceed courageously to rescind previous church council actions so as to return to the biblical practice long maintained by the Adventist pioneers? or (2) Should the church insist that there is "no turning back" on the tax-benefit redefinition of its ordination theology and, on that assumption, continue to seek creative ways to reinterpret biblical passages that the Adventist pioneers understood as prohibiting women from serving in the headship roles of elders and pastors? These two options comprise the church's hermeneutical dilemma.[44]

Among those urging the second option are the advocates of the historical-critical method. For example, using higher-critical assumptions, some of the essays in the pro-ordination book, *The Welcome Table,* seek to reinterpret the crucial biblical passages (e.g., 1 Tim 2:11ff.; 1 Cor 14:34-35; 1 Tim 3:2; Titus 1:6) by arguing that they are culturally conditioned to the times of the Bible writers. Before looking at the hermeneutical issues raised by these recent reinterpretations, we must state two important conclusions from our brief background discussion in the preceding pages.

Summary. While tax considerations provided the crucial *motivation* to redefine our practice and theology of ordination, the Scriptures and the long history of Adventist understanding and practice stood in the way of this redefinition. However, the agenda of some proponents of women's ordination intersected with the desire of church leaders to solve their tax problems when higher-critical scholars offered a welcome ideological *method* for reinterpreting the Scriptures. In this way they attempted to bring the Bible into harmony with the revised theology of ordination.

In short, the present agitation to ordain women as pastors and to issue them ministerial *credentials* is a departure from the long-standing Adventist understanding and practice. More significantly, ordaining women as elders or pastors also raises some critical questions about biblical interpretation.

Key Hermeneutical Questions. The following questions beg for biblically consistent answers: Is the requirement that an elder or pastor be a male (1 Tim 3:2; Titus 3:2) culturally conditioned? Also, when Paul wrote that women are to "keep silence in the churches; for it is not permitted unto them to speak; but they are commanded to be under obedience, as also saith the law. . ." (1 Cor 14:34-35), are we to interpret the *prohibition* as Paul's "opinion," the *command* as Paul's personal "suggestion," and *the law* as the imposition of some "Jewish law" upon the *Corinthian* church as well as upon believers "in the churches" (including non-Jewish churches)? This is the position of one Adventist scholar.[45]

Further, if the "law" referred to in 1 Corinthians 14:34 is not a "Jewish law," or even a "Corinthian law," but is a reference to the Old Testament Scriptures, as the use of the word "law" in verse 21 suggests, did Paul concoct an Old Testament justification to put women down? In the two texts that seem to link the headship role of elder/pastor to gender (1 Cor 14:34-35 and 1 Tim 2:11-14), did the apostle use a rabbinic, or even distorted, logic in an effort to make his point? That is, did Paul use the Old Testament wrongly in advancing his argument? How do we know? Can today's uninspired interpreters claim to understand the Old Testament better than the inspired Bible writers did? Was Paul forced to compromise the ethical ideal of "equality" (redefined as obliterating gender role differentiation) when he apparently taught role differences between male and female? And were his views merely an adaptation to the cultural beliefs, mores, and practices of people he wanted to win?

The answers implied in the above hermeneutical questions expose the higher-critical assumptions of some proponents of women's ordination.

Was Paul Inconsistent? For example, in his attempt to address some of the key questions above, one Adventist professor of ethics intimates that Paul "violated" ethical principle in 1 Corinthians 14:34 and 1 Timothy 2:11, 12: "Paul appears to violate this [ethical] principle on two occasions by making gender, not gifts the determining factor" for women aspiring to be elders/pastors. He explains that given the time in which the apostle lived, these ethical concessions can be excused: "Paul made as few ethical concessions to current practice as possible, and as many as necessary. If he were alive today, he would not ask us to reiterate everything he did in his time. He would ask us to travel as far and as fast as possible in the direction he was moving in the hope that in our time we will move closer to the full recovery of equal partnership between Man and Woman than he could in his."[46]

What the above writer fails to address is why Paul presents his alleged inconsistent ethical conduct as a command to be followed by believers in "all the churches" (1 Cor 14:34) and as "a command of the Lord" (14:37).

Was Paul's Teaching Culturally Conditioned? A former associate editor of a church publication takes up this issue in discussing 1 Corinthians 14:34, 35 ("Let your women keep silence in the churches: for it is not permitted unto them to speak; but they are commanded to be under obedience, as also saith the law . . ."), and on 1 Corinthians 9:19-23 ("To the Jews I became as a Jew, in order to win Jews. . . . To those outside the law I became as one outside the law . . . that I might win those outside the law").

According to this Adventist editor, these texts indicate that Paul accommodated his *teaching* and *lifestyle* to his culture. What he fails to address is whether Paul compromised the *truth* by "accommodating" to culture—the crucial question distinguishing proponents of the historical-critical method from Bible-believing Adventists.

He explains Paul's "seemingly inconsistent conduct under varying cultural circumstances" in this manner: "Beyond any question, Paul's personal conduct [1 Cor 9] and his counsel [1 Cor 14] as a representative of Jesus Christ were both culturally conditioned to the circumstances in which he found himself and to which he addressed his teaching. *The important thing—the principle involved— was an adaptation of his own lifestyle and his directives to the culture-conditioned beliefs, mores, and practices of the people he aspired to win to Christ.*"[47]

Some may wonder whether indeed this author's opinion is "beyond any question." Our concern, however, is how he arrived at "the principle involved" in Paul's "seemingly inconsistent conduct under varying cultural circumstances."

Did Paul Err? Another question deserves a response: Did Paul err in his understanding and interpretation of the Old Testament? Aside from the contentious issue of what is involved in Paul's prohibition of women to "teach and have authority over man," when the apostle forbids such "teaching and authority" to a woman on the grounds that "Adam was first formed, then Eve. And Adam was not deceived, but the woman . . ." (1 Tim 2:11-14), can we dismiss this statement as culturally conditioned to Paul's time?[48] Can the Christian accept the suggestion by some that Paul's argument—which is not cultural but theological, grounded in Creation and the Fall—is not God's logic but Paul's? Is it merely an example of the rabbinic midrash that was in vogue in his day?[49]

Refuting Gnostic (Feminist) Heresy? A retired professor of religion voices the same "culturally-conditioned" argument. He bases his argument upon the questionable work of a non-Adventist scholar who theorizes that in 1 Timothy 2 Paul was responding to a Gnostic heresy in Ephesus, which held that woman (not man) was created first and that man (not woman) was deceived. This hypothetical, syncretistic theology allegedly encouraged women to domineer over men in public church meetings. On this fanciful speculation, our own professor suggests that the apostle's teaching regarding male-female relationships is culturally conditioned to the local situation in Ephesus. Therefore, he claims, it may not have validity today: "The passage does not give a universal prohibition of women from the ministry, but instead is a refutation of Gnostic error."[50]

The crucial hermeneutical question is not addressed: Was Paul inspired when he apparently saw the male-female relationship established at creation *before* the fall ("Adam was formed first"), and confirmed *after* the fall (Eve "being deceived . . .")? Should we accept the suggestion that an alleged Gnostic heresy is the basis for Paul's statement rather than the Old Testament account of the creation and fall as Paul himself maintains? How can Adventist scholars continue to recycle the discredited Gnostic hypothesis when it has been shown convincingly to be founded on disputable assumptions and questionable inferences?[51]

In view of the ideological dogmatism and fanciful speculations attending the interpretation of 1 Timothy 2, Adventists desiring to speak knowledgeably on 1 Timothy 2:11ff. will benefit greatly from consulting the excellent review of the arguments and literature in the recent book *Women in the Church: A Fresh Analysis of 1 Timothy 2:9-15.*[52]

Summary. After all the flamboyant hermeneutical phrases are stripped away, and after all the high-sounding but superficial references to "ethical principles" ("equality," "justice," and "fairness") are examined in the light of biblical testimony, the hermeneutical questions concerning 1 Corinthians 14:34-35 and 1 Timothy 2:11-14 still remain: Should today's interpreters accept Paul as an inspired and trustworthy writer of Scripture, or not? Shall we accuse the apostle of faulty logic, midrashic or rabbinic interpretation, adapting his lifestyle to his culturally-conditioned beliefs, mores, and practices, and violating ethical principle (the best he could do under those circumstances)? Are his statements inspired commands, or are they merely expressions of uninspired personal opinions—opinions that reflect his culture and hence do not apply to us?

Some even argue that in these texts bearing on male-female role differences, "God constantly adapts to sinful human conditions," or that the "specific passages [were] addressed to specific cultural situations."[53] *How can a "command of the Lord," addressed to "all the churches," referred to as "the law," and grounded in the fact of "creation," be a sinful practice and hence culturally conditioned?*

In short, certain significant Bible passages (like Eph 5:22-33; Col 3:18-19; 1 Pet 3:1-7; 1 Cor 11:3, 11-12; 14:34-35; 1 Tim 2:11-14; 3:2; and Titus 1:6) seem clearly to teach that within the loving relationship of male-female equality and complementarity, the man has been called upon to be head of the home and the church. Can Bible-believing Christians accept the assertion that these passages do not apply to us today? Shall we reject them because we claim that (1) they reflect God's adaptation to sinful situations in the Greco-Roman world or (2) even if they are not accommodations to sinful situations, they are only for the times in which they were uttered?

Inspiration and Relevance of Ellen G. White's Writings. But just as historical-critical assumptions influence scholars' treatment of the inspired writers of the Bible, so also do these assumptions shape views on Ellen White's writings. To diminish the binding authority of the Spirit of Prophecy, some apply the cultural-conditioning argument to the Spirit of Prophecy.

"Massive Re-Education." Thus, a former college president, now a professor of English in an Adventist university, has urged the church to "take a serious

look at the entire issue of Ellen White's inspiration. As a church we have never yet formed a definitive position relative to *revelation found in her writings as differentiated from her devotional messages."* Such a course, he explains, "would require massive re-education of church leadership, church ministry, and laity." Adopting this suggestion, he concludes, "would force us to say that *The Great Controversy,* including specific teaching relative to last-day events, *represents the conviction of its author, who might have written otherwise today.* Such a position would seriously trouble those who have been conditioned to believe that while Ellen White's writings may be a lesser light than the Bible, they are *all* still sacred in a revelational way."[54]

Is such a "massive re-education of church leadership, church ministry, and laity" underway? Today we hear increasingly that the message of Ellen White was conditioned by her "Victorian culture." Consequently, we are told, we can no longer take all her writings seriously; they are good as "devotional messages," but we cannot take all her writings "in a revelational way." When the author states that "revelation [is] found in her writings," he is actually saying what others say about all inspired writings—the Bible or Spirit of Prophecy— namely, we cannot take everything as inspired. Some things in Scripture and the Spirit of Prophecy are not inspired. Since some portions are inspired and others are not, we need the enlightened scholar's "massive re-education" to know how to pick and choose the inspired writings. The Bible is not an inspired Book; rather it is an inspiring booklet. Pick your favorite parts, cafeteria style.[55]

New Views of the Spirit of Prophecy. To help in the "massive re-education" concerning the writings of Ellen White, a chaplain and teacher at an Adventist university who holds a "dynamic," "developmental," and "Christ-centered view of inspiration"[56] has proposed re-conceptualizing the Adventist understanding of the Spirit of Prophecy: "Ellen White must be seen as a uniquely gifted woman who used the talents she was given to God's glory, just as other women in the church may do with their respective gifts if they are properly recognized. The church has traditionally set her too far apart from other women, and all other human beings for that matter, by claiming too much for her, and by claiming too much for what the gift of prophecy entails."[57]

Does this mean that all individuals who fully employ their "gifts" and "talents" to the glory of God have the gift of prophecy? Is that the sense in which we are to understand the prophetic ministry of Ellen White?

According to the above author, "Adventists, who accept Ellen White as a post-Biblical prophet, would also recognise the prophetic ministry of individuals such as Joan of Arc, Martin Luther, John Wesley, Martin Luther King [Jr.], Desmond Tutu, etc. These individuals have not only issued radical calls for repentance and justice, but more importantly from a Christian perspective have pointed humanity back to Jesus Christ as the only perfect source of truth."[58] A former book editor of one of the church's publishing houses made this point explicit: "Beyond her [Ellen White's] visions, *I have no reason to believe she was more of a prophet than Martin Luther or Mother Theresa.* But I do have reason to believe she was a prophet nonetheless. And a mighty one at that. . . . Why do I believe she was a prophet? For one thing, *she was a mystic, and I think people who enjoy a direct, unmediated connection to God are prophets prima facie.*"[59]

Notice the implication. If Ellen White's "prophetic ministry" is little or no different from that of Martin Luther, Mother Theresa, and "all other human beings for that matter," it stands to reason that we must treat her writings in much the same way as we do other human books. Her writings are "inspired" in the sense that they are inspiring—or if at all uniquely "inspired," they are not *fully* inspired.

Also, since Ellen White is compared to the biblical prophets, it stands to reason that their writings also will not be fully inspired; some things in them are inspired and others are culturally conditioned by the limitations and mistakes of their times: "The writings of Ellen White contain historical, scientific, medical, theological and other informational errors, which reflect the misconceptions that existed in her day. Her writings fit well with the thinking of her age, and did not contain significant ideas which were unheard of at that time."[60]

Summary. Let us briefly summarize the new understanding of the "prophetic ministry" of Ellen White, and for that matter our own gifts of prophecy. Prophetic ministry is using one's unique gifts and talents to their highest potential, having vision (as opposed to visions) and courage to address the important issues of one's day. In the case of Ellen White, it meant that she made "mistakes" and "misquoted and misinterpreted scripture (also as did Bible writers)."[61] Later in this chapter, we shall point out the implications of this new view of Ellen White's writings. Right now, however, we should only note that this understanding of the nature of inspired writings stems from higher-critical assumptions which many scholars have embraced.

In fact, the Adventist university chaplain cited earlier states that the new view of inspiration is the result of "a broader understanding of the nature of inspiration that has come through Adventism's exposure to higher education, and the application of the historical-critical method to both Scripture and the writings of Ellen White."[62]

A Bible-Believing Adventist Response

As we have noted earlier, many of the "culturally conditioned" arguments are based on the myth of evolutionism which maintains that the inspired writers were "primitive" or even "barbarians." Roland M. Frye's response to this chronological snobbery is apt: "The barbarian blindly asserts the primacy of his own temporal and cultural provincialism in judging and understanding and interpreting all that occurs, and the *learned* barbarian does precisely the same thing, but adds footnotes."[63]

The Bible Writers' View. Peter provided the best response to the "culturally-conditioned" argument: "Knowing this first, that no prophecy of the scripture is of any private interpretation. *For the prophecy came not in old time by the will of man; but holy men of God spake as they were moved by the Holy Ghost*" (2 Pet 1:20-21).

The oft-made suggestion that Paul's statements on such issues as Christian dress, sexual role differentiation, and homosexuality (1 Tim 2:9-14; 1 Cor 14:34-35; 11:3, 8-12; Rom 1:21-32) are "culturally conditioned" flies in the face of his own protest: "For this I was appointed a preacher and apostle (*I am telling the truth, I am not lying*), a teacher of the Gentiles in faith and *truth*" (1 Tim 2:7, emphasis supplied).[64] The Bible does not teach that some parts of Scripture are not inspired, while others are. Who decides which portions of Scripture are inspired and which are not?

The apostle Paul adamantly insists that his messages were not tainted by faulty logic of human wisdom or words distorted by the culture of their times. Instead, the Spirit who revealed the message to the Bible writers also enabled them to communicate it accurately: "When I came to you, brothers, I did not come with eloquence or superior wisdom as I proclaimed to you the testimony about God. . . . My message and my preaching were not with wise and persuasive words, but with a demonstration of the Spirit's power, so that your faith might not rest on men's wisdom, but on God's power. . . . This is what we speak, not in words taught us by human wisdom but in words taught by the Spirit, expressing spiritual truths in spiritual words" (1 Cor 2:1, 3, 13 NIV).

Those who are tempted to fault the Bible writers' logic and understanding of spiritual truths, dismissing their teachings as culturally conditioned, need to be reminded of Paul's statement: "The man without the Spirit does not accept the things that come from the Spirit of God, for they are foolishness to him, and he cannot understand them, because they are spiritually discerned" (1 Cor 2:14 NIV).

Ellen White's Position. Ellen White rejected the "culturally-conditioned" argument of modern scholars. She asserted that the Holy Spirit guided the Bible writers to record their accounts with such an "exact fidelity" that the Holy Scriptures are to be deemed as "truthful history of the human race, one that is unmarred by human prejudice or human pride" (*Testimonies for the Church,* 4:370; *Fundamentals of Christian Education,* pp. 84-85; cf. *Education,* p. 173). Though uninspired historians are so partial that they are unable to record history without their biases, the inspired writers "did not testify to falsehoods to prevent the pages of sacred history being clouded by the record of human frailties and faults. The scribes of God wrote as they were dictated by the Holy Spirit, having no control of the work themselves. They penned the literal truth, and stern, forbidding facts are revealed for reasons that our finite minds cannot fully comprehend" (*Testimonies for the Church,* 4:9-10).[65]

The Question of the Human and Divine. Besides the questionable "culturally-conditioned" argument, some also attempt to separate the human and divine elements in Scripture and classify some parts (the so-called human portions) as not fully inspired. But arguing that to be human necessarily means to be sinful and thus to err and to make mistakes is wrong biblically. "Human nature does not per se include sin. If that were the case, Jesus Christ who was the 'second Adam,' the real Man, who was truly human should have sinned. But according to Scripture, Jesus never sinned . . . (Heb 4:15). Thus a true Incarnational model of the Bible reflects that the Bible is indeed the Word of God, it is indeed exactly as Christ is, truly divine and truly human, and both together form an inseparable unity. The Bible is not mistaken in what it tells us as He was not mistaken in what He told us. It is fully trustworthy in what it says—it is without 'sin' to use the analogical term. In the same way that Jesus did not sin intentionally nor unintentionally Scripture does not give wrong information—intentionally or unintentionally."[66]

Ellen White challenged the tendency of some scholars to separate the human and divine elements in Scripture, conferring uninspired or fallible status upon some portions of the written Word. "The union of the divine and the human, manifest in Christ, exists also in the Bible. . . . And this fact, so far from being an argument against the Bible, should strengthen faith in it as the word of God. Those who pronounce upon the inspiration of the Scriptures, accepting some portions as divine while they reject other parts as human, overlook the fact that Christ, the divine, partook of our human nature, that He might reach humanity. In the work of God for man's redemption, divinity and humanity are combined" (*Testimonies for the Church,* 5:747; cf. *The Great Controversy,* p. vi).[67]

Bible-believing Adventists recognize the impossibility of separating what is divine from what is human in Scripture. They also recognize that attempting to do so denies the basic *unity* of Scripture. Against this liberal view, they assert that the Bible is ultimately the product of one divine mind, the Holy Spirit;

hence, a theological unity runs through the Bible from Genesis to Revelation. This unity means that we may compare Scripture with Scripture to arrive at correct doctrine. It makes the later inspired writers the best interpreters of earlier inspired writers.

A Warning. Because the entire Scripture is inspired, Ellen White warned: "Do not let any living man come to you and begin to dissect God's Word, telling what is revelation, what is inspiration and what is not, without a rebuke. . . . We call on you to take your Bible, but do not put a sacrilegious hand upon it, and say, 'That is not inspired,' simply because somebody else has said so. Not a jot or tittle is ever to be taken from that Word. Hands off, brethren! Do not touch the ark. . . . When men begin to meddle with God's Word, I want to tell them to take their hands off, for they do not know what they are doing" (*Seventh-day Adventist Bible Commentary,* 7:919-920). Again she wrote: "Brethren, cling to your Bible, as it reads, and stop your criticisms in regard to its validity, and obey the Word, and not one of you will be lost" (*Selected Messages,* 1:18).

NOTES

1. Besides dreams and visions, methods of revelation include: direct [theophanic] revelation (Ex 3:1-4:23; 20; 1 Kings 19:9-18; Rev 1:11-3:22), historical research (Luke 1:1-4), memory (John 14:26), and the use of the Bible writers' own judgment (1 Cor 7:12). All these are consistent with God's ways, since He Himself can choose to lead the inspired writers to discover the truths He has already revealed in nature, history and human experience (Ps 19; Rom 1, 2; Heb 1:1-2). It was the Spirit of God who illumined the natural faculties of Bible writers to present messages that have been kept for our benefit in such books as Job, Proverbs, Ecclesiastes, Luke, Acts, etc. Even references to uninspired pagan philosophers (e.g., Acts 17:22-28), as well as the "fights" and moral failures or shortcomings of Bible writers have all been recorded for our learning (see Acts 15; Jonah; Gal 2:11-14; Matt 16:21-23). Some of the Bible records also include things dealing with common or personal aspects of life. For example, 2 Timothy 4:13 talks about Paul's "pedestrian" request to Timothy to bring along his winter coat and books.

2. Such an argument has been articulated by a chaplain and teacher in an Adventist university. See Steve Daily, *Adventism for a New Generation* (Portland, Ore.: Better Living Publishers, 1993), pp. 296-298, 20. More will be said about this book in part 6 of this chapter.

3. Dennis E. Nineham, *The Use and Abuse of the Bible* (London: Macmillan; New York: Barnes and Noble Books, 1976), p. 28.

4. For helpful discussion of the incarnational analogy between Scripture and the incarnate Jesus Christ, see René Pache, *The Inspiration and Authority of Scripture,* transl. Helen I. Needham (Chicago: Moody Press, 1969), pp. 35-42.

5. Frank M. Hasel, "Reflections on the Authority and Trustworthiness of Scripture," in *Issues in Revelation and Inspiration,* ed. Frank Holbrook and Leo Van Dolson (Berrien Springs, Mich.: Adventist Theological Society Publications, 1992), pp. 208-209.

6. Alden Thompson, *Inspiration: Hard Questions, Honest Answers* (Hagerstown, Md.: Review and Herald, 1991), pp. 121, 125, cf. 147-150.

7. Ibid., pp. 53, 261, 70.

8. For a scholarly critique of the so-called "Incarnational model" of Scripture presented by the author of *Inspiration,* see Norman Gulley, "An Evaluation of Alden Thompson's 'Incarnational' Method

in the Light of His View of Scripture and Use of Ellen White," in *Issues in Revelation and Inspiration,* ed. Frank Holbrook and Leo Van Dolson (Berrien Springs, Mich.: Adventist Theological Society Publications, 1992), pp. 69-90; see also Frank M. Hasel, in his chapter "Reflections on the Authority and Trustworthiness of Scripture," in *Issues in Revelation and Inspiration,* pp. 206-209.

9. Thompson, *Inspiration,* pp. 123-126, 147-150.

10. The above professor of history initiated a dialogue with the author on the relationship between the inspiration of the Bible writers and Ellen G. White. He stated his "structural view" of inspiration in a letter (dated October 13, 1992) to this author following the published critique of Thompson's *Inspiration* "casebook" approach to Scripture (see Holbrook and Van Dolson, eds., *Issues in Revelation and Inspiration*).

11. Gary Land, "Adventists In Plain Dress," *Spectrum* 20/2 (1989):42-48.

12. Madelynn Jones-Haldeman, "Adorning the Temple of God," *Spectrum* 20/2 (1989):54-55.

13. For more on this, see John Piper, "A Vision of Biblical Complementarity: Manhood and Womanhood Defined According to the Bible," in Piper and Wayne Grudem, eds., *Recovering Biblical Manhood and Womanhood: A Response to Evangelical Feminism* (Wheaton, Ill.: Crossway, 1991), pp. 31-59; cf. Vern Sheridan Poythress, "The Church as Family: Why Male Leadership in the Family Requires Male Leadership in the Church," in John Piper and Wayne Grudem, eds., *Recovering Biblical Manhood and Womanhood* (Wheaton, Ill.: Crossway, 1991), pp. 233-247; cf. Samuel Koranteng-Pipim, *Searching the Scriptures* (Berrien Springs, Mich.: Adventists Affirm, 1995), pp. 45-55.

14. Ministerial Association of the General Conference of Seventh-day Adventists, *Seventh-day Adventists Believe . . . : A Biblical Exposition of 27 Fundamental Doctrines* (Hagerstown, Md.: Review and Herald, 1988), p. viii. For the place of this volume in contemporary Adventist theology see the opening pages of the book (ibid., pp. iv-viii). The biblical doctrine of headship is set forth in the volume's discussion of the responsibilities of fathers and mothers in the family (ibid., pp. 303-305; cf. note 3).

15. Sheryll Prinz-McMillan, "Who's in Charge of the Family?" in *The Welcome Table: Setting A Place for Ordained Women,* edited by Patricia A. Habada and Rebecca Frost Brillhart (Langley Park, Md.: TEAMPress, 1995), pp. 209-212, 212, emphasis supplied.

16. Lourdes E. Morales-Gudmundsson, "Preface," *Women and the Church: The Feminine Perspective,* ed. Lourdes E. Morales-Gudmundsson (Berrien Springs, Mich.: Andrews University Press, 1995), p. x. C. Raymond Holmes has aptly described the issue as "the tip of an iceberg" (see his book by that title).

17. See note 15.

18. The Bible teaches that, despite their significant role in ministry, women in Old Testament times were not ordained as priests. Also, though they made major contributions to the ministry of Christ, He did not appoint a single one of them as an apostle; further, when a replacement apostle was sought (Acts 1:15-26), even though women were present and surely met most of the requirements set (vv. 21-22), it was a male who was chosen. In addition, we have no record of any woman's being ordained as an elder or pastor in the New Testament church. Why was this so?

19. Despite the active involvement of women in ministry in the apostolic church, Paul's pastoral epistles to Timothy and Titus (letters specifically written to pastors and laity) contain instruction that only men may aspire to the office of elder or pastor. "I permit no woman to teach or to have authority over men" (1 Tim 2:12; cf. 1 Cor 14:34, 35); "a bishop [or elder] must be . . . the husband of one wife" (1 Tim 3:2; Titus 1:6). These passages all use the same Greek word for "man" and "husband." It is *not* the generic term *anthropos,* from which the English word "anthropology" derives and which refers to human beings, male or female, without regard to gender. Rather, Paul employed the specific word *aner,* a term that means a male person in distinction from a woman (cf. Acts 8:12; 1 Tim 2:12), one capable of being a husband (see Matt 1:16; John 4:16; Rom 7:2; Titus 1:6). Why did Paul prohibit women from exercising the headship/leadership role of elder or pastor?

20. The Bible clearly teaches that women have been called to the work of soul-winning ministry as surely as have men. In the Old Testament, women participated in the study and teaching of the law (Neh 8:2; Prov 1:8; Deut 13:6-11), in offering prayers and vows to God (1 Sam 1:10; Num 30:9; Gen 25:22; 30:6, 22; 2 Kings 4:9-10, 20-37), in ministering "at the entrance to the tent of meeting" (1 Sam

2:22), in singing at the worship of the temple service (Ezra 2:65), and in engaging in the prophetic ministry of exhortation and guidance (Ex 15:20; 2 Kings 22:14-20; 2 Chron 34:22-28; Judges 4:4-14). Of this latter group, especially prominent are Deborah, "a prophetess . . . [who] was judging [NIV "leading"] Israel at that time" (Judges 4:4), and Huldah, the prophetess to whom Josiah the king and Hilkiah the high priest looked for spiritual guidance (2 Kings 22).

The New Testament portrays women fulfilling vital roles in ministry. Besides Mary and Martha, a number of other women, including Joanna and Susanna, supported Jesus with their own means (Luke 8:2-3). Tabitha ministered to the needy (Acts 9:36). Other women, including Lydia, Phoebe, Lois, and Eunice, distinguished themselves in fulfilling the mission of the church (Acts 16:14-15; 21:8-9; Rom 16:1-4, 12). Of these, many were Paul's co-workers in ministry. Priscilla apparently was well educated and an apt instructor in the new faith (Rom 16:3; Acts 18:26); Paul calls Phoebe "a servant of the church" and a "succourer of many, and of myself also" (Rom 16:1, 2); Mary, Tryphena, Tryposa, and Persis all "worked very hard in the Lord" (Rom 16:6, 12); Euodia and Syntyche were women "who have contended at my side in the cause of the gospel" (Phil 4:3 RSV); and Junia, who suffered imprisonment with Paul, received commendation as someone "of note among the apostles" (Rom 16:7).

21. Ellen G. White strongly encouraged women in ministry. "There are women who should labor in the gospel ministry. In many respects they would do more good than the ministers who neglect to visit the flock of God" (*Evangelism,* p. 472). "The Lord has a work for women as well as for men. . . . The Saviour will reflect upon these self-sacrificing women the light of His countenance, and will give them a power that exceeds that of men. They can do in families a work that men cannot do, a work that reaches the inner life. They can come close to the hearts of those whom men cannot reach. *Their labor is needed"* (ibid., pp. 464-465, emphasis added). Seventh-day Adventist history and current practice illustrate the biblical truth that indeed women have a role in ministry.

22. Several Greek words in the New Testament are translated "ordain" (KJV); they convey such meanings as to "choose," "appoint," or "set apart." For example, Jesus "ordained (*poieo*) twelve" (Mark 3:14); Paul himself was "ordained (*tithemi*) a preacher and an apostle" (1 Tim 2:7; cf., 4:14; 5:22); Titus was urged to "ordain (*kathistemi*) elders in every city" (Titus 1:5). Each of these three Greek words carries the sense of "appoint," "place," or "establish." Another word used in the New Testament for the act of ordination is *cheirotoneo,* which can mean "to stretch forth the hand," or "elect" or "appoint." Thus Paul and Barnabas *"ordained* them elders in every church" (Acts 14:23); and when Titus was appointed by the churches to travel with Paul to Jerusalem, we are told that he was *"chosen* of the churches" (2 Cor 8:19). The compound form of the word, *procheirotoneo,* appears in Acts 10:41, where it describes God's prior appointment of the apostles. Thus, ordination is the act of the church in choosing, appointing, and setting apart through the laying on of hands certain individuals to perform specific functions on behalf of the church (cf. *The Acts of the Apostles,* p. 161). Rightly understood, both male and female can be ordained to do some assigned tasks (i.e., both male and female, through an act of dedication, can be commissioned to do *specific assigned tasks;* cf. Ellen G. White, *The Advent Review and Sabbath Herald,* July, 9, 1895, p. 434). The question is whether those tasks include the headship role of elder/pastor. For more on this, see our *Searching the Scriptures,* (Berrien Springs, Mich.: Adventists Affirm, 1995), pp. 21-23; cf. ibid., p. 24 note 6.

23. Samuel Koranteng-Pipim, *Searching the Scriptures,* p. 23.

24. For the arguments for and against the headship principle, see *Searching the Scriptures,* pp. 45-55; cf. "Q & A: The Request From North America," *Adventist Review,* May 1995, pp. 14-15; C. Raymond Holmes, "Post-Utrecht: Conscience and the Ecclesiastical Crisis," *Adventists Affirm* 10/1 (Spring 1996):49.

25. Koranteng-Pipim, *Searching the Scriptures,* pp. 45-55. Based on an analysis of the biblical data, we have concluded: "Thus, with respect to the attempt to ordain women, just as with the bid to change the Sabbath from Saturday to Sunday, we respond that the testimonies of Scripture indicate that God the Father *did not* do it; the Old Testament is clear that the patriarchs, prophets and kings *never did* do it; the gospels reveal that Jesus, the Desire of Ages, *would not* do it; the epistles and the acts of the apostles declare that the commissioned apostles *could not* do it; Ellen White, with a prophetic vision of the great controversy between Christ and Satan, *dared not* do it. Should we who live at the turn of another millennium do it?" (ibid., p. 65).

26. See Gerhard F. Hasel's 56-page document, "Hermeneutical Issues Relating to the Ordination of Women: Methodological Reflections on Key Passages," May 23, 1994, available at the Adventist Heritage Center, James White Library, Andrews University.

27. The Greek phrase, *mias* [of one] *gunaikos* [woman] *andra* [man], literally translates as a "man of one woman," or "one-woman-man," meaning "a *male* of one woman." When used of the marriage relation, it may be translated "husband of one wife" (KJV) or "husband of but one wife" (NIV). Because in this passage the words for "man" and "woman" do not have the definite article, the construction in the Greek emphasizes character or nature. Thus, "one can translate, 'one-wife sort of a husband,' or 'a one-woman sort of a man.' . . . Since character is emphasized by the Greek construction, the bishop should be a man who loves only one woman as his wife" (see Kenneth S. Wuest, *The Pastoral Epistles in the Greek New Testament for the English Reader* [Grand Rapids, Mich.: Eerdmans, 1952], p. 53). Also, because the word "one" (*mias*) is positioned at the beginning of the phrase in the Greek, it appears to emphasize the *monogamous* nature of this relationship. Thus, the phrase "husband of one wife" is calling for *monogamous fidelity*—that is to say, an elder must be "faithful to his one wife" (NEB). For an excellent summary of the various interpretations of this text, see Ronald A. G. du Preez, *Polygamy in the Bible with Implications for Seventh-day Adventist Missiology* (D.Min. project dissertation, Andrews University, 1993), pp. 266-277.

28. See *Searching the Scriptures*, pp. 27-28, 32-33, especially p. 32, note 1; 78-79; cf. 21-23.

29. In certain oversimplified analyses of the hermeneutical issues regarding women's ordination some have misunderstood the crucial distinction between the prophetic office and that of pastor/elder. See, for example, George R. Knight's, "Proving More Than Intended," *Ministry,* March 1996, pp. 26-28.

30. Unsigned editorial, "Woman's Place in the Gospel," *The Signs of the Times,* Dec. 19, 1878, p. 380. The editors were James White, J. N. Andrews, and Uriah Smith. The resident editor and presumed author of the editorial was J. H. Waggoner.

31. Ibid., emphasis original. Cf. Uriah Smith, "Let Your Women Keep Silence in the Churches," *Review and Herald,* June 26, 1866, p. 28.

32. For a helpful summary of the views of Adventist pioneers on 1 Tim 2:11ff. and 1 Cor 14:34, see Laurel Damsteegt, "Shall Women Minister?" *Adventists Affirm* 9/1 (Spring 1995):4-16. She lists the following sampling of articles from Adventist periodicals relating to women speaking in church: S. C. Welcome, "Shall the Women Keep Silence in the Churches?" *Review and Herald,* February 23, 1860, pp. 109-110; J. A. Mowatt, "Women as Preachers and Lecturers," ibid., July 30, 1861, p. 65; "Shall Women Speak in the Church?" ibid., Mar. 14, 1871; I. Felkerhoof, "Women Laboring in Public," ibid., Aug. 8, 1871, p. 58; "Shall Women Speak in the Church?" *Signs of the Times,* Aug. 17, 1876, p. 277; [J. H. Waggoner,] "Woman's Place in the Gospel," ibid., Dec. 19, 1878, p. 380; J. White, "Women in the Church," *Review and Herald,* May 29, 1879, p. 172; N. J. Bowers, "May Women Publicly Labor in the Cause of Christ?" ibid., June 14, 1881, p. 372; Uriah Smith, "Let Your Women Keep Silence in the Churches," *Review and Herald,* June 26, 1866, p. 28.

33. We have dealt with this in greater detail in *Searching the Scriptures* (Berrien Springs, Mich.: Adventists Affirm, 1995). The following two paragraphs are from p. 30 of that work, reproduced here without their supporting endnotes:

When the Bible urges women to "keep silence" in church (1 Cor 14:34), it does not mean that women cannot pray, prophesy, preach, evangelize or teach in the church. In the *same letter* to the Corinthians in which Paul told women to keep silence in the church, he indicated that women may pray and prophesy, provided they are dressed appropriately (1 Cor 11:2-16). And he said that the one who prophesies speaks "edification, and exhortation, and comfort" (14:3). Also, just like the command in the *same chapter* that those who speak in tongues should "keep silence in the church" if no interpreter was present (1 Cor 14:28), the instruction that women should "keep silence in the churches" suggests that Paul wants women to exercise their gift to speak within certain appropriate guidelines. Further, the same Paul who urged women "to learn in silence" (1 Tim 2:11) and who did not permit women to "teach or to have authority over men" (1 Tim 2:12 RSV) apparently approved the "teaching" ministry of Priscilla and Aquila in their instruction of Apollos (Acts 18:26). Paul also *required* women to do a certain kind of teaching: "Bid the older women . . . to teach what is good, and so train the young women to love their husbands and children" (Titus 2:3-5 RSV).

These texts should alert the Bible student that the prohibition of women "to teach or to have authority over men" does not forbid to women every form of teaching. Unlike other terms used in the New Testament to communicate the idea of teaching, the Greek word *didasko* used in this passage carries the force of authoritative teaching entrusted to a person—particularly someone in the leadership role in the church (cf. 1 Tim 3:2; 4:11; 6:2; 2 Tim 2:2). In light of the wider context of Paul's pastoral epistles to Timothy and Titus, as well as the immediate context which links this form of teaching with exercising "authority over men," we may conclude that Paul is here prohibiting women from the kind of teaching done in the capacity of a leader of the church. In other words, the apostle Paul is not forbidding all teaching to women, but only the kind of "teaching" in the church which gives women a position of authority over men.

34. See Kit Watts, "Ellen White's Contemporaries: Significant Women in the Early Church," in *A Woman's Place: Seventh-day Adventist Women in Church and Society,* ed. Rosa T. Banks (Hagerstown, Md.: Review and Herald Publishing Assn., 1992), pp. 41-74; Laurel Damsteegt, "S. M. I. Henry: Pioneer in Women's Ministry," *Adventists Affirm* 9/1 (Spring 1995):17-19, 46. The spirit of the early Adventist women is also reflected in the soul-winning ministries of women in Africa and many other parts of the world. See, for example, J. J. Nortey, "The Bible, Our Surest Guide," *Adventists Affirm* 9/2 (Spring 1995):47-49, 67; cf. Terri Saelee, "Women of the Spirit," *Adventists Affirm* 9/2 (Fall 1995):60-63. But contrary to revisionist interpretations of Adventist history, none of these roles required women to be ordained as elders or pastors (see William Fagal, "Ellen White and the Role of Women in the Church," available from the Ellen G. White Estate, and adapted as chapter 10 in Samuele Bacchiocchi's *Women in the Church* (Berrien Springs, Mich.: Biblical Perspectives, 1987); a summary version of Fagal's work is found in his "Did Ellen White Call for Ordaining Women?" *Ministry,* December 1988, pp. 8-11, and "Did Ellen White Support the Ordination of Women?" *Ministry,* February 1989, pp. 6-9; cf., Samuel Koranteng-Pipim, *Searching the Scriptures,* pp. 70-83, where we discuss "Restless Eves" and "Reckless Adams."

35. The 1881 General Conference session considered a resolution to permit ordaining women to the gospel ministry (*Review and Herald,* Dec. 20, 1881, p. 392). The minutes clearly show that instead of approving the resolution (as some today have erroneously claimed), the delegates referred it to the General Conference committee. There it died; neither Ellen G. White nor the other pioneers brought it up again. The issue did not resurface until recent decades. See the work of William Fagal, referenced in the previous note.

36. A number of dedicated women who worked for the church in the late 1800's and early 1900's were issued ministerial licenses. Ellen White was issued ministerial credentials from 1871 until her death in 1915. Three of her ministerial credential certificates—dated 1883, 1885, and 1887—are still in the possession of the Ellen G. White Estate.

It is interesting to note that on one of them (1885) the word "ordained" is neatly crossed out, but on the other two certificates it is not. Does this mean that Ellen White was "ordained" in 1883, "unordained" in 1885, and "re-ordained" in 1887? Obviously not. Rather, the crossing out of "ordained" in 1885 highlights the awkwardness of giving credentials to a prophet. No such special category of credentials from the church exists. So the church utilized what it had, giving its highest credentials without an ordination ceremony having been carried out. In actuality, the prophet needed no human credentials. She functioned for more than twenty-five years (prior to 1871) without any.

For more on this, see William Fagal's "Was Ellen White Ordained?" in his "Ellen White and the Role of Women in the Church," available from the Ellen G. White Estate. This paper was adapted for two published articles: "Did Ellen White Call for Ordaining Women?" *Ministry,* December 1988, pp. 8-11; "Did Ellen White Support the Ordination of Women?" *Ministry,* February 1989, pp. 6-9.

37. See note 34.

38. Bert Haloviak, "The Adventist Heritage Calls for Ordination of Women," *Spectrum* 16/3 (August 1985):52. More examples of such revisionist interpretation of Seventh-day Adventist history can be found in some pro-ordination works, which leave readers with the false impression that the issu-

ance of ministerial licenses to dedicated Adventist women of the past implied that they labored as ordained ministers. See, for example, Josephine Benton, *Called by God: Stories of Seventh-day Adventist Women Ministers* (Smithsburg, Md.: Blackberry Hill Publishers, 1990). Cf. the following articles in *The Welcome Table:* Bert Haloviak, "A Place at the Table: Women and the Early Years," pp. 27-44; idem, "Ellen G. White Statements Regarding Ministry," pp. 301-308; and Kitt Watts, "Moving Away from the Table: A Survey of Historical Factors Affecting Women Leaders," pp. 45-59; cf. "Selected List of 150 Adventist Women in Ministry, 1844-1994," Appendix 6.

While in early Adventist records, full-time workers carrying ordained ministers' *credentials* were listed as "Ministers," for un-ordained workers (women and some men) with ministerial *licenses*, the term "Licentiates" was used. In later *Yearbooks* of the church, the terms "Ordained Ministers" and "Licensed Ministers" were employed for these two categories of church workers. Both the early and later distinctions between the two groups of full-time workers ensured that under no circumstance could unordained laborers in the soul-winning ministry be confused with ordained ministers. There is, therefore, no valid justification for some contemporary writers to suggest or create the impression that women listed as "licensed ministers" performed the functions of ordained ministers, or that women today seeking to do full-time work in the gospel ministry must be ordained as elders/pastors. The facts from the "historical heritage of the Seventh-day Adventist Church" do not support such a conclusion.

39.   For a helpful corrective to the historical revisionism of some contemporary writers on the issue of ordination (see note 38 above), refer to the careful work by William Fagal "Ellen White and the Role of Women in the Church," available from the Ellen G. White Estate; a summary version of Fagal's work is found in his "Did Ellen White Call for Ordaining Women? *Ministry,* December 1988, pp. 8-11; "Did Ellen White Support the Ordination of Women? *Ministry,* February 1989, pp. 6-9; cf. Samuel Koranteng-Pipim, *Searching the Scriptures,* pp. 70-83, where we discuss "Restless Eves" and "Reckless Adams."

40.   Rose Otis, "Ministering to the Whole Church," *Elder's Digest,* Number Nine, p. 15. *Elder's Digest* is published by the General Conference Ministerial Association. As in this article, one statement from Ellen White has often been taken out of context and misused to claim support for ordaining women as elders or pastors: "Women who are willing to consecrate some of their time to the service of the Lord should be appointed to visit the sick, look after the young, and minister to the necessities of the poor. *They should be set apart to this work by prayer and laying on of hands.* In some cases they will need to counsel with the church officers or the minister; but if they are devoted women, maintaining a vital connection with God, they will be a power for good in the church" (Ellen G. White, *The Advent Review and Sabbath Herald,* July 9, 1895, p. 434, emphasis supplied).

Evidence that this statement may not be applied to ordination of women *as pastors or elders* may be found within the passage itself. (1) This is a part-time ministry, not a calling to a lifework. "Women who are willing to consecrate some of their time . . . ." (2) The work is not that of a minister or a church officer. "In some cases they will need to counsel with the church officers or the minister." Evidently this work is not that of an elder or minister. (3) It was a ministry different from what we were already doing. The portion quoted here is followed immediately by, "This is another means of strengthening and building up the church. We need to branch out more in our methods of labor." (4) It appears in an article entitled, "The Duty of the Minister and the People," which called upon ministers to allow and encourage the church members to use their talents for the Lord. The last sentence of the quoted paragraph reflects this thrust: "Place the burdens upon men and women of the church, that they may grow by reason of the exercise, and thus become effective agents in the hand of the Lord for the enlightenment of those who sit in darkness."

This is the only statement from Mrs. White addressing laying on of hands for women. The statement and its context clearly indicate that these women were being dedicated to a specific *lay* ministry, not the ministry of elders or pastors. For more on this, see William Fagal's work cited in the previous note; see also Samuel Koranteng-Pipim, *Searching the Scriptures*, pp. 21-23.

41.   A copy of her Biographical Information Blank may be found in Document File 701 at the Ellen G. White Estate Branch Office, James White Library, Andrews University. Arthur L. White published the information regarding these matters in the introduction to his article, "Ellen G. White the Person," *Spectrum* 4/2 (Spring, 1972):7.

42. See note 36 above.

43. In 1965, the United States Internal Revenue Service (IRS) ruled that in order for licensed ministers (i.e., full-time, non-ordained men and women workers of the church) to continue receiving parsonage allowance and other tax benefits reserved only for ordained ministers, and for their employing organizations not to be required to pay substantial Social Security taxes for them, they must be "fully qualified to exercise all of the ecclesiastical duties" of the ordained ministry. Space limitations prevent our going into the history of how, beginning in 1966, the desire to continue enjoying the U.S. tax benefits influenced administrators at church council meetings in 1970, 1973, 1974, 1975, 1976, 1977, 1984, and 1989 gradually to change the long-standing Adventist theology of the ordained ministry. Bert B. Haloviak provided a brief account in "The Internal Revenue Service and the Redefinition of Adventist Ministry," *Adventist Today* (May-June 1996), pp. 12-15. Haloviak concluded with this perceptive comment: "The interrelationship between money, theology, the IRS, and church administration had converged to create a moral dilemma within the Seventh-day Adventist Church" (ibid., p. 15). With the hindsight of considering the tumultuous events leading up to and following the women's ordination debates at the 1990 and 1995 General Conference sessions, one wonders if the desire for tax benefits in a particular country was sufficient reason to plunge the worldwide church into a theological, hermeneutical, and ecclesiastical crisis.

44. With respect to the first option, *Adventists Affirm,* with contribution and counsel of other Adventist scholars and church leaders, prepared an appeal to church leadership in 1989 which said in part: "The United States tax code problem which prompted the 1977 action no longer exists. Would it not be simpler to rescind our action and return to the practice the church had long maintained, and which it still follows in most of the world? This would provide one policy for the unity of the world church, remove the unequal treatment of unordained men and women serving in their various pastoral roles, and restore something of the significance of ordination in North America" (see "An Appeal to the World Field Regarding the Ministry of Women in the Church," *Adventists Affirm* 3/2 [Fall 1989]:11). This appeal, however, went unheeded by those who favored option two. Thus in the events leading to the 1995 Utrecht General Conference session, the North American Division still argued for "No Turning Back" on the ordination of women as elders and pastors. See, for example, Alfred C. McClure, "NAD's President Speaks on Women's Ordination: Why Should Ordination be Gender Inclusive?" *Adventist Review* [NAD edition], February 1995, pp. 14-15; cf. Gary Patterson, "Let Divisions Decide When to Ordain Women," *Spectrum* 24/2 (April 1995), pp. 36-42. For responses to the above view, see the articles by Ethel R. Nelson, "'No Turning Back' on Ordination?" and C. Mervyn Maxwell, "Response to NAD President's Request to Annual Council" in *Adventists Affirm* 9/1 (Spring 1995):42-46, 30-37, 67; cf. *Searching the Scriptures,* pp. 9-14, 88-90.

45. David R. Larson, "Man and Woman as Equal Partners: The Biblical Mandate for Inclusive Ordination," in *The Welcome Table,* p. 132.

46. Ibid., pp. 131, 133.

47. Raymond F. Cottrell, "A Guide to Reliable Interpretation," *The Welcome Table,* p. 87, emphasis supplied. For a brief discussion of the crucial hermeneutical issues at stake in our treatment of the key New Testament passages relating to the roles of male and female in the church (1 Cor 14:34-35; 1 Tim 2:11ff.; 3:2; Titus 3:2; Acts 1:21-25), see Samuel Koranteng-Pipim, *Searching the Scriptures,* pp. 56-69; C. Raymond Holmes, *The Tip of An Iceberg,* pp. 133-155; Gerhard F. Hasel, "Hermeneutical Issues Relating to the Ordination of Women: Methodological Reflections on Key Passages," May 23, 1994, available at the Adventist Heritage Center, James White Library, Andrews University.

48. Those desiring to explore 1 Tim 2:11ff. in greater depth will benefit from the following works: Andreas J. Köstenberger, Thomas R. Schreiner, and H. Scott Baldwin, eds., *Women in the Church: A Fresh Analysis of 1 Timothy 2:9-15* (Grand Rapids, Mich.: Baker, 1995), a ground-breaking work that takes a closer look at the background, lexicography, grammar, and exegesis of 1 Tim 2:9-15. Two articles in this volume deserve special mention. First, H. Scott Baldwin's "A Difficult Word in 1 Timothy 2:12" offers a compelling argument that the Greek word *authentein* can only be translated as "to have authority over"; this decisively excludes meanings such as "instigate violence," "murder," or "proclaim oneself author of a man." Second, Andreas J. Köstenberger's "A Difficult Sentence

Structure in 1 Timothy 2:12" analyzed the syntactical structure of Paul's statement, "I do not permit a woman to teach or to have authority over a man," showing that the grammatical structure in the Greek ("not + [verb 1] + neither + [verb 2]") suggests that if "teach" is viewed positively in 1 Timothy (which it is), then "have authority" must also be an action that is viewed positively, but prohibited for reasons other than the inherent wrongness of the activity of "having authority" in itself. This powerful argument discredits interpretations such as "domineer" or "instigate violence." Another significant work is Wayne Grudem's "The Meaning of '*kephale*,' ('head'): A Response to Recent Studies," appendix in *Recovering Biblical Manhood and Womanhood: A Response to Evangelical Feminism,* ed. John Piper and Wayne Grudem (Wheaton, Ill.: Crossway, 1991), pp. 425-468; this work challenges the unfounded speculation that the Greek word *kephale* (head) should be translated as "source" rather than its real meaning as "authority." Bruce Waltke, "1 Tim. 2:8-15: Unique or Normative?" *Crux* 28/1 (March 1992):22-27, answers the common objection that 1 Timothy 2:8-15 only applies to a particular situation at that time, and not to all churches for all time; cf. Wayne Grudem, "Why Paul Allows Women to Prophesy but not Teach in Church," *Journal of the Evangelical Theological Society* 30/1 (March 1987):11-23; cf. Douglas Moo, "What Does It Mean Not to Teach or Have Authority Over Men?: 1 Timothy 2:11-15," in *Recovering Biblical Manhood and Womanhood,* pp. 179-193; D. A. Carson, "'Silent in the Churches': On the Role of Women in 1 Corinthians 14:33b-36," in *Recovering Biblical Manhood and Womanhood,* pp. 140-153. Finally, Guenther Haas, "Patriarchy as An Evil that God Tolerated: Analysis and Implications for the Authority of Scripture," *Journal of the Evangelical Theological Society* 38/3 (September 1995):321-326, shows how rejecting the biblical teaching of headship has far-reaching implications for one's view of God and the authority of Scripture.

49. Thompson, *Inspiration,* p. 98; cf. Fritz Guy, "The Disappearance of Paradise," in *The Welcome Table,* pp. 142-143.

50. Ralph E. Neall, "Ordination Among the People of God," *The Welcome Table,* p. 264. Neall admits that his article is built on the work of Catherine and Richard Kroeger, *I Suffer Not a Woman: Rethinking 1 Timothy 2:11-15 in Light of Ancient Evidence* (Grand Rapids, Mich.: Baker, 1992). For a succinct critique of Neall's work, see Keith Burton, "At God's Table, Women Sit Where They Are Told," *Spectrum* 25/3 (March 1996):55-57, especially note 16. Adventists who join Catherine Kroeger, President of Christians for Biblical Equality, and her husband Richard in advancing a Gnostic hypothesis as an explanation of Paul's statement in 1 Tim 2:11ff. are apparently unaware of the serious flaws in the hypothesis. A helpful critique can be found in Stephen Baugh, "The Apostle Among the Amazons" (a review of Richard and Catherine Kroeger, *I Suffer Not a Woman* (Baker, 1992), *Westminster Theological Journal* 56 (1994):153-171; Albert Wolters, review of *I Suffer Not a Woman,* *Calvin Theological Journal* 28 (1993):208-213; Robert W. Yarbrough, "I Suffer Not a Woman: A Review Essay," *Presbyterion* 18/1 (1992):25-33; Richard Oster, review of *I Suffer Not a Woman,* *Biblical Archaeologist* 56/4 (1993):225-227.

51. See note 50. A Gnostic/feminist hypothesis similar to that of the Kroegers is found in Sharon Marie Hodgin Gritz's *A Study of 1 Timothy 2:9-15 in Light of the Religious and Cultural Milieu of the First Century* (Ph.D. dissertation, Southwestern Baptist Theological Seminary, 1986). For a detailed critique and correction of works such as the Kroegers' and Gritz's, see Stephen Baugh's "A Foreign World: Ephesus in the First Century" in Andreas J. Köstenberger, Thomas R. Schreiner, and H. Scott Baldwin, eds., *Women in the Church: A Fresh Analysis of 1 Timothy 2:9-15* (Grand Rapids, Mich.: Baker, 1995), pp. 13-52. Baugh's 40-page analysis of Ephesus in the First Century dismisses the unfounded speculations of such works. Cf. C. Mervyn Maxwell, "Women in the Greco-Roman World," a study paper for the Biblical Research Institute, revised and corrected edition, March, 1988; Douglas Moo, "What Does It Mean Not to Teach or Have Authority Over Men?: 1 Timothy 2:11-15," in John Piper and Wayne Grudem, *Recovering Biblical Manhood and Womanhood: A Response to Evangelical Feminism* (Wheaton, Ill.: Crossway, 1991), pp. 179-193.

52. See especially the essays by Thomas Schreiner ("An Interpretation of 1 Timothy 2:9-15: A Dialogue with Scholarship," pp. 105-154), Robert W. Yarbrough ("The Hermeneutic of 1 Timothy 2:9-15," pp. 155-196), and Daniel Doriani ("A History of the Interpretation of 1 Timothy 2," pp. 213-

267) in *Women in the Church: A Fresh Analysis of 1 Timothy 2:9-15*, ed. Andreas J. Köstenberger, Thomas R. Schreiner, and H. Scott Baldwin (Grand Rapids, Mich.: Baker, 1995).

53. Andrew Bates (pseudonym), "The Jerusalem Council: A Model for Utrecht?" *Ministry*, April 1995, p. 22. For a brief response to the main arguments of this article, see Samuel Koranteng-Pipim, "The Spirit's Guidance at a Church Council," in *Searching the Scriptures*, pp. 42-44 (note carefully endnotes 3, 4, and 5 on page 44).

54. Frank A. Knittel, "The Great Billboard Controversy," *Spectrum* 23/1 (May 1993):56. See also his interview with Jim Walters, "Observations of a President, Pastor, Entrepreneur," *Adventist Today*, November-December, 1995, p. 12; cf. Sakae Kubo's call for a "re-evaluation" of Ellen White in the light of source-critical findings (see Scott Moncrieff's summary of Kubo's views, "Adventist Issues for the '90s," *The Student Movement* [Andrews University student newsaper], November 8, 1989, pp. 7, 15).

55. For more on this, see Samuel Koranteng-Pipim, "Inspired Book or Inspiring Booklet," *Adventists Affirm* 9/1 (Spring 1995):20-29.

56. Steven G. Daily, *Adventism for a New Generation* (Portland/Clackamas, Ore.: Better Living Publishers, 1993), pp. 77-78.

57. Steven G. Daily, "Towards An Adventist Theology of Liberation," a paper presented to the Association of Adventist Women and the Association of Adventist Forums in Loma Linda, Calif., on March 18, 1984, and reproduced as appendix B in his "The Irony of Adventism: The Role of Ellen White and Other Adventist Women in Nineteenth Century America (D.Min. project, School of Theology at Claremont, 1985), p. 324; cf. pp. 302-306.

58. Steven G. Daily, *Adventism for a New Generation*, p. 188.

59. Max Gordon Phillips, "The Church: Leave It *and* Love It?" *Adventist Today*, March-April 1996, pp. 12-13, emphasis supplied.

60. Steven G. Daily, *"How Readest Thou:* The Higher Criticism Debate in Protestant America and Its Relationship to Seventh-day Adventism and the Writings of Ellen White, 1885-1925," M.A. Thesis, Loma Linda University, 1982, p. 133. The view expressed above is built upon the "historical research" of men like Ronald Numbers, Walter Rea, and Don McAdams (ibid., p. 132).

61. Ibid.; cf. p. 125, where Daily writes that "errors can be found in Scripture." Cf. his *Adventism for a New Generation*, pp. 186-188; George R. Knight, *Anticipating the Advent: A Brief History of Seventh-day Adventists* (Boise, Id.: Pacific Press, 1993), pp. 106-107, who intimates that while both the Bible and the writing of Ellen White are infallible in the realm of salvation, they are not "beyond any possibility of factual difficulties or errors."

62. Steven Daily, "The Irony of Adventism: The Role of Ellen White and Other Adventist Women in Nineteenth Century America (D.Min. project, School of Theology at Claremont, 1985), p. 327. More will be said on this point later in the chapter.

63. Roland M. Frye, "A Literary Perspective for the Criticism of the Gospels," in Donald G. Miller and Dikran Y. Hadidian, eds., *Jesus and Man's Hope*, vol. 2 (Pittsburgh: Pittsburgh Theological Seminary, 1971), p. 198, emphasis supplied. Readers will greatly benefit from David R. Hall's *The Seven Pillories of Wisdom* (Macon, Ga.: Mercer University Press, 1990), pp. 37-54. With wit and good humor, Hall demolishes seven shaky foundations of the modern approaches to Scripture. This is a "must read" for all.

64. For a response to this "culturally-conditioned" argument in the women's ordination debate, refer to my *Searching the Scriptures*, pp. 62-66.

65. See also P. Gerard Damsteegt, "The Inspiration of Scripture in the Writings of Ellen G. White," *Journal of the Adventist Theological Society* 5/1 (1994):155-179.

66. Frank M. Hasel, "Reflections on the Authority and Trustworthiness of Scripture," in *Issues in Revelation and Inspiration*, p. 209.

67. Cf. Peter van Bemmelen, "The Mystery of Inspiration: An Historical Study of the Doctrine of Inspiration in the Seventh-day Adventist Church, With Special Emphasis on the Decade 1884-1893," (paper, Andrews University, 1971), available at the James White Library, Andrews University.

DEPARTING FROM THE WORD

PART III

The Bible—
Fully or Partially Trustworthy?

Objective. In this section we shall explore to what extent higher-critical assumptions are influencing Seventh-day Adventist views on the reliability of the Bible writers' accounts, Ellen White's position on the Bible's trustworthiness, the New Testament's use of the Old Testament, and the alleged contradictions in parallel accounts in the Bible.

Key Issue. Is the Bible fully or partially trustworthy?

Traditional Adventist Belief. Bible-believing students accept the Bible's full reliability in matters of salvation as well as on any other subject the Bible touches upon. When the Bible writers describe an account as actually taking place, we are to believe it as trustworthy. The apostle Peter wrote: "For *we have not followed cunningly devised fables,* when we made known unto you the power and coming of our Lord Jesus Christ, but were eyewitnesses of his majesty" (2 Pet 1:16; cf. 1 Cor 2:10-13). John wrote: *"The man who saw it has given testimony, and his testimony is true. He knows that he tells the truth,* and he testifies so that you also may believe" (John 19:35 NIV); and Luke stated: "Therefore, since I myself have *carefully investigated everything* from the beginning, it seemed good also to me to write an orderly account for you. . ." (Luke 1:3 NIV).

Mainstream Adventism believes that the biblical accounts—including those touching upon science, history, geography, and other matters—are fully reliable and trustworthy. When the Bible says that the creation took six literal days, that there was a universal flood in Noah's day, an exodus of some 600,000 men from Egypt, and that the sun stood still in Joshua's day, we are to believe that the events actually took place. When the New Testament writers pointed to events in their day as fulfilling Old Testament prophecies, they were not mistaken, nor did they read the Old Testament out of context.

The first article of Seventh-day Adventists' "Fundamental Beliefs" emphasizes the trustworthiness of Scripture by stating: "The Holy Scriptures are the infallible revelation of His will. They are the standard of character, the test of experience, the authoritative revealer of doctrines, and *the trustworthy record of God's acts in history.*" Ellen G. White wrote that the Holy Scriptures "are to be accepted as an authoritative, infallible revelation of His [God's] will" (*The Great Controversy,* p. vii; cf. pp. 68, 102); they are "the only infallible authority in religion" (ibid., p. 238; see also pp. 89, 177), and "the only sufficient, infallible rule" (ibid., p. 173).

For Ellen White, Scripture shares in the infallibility of God. "God and heaven alone are infallible" (*Selected Messages,* 1:37; cf. *Testimonies to Ministers,* pp. 30, 105). "Man is fallible, but God's Word is infallible" (*Selected Messages,* 1:416). She left no doubt that the Bible is "an unerring counselor and infallible guide" and the "perfect guide under all circumstances of life";[1] "an unerring guide," "the one unerring guide," "the unerring standard," "an unerring light," "that unerring test," and "the unerring counsel of God."[2]

Theological Assumption. The theological assumption undergirding the trustworthiness of Scripture is the character of the triune God. Since what a person says reflects his character, we would expect that if God is the God of truth (Ex 34:6; Deut 32:4), if Jesus is Truth (John 14:6), and if the Holy Spirit is Truth (John 14:17), then the Triune God who has spoken in Scripture must speak the truth. Because God's Word says that God does not lie (Num 23:19; 1 Sam 15:29; Titus 1:2; Heb 6:18), Bible-believing Christians maintain that His inspired Word speaks the truth.

But in their efforts to appear "scientific," theological liberals do not accept the reliability of the accounts in Scripture. They seek to reconstruct the Bible according to what they think probably happened, and in some cases they argue that the inspired New Testament writers were wrong in how they used the Old Testament.

How are historical-critical assumptions influencing Adventist views on Scripture's trustworthiness?

Effect of the Liberal Approach

While our scholars who subscribe to contemporary higher criticism reject some of the anti-supernatural presuppositions of "radical" liberals and hence give an appearance of being Bible-believing Adventists, they maintain nonetheless that the Bible is not fully reliable since it contains some "mistakes" or "exaggerations." The alleged "mistakes" include so-called "discrepancies," "inconsistences," and "inaccuracies" in its statements about chronology, numbers, genealogy, history, geography, and science. Believing that they can use the historical-critical method without adopting the skeptical and naturalistic assumptions on which it is based, proponents of the method resort to *reconstructing* or reinterpreting the biblical accounts.

First, they downgrade biblical certainties into probabilities and probabilities into possibilities. Then they upgrade the possibilities of their reconstructed accounts into probabilities and probabilities into certainties. They present the result of this "objective" or "scientific" historical inquiry to unsuspecting church members as a mark of scholarly enlightenment. And anyone who does not accept these reconstructions is classified as "narrow-minded," "literalistic," or "fundamentalistic" in thinking!

The Biblical Accounts. The book *Inspiration,* for example, denies the trustworthiness of certain scriptural accounts. In it (a) the author makes a dichotomy between saving acts and factual statements, so that in scriptural accounts some things are "essential" and others are "debatable";[3] (b) he rejects the Bible's claim that the original sanctuary in the wilderness was constructed as a copy of the heavenly (Ex 25:40), suggesting that the idea was borrowed from surrounding Canaanites and that the book of Hebrews interprets the "heavenly" sanctuary in terms of Platonic dualism;[4] (c) he accepts the miracle of the Exodus but maintains that the exact "number of people involved in the Exodus is not that crucial";[5] (d) he acknowledges a miraculous flood in Noah's day but holds that the biblical flood was "less than [a] universal event";[6] (e) he believes in biblical history and yet argues that information on numbers, genealogies, and dates may have been "distorted."[7] Do Seventh-day Adventist interpreters do well to deny or question the trustworthiness of Scripture?

Revising of Ellen White's View. Some Adventist scholars subtly suggest that while the Bible is infallible in matters of salvation, the same cannot be said about the factual, historical, or scientific accounts in Scripture. An Adventist historian who offers a nuanced endorsement of *Inspiration* even goes so far as to make Ellen G. White a party to his own "moderate stance on inspiration," which he also terms a "common-sense flexibility on inspiration." Without any shred of support from Ellen White and contrary to what she unambiguously asserted in several places in her works, he popularizes his revisionist reinterpretation of Ellen White's position: "The Bible, she held, was infallible in the realm of salvation, but it was not infallible or inerrant in the radical sense of being beyond any possibility of factual difficulties or errors"![8] One searches in vain for such a statement from Ellen White.

The Genesis Account. In the same spirit of distinguishing between the Bible's theological statements as infallible and the accompanying historical facts as debatable, a contributor to the book, *The Welcome Table,* uses "sanctified imagination" to assert: "First we need to make clear what Genesis 2 is and what it isn't. It is a story of beginnings, a story to instruct and even entertain, told in such a fashion as to be easily remembered and retold. *It is not history or science.*"[9] In other words, we cannot always trust the historical or scientific accuracy of Genesis 2.

Also, contrary to the Bible's clear teaching that Adam was a male, this writer states: "Even though we may *deduce* that the first human being was a male being, the storyteller does not specifically say so." She suggests that Adam is presented as *"an androgynous being"* (i.e. bisexual)![10]

The obliteration of gender differentiation in Genesis 2 is only a few steps away from positing homosexuality or bisexuality in the first created pair. And since human beings were created in God's image, if Adam was "an androgynous being" does it not mean that God also is androgynous? One wonders what is really behind the gender-inclusive reconstructions of the Bible: "*Son* of God" becomes "*Child* of God"; "*Son* of Man" becomes "*Human* one"; "our heavenly *Father*" becomes "our heavenly *Parent*."[11] Is this also the reason why an Adventist author promotes the Holy Spirit as the female member of the Godhead and repeatedly refers to the Creator as "He/She"?[12]

The New Testament Use of the Old. Scholars highlight the alleged distortion of the biblical message when they express their views on how New Testament writers used the Old Testament. They maintain that, using rabbinic methods current in their times, the writers of the New Testament sometimes read back into Old Testament passages meanings that were foreign to the original meaning.[13] This implies that we cannot always trust the New Testament writers, since they allegedly took texts out of context and imposed their own meanings upon them.

Apparently believing that he understands the Old Testament better than the apostle Paul did, one author maintains that Paul misused Isaiah 64:4 in his quotation of 1 Corinthians 2:9: "It appears Paul used Old Testament verses out of context on occasion as he wrote in the New Testament!"[14] Similarly, others suggest that though the inspired writer Matthew cited Isaiah 7:14, Hosea 11:1, and Jeremiah 31:15 as prophecies in connection with Jesus's birth, childhood, and flight to Egypt to escape Herod's massacre, each of the Old Testament verses was "not intended as a prophecy at all." In other words, Matthew used the Old Testament out of context.[15]

What makes these authors think they have a better understanding of the Old Testament than the inspired writers of the New Testament had?

Alleged Contradictions in Parallel Accounts. Another effort to undermine the trustworthiness of Scripture is the suggestion that there are discrepancies or contradictions in parallel accounts of the Bible. The euphemistic term often employed is "diversity" or "differences" in Scriptures. For instance, one teacher and Adventist university chaplain cites as an "obvious example" of "theological contradictions in the Bible" the *apparent* discrepancy between 2 Samuel 24 and 1 Chronicles 21, a point that is also made in *Inspiration.*[16] In Chapter Ten we shall show that the so-called "theological contradiction" does not reside in the biblical texts, but rather in the imagination of scholars conditioned by the historical-critical methodology.

Similarly, an Adventist New Testament scholar employs redaction criticism (an aspect of the historical-critical method) in his book, *Luke, A Plagiarist?* He attempts to show that the gospel writers performed major "surgery" on the sayings of Jesus which they reported. Differences between parallel accounts in Matthew, Mark, Luke and John are the result of these writers' editorial genius in deliberately introducing some "minor" or "even more radical" "discrepancies" or "changes" into their sources (the actual teachings of Christ). The author explains that "each change makes a contribution to what the writer is saying about Jesus." Thus, two of his chapter titles are: "Small, Unimportant Changes" and "Large, Important Changes."[17]

Unlike the publishers of *Inspiration,* who apparently did not recognize that the book was the product of historical-critical viewpoints,[18] the publishers of *Luke, A Plagiarist?* judiciously included a disclaimer: "The purpose of this book is to investigate a concept of inspiration not generally held by most Seventh-day Adventists. . . . This book does not represent an official pronouncement of the Seventh-day Adventist Church nor does it necessarily reflect the editorial opinion of the Pacific Press Publishing Association." In any case, both historical-critical works from Adventist publishing houses suggest that differences in parallel accounts in the Bible constitute contradictions.

In a similar fashion, the author of *Inspiration,* building his "incarnational view of inspiration" on alleged discrepancies in Scripture (technically referred to as the "phenomena" of Scripture), writes: "Certainly the differences between the two editions of the decalogue (Exodus 20 and Deuteronomy 5) suggest that we do not know precisely what came from God's finger when he inscribed the law on tables of stone, yet we would certainly say that the decalogue is 'revelation.'" He also maintains that "the gospel writers could differ from one another in their recording and interpreting of Gospel traditions, being more concerned about practical application than *absolute historical precision.*"[19] The coded message is that we may not always rely on the accounts of Moses and the gospel writers as fully trustworthy.

If the content of the Ten Commandments cannot be known precisely, on what basis was Paul led to declare the law "holy, and just, and good" (Rom 7:12)? And how can human beings be expected to obey a law of which they are not sure?

Many more examples can be cited to show how higher-critical assumptions are shaping the views of some regarding the reliability or trustworthiness of parallel biblical accounts. The allegation that there are two different, even contradictory, creation accounts (Gen 1 and 2) and flood narratives (Gen 6-9) provides two more examples that are often cited.[20] But the above are enough to illustrate our point.

Notice the three major implications of maintaining that the differences in parallel accounts are contradictions. First, it suggests that today's scholar may use historical-critical principles of interpretation to determine the factual trustworthiness of biblical accounts.[21] Second, attempts by Bible-believing Adventists to harmonize *apparent* discrepancies in parallel accounts of Scripture are often dismissed as "proof-text" method. Third, since in the Bible we supposedly find evidence of inspired writers holding contradictory views, the Adventist church should allow "diversity" of views (i.e., contradictory theologies) in the church. This is the recipe for theological pluralism, which holds that conflicting theological views are legitimate and must be allowed to cohabit in the same church.[22]

A Bible-Believing Adventist Response

How should Bible-believing Seventh-day Adventists respond to such an approach? Proponents of the historical-critical method claim that "objectivity in exegesis [interpretation]" and not "proof-text subjectivity" is the goal of biblical study.[23] Yet their approach is a true expression of "proof-text subjectivity." For instead of *exegesis* (reading out of the text what is already there), they practice *eisegesis* (reading into the text what was not originally there). Instead of a faithful *exposition* of the biblical text, they make an *imposition* on the text, as we have shown in the several preceding pages. How can the historical-critical method be "objective" when speculation overshadows evidence and when twentieth-century liberal assumptions reduce the inspired message to a mere reflection of the scholars' own ideological convictions? To the extent that it does this, the historical-critical method is the worst kind of proof-texting.

Historical Trustworthiness. Bible-believing Adventists welcome the inquiry of those who accept what Scripture says as trustworthy and who desire simply to learn its meaning. What they reject is the intrusion of unbiblical assumptions drawn from secular thought (e.g., Romantic philosophy and evolutionary philosophy) as the basis to judge the credibility of the biblical record and to reconstruct what actually happened. The "historical" interpretation of the historical-critical method, if adopted, will breed a "new papalism" of scholars, since ordinary laypeople who are not trained as "historians" will be expected to depend on the experts for understanding the contents of the Christian faith. Besides, such a historical approach fails to show a way out should the "historical" experts disagree.

Ellen White expressed the conviction of Bible-believing students when she argued for the trustworthiness of Scripture in all that it teaches and touches upon—whether in the realm of salvation or in the sphere of history, science, etc. Against those who questioned the historical reliability of Scripture, she asserted that because the Holy Spirit "guided the pens of the sacred historians" (*Gospel Workers,* p. 286), biblical history is truthful, authentic, and reliable (*Fundamentals of Christian Education,* pp. 84-85; *Testimonies for the Church,* 4:9-10). The accounts in the Bible are not sullied by human pride or prejudice (*Education,* p. 173; *Patriarchs and Prophets,* p. 596; *Testimonies for the Church,* 5:25). "The unerring pen of inspiration" traces biblical history with "exact fidelity" (ibid., 4:370). The Bible is equally trustworthy even in its statements having to do with scientific issues—e.g., questions about origins and geology (*Education,* pp. 128-130).[24]

Summarizing his findings from an extensive study of Ellen White's writings, a knowledgeable Adventist professor of church history and historical theology writes: "Although Ellen White recognized the existence of *difficulties* in Scripture, I have been unable to find any instance in which she mentioned specific factual errors in the Scriptures. As silent as the writers of the New Testament had been in pointing out factual errors in the Old Testament, so was Ellen White in regard to the total canon of Scripture."[25] In other words, if none of the inspired prophets felt himself authorized to criticize alleged "errors" of his predecessors, why should we? Are we more enlightened for such a task than the prophets themselves?

Bible-believing Adventists, therefore, reject the kind of thinking that does not want to accept or obey what Scripture explicitly affirms. They also reject the kind of "sanctified reason" which does not make logically correct deductions from Scripture itself, and which makes an uninspired interpreter sit in judgment over God's Word to decide what to accept as true. Such "sanctified reason" does not merit the label of "science" or "Christian." It is not "scientific" because, rather than being a scientific inquiry into the truths of God's Word, it sets about "dissecting, conjecturing, reconstructing" the Bible (see *The Acts of the Apostles,* p. 474). And it is not "Christian," because instead of submitting to the Book that will judge human reason, it dares to sit in judgment and overthrow the authority of the Bible.

Critical Thinking. In opposition to "Methods of Bible Study" (the Rio document that urged Adventist scholars not to use the historical-critical method in any of its forms), a proponent of modern higher criticism gives the impression that the church is opposed to "critical thinking," understood as objective thinking. He explains that the goal of historical-critical Adventist scholars was to be "'critical' in the sense that it attempted to discriminate between fact and fiction. The idea that the word 'critical' in the term 'historical-critical' expresses a critical attitude toward the inspiration and authority of the Bible reflects the uninformed thinking of those who do not understand the nature and purpose of the method or who have ulterior motives for opposing it."[26]

Does rejecting the historical-critical method reflect "the uninformed thinking" of Bible-believing Adventists who are against the use of liberal methodology? Not so.

The difference between the traditional Adventist plain reading of Scripture and the contemporary liberal approach is not that the latter is "critical" while the former is not; both are "critical," depending upon how one defines the term.

If by *critical* interpretation we mean the answering of questions about the date, place, sources, background, literary character, credentials, and purposes of each biblical book or composition, then Bible-believing Adventists will have no difficulty in describing their own approach as "critical." If, however, the term implies *charging the Bible with untrustworthiness or fraudulence of any kind* (which is what proponents of the historical-critical method intimate), then Bible-believing Adventists are opposed to it.

Christians who are tempted to adopt historical-critical reasoning face a major dilemma. How do they exalt the Bible as the judge of human errors and at the same time keep the human interpreter as the arbiter of Scripture's errors? How can they commend the Bible as a true witness yet charge it with falsehood? Is this not theological double-talk?

Careless and Superficial Analysis. Superficial works may fill useful functions. But it is always regrettable when superficial analyses of parallel accounts are presented to unsuspecting church members as though they were biblically profound works. Later in this book, we shall take a look at some of the biblical passages alleged to be contradictions. Presently, however, we must only remind ourselves of a statement by Ellen White: "As several [Bible] writers present a subject under varied aspects and relations, *there may appear, to the superficial, careless, or prejudiced reader, to be discrepancy or contradiction, where the thoughtful, reverent student, with clearer insight, discerns the underlying harmony*" (*The Great Controversy*, p. vi, emphasis supplied).

"Men of ability have devoted a lifetime of study and prayer to the searching of the Scriptures, and yet there are many portions of the Bible that have not been fully explored. Some passages of Scripture will never be perfectly comprehended until in the future life Christ shall explain them. There are mysteries to be unraveled, statements that human minds cannot harmonize. And the enemy will seek to arouse argument upon these points, which might better remain undiscussed" (*Gospel Workers,* p. 312).

Need for Caution. The history of biblical interpretation teaches us that some Bible difficulties that once appeared to be "contradictions" or "errors" were nothing more than optical illusions. For this reason, we must be careful that in our haste to obtain an "objective" or "scientific" explanation we are not tempted to declare those unresolved Bible difficulties as "distortions," "contradictions," "inconsistencies," or "demonstrable errors of fact."

Instead, when faced with unresolved Bible difficulties, we should make a painstaking and prayerful effort to study them in the light of Scripture itself. We should look at what other scholars and Bible students have said about the same subject to ascertain the extent to which their solutions are in agreement with the Bible itself. We should also pay close attention to what Ellen G. White has to say on the issue since we believe that an inspired writer is always a more dependable interpreter of a Bible passage than are contemporary scholars. If we still do not get a handle on the difficulty, we should suspend judgment till such a time as the Lord sheds further light on the problem passage. And He does![27]

NOTES

1.   *Fundamentals of Christian Education,* p. 100.

2.   *The Acts of the Apostles,* p. 506; *Testimonies for the Church,* 5:389; *The Ministry of Healing,* p. 462; *Testimonies for the Church,* 5:247, 192; ibid., 4:441.

3.   Alden Thompson, *Inspiration: Hard Questions, Honest Answers* (Hagerstown, Md.: Review and Herald, 1991), p. 248. For a response to this book, see the collection of essays in *Issues in Revelation and Inspiration,* ed. Frank Holbrook and Leo Van Dolson (Berrien Springs, Mich.: Adventist Theological Society Publications, 1992).

4.   Thompson, *Inspiration,* p. 202.

5.   Ibid., p. 222.

6.   Ibid., pp. 247, 248, 229. For a Bible response to the "local flood" theory, see the article by Gerhard Hasel in a forthcoming "Science-Theology" book by the Adventist Theological Society.

7.   Thompson, *Inspiration,* pp. 222, 214-236. For a Bible-believing Adventist response, see Randall W. Younker, "A Few Thoughts on Alden Thompson's Chapter: Numbers, Genealogies, Dates," *Issues in Revelation and Inspiration,* pp. 173-199.

8.   George R. Knight, *Anticipating the Advent: A Brief History of Seventh-day Adventists* (Boise, Id.: Pacific Press, 1993), pp. 106-107. He writes: "The loss of Ellen White's and Adventism's moderate stance on inspiration during the 1920s set the church up for decades of difficulties in interpreting the Bible and the writings of Ellen White. The resulting problems have led to extremism, misunderstandings, and bickering in Adventist ranks that exist, unfortunately, until the present" (ibid., p. 107). Knight's nuanced endorsement of Alden Thompson's book is found on the jacket cover of the latter's *Inspiration.* For helpful correction to the above reinterpretation of Ellen White's and Adventism's position, see James H. Burry, "An Investigation to Determine Ellen White's Concepts of Revelation, Inspiration, 'The Spirit of Prophecy' and Her Claims About the Origin, Production and Authority of Her Writings," M.A. Thesis, Andrews University, 1991. Cf. P. Gerard Damsteegt, "The Inspiration of

Scripture in the Writings of Ellen G. White," *Journal of the Adventist Theological Society* 5/1 (Spring 1994):155-179; Peter van Bemmelen, "The Mystery of Inspiration: An Historical Study About the Development of the Doctrine of Inspiration in the Seventh-day Adventist Church, With Special Emphasis on the Decade 1884-1893," unpublished manuscript (1971), available at the James White Library, Andrews University. In a later chapter, "Liberating the Word," we shall take a closer look at the theological implications of driving a wedge between statements of salvation (deemed to be infallible) and other statements (believed to be ridden with "possible factual difficulties or errors").

9.   Jeane Haerich, "Genesis Revisited," in *The Welcome Table,* pp. 99-100, emphasis supplied. For a biblical response to this liberal view, see Gerhard F. Hasel, "The 'Days' of Creation in Genesis 1: Literal 'Days' or Figurative 'Periods/Epochs' of Time?" *Origins* 21/1 (1994):5-38.

10.   Haerich, "Genesis Revisited," in *The Welcome Table,* pp. 101, 100.

11.   For more on this, see Wayne Grudem's 22-page article, "What's Wrong with Gender-Neutral Bible Translations? A Critique of the *New Revised Standard Version,*" available through The Council on Biblical Manhood and Womanhood (CBMW), P. O. Box 317, Wheaton, IL 60189 or E-mail: CBMWHendo@aol.com. See also William Oddie, *What Will Happen to God?: Feminism and the Reconstruction of Christian Belief* (San Francisco: Ignatius Press, 1988)

12.   Steve Daily, *Adventism for a New Generation* (Portland/Clackamas, Ore.: Better Living Publishers, 1993), pp. 88, 105, 113.

13.   Thompson, *Inspiration,* p. 208.

14.   Steve Case, "Thinking About Jewelry: What the Bible (Really) Says," in *Shall We Dance: Rediscovering Christ-Centered Standards,* ed. Steve Case (Riverside, Calif.: La Sierra University Press, 1996), p. 185, note 2. For a response to such arguments, see Samuel Koranteng-Pipim, "Paul's Use of Deut. 25:4 in 1 Cor. 9:9ff: Its Implications for Biblical Inspiration and Hermeneutics," paper, Andrews University, 1989, available at the Adventist Heritage Center, James White Library, Andrews University.

15.   Craig Kinzer and Sylvia Nelson Clarke, "Joseph, Jesus, and the Old Testament," *Collegiate Quarterly,* October-December, 1995, p. 75. For a discussion and response to similar views expressed in *Inspiration,* see Richard Davidson, "Revelation/Inspiration in the Old Testament," in *Issues in Revelation and Inspiration,* pp. 127-130.

16.   Steven G. Daily, *Adventism for a New Generation* (Portland/Clackamas, Ore.: Better Living Publishers, 1993), p. 78; cf. Thompson, *Inspiration,* pp. 174-182.

17.   George E. Rice, *Luke, A Plagiarist?* (Mountain View, Calif.: Pacific Press, 1983), pp. 71, 82, 83, 84, 88.

18.   This fact has been confirmed in official correspondence (dated July 14, 1992) to the present writer from Richard W. Coffen, at the time the Associate Book Editor of Review and Herald. He indicates that only six out of twenty-eight reviewers of the *Inspiration* manuscript responded negatively to the publication of the book.

19.   Alden Thompson, "Are Adventists Afraid of Bible Study?" (a review of George E. Rice's *Luke, A Plagiarist?*), *Spectrum,* April 1985, pp. 57, 58, emphasis supplied. Elsewhere others have offered an analysis and evaluation of Thompson's "incarnational view of inspiration" (see *Issues in Revelation and Inspiration*).

20.   This is the so-called documentary hypothesis. According to this liberal theory, Moses did not write the first five books of the Bible. The scholars hypothesize that they were written roughly between the time of David and the second century B.C. by many authors and compilers. One hypothetical author is called **J**, because he always called God "Jehovah." Another is known as **E**, because he chose the Hebrew word *Elohim* for God. There was also **D**, who is believed to have written Deuteronomy, and **P**, from the priestly class. Based on this hypothesis, higher-critical scholars chop up the Bible into pieces according to whether the section uses the word Jehovah or Elohim, or if it contains references to priestly activity or concerns. This is one reason why Genesis 1 and 2 are supposed to contain two different, even contradictory, creation accounts. Of course, within each imaginary compiler, there were a lot of other members so that documents like D could be split into D the first, D the second, etc. Those who desire to pursue a discussion of this issue will greatly benefit from Gerhard

Hasel's *Biblical Interpretation for Today* (Washington, D.C.: Biblical Research Institute, 1985); cf. also his *Understanding the Living Word of God* (Mountain View, Calif.: Pacific Press, 1980), pp. 218-228; Peter M. van Bemmelen, "The Authenticity and Christo-Centricity of the Pentateuch According to the Writings of Ellen G. White," unpublished paper (1978), available at the Ellen G. White Research Center of the James White Library, Andrews University, in Document File 391-f-5. For a discussion of the complementary accounts in Genesis 1 and 2, see Jacques B. Doukhan, *The Genesis Creation Story: Its Literary Structure,* Andrews University Seminary Doctoral Dissertation Series, vol. 5 (Berrien Springs, Mich.: Andrews University Press, 1978).

21.   In his review article, "Are Adventists Afraid of Bible Study?" p. 58, Alden Thompson writes: "Adventist scholars could indeed use the descriptive method [e.g., source criticism, redaction criticism, etc.] without adopting the naturalistic presuppositions affirmed by the thorough-going practitioners of the method."

22.   Writing on the theological pluralism in the church, one North American church administrator suggested that the church should "allow tensions in our belief system as we continue to grow in an understanding of God. If we are on a spiritual journey together, we will create room for *diversity of thought and opinion, perhaps even interpretation.*" See Bj. Christensen, "Dialogue or Ballots?" *Adventist Today,* January/February 1994, p. 15, emphasis supplied. Cf. Gerhard van Wyk, "Dealing with Pluralism," *Ministry,* March 1995, pp. 6-9. A brief but excellent critique of theological pluralism is found in John Fowler's letter to the editor, "Dealing with Pluralism," *Ministry,* December 1995, p. 2. For a detailed discussion and evaluation, see Winfried Vogel, "Man and Knowledge: The Search for Truth in a Pluralistic Age," to be published in the forthcoming Autumn 1996 issue of *Journal of the Adventist Theological Society.*

23.   Raymond F. Cottrell, "Blame It On Rio: Annual Council Statement on Methods of Bible Study," *Adventist Currents,* March 1987, p. 33.

24.   A detailed discussion of the Seventh-day Adventist pioneers' attitude toward higher criticism can be found in Peter van Bemmelen's paper, "Seventh-day Adventists and Higher Criticism in the Nineteenth Century," Andrews University, 1977, available at the Ellen G. White Research Center of the James White Library, Andrews University, in Document File 391-h.

25.   Alberto R. Timm, "History of Inspiration in the Adventist Church (1844-1915)," *Journal of the Adventist Theological Society* 5/1 (Spring 1994):189-190, emphasis his.

26.   Raymond F. Cottrell, "Blame It On Rio: Annual Council Statement on Methods of Bible Study," *Adventist Currents,* March 1987, p. 33.

27.   In chapters 9 and 10, we shall not only offer principles for interpreting the Bible, but we shall also attempt to explain some of the problem passages of Scripture.

The Bible—Progressive Revelation or Progressive Ideas?

Objective. In this section we shall examine to what extent higher-critical assumptions are influencing Seventh-day Adventist views on human relationships, the Spirit's ongoing divine guidance, concepts of God, divine judgment, the doctrine of hell, and the nature of "present truth."

Key Issue. How should we understand the nature of "progressive revelation"? Is it an unfolding of the meaning and import of previously disclosed truth, or is it a revelation of new truths that are not already present in the Bible?

Traditional Adventist Belief. Historically, Adventists have understood "progressive revelation" to mean an ever increasing unfolding or expansion of what *was previously revealed.* They have often referred to this as "present truth," arguing that new truth does not contradict previously revealed truth.[1] Thus, the preamble to our Fundamental Beliefs speaks of how "the church is led by the Holy Spirit to a fuller understanding of *Bible truth* or finds better language in which to express *the teachings of God's Holy Word.*"

But as is common in liberal theology, proponents of the historical-critical method have taken this good concept and *redefined* it according to the myth of evolutionism. To promote their "dynamic concept of truth," they disguise it as the "Holy Spirit's leading"—when it is actually the spirit of the modern age which is driving them. They claim that "progressive revelation" is the Holy Spirit's guidance into truths that were *not* previously revealed by the Bible writers, and which may at times be contradictory to established Bible truth. Thus they abandon God's absolute truth for liberalism's "dynamic truth"; and they replace the true progressive (i.e. unfolding) revelation of His written Word with the allegedly "progressive" ideas of our contemporary culture.

How are historical-critical assumptions shaping Adventist views on the interpretation of Scripture?

Effect of the Liberal Approach

Reinterpreting progressive revelation to mean the disclosure of new truths to supplant old ones is another variation of the cultural conditioning argument discussed in part two of this chapter. In this respect, those who maintain that some parts of the Bible are culturally conditioned will also tend to hold the new views regarding progressive revelation.

Human Relationships. Proponents of the new approaches to the Bible do not overtly deny the absolute nature of Biblical truth. Yet by viewing truth as dynamic or evolutionary—at least in such matters as male-female roles, polygamy, and homosexuality—they are leaning in that direction.

For example, although they acknowledge that male headship and the female supportive roles are taught in both the Old and New Testaments, they argue that these directives were not meant for all time. The teachings were meant to *evolve* and change with culture. Another example is marriage, which they believe to have evolved from the widespread polygamy in the Old Testament (Abraham, Jacob, Isaac, David, etc.)[2] towards monogamous relationships in the New Testament, and now, some would argue, should include a closed couple homosexual relationship.[3]

Even when confronted with the evidence that, in Eden prior to the fall, God instituted male-female role differentiation and monogamous (not polygamous), heterosexual (not homosexual) marriage, such proponents may respond that Genesis 1 and 2 are not historical; and even if they are historical, Adam was androgynous (bisexual). An un-historical creation account and an androgynous Adam both nullify the biblical case for divinely instituted role differences and a monogamous heterosexual relationship.

A few examples will illustrate this new understanding of "progressive revelation."

The Spirit's Guidance Today. Bible-believing Adventists hold that there are no theological contradictions or discrepancies in Scripture. However, a historical-critical proponent responds: "The objection to such a view of inspiration would be that it does not recognize the developmental process behind doctrinal truths which unfold in Scripture, and fails to account for theological contradictions in the Bible."[4]

A favorite illustration for liberalism's "dynamic truth" of progressive revelation[5] is how the Holy Spirit allegedly guided Paul to contravene His explicit instructions at the Jerusalem Council. In Acts 15:28, 29, the Spirit guided the Jerusalem Council to lay down as a binding obligation to Christians that they should abstain from "meats offered to idols, and from blood, and from things strangled, and from fornication." These "necessary" prohibitions were binding on all churches (Acts 15:28; 16:4; 21:25; Rev 2:14, 20).[6] But in 1 Corinthians 8 and 10, Paul *appears to* set aside the Spirit-inspired command of Acts 15 when he stated that the Corinthians could eat meat offered to idols.

To some Adventist scholars, this is a prime example of how the Holy Spirit overrules a binding *moral* command given in an earlier time.[7] It could also suggest to them that what may be morally forbidden to Christians in one culture could be morally acceptable in another.

Notice, however, that a careful study of 1 Corinthians 8 and 10 does not validate the conclusions of these scholars.[8] This reinterpretation of progressive revelation is based on an assumption that there is no underlying unity in the various parts of Scripture. If we view the Scriptures as a divine document as much as human, we will seek to discover the underlying harmony among Scriptures that may at first seem contradictory.

But under the impact of historical-critical assumptions, some scholars cast doubt on the basic unity of the Bible. One Adventist scholar dismisses it as "the traditional theoretical model of the unity of Scripture." In his opinion there are "differences" in the Bible, a euphemism for alleged contradictions, discrepancies, and mistakes.[9]

Denying the Bible's unity makes it impossible to maintain the validity of comparing Scripture with Scripture as Jesus did on the road to Emmaus (Luke 24:27). Can this explain the uneasiness of some scholars to do topical Bible study, dismissing it as a "proof-text" or "key-text" method? Can this also explain the claim by some that later Bible writers cannot be reliable interpreters of earlier inspired writers?

A God Who Keeps Changing. Rejecting the internal unity of Scripture, one "progressive Adventist" professor takes a "dynamic" view of Scripture. The picture of God revealed in both Testaments, she says, was merely the views of the Bible writers as they understood God in their times. Thus, in the Bible we find God evolving from the violent, blood-thirsty God of the Old Testament to the kind and gentle God of the New. She writes: "The belief in progressive revelation makes us aware that our *pictures of God keep changing.* . . . There is enough internal evidence, as scholars have shown, to suggest that as one reads through the Bible, a loving monotheistic God emerges from a pantheon of warlike gods. The progressive Adventist believes that the picture of God blotting out populations either by the sword of man, or by fires, earthquakes, catastrophic storms, and volcanic eruptions, demonstrates that man has indeed made god in his own image."[10]

This "progressive Adventist" belief is a variation of the cultural conditioning argument, claiming that the inspired accounts in the Old Testament were colored by the Bible writers' cultural understanding of God; the Old Testament pictures of God were a creation in their "own image." The above scholar's idea that there are "differences" between the Old and New Testament pictures of God is an old heresy—Marcionism—being recycled as new truth for our enlightened age.

How can the biblical God who says "I am the Lord, I change not" (Mal 3:6) evolve from a "pantheon of warlike gods" into the "loving monotheistic God" that we know Him to be? Can such a God be trusted? Can we place our future into His hands? When friends and loved ones we trust change, we are disappointed. How can we be sure that the God we know today will not change tomorrow?

An Open View of God. The above questions are partly answered in another example, a more technical book based on essentially the same idea of "progressive revelation." In this controversial book, *The Openness of God: The Relationship of Divine Foreknowledge and Human Free Will,* a professor of theology proposes an "open view of God" on the basis of the evolutionary philosophy called "process theology." He sees God as evolving in His knowledge of things: though God knows everything that has happened in the past, He does not know absolutely what will take place in the future. He only knows "possible" things that may happen in the future, but not necessarily exactly how they will be.

The author says: "The central claim of this alternative view is that God's experience of the world is open rather than closed. God's experience does not consist of one timeless intuition. He does not have one eternal perception of all reality, past and future. . . . Another way to make the point is to say that time is real for God. His experience is the *infallible* register of temporal reality. It reflects every event and development in the temporal world. All that happens enters His memory, is retained forever. Nothing escapes His notice." In other words, God knows perfectly what has happened in the past.

But now notice what follows: "But God's experience is also the *progressive* register of reality. Events enter His experience as they happen, not before [meaning God does not know perfectly what will happen in the future]. This means that God experiences the past and the future differently. They are not the same for Him. He remembers the past exhaustively, in all its detail. Every aspect is vividly present to His mind. But His experience of the future is different. He anticipates the future, to be sure, and in a way unique to Him, as we shall see. But the future retains its essential indefiniteness from God's perspective as well as from ours."[11]

When one accepts the logic of an "open view of God," the prophecies of Daniel, Revelation, and *The Great Controversy* become essentially untenable![12]

If God does not know the future perfectly, either these "prophecies" were written after the events took place, or at best, they are accurate "guesses" by God.

For this theology professor, "the future is not absolutely foreknowable" even to God. Rather, God "faces the future with *complete foresight*" or an "anticipation" which involves His "knowing what *might* happen" and how He should respond. God merely knows "a great deal about the future" as determined by past and present human causes. God "knows exactly what some of His own future actions will be" when they are not dependent on human actions. But "God does not know the future absolutely. He nevertheless anticipates it perfectly. But it [God's perfect anticipation] does *not* consist in knowing everything that actually will happen."[13]

Many questions still remain: If God does not know the future in all its details, can we really speak about Bible prophecies at all? How was God able to guarantee to Nebuchadnezzar through Daniel, "The dream is *certain,* and the interpretation thereof *sure*" (Dan 2:45)? Can God give accurate prophecies about end-time events, such as the final conflict between God's last-day remnant church and the apostate powers of the enemy?

Are such "progressive" reinterpretations of God an underlying reason why some of our scholars are repudiating traditional Adventism's doctrine of last-day events (eschatology)? One historical-critical author asserts: "It is a sobering and scary thought to conclude that our eschatology has been built on an unsound foundation, and that it has ultimately done us more harm than good. In a word, it has made us an 'ethnocentric' people."[14]

A "Friendly" God Who Doesn't Destroy. Offended by the apparent biblical teaching that God sometimes expresses His divine "wrath" upon sinners by acts of divine retribution, some Adventist authors see such acts of God as merely disciplinary, or at best as simply figures of speech.

In an influential book, *Servants or Friends? Another Look at God,* an Adventist scholar rejects the Bible's assertions that God actually punishes sinners in retributive judgment, even at the end of the world. In his opinion, the references in the Bible that speak of God's displaying His wrath in retribution on sinners are examples of His communicating to us "in our ignorance and immaturity"—using "dark speech" that God's "friends" know how to explain.

Based on his "matured" view of God as our "friend," this scholar explains that the "many references in the Bible to God's destruction of the wicked" must be understood as God's "just using a figure of speech."[15]

Commendably, this progressive reinterpretation of the Bible seeks to move beyond the "more ferocious" and "cruel" picture of God that many see in Scripture to a more "friendly" one. But in using as its measure such human standards as how a mother would treat her misbehaving children, it casts God in man's image and seeks to explain away Bible evidence contrary to its attractive conclusions.

This view necessarily affects one's understanding of our Savior's work. If God chooses not to punish sinners retributively, and if the biblical references to God's doing so are mere metaphors, then for this scholar, Jesus could not have experienced God's retributive punishment for our sin. In short, this teacher's view of God has led him and others to reinterpret the biblical doctrine of the substitutionary atonement of Christ (found in, for example, Isa 53:4-12, 2 Cor 5:21; cf. *The Desire of Ages,* p. 25 ["Christ was treated as we deserve . . ."]).[16]

New Teaching on Hell. "Progressives" who hold to the "friendly" view of God tend to reinterpret the biblical doctrine of hell. One such scholar understands hell as merely a "vision of reality" that "fills the wicked with intense mental anguish and remorse. Their mental suffering, like the suffering of Jesus—who died on Calvary from a broken heart—surpasses any kind of physical suffering and is the direct result of sin. This is the agony of Hell. God does not add any kind of punishment to the consequences of sin to make Hell worse than it already is, any more that [*sic*] a loving parent would spank the scalded body of a disobedient child who pulled a boiling kettle off the stove. Hell is full realization of sin."[17]

A 1986 Seventh-day Adventist devotional book, translated into several languages and read by thousands of Adventists around the world, also rejects the Bible's teaching that sinners will ultimately be destroyed in hell-fire. *His Healing Love* explains that hell is merely a separation or disconnection from God. In answer to his own question, "How hot is hell?" the author employs the analogy of a light bulb and its power source:

"The day will come when those who refuse His [God's] gracious invitation for friendship will be given what they have chosen: *separation from Him.* When you unplug your lamp, it doesn't explode. The light just goes out. Nor do you need to beat on the bulb in anger for its ceasing to give light. That's simply what happens when it is disconnected. By the same token, when one breaks union with God, life ceases. God does not, in anger, need to crush it out. . . . To be separated from the Life-giver is to be dead eternally."[18]

In his opinion the biblical references to hell-fire are metaphors or imageries God employed to communicate to an immature people: "The people God was addressing in Biblical times did not always understand this cause-effect principle [of the power-source/lamp analogy]. It was difficult for them to appreciate the destructiveness of being out of harmony with God. And so the Bible writers employed the imagery of consuming flames to describe the sureness and completeness of the destruction of life apart from God. But being apart from God is in itself the worst thing that could ever happen to a person. God doesn't need to torch hellish fires to enhance what is already so terrible."[19]

In summary, the liberal reinterpretation of progressive revelation is the hermeneutical foundation undergirding attempts by some Adventists to view God as One who is ever changing, does not know the future absolutely, would not visit retribution on sinners, and consequently, could not have given His Son to die as the sinners' substitutionary atonement. In this "mature" view of God, hell-fire is often reinterpreted as merely an intense mental anguish and remorse experienced by sinners when they are ultimately disconnected from God. But liberalism's theory of progressive revelation also underlies recent reinterpretations of the Adventist view of "present truth" and "new light."

"Progressive" Scholars and "Present Truth." A widely circulated document by an influential North American Conference endorsing women's ordination redefines the ideas of "progressive revelation" and "present truth":

"The essential presupposition of the idea of 'the great controversy' is that God is active throughout history, bringing new truths to light. Historically, Adventists have understood that God is active in our own time, using the term 'present truth' to denote *truths which were not present in earlier times, but which God has led his people to discover.* Further, there is the parallel idea of 'progressive revelation,' which suggests that *God has not revealed all truth at some previous time, that revelation is not confined to the thought and behavior patterns of the prophets and disciples of old, but that God lives and is active today and tomorrow.* Most importantly, *this dynamic character of truth* is the undergirding theological rationale for the very existence of Seventh-day Adventism. Thus the notion of Scriptural literalism is essentially un-Adventist."[20]

Contrary to what Adventists have always believed, "present truth" is here defined along historical-critical lines as "truths that were not present in earlier times,"—i.e., "the prophets and disciples of old" were not privileged to have the "new light" that our twentieth century progressive culture needs. In this way truth is seen as "dynamic." In other words, God by-passed Peter, James, John, Paul, and Ellen White, in order to reveal to the "progressive Adventist" scholars "present truths" which we cannot evaluate by prior revelation in the "prophets and disciples of old." Then how can one "prove all things" and "hold fast that which is good" (1 Thess 5:21)? How does one "try the spirits whether they are of God" (1 John 4:1)?[21]

The above view of progressive revelation and present truth finds expression in an article entitled "Equality Is Present Truth." In this work, the editors of *Adventist Today* also explain that in "present truth" "God reveals new concepts of truth not known previously."[22]

If "present truth" is a revelation of truth "not known previously," and if "equality is present truth," does it mean that the inspired Bible writers did not teach the concept of equality? Or is it more accurate to say that while they had much to say about true equality, they did not teach the kind of equality being advanced today by "progressive" scholars?[23]

This liberal reinterpretation of "present truth" to mean "dynamic truth" not contained in Scripture is the foundation upon which some want to construct an Adventist theology for the next millennium. For example, at a recent meeting of the Association of Adventist Forums ("an organization concerned with the reform of Adventism and the creation of progressive community within the church"[24]), one systematic theologian stated: "My first proposal is that we *revitalize our theology.* In order to do this, we need to recover the idea of 'present truth'—*truth that is not closed but open, not changeless but dynamic.*"[25]

What scholars of "dynamic truth" apparently overlook is the contradictory logic inherent in their assertion that truth is "not changeless." For if truth is not changeless, then the "progressive" scholar's own statement that truth "is not closed but open, not changeless but dynamic" is itself not a changeless truth! Why should we accept as "truth" what is not a changeless truth? Which theology needs "revitalizing"—Adventism's historic theology which is based on the solid Rock of absolute truth, or historical-critical theology which is established on the shifting sand of "dynamic" truth? Against these contemporary reinterpretations, we must assert that truth is an *unchanging* reality, for God is truth, and He does not change; His Word is truth, and it does not change.

Revision of Ellen White's View. Another author argues for a dynamic concept of "present truth" by claiming that even the early Adventist pioneers, including Ellen White, did not believe that truth was static.[26] As is often the case in such efforts to revise the interpretation of Adventist history, one fails to find support in the Ellen White sources the author cites! Contrary to the impression the author creates, Ellen White did not state that what was present truth a hundred years ago might not be present truth today.

What she actually wrote is this: "The present truth, which is a test to the people of this generation, was not a test to the people of generations far back" (*Testimonies for the Church,* 2:693). The point is not that truth in this generation was not truth in an earlier generation. Her emphasis was on *testing* truth. Each generation, each time, has its testing truth. But it is the same old truth of Scripture forcefully brought to bear on an individual or group at a particular time and place, testing their loyalty or faithfulness to the God who has beamed His searchlight on an old truth.

As one Bible-believing scholar correctly noted, "To say, then, that something is 'present truth' should not imply that what is truth today was not truth in previous generations. Rather, truth that Scripture taught but which had been overlooked or forgotten now shines with new luster. When this happens, God does not condemn the previous generations. 'The times of this ignorance God winked at; but *now commandeth all men everywhere to repent'* (Acts 17:30)."[27] However, this "present truth" never contradicts an old truth, despite what scholars often suggest who argue for a dynamic concept of present truth (cf. *Selected Messages,* 1:161-162; *Review and Herald,* June 29, 1886, par. 9).

A Bible-Believing Adventist Response

The Bible teaches: "To the law and to the testimony; if they speak not according to this word, it is because there is no light in them" (Isa 8:20). Even the three angels' messages were considered "present truth" only because they were an aspect of "the *everlasting* gospel." They were not brand new truths without a basis in prior biblical revelation. They were not the product of an anti-Catholic nineteenth-century culture.

If "present truth" were an evolving, "progressive," or "dynamic" truth, it would follow logically that other Christian doctrines may also be evolving. Adventists would therefore be justified in challenging the church's long-held teaching on sexual morality, homosexuality, divorce and remarriage, clean and unclean foods, use of alcohol, wearing of jewelry, the concept of the remnant, and other matters, as some are already doing. In all these cases the liberal concept of "progressive revelation" assumes that truth is relative; *the cases differ only in degree of application.*

Ellen White discredits the claims of the revisionist proponents of "present truth" or "progressive revelation." Anticipating the modern reinterpretations and applications of Scripture which contradict Scripture, she wrote: "When the power of God testifies as to what is truth, that truth is to stand forever as the truth. No after suppositions contrary to the light God has given are to be entertained. Men will arise with interpretations of Scripture which are to them truth, but which are not truth. The truth for this time God has given us as a foundation for our faith. One will arise, and still another, with new light, which contradicts the light that God has given under the demonstration of His Holy Spirit. . . . We are not to receive the words of those who come with a message that contradicts the special points of our faith" (*Selected Messages,* 1:161).

If accepted, the new view of "progressive revelation" will result in pluralism in doctrine, lifestyle, and interpretation. Everyone will claim a right to his or her "new light" (the new expressions are "unity in diversity" or "openness to other people's ideas").

One church administrator has already endorsed such an outcome in print: "If we truly believe in the notion of progressive revelation (as claimed by the preamble of the Statement of Fundamental Beliefs), *we will allow tensions in our belief system* as we continue to grow in an understanding of God. If we are on a spiritual journey together, *we will create room for diversity of thought and opinion, perhaps even interpretation."*[28] In other words, "progressive revelation" should allow for pluralism in belief and interpretation.

To accept a system of multiple interpretations (hermeneutical pluralism) requires one to assume that there is no underlying unity or harmony in Scripture, that Scripture can be interpreted in many different yet equally truthful ways. Is this not a recipe for theological pluralism, which breeds uncertainty of faith and relativism in ethics? Should Seventh-day Adventists really go this way, even claiming that the Holy Spirit is an ally to this?

For Ellen White, the answer is very simple: "The Spirit was not given—nor can it ever be bestowed—to supersede the Bible; for the Scriptures explicitly state that the word of God is the standard by which all teaching and experience must be tested" (*The Great Controversy,* p. vii). Again, "The old truths are essential; new truth is not independent of the old, but an unfolding of it. It is only as the old truths are understood that we can comprehend the new" (*Christ's Object Lessons,* pp. 127-128). "In all His teachings He [Christ] dwelt upon the *unchangeable positions* of Bible truth" (*The Upward Look,* p. 313, emphasis supplied).

NOTES

1. For a detailed discussion, refer to P. Gerard Damsteegt's excellent articles "New Light in the Last Days," *Adventists Affirm* 10/1 (Spring 1996):5-13; "Seventh-day Adventist Doctrines and Progressive Revelation," *Journal of the Adventist Theological Society* 2/1 (1991):77-92.

2. Ronald A. G. du Preez, *Polygamy in the Bible with Implications for Seventh-day Adventist Missiology* (D.Min. project dissertation, Andrews University, 1993), offers an excellent review of what Seventh-day Adventist scholars have said on the issue of polygamy. His work not only challenges the cultural conditioning argument, but also presents a biblically consistent interpretation of polygamy in the Bible.

3. David Larson, "Sexuality and Christian Ethics," *Spectrum* 15/1 (May 1984):16.

4. Steve Daily, *Adventism for a New Generation* (Portland/Clackamas, Ore.: Better Living Publishers, 1993), pp. 77-78.

5. Dismissing Bible-believing Adventism "for its 'proof text' approach to Scripture, and its uncompromising emphasis on 'correct doctrine' or 'objective truth'," Daily asserts: "Jesus Himself was not the author of a static written code [a body of objective doctrines]. His revelation of truth was a dynamic, living revelation" (ibid., pp. 36, 47).

6. The four categories of prohibited things correspond to the instructions Moses gave in Leviticus 17 and 18, which include reference not only to the Israelites but to the "strangers which sojourn among you" (17:8, 10, 12, 13, 15; 18:26). In the letter that went out to the churches, these items are even listed in the same order as they appear in Leviticus (see Acts 15:29). That the council did not require circumcision of the Gentiles seems to indicate a recognition that this sign was given to the Israelites but not to the "strangers which sojourn among you," unless they should choose to become Jews. The Jerusalem Council ruled, in effect, that Gentiles did not have to become Jews in order to be Christians and experience Jesus' salvation. As with matters of the ceremonial law, circumcision was not to be expected of the

Gentile Christians. Paul himself made the Christian perspective explicit: "Circumcision is nothing and uncircumcision is nothing. Keeping God's commands is what counts" (1 Cor 7:19 NIV).

7. See Andrew Bates (pseudonym), "The Jerusalem Council: A Model for Utrecht?" *Ministry,* April 1995, pp. 18-23; cf. Alden Thompson, *Inspiration: Hard Questions, Honest Answers* (Hagerstown, Md.: Review and Herald, 1991), pp. 149-150. Thompson writes: "At least one culturally conditioned requirement of Acts 15, food offered to idols, was already in the process of being set aside, even while the brethren voted on it" (ibid., p. 149). For a response to the above interpretation of the Jerusalem Council of Acts 15, see our *Searching the Scriptures* (Berrien Springs, Mich.: Adventists Affirm Publications, 1995), pp. 42-44.

8. A careful study of chapters 8-10 of 1 Corinthians will reveal that Paul did not violate the council's decision. Paul addressed three issues regarding food offered to idols: (a) Could Christians accept invitations from their friends and relatives to eat these foods *in pagan temples?* (b) Could they buy such food if it was sold *in the market?* and (c) If the food was *brought home,* was it all right to eat it? Paul answered that: (i) Christians could *not* go to pagan temples and eat these foods (1 Cor 8:10; cf. 10:19-21); (ii) they *could* buy these foods in the market—unless it violated the consciences of those who called attention to it (1 Cor 10:27-33); (iii) they *could* eat the foods in their homes, since idols were really nothing (1 Cor 10:25-26; cf. 8:1ff.). Eating the foods at the temple was incompatible with Christianity, since it implied worship of those gods. This seems to be the thrust of the Jerusalem Council's decree (cf. Rev 2:14, 20; see also Lev 17:7; 18:24-30). Likewise, if others might construe that homage was being offered to the gods, the Christian should not buy the foods in the market. At home, where worship was not implied, eating the foods would compromise neither conscience nor witness. Thus, Paul did not contravene the prohibitions of the Jerusalem council decision, but rather established a theological explanation of the spirit behind the decision (1 Cor 8-10) and how Christians should implement it, balancing freedom and responsibility (1 Cor 8:9, and following through ch. 9).

9. Thompson, *Inspiration,* p. 142; cf. pp. 144-145; 249-250.

10. Madelynn Jones-Haldeman, "Progressive Adventism: Dragging the Church Forward," *Adventist Today,* January/February 1994, p. 11.

11. Richard Rice, *The Openness of God: The Relationship of Divine Foreknowledge and Human Free Will* (Washington, D.C.: Review and Herald, 1980), pp. 21-22. For a sympathetic yet revealing discussion of the controversy generated by the publication of Rice's book, see Richard Emmerson, "The Continuing Crisis (and also The Atlanta Affirmation)," *Spectrum* 12/1 (September 1981):40-44.

12. For more on this, see Alberto R. Timm, "Divine Foreknowledge: Relative or Absolute?" (May 1989), a 40-page paper available as document VFM 6886, at the Adventist Heritage Center, James White Library, Andrews University. It was originally presented in Portuguese ["Presciência Divina—Relativa ou Absoluta?"] as a partial fulfillment of the requirements for the Master in Theology course at Instituto Adventista de Ensino, Brazil College, May 1987. An earlier version of this work was published as an article in *O Ministério Adventista,* November-December 1984, pp. 13-22.

13. *The Openness of God,* pp. 47-50, emphases supplied (1st) and original (2nd and 3rd).

14. Steve Daily, *Adventism for a New Generation,* p. 314; cf. pp. 312-316.

15. Graham Maxwell, *Servants Or Friends? Another Look At God* (Redlands, Calif.: Pineknoll Publications, 1992), pp. 98, 177, 73-75.

16. Graham Maxwell, *Servants or Friends?* pp. 5-6, 117-136; Jack Provonsha, *You Can Go Home Again* (Review and Herald, 1982); *God Is With Us* (Review and Herald, 1974); cf. Dick Winn, "Discovering Forgiveness," *Insight,* May 14, 1983, pp. 6-7; *God's Way to a New You* (Pacific Press, 1979). For a Bible-believing conservative understanding of the wrath of God, see Frank M. Hasel's penetrating article, "The Wrath of God," *Ministry,* November 1991, pp. 10-12. For a critique of the view of atonement held by Graham Maxwell and others, see Norman Gulley, "A Look at the Larger View of Calvary: An Evaluation of the Debate in the Seventh-day Adventist Church," *Journal of the Adventist Theological Society* 3/1 (1992):66-96; cf. his "Toward Understanding the Atonement," *Journal of the Adventist Theological Society* 1/1 (1990):57-89; cf. Martin Weber, *Who's Got the Truth?* (Silver Spring, Md.: Home Study International Press, 1994), pp. 14-34.

17. Daily, *Adventism for a New Generation,* p. 156.

18. Dick Winn, *His Healing Love* (Washington, D.C.: Review and Herald, 1986), p. 332.

19. Ibid.; cf. p. 180.

20. In a letter dated June 1, 1995, given out to delegates at the 1995 GC Session in Utrecht, the president of this influential North American Conference states: "With this letter we have attached several position papers that we have prepared. We trust that they will help clarify our perspective on ordination and the ministry of women." The statement cited on "progressive revelation" and "present truth" comes from one of the position papers prepared by a team of thought leaders, Larry Christoffel, Fritz Guy, Audray Johnson, Lynn Mallery, Penny Miller, and James Walters, "An Attempt to Justify Gender Discrimination in Ministry," p. 2. The above paper was subtitled "A Brief Response to *Searching the Scriptures: Women's Ordination and the Call to Biblical Fidelity.*" Readers may wish to evaluate the response against the content of the book it purports to review. As to whether the restatement of the Adventist understanding of "present truth" and "progressive revelation" represents the historic Adventist position, see P. Gerard Damsteegt, "Seventh-day Adventist Doctrines and Progressive Revelation," *Journal of the Adventist Theological Society* 2/1 (1991):77-92.

21. P. Gerard Damsteegt, "New Light in the Last Days," *Adventists Affirm* 10/1 (Spring 1996):5-13, provides a careful summary of what Ellen G. White taught about "new light."

22. The Editors [Jim Walters and Raymond Cottrell], "Equality Is Present Truth," *Adventist Today,* September-October, 1995, p. 4.

23. Observe that Bible-believing students uphold the biblical teaching on *ontological* equality, which suggests that human beings are equal in their standing before God, in that they were all created in His image, they all need salvation through Christ, and they all have been called to the same destiny (Gen 1:26, 27; Gal 3:28; 1 Pet 3:7). Ontological equality refers solely to God's action and purposes, and not to any intrinsic qualities that human beings possess by themselves; it is a gift of God to every member of the human race—regardless of ethnicity, status or gender. This is what Paul had in mind when he wrote in Galatians 3:28 that "in Christ Jesus," there is "neither Jew nor Greek, neither slave or free, neither male nor female." This statement on ontological equality did not, however, do away with functional role distinctions. Thus, ontological equality must not be confused with *functional* equality—the view that there is equality of ability, skill, gifts, office or position. The Bible does *not* teach functional equality, since the Holy Spirit gives to each "severally as He wills" (cf. 1 Cor 12; Rom 12: 3-8). This understanding will correct some of the excesses of the various (racial or gender) "equal rights" movements. See Samuel Koranteng-Pipim, "The Triumph of Grace Over Race," *Adventists Affirm* 9/2 (Fall 1995):42-43.

24. Gary Chartier, "Welcoming the Third Millennium," *Spectrum* 25/4 (June 1996):23. The conference took place on March 14-17, 1996 at San Diego, California. Chartier explains: "This was a progressive gathering, responding to the challenges posed by a conservative [Adventist] community" (ibid.). He provides highlights of the meeting and a summary of each speaker's vision for 21st-century Adventism (ibid., pp. 21-24).

25. Fritz Guy, "Four Ways Into the Next Millennium," *Spectrum* 25/4 (June 1996):25, emphasis supplied. Cf. Dalton Baldwin's "Revelation and the Development of the Biblical Concept of God," previewed in the Newsletter of the Association of Adventist Forums, San Diego chapter, September 1996.

26. George R. Knight, "Adventists and Change," *Ministry,* October 1993, p. 14. For some helpful comments on the early Seventh-day Adventist understanding of "present truth," see Alberto R. Timm, "The Sanctuary and the Three Angels' Messages, 1844-1863: Integrating Factors in the Development of Seventh-day Adventist Doctrines" (Ph.D. dissertation, Andrews University, 1995), pp. 184-186, 420-423; P. Gerard Damsteegt, "Seventh-day Adventist Doctrines and Progressive Revelation," *Journal of the Adventist Theological Society* 2/1 (1991):77-92.

27. P. Gerard Damsteegt, "New Light in the Last Days," *Adventists Affirm* 10/1 (Spring 1996): 7, emphasis his. Readers will benefit greatly from the article's prudent summary of Ellen G. White's views about "new light" (pp. 5-13).

28. Bj. Christensen, "Dialogue or Ballots?" *Adventist Today,* January/February 1994, p. 15, emphasis supplied.

DEPARTING FROM THE WORD

PART V

The Bible— "Literal" or "Principle" Approach?

Objective. In this 'section we shall investigate the extent to which higher-critical assumptions are influencing Seventh-day Adventist views regarding the validity of the Ten Commandments, the Sabbath, end-time prophecy, Jesus' second coming, the sanctuary doctrine, the substitutionary atonement of Christ, and issues dealing with Adventist lifestyle.

Key Issue. How should we interpret the Bible—with a "literal" or a "principle" approach?

Traditional Adventist Belief. Seventh-day Adventists have always maintained that one finds the true meaning of Scripture by seeking the plain, obvious sense of the text. Interpreting Scripture literally does not mean blind, rigid literalism. Literal interpretation means we understand a given passage in its natural or normal sense. We must understand the words just as we would interpret the language of normal discourse.

From the literal meaning of the biblical text, we can derive appropriate principles for today's living. These principles must be faithful to the literal meaning and must not contradict any established biblical teaching or truth. The details of the traditional Adventist approach to interpretation are described in "Methods of Bible Study" (see Appendix C).

Theological Assumption. The theological assumption behind interpretation based on the plain literal meaning of Scripture is this: though the Bible's content is profound, it came from a perfect Communicator. God has done what all good communicators do—He has spoken in the language of the listener. God has used the expressions of normal people, however imperfect, so that "the wayfaring men, though fools, shall not err therein" (Isa 35:8).

Rather than speaking in grand superhuman language, "The Lord speaks to human beings in imperfect speech, in order that the degenerate senses, the dull, earthly perception, of earthly beings may comprehend His words. Thus is shown

God's condescension. He meets fallen human beings where they are. . . . Instead of the expressions of the Bible being exaggerated, as many people suppose, the strong expressions break down before the magnificence of the thought, though the penmen selected the most expressive language" (*Selected Messages,* 1:22).

"The Bible is not given to us in grand superhuman language. Jesus, in order to reach man where he is, took humanity. The Bible must be given in the language of men. Everything that is human is imperfect. Different meanings are expressed by the same word; there is not one word for each distinct idea" (ibid., 1:20). God's use of "imperfect" human language to communicate does not mean that the truthfulness of Scripture's message is compromised. Rather, it simply means that "infinite ideas cannot be perfectly embodied in finite vehicles of thought" (ibid., 1:22). In their attempt to communicate infinite ideas in finite human language, the inspired writers sometimes employed figures of speech, like parables, hyperbole, simile, metaphor, and symbolism. But even this figurative language conveys clear, literal truth.

Literal Understanding. Thus, apocalyptic books like Daniel, Zechariah, Ezekiel, and Revelation, which employ figures and symbols, must be studied carefully to discover the literal truth they convey. The same applies to the parables. They are stories used to illustrate spiritual truth. Though the details regarding people, events, times, and places in the parables may not be actually historical, the spiritual truths they convey are always literal and real.

Literal interpretation, therefore, means first understanding Scripture in its plain, normal sense. The interpreter then proceeds to apply the literal meaning to the contemporary situation of the interpreter. Those who reject literal interpretation have no objective control for wild imaginations, no safeguard against fanciful spiritualizing, allegorizing, and relativizing biblical truth. This is why responsible Bible students insist that the "principle" of application must always be controlled by the literal, plain reading of the text. Otherwise we tend to pick and choose only the supposed principles of the Bible palatable to our taste.[1]

When liberalism relativizes Scripture, it uses the Bible selectively, choosing a "key point," "central concept," or "principle" in Scripture by means of which it decides what is abiding or relevant in the Bible. In other words, the new views of Scripture seek to establish a "canon within the biblical Canon" (i.e., an inspiring booklet within the inspired Book). Without the literal reading of the biblical text, they spiritualize away, through fanciful interpretations, the plain meaning of the Scriptures.

How are historical-critical assumptions on these matters affecting the Adventist church?

Effect of the Liberal Approach

To justify setting aside the plain, literal reading of Scripture, expressions like these are now being used: "trajectory of Scripture," the "flow of Scripture," the "plot of Scripture," "Scripture as a whole" (not "the whole Scripture"), "the primary emphasis" of Scripture, "the positive principles" of Scripture, etc. In any case, it is the interpreter who decides what is the central concept which controls the selection process. Those who adopt these approaches to Scripture reinterpret the Bible and make applications of Scripture that lead away from established truths.

"Positive Principle." For example, one Adventist Old Testament scholar develops a three-tier "law pyramid" which places the principle of love at the apex of the pyramid as the highest norm. Below it are the two laws—love to God and love to neighbor, and at the bottom is the Ten Commandments. His pyramid then consists of "The one, the two, and the ten." He writes: "A key principle undergirds the concept of law pyramid: *some of God's laws are more important than others.*"[2]

But how do we know which of God's laws are more important than others? He explains: "The key point [of the casebook approach] is that the *positive principles* embedded in the one, the two, and the ten are absolute and enduring, but the specific applications are not."[3] None of the Ten Commandments, then, is absolute or enduring, but only the "positive principles" found in them. Adopting this kind of methodology, each student of the Bible could decide for himself what constitutes those "positive principles."[4]

Sabbath "Principle." What happens when one interprets Scripture according to the "positive principle" approach? The Worldwide Church of God, publisher of the *Plain Truth* magazine and until recently a Sabbath-keeping church, has given up its historic teaching on the validity of the seventh-day Sabbath. The reason may be of interest to Adventists tempted to look only for the "positive principles" within the Ten Commandments.

Under the influence of well-educated moderate liberal scholars, the leaders of the Worldwide Church of God came to believe that the "seventh-day" component of the fourth commandment is not as relevant as the "positive principle" of the Sabbath commandment. They argue on the basis of their "New Covenant" theology that observing the Sabbath on the seventh day is no longer as important as the "principle" of observing *a day of rest after six days of labor;* the Sabbath can be any day.[5]

Among Seventh-day Adventists, the historic method of interpreting Scripture—what historical-critical scholars refer to as the "literal-based approach"—

insists that the "seventh-day" (Saturday) is to be observed as the Sabbath. The "principle-based approach," however, may eventually lead to the "positive principle" of the Sabbath—one day of rest in seven, as has happened in the World-wide Church of God, and as is being advocated by two former Adventists, a pastor and a Bible scholar.[6]

With such an approach, the Sabbath/Sunday issue raised in Daniel, Revelation, and *The Great Controversy* becomes obsolete for today's anti-apocalyptic culture. Our claim to be the "remnant" becomes mere triumphalism and, hence, our opposition to joining the ecumenical movement is nothing more than religious bigotry or intolerance. This point will become clearer in part six of this chapter when we take a look at a proposal being suggested as an "Adventism for a New Generation."

Apocalyptic Prophecy. Already, one scholar and church administrator has called for "a fresh approach" to our understanding of end-time prophecy as a means to overcome the increasing theological pluralism in the church. He argues mistakenly that the "general anti-Catholic climate which prevailed in the United States in the 1830s through the 1850s" and the "uncritical adoption" of "William Miller's hermeneutical method in dealing with apocalyptic Bible prophecy" were the reasons behind Adventism's understanding of last-day events.

He expresses his discomfort with the "more conservative Adventists [who] insist that Adventism must continue to subscribe to its traditional interpretations of prophecy, with the corresponding condemnation of Roman Catholicism and other Christian churches." Against these conservative Adventists who "insist that 'the old landmarks' of the Adventist faith must be zealously guarded and are unwilling to re-think or modify traditional views," he sides with the "more 'progressively' inclined [who] are increasingly open to emphasizing the common bond with other Christians and [who] tend to feel uncomfortable with traditional attitudes." In his opinion the way to make Adventism "more relevant to this generation" is to adopt a "fresh approach that will re-evaluate the traditional Adventist views in the context of time."[7]

Thus, a growing body of Adventist scholars are saying: "We must become facilitators of 'spiritual ecumenicity' [of the charismatic movement] (as opposed to institutional ecumenicity [of the World Council of Churches]), so that we can respond to Christ's last prayer for unity (John 17:21) by breaking down the barriers of denominationalism rather than helping to build them up. . . . We must open ourselves to the possibility of new and different eschatological [end-time] scenarios so that we do not enter the twenty-first century with a nineteenth-century view of prophecy."[8]

Spiritual Second Coming Principle. Observe that if one's "fresh approach" to Scripture follows some ambiguous "positive principle" method, there are several ways in which one can "re-think" or "modify" Adventist doctrine. For example, a former book editor of one of our church's publishing houses has identified "the 'spiritual Second Coming' principle" (as he calls the real "principle" behind the Bible's "literal" teaching of a second Advent) as the belief that "Jesus has come in your hearts."

He continues: "The Second Coming can be accepted as symbolic or typical of the consummation of your religious experience, an event judging and justifying your spiritual connection with God. You may or may not choose to deal with the question of literality [the literal-based approach?]. But in spite of everything, you can maintain your spiritual existence, which I submit, is far more vital than settling any questions of literality! . . . Once the principle of symbolic interpretation is accepted, one can see many Second Comings."[9]

The "spiritual Second Coming principle" that leads one to see "many Second Comings" in Scripture is the same approach that undergirds the "apotelesmatic principle" (multiple fulfillment principle) or "idealist" principle of interpretation of Desmond Ford, the Seventh-day Adventist scholar who in the 1970s and 1980s departed from our historic teaching on the sanctuary doctrine, prophetic interpretation, and the Spirit of Prophecy.[10]

Clearly, the so-called "principle-based approach," which may be another name for the historical-critical method, does indeed affect the interpretation of Bible prophecy. Against the literal or plain reading of the Bible, this liberal way of studying the Bible seeks the "positive principle" of the Scripture. It is a sophisticated way to spiritualize away the apocalyptic prophecies of Daniel and Revelation and their interpretations as found in *The Great Controversy.*

This explains why the Rio document, "Methods of Bible Study," stated that "The historical-critical method *minimizes the need for faith in God and obedience to His commandments.* In addition, because such a method de-emphasizes the divine element in the Bible as an inspired book (including its resultant unity) and *depreciates or misunderstands apocalyptic prophecy and the eschatological portions of the Bible,* we urge Adventist Bible students to avoid relying on the use of the presuppositions and the resultant deductions associated with the historical-critical method."[11] Regrettably, as we have seen, many Adventist scholars still use the historical-critical method—disguised under different labels.

The Sanctuary Doctrine. According to the former book editor mentioned above, the Adventist critics' suggestion that the sanctuary doctrine is "seriously flawed" is "an understatement!" He writes: "Fashioned not to save souls, but to save our collective, wounded ego in the wake of a 'great disappointment' (as though God could be guilty of 'standing us up'!), it [the sanctuary doctrine] is actually destructive to the individual soul."[12] He cites another writer to explain his own attitude toward the sanctuary doctrine: "Discard the damaging. And shop elsewhere to meet unfulfilled needs."[13] The unwritten "principle" to rehabilitate the sanctuary doctrine, if it is possible at all, is "the fulfilment of needs."

If the statement of a former associate editor of the *Review and Herald* and current editor of *Adventist Today* is anything to go by, then a significant number of scholars and church administrators, including himself, seek to revise our traditional Sanctuary doctrine (Article 23 of our Fundamental Beliefs).[14] It is understandable that he would take exception to this fundamental pillar of our faith, given his favorable disposition towards the historical-critical method.[15]

Among those who are seeking to revise the traditional sanctuary doctrine is a theology professor. Seeking to move beyond the "maddening literalization of the rituals of Leviticus" and "cabalistic numerology" (1844?), he builds upon a non-Adventist's work and intimates that we must "re-vision" our historic sanctuary doctrine around a socio-political axis. Believing that his approach will make the sanctuary doctrine "relevant," he suggests that God's "presence" in the sanctuary (Lev 26:11) should be understood as His presence in the church on earth; the "defilement" of the sanctuary (Lev 26:31) should be understood as God's forced withdrawal, occasioned by physical and moral pollution of the earth (oil spills, acid rain, ozone depletion, nuclear waste, killing of innocent people in wars, starvation, etc.); the "restoration" (Lev 26:42ff.) means that the church should become a place for the "hurting, the marginalized, the disappointed," a refuge where people can "openly express anger and fear and doubt, and even heresy—otherwise the church will always remain a court of law rather than a place of safety."[16]

Does one need to go "beyond literalization" in order to affirm these relevant issues of social ethics?

The Substitutionary Atonement of Christ. For one Adventist theologian and college administrator, the "principle" in Christ's atonement is "social justice." On the basis of this "principle," he denies the penal substitutionary atonement of Christ, the teaching that Jesus Christ died in our stead, taking upon Himself the penalty of death that we deserved. The titles of his two articles summarize his views: "God's Justice, Yes; Penal Substitution, No"; ". . . Penal Substitutionary Atonement is Still Unbiblical."[17]

Notice that the above author's "principle" of "justice" essentially repudiates the historic Adventist understanding of Christ's atonement as stated in our Fundamental Beliefs, No. 9 and beautifully captured by Ellen White: "Christ was treated as we deserve, that we might be treated as He deserves. He was condemned for our sins, in which He had no share, that we might be justified by His righteousness, in which we had no share. He suffered the death which was ours, that we might receive the life which was His. 'With His stripes we are healed'" (*The Desire of Ages,* p. 25).

Sad to say, another influential Adventist theologian rejects this substitutionary atonement of Christ on the grounds that if we are saved because of Christ's death, it would in principle be salvation by works—Christ's works![18] The author of the devotional book, *His Healing Love,* echoes this sentiment when he asks rhetorically: "Who needs Christ's merits?"[19]

Adventist Lifestyle. Traditional Adventist practices like abstinence from the use of unclean foods, jewelry, and alcohol are also coming under fire as the "principle" approach gains acceptance in the church. Thus, a growing number of Adventist scholars are asking, "What's the big deal about these lifestyle issues?" To such, pork and jewelry are not biblical mandates, but rather are, at best, sociological symbols that our nineteenth-century colonial Adventists instituted as "markers" to identify those who belong to their faith.[20] Even on the question of whether the Bible condemns alcohol *use* or its *abuse,* some suggest that the answer depends heavily on one's present "bias."[21]

1. Clean and Unclean. Since some Adventist scholars believe that there is no clear scriptural mandate for our lifestyle practices, we should observe how their own "positive principle" conditions their interpretation of Scripture on these issues. One Adventist scholar asks: "Should Adventists use Leviticus 11 to support the prohibition of pork and other foods listed there as 'unclean'?" He answers No. In his opinion, "only a penchant for proof texting" will lead one to continue upholding the clean/unclean distinction. Arguing on the basis of a "more principled biblical-theological foundation" rather than on "dubious proof-texts," he concludes that Adventists "will refrain from eating pork, not because the laws concerning clean and unclean in Leviticus are still binding on Christians," but because "pork is especially unhealthful."[22]

The author of *Inspiration* echoes the same "principle" approach to Scriptures. Since the "principle" against eating unclean animals (Lev 11; Deut 14) is believed to be "health," he suggests that when threatened by starvation, one could "eat everything possible to enhance and preserve life."[23] Did the Bible cite "health" as the reason for prohibiting unclean animals for food, so that if one could raise pigs, snakes, lizards, earthworms, cockroaches, or vultures in a sanitized environment, their carcasses would be "clean" for food? Did not God give His own reason for designating some animals as unfit for food (cf. Deut 14:2, 3)?

2. Jewelry. The new method of interpretation is also shaping the way we relate to the jewelry issue. This is best illustrated by calling attention to the revealing conclusion of an article titled, "Thinking About Jewelry: What the Bible (Really) Says," written by the editor of the recent book, *Shall We Dance.* "If you utilize key-text hermeneutics to study the issue of jewelry, you can develop a good biblical case against wearing it. If you employ contextual hermeneutics, the case against it is less compelling. If you're a Seventh-day Adventist, you probably hold the Bible as the final authority for truth. Some have suggested that if your training in Seventh-day Adventism pre-dates 1970, you're likely [to] prefer key-text hermeneutics. If your higher education dates after 1970, you probably prefer contextual hermeneutics. When it comes to jewelry, it's not a matter of whether or not you follow the Bible; it's often more a matter of the way you use the Bible to establish your standards."[24]

It appears that the "key-text" designation is a new way of saying "proof-text" method, a label mistakenly applied to those who still uphold the long-standing Seventh-day Adventist plain meaning of Scripture. According to the article's author, among those who employ the "key-text" method are: (a) "those opposed to the ordination of women at the General Conference session in 1995"; (b) the publishers of *Bible Readings for the Home* (Review and Herald, 1914, 1935, 1942, 1958, 1963); and (c) "a number of the biblical writers"—notably, the apostle Paul: "It appears Paul used Old Testament verses out of context on occasion as he wrote in the New Testament!"[25]

It is, at least, encouraging that the apostle Paul is bracketed among those who employ the "key-text" method. Could it be that those who use this "pre-1970" approach are on more solid ground than the practitioners of the post-1970 "contextual" approach, the historical-critical method? The choice for Adventists is really between the approach marked out by the ancient Bible writers and that employed by the so-called "post-1970" scholars. In any case, only on the basis of the "positive principles" of the latter approach can one endorse the use of jewelry.

3. Other Issues. For pro-abortionists, the "principle" of selectivity is "choice," understood to be the right to terminate a pregnancy, even if the baby's choice is denied.[26] For biblical feminists, the "principle" is "equality," defined as the absence of role differentiation between men and women in both the home and the church.[27] For libertarians or situation ethicists, the "principle" is "love," even if it includes such things as divorce and remarriage on non-biblical grounds, breaking the Sabbath, cheating, stealing, lying, discriminating against other races, pre- and extra-marital sex—as long as these things are done for "loving" reasons.[28] And for those sympathetic to homosexual theology, the "principle" may be "acceptance" and "compassion."[29]

Deriving the "Positive Principle." How can one decide which "principle" applies? The author of *Inspiration* suggested that "reason in dialogue with the

Spirit, determines which of those cases [in Scripture] are most helpful in informing the decisions we make day by day."[30] Instead of submitting to God's Word, human reason engages in a "dialogue" with the Spirit. The author makes this point more explicit, stating that in his "casebook approach" to biblical interpretation he will *"never take an inspired writer to be a final interpreter of a passage written by another inspired writer,"* and that he will accept inspired interpretations as valid only when they are in harmony with his own scholarly "rules" of interpretation.[31] Apparently, today's scholar is more apostolic than the apostles!

A professor of history in an Adventist university takes up this point in connection with issues raised by *Inspiration:* "I don't think it is possible for us to totally subject human reasoning to the higher authority of the Bible. We are, after all, humans."[32] Instead of submitting to Scripture, proponents of the historical-critical method want to "dialogue" with Scripture. However, when they find its message unpalatable, they quarrel with Scripture and criticize it. But the prophet Isaiah declares: "Woe to him who quarrels with his Maker" (Isa 45:9 NIV; cf. Rom 9:20-21).

A Bible-Believing Adventist Response

The "principle-based approach" is a sophisticated attempt to relativize the Bible. It is a form of situation ethics—the ethical system that says rightness or wrongness is determined by what is "loving"—designed for those who consider themselves "mature" Christians. Notice how the author of *Inspiration* contrasts his "casebook approach" with the "codebook" approach (what some today would call the "literal-based approach"):

"Admittedly, what I have outlined is a sophisticated approach to the law, one that requires a rather advanced level of mental and Christian maturity. We would not expect young children or new Christians to be able to function at that level. For that very reason, God has given rules and adaptations—codebook, if you please, for those who need them. And the church, as a body of Christ, responsible for believers of every shape and capability, will always have a list of rules to get us started, so to speak."[33] Observe how similar the above "casebook approach" is to the "principle-based approach"—requiring "a high level of abstract thinking" believed to be favored by those who live in regions where the church has "matured for a century and half."[34]

Principles Dependent on Literal Meaning. It appears that the "principle-based approach" is a subtle way of finding fault with the Bible by allowing human reason to be the ultimate judge. But a true understanding of biblical principles does not create its own artificial "principles"; rather, it is based on a literal understanding of the Bible, ascertained by carefully using the literary, grammatical, and historical information contained in the Bible itself, consistent with Scripture's nature as fully inspired, trustworthy, and authoritative. The true Seventh-day Adventist method is *a principled approach to the literal meaning of the text.*

Illumined Rationality, Not Perverted Rationalism. The Bible teaches that because of the basic difference between God and human beings (i.e., because God is so much greater than we are), and because of the problems of sin and the unwillingness of unconverted human reason to surrender to God, there are limits to reason (Isa 55:8, 9; Rom 11:33; 2 Cor 4:4; 1 Cor 2:14). The greatest mind, unless guided by the Word of God, becomes bewildered; human rationality will become perverted into rationalism. The Bible's prescription for autonomous human reason is conversion, renewing the mind and transforming it into conformity with His will (Rom 12:2). When this happens, Spirit-regenerated human reason delights to submit totally to the higher authority of the Bible.

Against those who contradict established Bible truths by their re-interpretations and re-applications of Scripture, Ellen White wrote: "We are not to receive the words of those who come with a message that contradicts the special points of our faith. They gather together a mass of Scripture, and pile it as proof around their asserted theories. This has been done over and over again during the past fifty years. And while the Scriptures are God's word, and are to be respected, the application of them, if such application moves one pillar from the foundation that God has sustained these fifty years, is a great mistake. He who makes such application knows not the wonderful demonstration of the Holy Spirit that gave power and force to the past messages that have come to the people of God" (*Selected Messages,* 1:161).

God Never Contradicts Himself. If a scholar arises with an interpretation of Scripture, even one disguised as new light from a "principled-approach," and it contradicts the established truths of our faith, we are urged: "We must be decided on this subject; for the points that he is trying to prove by Scripture are not sound. They do not prove that the past experience of God's people was a fallacy. We had the truth; we were directed by the angels of God. It was under the guidance of the Holy Spirit that the presentation of the sanctuary question was given. It is eloquence for every one to keep silent in regard to the features of our faith in which they acted no part. *God never contradicts Himself.* Scripture proofs are misapplied if forced to testify to that which is not true. Another and still another will arise and bring in supposedly great light, and make their assertions. But we stand by the old landmarks" (*Selected Messages,* 1:161-162, emphasis supplied).

At a time when "to many the Bible is as a lamp without oil, because they have turned their minds into channels of speculative belief that bring misunderstanding and confusion," and at a time when "the work of higher criticism, in dissecting, conjecturing, reconstructing, is destroying faith in the Bible as a divine revelation . . . robbing God's word of power to control, uplift, and inspire human lives" (*The Acts of the Apostles,* p. 474), Bible-believing Adventists must affirm with Ellen White: "Reason must acknowledge an authority superior to itself. Heart and intellect must bow to the Great I AM" (*The Ministry of Healing,* p. 438). In studying the Scriptures, reason must be humble enough to accept and obey what it finds in those sacred pages and must not seek to circumvent biblical teaching by resorting to abstract "positive principles."

NOTES

1. For more on this, see Samuel Koranteng-Pipim, "Inspired Book or Inspiring Booklet?" *Adventists Affirm* 9/1 (Spring 1995):20-29.

2. Alden Thompson, *Inspiration: Hard Questions, Honest Answers* (Hagerstown, Md.: Review and Herald, 1991), pp. 114, 116 (italics are his).

3. Ibid., pp. 120-121, emphasis supplied.

4. A penetrating critique of the "law pyramid" has been offered by Gerhard F. Hasel, "Reflections on Alden Thompson's 'Law Pyramid' Within a Casebook/Codebook Dichotomy," in *Issues in Revelation and Inspiration,* ed. Frank Holbrook and Leo Van Dolson (Berrien Springs, Mich.: Adventist Theological Society Publications, 1992), pp. 137-171.

5. For an update on these developments in the Worldwide Church of God (WCG), see the editorial of the church's president, Joseph Tkach, Jr., "A Church Reborn," *The Plain Truth,* February 1996, pp. 1, 26. For a detailed analysis of the factors leading to the crisis in the WCG, see Samuele Bacchiocchi's illuminating articles, "A Church in Crisis: Causes and Lessons," *Adventists Affirm* 9/2 (Fall 1995):49-55; "Lessons from a Church Meltdown," *Adventist Review,* April 18, 1996, pp. 25-28.

6. The "New Covenant" Sabbath theology recently adopted by the Worldwide Church of God is the same as that of Dale Ratzlaff, a former Adventist pastor (see Ratzlaff, "The Sabbath: A Shadow of Grace," *Adventist Today,* July-August 1996, pp. 11-14). Similarly, a former Adventist professor of theology has given up on the seventh-day Sabbath and now pastors the First Christian Church (Disciples of Christ). The influence of the historical-critical method on this Bible scholar's view of the Bible Sabbath is evident in his recent article arguing that "diversity" in the New Testament allows for "at least three views of the Sabbath, all of which may claim roots in the primitive church" (see Jerry Gladson, "The Sabbath in Christian Life: A Reconsideration," *Adventist Today,* July August 1996, p. 16). Gladson's favorable view of the historical-critical method is reflected in an article he wrote while an Adventist. See Jerry Gladson, "Taming Historical Criticism: Adventist Biblical Scholarship in the Land of Giants," *Spectrum* 18/4 (April 1988):19-34.

7. Reinder Bruinsma, *Seventh-day Adventist Attitudes Toward Roman Catholicism 1844-1965* (Berrien Springs, Mich.: Andrews University Press, 1994), pp. 295, 301-302.

8. Steve Daily, *Adventism for a New Generation* (Portland/Clackamas, Ore.: Better Living Publishers, 1993), pp. 201-202; cf. pp. 312-316. Another recent work that essentially reflects the same outlook as Reinder Bruinsma and Steve Daily is Rolf J. Pöhler, "Change in Seventh-day Adventist Theology: A Study of the Problem of Doctrinal Development" (Th.D. dissertation, Andrews University, 1995). Readers will greatly benefit from Winfried Vogel's excellent portrayal and evaluation of the theological pluralism that has infected many Adventist publications. See Winfried Vogel, "Man

and Knowledge: The Search for Truth in a Pluralistic Age," scheduled for publication in the forth-coming Autumn 1996 issue of *Journal of the Adventist Theological Society.*

9.   Max Gordon Phillips, "1844: No Disappointment," *Adventist Today,* November-December, 1995, pp. 18-19. For an insightful article documenting the devastating results of the historical-critical method in eschatology, see Norman Gulley, "The Battle for Biblical Eschatology in the End-Time," *Journal of the Adventist Theological Society* 1/2 (1990):22-36.

10.   Desmond Ford, *Daniel* (Nashville, Tenn.: Southern Publishing Association, 1978), pp. 65-70. We have commented on the theological and hermeneutical issues raised by Ford's challenge to the sanctuary doctrine; see chapter 4, note 10. For a discussion of the different approaches to the interpretation of Bible prophecies, see William Shea, "Making Sense of Bible Prophecy," *Dialogue* 5/2 (1993):5-8.

11.   "Methods of Bible Study," *Adventist Review,* January 22, 1987, pp. 18-20 (reproduced in Appendix C of this book).

12.   Max Gordon Phillips, "The Church: Leave It *ard* Love It?" *Adventist Today,* March-April, 1996, pp. 12-13.

13.   Ibid., citing Richard Winn's "When the Pew Gets Uncomfortable," *Adventist Today,* September-October, 1995.

14.   Raymond Cottrell, "1844 Revisionists Not New: President Indicts the Church's Scholars," *Adventist Today,* January-February, 1995, p. 16. Cottrell is the editor of *Adventist Today.* Perceptive readers of Cottrell's article in the widely promoted book, *The Welcome Table,* will notice that his analysis of Daniel 9:25 repudiates the Adventist belief that the 2300 day prophecy of Daniel 8:14 ended in 1844 (see Cottrell, "A Guide to Reliable Interpretation," *The Welcome Table,* pp. 74-75). The front cover of the defunct *Adventist Currents* (October 1983) places Cottrell's picture alongside "some of the Seventh-day Adventist leaders who either doubted or discarded the traditional teaching of the sanctuary: O. R. L. Crosier, D. M. Canright, E. J. Waggoner, A. F. Ballenger, J. H. Kellogg, A. T. Jones, L. R. Conradi, W. W. Prescott, Raymond Cottrell, Desmond Ford" (p. 3). Careful readers can discern Cottrell's "revised" views on the sanctuary doctrine by reading his assessment of Ford's position in the same issue of *Adventist Currents* in which his picture appears on the cover page. See Raymond F. Cottrell, "'Variant Views' Digested," *Adventist Currents,* October 1983, pp. 4-9, 34. For a response to the concerns often raised against the historic Adventist doctrine of the sanctuary, see Brempong Owusu-Antwi, *The Chronology of Daniel 9:24-27* (Berrien Springs, Mich.: Adventist Theological Society Publications, 1995); William Shea, *Selected Studies on Prophetic Interpretation* (Washington, D.C.: General Conference of Seventh-day Adventists, 1982); Arnold V. Wallenkampf and Richard W. Lesher, eds., *The Sanctuary and the Atonement: Biblical, Historical, and Theological Studies* (Washington, D.C.: Review and Herald, 1981); Frank Holbrook, ed., *The Seventy Weeks, Leviticus, and the Nature of Prophecy* (Washington, D.C.: Biblical Research Institute, 1986); Frank Holbrook, *The Atoning Priesthood of Jesus Christ* (Berrien Springs, Mich.: Adventist Theological Society Publications, 1996).

15.   In recent times Cottrell has called his method "the historical method," arguing that "no Adventist Bible scholar subscribes to that [historical-critical] method, or to its presuppositions or conclusions" (see his article in *The Welcome Table,* pp. 79, 84, 80). This contradicts his earlier assertion that, with the exception of "all but a few," the historical-critical method is the method that had been employed by Adventist scholars since the 1930s. Evidence of his own historical-critical leanings can be found in his "Blame It On Rio: The Annual Council Statement on Methods of Bible Study," *Adventist Currents,* March 1987, p. 33. For a detailed discussion of the changing terminology for the historical-critical method, see chapter 4.

16.   Glen Greenwalt, "Sanctuary In the Year 2000," *Adventist Today,* November-December 1994, pp. 6-9. For a critical response to this "re-visionment" by Greenwalt, see Roy Gane, "Sanctuary of Hope: A Response to Glen Greenwalt," ibid., p. 10. Also, the entire issue of *Adventists Affirm* 8/2 (Fall 1994) is devoted to the relevance of the historic Adventist sanctuary doctrine; cf. *Adventists Affirm,* Fall 1992, an issue also devoted to the sanctuary. A detailed work has been provided by Richard M. Davidson, "In Confirmation of the Sanctuary Message," *Journal of the Adventist Theo-*

logical Society 2/1 (Spring 1991); Frank B. Holbrook, ed., *Doctrine of the Sanctuary: A Historical Survey,* Daniel and Revelation Committee Series, vol. 5 (Silver Spring, Md.: Biblical Research Institute, General Conference of Seventh-day Adventists, 1989); C. Mervyn Maxwell, *Magnificent Disappointment: What Really Happened in 1844 and Its Meaning for Today* (Boise, Id.: Pacific Press, 1994); Clifford Goldstein, *1844 Made Simple* (Boise, Id.: Pacific Press, 1988).

17. See Charles Scriven, "God's Justice, Yes; Penal Substitution, No," *Spectrum,* October 1993, pp. 31-38; see also his follow-up letter, "Scriven Says Penal Substitutionary Atonement is Still Unbiblical," *Spectrum,* July 1994, pp. 63-64. For a brief analysis and critique of these works, see Samuel Koranteng-Pipim, "A Critique of Dr. Charles Scriven's 'God's Justice Yes: Penal Substitution, No'," unpublished manuscript, December 1994, available at the Adventist Heritage Center, James White Library, Andrews University. For a detailed discussion of the historic Adventist position on the penal substitutionary atonement of Christ, see Angel Manuel Rodriguez, "Salvation by Sacrificial Substitution," *Journal of the Adventist Theological Society* 3/2 (Autumn 1992):49-77; Gerhard F. Hasel, "Salvation in Scripture," *Journal of the Adventist Theological Society* 3/2 (Autumn 1992):17-48.

18. Jack Provonsha, *You Can Go Home Again* (1982), p. 94. He writes: "Nobody has to (or can) pay for it [salvation], or work for it. The cross rejects salvation by works *in principle.* It was a demonstration, not a payment. Golgotha is not a question of *whose* merits *earn* our salvation, but a rejection of the merit-earning formula itself" (ibid.). His theory of atonement is a version of the moral influence theory advocated by Peter Abelard (1079-1142). This view says that Jesus' death did not pay the legal debt of our sins, but rather it was simply a demonstration of God's love designed to awaken a response in us (ibid., pp. 20, 95); cf. Graham Maxwell, *Servants or Friends? Another Look At God* (Redlands, Calif.: Pineknoll Publications, 1992), pp. 117-136. For a helpful summary and evaluation of this theory, see Richard Fredericks, "The Moral Influence Theory—Its Attraction and Inadequacy," *Ministry,* March 1992, pp. 6-10; Raoul Dederen, "Atoning Aspects in Christ's Death," *The Sanctuary and the Atonement* (Washington, D.C.: Review and Herald, 1981), pp. 292-325; Norman Gulley, "A Look at the Larger View of Calvary: An Evaluation of the Debate in the Seventh-day Adventist Church," *Journal of the Adventist Theological Society* 3/1 (1992):66-96.

19. Dick Winn, *His Healing Love* (Washington, D.C.: Review and Herald, 1986), p. 55.

20. See Ernest J. Bursey, "The Big Deal About Pork and Jewelry," *Spectrum* 22 (May 1992):43-46; Gregory A. Schneider, "If Pork and Rings Are a Big Deal, We Have to Give Fundamental Reasons," *Spectrum* 22 (May 1992):47-48; cf. Charles Scriven, "I Didn't Recognize You With Your Ring On," *Spectrum* 20/2 (1989):56-59; Carl G. Tuland, "Let's Stop Arguing Over the Wedding Ring," *Spectrum* 8/2 (1977):59-61. Another writes: "We must give up our preoccupation with externals and our obsession with control. It is not the business of the church to prescribe for its members how they should behave on Sabbath, what foods they should eat, in what forms of recreation or entertainment they may participate, what books they can read, how they should dress, if they can wear jewelry, or how they should think" (Steve Daily, *Adventism for a New Generation,* p. 20).

21. Steve Case, "Mixing Alcohol, Abstinence, and the Bible," in *Shall We Dance: Rediscovering Christ-Centered Standards,* ed. Steve Case (Riverside, Calif.: La Sierra University Press, 1996), p. 313.

22. John C. Brunt, "Unclean or Unhealthful? An Adventist Perspective," *Spectrum* 11/3 (1981):21-23; see especially p. 23, note 9.

23. Thompson, *Inspiration,* p. 129. Notice that Gerhard F. Hasel, "Clean and Unclean Meats in Leviticus 11: Still Relevant?" *Journal of the Adventist Theological Society* 2/2 (1991):91-125, has offered solid biblical reasons for the continued relevance of the clean and unclean distinction.

24. Steve Case, "Thinking About Jewelry: What the Bible (Really) Says," *Shall We Dance,* p. 193; cf. p. 182. For careful discussion of the jewelry question, see Angel Manuel Rodriguez, "Jewelry in the Old Testament: A Description of Its Functions," unpublished article (1996); cf. Samuele Bacchiocchi, *Christian Dress and Adornment* (Berrien Springs, Mich.: Biblical Perspectives, 1995).

25. Case, *Shall We Dance,* p. 185, notes 1 and 2.

26. The principle of "choice" is one of the assumptions underlying the ambivalent "Abortion Guidelines" of the church. See also, Ginger Hanks-Harwood, "A Higher Calling," *Adventist Today,*

May-June 1993, p. 18. For an insightful history of the abortion debate in the Adventist church, refer to George B. Gainer, "Abortion: History of Adventist Guidelines," *Ministry,* August 1991, pp. 11-17. For a contemporary discussion of the issue, see David R. Larson, ed., *Abortion: Ethical Issues & Options* (Loma Linda, Calif.: Loma Linda University Center for Christian Bioethics, 1992). A summary and critique of this latter work can be found in Samuel Koranteng-Pipim, "Review of *Abortion: Ethical Issues & Options,*" in *Dialogue* 6/3 (1994):26-27. An in-depth study of a key biblical text in the abortion debate, Exodus 21:22-25, has been provided by Ronald A. G. du Preez, "The Status of the Fetus in Mosaic Law," *Journal of the Adventist Theological Society* 1/2 (1990):5-21; a summary can be found in his "The Fetus in Biblical Law," *Ministry,* September 1992, pp. 11-14. For biblically consistent positions in the book, *Abortion: Ethical Issues & Options,* see Niels-Erik Andreasen, "A Biblical Perspective on Abortion," pp. 43-53; Teresa Beem, "The 'Hard Cases' of Abortion," pp. 155-169; Sara K. Terian, "Communicating Grace: The Church's Role in the Abortion Controversy," pp. 205-220.

27. On the feminist interpretation of the Bible, see Gerhard F. Hasel, "Biblical Authority and Feminist Interpretation," *Adventists Affirm* 3/2 (Fall 1989):12-23. For a more detailed discussion, refer to his "Hermeneutical Issues Relating to the Ordination of Women: Methodological Reflections on Key Passages" (unpublished document, May 23, 1994), available at the Adventist Heritage Center at Andrews University. See also Mary A. Kassian, *The Feminist Gospel: The Movement to Unite Feminism With the Church* (Wheaton, Ill.: Crossway, 1992).

28. For how the divorce issue has been discussed in the Adventist church, see Michael Pearson, *Millennial Dreams and Moral Dilemmas: Seventh-day Adventism and Contemporary Ethics* (New York: Cambridge University Press, 1990), pp. 182-228. On the Bible's position regarding the use of alcohol, see Samuele Bacchiocchi, *Wine in the Bible: A Biblical Study on the Use of Alcoholic Beverages* (Berrien Springs, Mich.: Biblical Perspectives, 1989); see also his *Christian Dress and Adornment* (Berrien Springs, Mich.: Biblical Perspectives, 1995). On the relevance of the "clean and unclean" teaching, see Gerhard F. Hasel, "Clean and Unclean Meats in Leviticus 11: Still Relevant?" *Journal of the Adventist Theological Society* 2/2 (Autumn 1991):91-125. On the question of racism and tribalism, see Samuel Koranteng-Pipim, "The Triumph of Grace Over Race," *Adventists Affirm,* Fall 1995, pp. 35-49; cf. "Saved by Grace and Living by Race: The Religion Called Racism," in *Journal of the Adventist Theological Society* 5/2 (Autumn 1994):37-78; "Racism and Christianity," *Dialogue* 7/1 (1995):12-15.

29. Cf. Special Issue of *Insight* (December 5, 1992) that was devoted to the question of homosexuality. The questions raised by this publication will require a detailed theological analysis and evaluation. In the meantime, those seeking a brief treatment of the Bible's position may benefit from Raoul Dederen's "Homosexuality: A Biblical Perspective," *Ministry,* September 1981, pp. 14-16; Ronald M. Springett, *Homosexuality in History and the Scriptures* (Washington, D.C.: Biblical Research Institute, 1988).

30. Thompson, *Inspiration,* p. 109. For a response to this, see *Issues in Revelation and Inspiration,* pp. 43-47, 137-171.

31. Thompson, *Inspiration,* pp. 252, 251, emphasis supplied. Despite his claim, his entire book is allegedly predicated on two Ellen G. White statements on Scripture. See Norman R. Gulley's critique, "An Evaluation of Alden Thompson's 'Incarnational' Method in the Light of His View of Scripture and Use of Ellen White," *Issues in Revelation and Inspiration* (Berrien Springs, Mich.: Adventist Theological Society Publications, 1992), pp. 69-90.

32. Taken from correspondence (dated October 13, 1992) with this professor of history in connection with issues raised by *Inspiration.*

33. Thompson, *Inspiration,* p. 118. For a critical examination of this approach see Samuel Koranteng-Pipim, "An Analysis and Evaluation of Alden Thompson's Casebook/Codebook Approach to the Bible," in *Issues in Revelation and Revelation,* pp. 31-67.

34. J. David Newman, "Stuck in the Concrete," *Adventist Today,* July-August, 1995, p. 13; cf. Jim Walters, "General Conference Delegates Say NO on Women's Ordination," *Adventist Today,* July-August, 1995, pp. 12-13.

DEPARTING FROM THE WORD

PART VI

Adventism for a New Generation— Perception or Deception?

Objective. In this section we shall draw out the implications of our discussion in the previous sections of this lenthy chapter, examining a recent proposal for an "Adventism for a New Generation."

Key Issue. What do the new approaches to Scripture imply for the life, mission, and identity of the church? What kind of Adventism do the new approaches to Scripture produce? How does this relate to the perceived polarization between "the church of the West" and "the rest of the church"? Is the reading of Scripture through higher-critical lenses evidence of true insight and clear *perception* or an omen of blindness and *deception*?

Introduction. Because many Bible scholars in Seventh-day Adventist institutions around the world are still faithfully employing traditional Adventism's plain reading of Scripture, they continue to uphold the biblical doctrines and practices of our faith. However, since at least in first-world countries a significant majority have embraced aspects of the higher-critical method, we need to know the destination of that approach to Scriptures. This chapter was designed to illustrate the need to "examine the full consequences of our theological method lest we prove more than we intend."[1]

In the course of our investigation, we have shown how wrong assumptions regarding the inspiration, trustworthiness, and the sole authority of Scripture result in *departing from the Word* and consequently from our distinctive Bible doctrines (e.g., the Sabbath, the sanctuary, atonement of Christ, second coming, spirit of prophecy, remnant, etc.). They also affect our views on issues of Christian lifestyle: abortion, polygamy, women's ordination, homosexuality, dress, clean food, jewelry, use of alcoholic beverages, war, etc.

What does this new trend mean for the identity and mission of the church? Will such published calls as we have examined here from various thought-leaders bring about a reformation in the church? Or do they lead away from what we have always known as the Seventh-day Adventist faith? What kind of Adventism is being created for our new generation?

The Need for Revival and Reformation. Many earnest Seventh-day Adventists, especially young people who have grown up in the church, feel increasingly disenchanted and disillusioned. They have observed that while we rightly affirm "the Bible and the Bible only," many of us do not have a living experience with the Bible's divine Author. Baptism seems more a graduation ceremony rather than the start of a new life in Christ. Our identity as God's "remnant" church makes us complacent instead of inspiring us to fulfill our divine mission to the world. We assert repeatedly that "we have the truth," but very often the truth does not have us. Our preaching, teaching, and evangelism may cram the mind with information but seldom bring about the deep soul searching and humility of heart that results in transforming the character. Our ethical positions on social issues reflect pragmatic concerns rather than fidelity to Scripture. And instead of our worship being reverently vibrant, it tends to be either dull and sterile or emotional and superficial.

The church's condition has led today's generation of Adventists to renew the call for a revival of primitive godliness. But while both mainstream and liberal Adventism correctly recognize this need for revival and reformation, the two theological camps offer totally different solutions to the problem.

Mainstream, Bible-believing Adventists hold that wherever the Word of God has been faithfully received, interpreted, and proclaimed, the Spirit of God has convicted men and women of their sin and led them to accept the Lamb of God who taketh away the sin of the world. Those who repented and believed were baptized, "and rose to walk in newness of life—new creatures in Christ Jesus; not to fashion themselves according to the former lusts, but by the faith of the Son of God to follow in His steps, to reflect His character, and to purify themselves even as He is pure. The things they once hated they now loved, and the things they once loved they hated. The proud and self-assertive became meek and lowly of heart. The vain and supercilious became serious and unobtrusive. The profane became reverent, the drunken sober, and the profligate pure. The vain fashions of the world were laid aside. Christians sought not the 'outward adorning of plaiting the hair, and of wearing of gold, or of putting on of apparel; but . . . the hidden man of the heart, in that which is not corruptible, even the ornament of a meek and quiet spirit, which is in the sight of God of great price.' 1 Peter 3:3, 4" (*The Great Controversy,* pp. 461, 462).

But liberal Adventism offers another kind of reformation, based on a skeptical view of Scripture and a reinterpretation of our biblical doctrine and lifestyle along the lines of contemporary higher criticism. Tragically, this theological experiment is being offered to our young people and other Adventists of our generation as the answer to their spiritual needs and concerns. Is this version of Adventism genuine or counterfeit?

Adventism for a New Generation?

The analysis in the various parts of this chapter has highlighted how a growing body of our influential authors seeks to make Adventism "relevant" to this generation. One scholar and church administrator represents this new trend of scholarship when he calls for a "fresh approach" to the historic Adventist understanding of end-time events so that the church will be more "open to emphasizing the common bond with other Christians," and in this way make Adventism "more relevant to this generation."[2] Such calls for "relevance" (some would say "liberation," "renewal" or even "reformation" within Adventism) have not gone unheeded.

An influential Adventist university chaplain and teacher has taken up this challenge and developed it in a well-crafted book, *Adventism for a New Generation.* Endorsed by prominent church administrators and educators, this work deserves some attention. It may represent the kind of Adventism toward which the *liberal left* seeks to move mainstream Adventism.[3]

New Generation Adventism? The book's author rejects historic Adventism's self-understanding as God's end-time remnant and its Bible-based lifestyle and morality, dismissing these beliefs and practices as culturally conditioned to the nineteenth-century Victorian age of Ellen G. White.

Believing that "our eschatology [our unique beliefs about last day events] has been built on an unsound foundation, and that it has ultimately done us more harm than good," he writes: "We must open ourselves to the possibility of new and different eschatological scenarios so that we do not enter the twenty-first century with a nineteenth-century view of prophecy."[4] He asks: "Why has the [Adventist] church rigidly clung to an outmoded view of eschatology which has focused on Sunday laws and Catholics rather then [*sic*] applying Christ-centered eschatological principles to our world today?" He maintains that the church has too often "overstated" its claims to remnant status. "Such claims, past and present, are unfortunate evidence of unhealthy and dysfunctional religion in Adventism."[5]

A New Lifestyle. The author of *Adventism for a New Generation* also challenges the church "to uplift and glorify Christ by calling all people to worship Him, and internalize the principles of His kingdom." He envisions an Adventism that is emptied of its Bible-based lifestyle: "As I have taught, counseled, and listened to Adventist young people over the last seventeen years and as I reflect on my own experience in our church's schools, it is clear to me that we must give up our preoccupation with externals and our obsession with control. It is not the business of the church to prescribe for its members how they should behave on Sabbath, what foods they should eat, in what forms of recreation or entertainment they may participate, what books they can read, how they should dress, if they can wear jewelry, or how they should think."[6]

Note that the new lifestyle was not developed from Scripture, but rather from empirical data (listening to "young people") and a reflection on "my own experience."

The author rejects conservative Adventism because "such religion is known for its 'prooftext' approach to Scripture, and its uncompromising emphasis on 'correct doctrine' or 'objective truth'."[7] Believing that the Bible "contains certain discrepancies in different ways" and "theological errors," he seeks a "dynamic" revelation of truth that is consistent with a "developmental process behind the doctrinal truths which unfold in the Bible" and which "account for theological contradictions in the Bible."[8]

A New Morality. On premarital sex and masturbation, this author wants to free the new generation of Adventists from "our Victorian heritage, which has been well preserved through the work of Ellen White. Most Adventists are not aware of what bizarre and extreme views of sexuality were commonly held by our nineteenth century ancestors. Books like *Messages to Young People* have served to perpetuate such baggage throughout much of the twentieth century as well. . . . I had a senior Bible teacher in academy in the 1970s who held similar views, teaching us (much to our amusement) that any physical contact with the opposite sex before marriage was wrong. Our Victorian heritage may be greater than we think."[9]

He continues: "Many Adventists have a 'masturbation-phobia' as a result of Ellen White's extreme pronouncements about the practice. Her teaching on this topic was rooted in a nineteenth century 'vital force' physiology which has no credibility in the medical community today, and stands in stark contrast to the Bible's silence concerning masturbation. A balanced Christian approach to sexual self-stimulation sees it as a potentially healthy form of sexual discovery, exploration and awareness. It can even be a healthy equalizing force in marriages where partners have significantly different amounts of sex drive."[10]

"Finally," he concludes, "the question of premarital sex is an important one. The biblical principle that sexual intercourse be reserved for a monogamous marital relationship (Gen. 2:24) is increasingly being viewed as obsolete or impractical by young Christians. One reason for this has been the church's tendency to address this issue in an 'all or nothing' context. Sexuality, like spirituality, communication, or any other aspect of a relationship, must develop and mature over time. Christian couples who have dated for a significant period need to honestly discuss their convictions and sexual boundaries. Sexual exploration and experimentation before marriage should respect these boundaries; one should never put a partner in the position of feeling guilty or sinful. We need to remember that God created sex to be an enjoyable, pleasurable activity."[11]

Young unmarried Christians must set their own boundaries in their sexual conduct. "In cases where [unmarried] couples do have intercourse before marriage, and wish to break this behavior pattern, I often recommend an exercise called 'sexual pleasuring' that is commonly prescribed in sexual therapy for impotence and premature ejaculation. These [unmarried] couples need to realize that there is a wide range of sexual activities that can be tremendously pleasurable and satisfying that do not involve sexual intercourse, and its accompanying risks. Christian young people in general need to know their individual boundaries . . . from their own study of scripture, and truly enjoy themselves in a guilt-free, balanced manner within those boundaries. Those who criticize such young people for not living up to *their* standards have no scriptural basis for their criticisms and no right to make themselves moral policemen for other Christians."[12]

A New Ecumenism. The book castigates the Adventist church for its opposition to ecumenism, saying that "there is a new ecumenism sweeping through much of the Christian church today, that Adventism cannot afford to ignore." This is not the ecumenism of the World Council of Churches, with its institutional and liberal political agenda. Instead, the "new ecumenism" is identified with the *charismatic movement.*[13]

This Adventist author embraces the charismatic movement not only because of its wonderful work of "intercessory prayer" in cities and communities, but also because of its charismatic worship style: "My thinking about worship was transformed several years ago when I attended the Anaheim Vineyard Fellowship. I was dumbfounded by what I saw. Thousands of people worshipping God with a passion that I had never witnessed in any other church. Some were standing, some were lifting up their arms, others were clapping, some were sitting quietly in prayer or meditation, a few were jumping, and several were kneeling, but they all seemed to be actively worshipping God. . . . Since that day, I have returned to the Vineyard many times for my own spiritual nourishment and have longed to see the same kind of worship emerge in Adventism. God's last people will be people who find worship to be the most exciting and meaningful experience in life."[14]

Motivation for Ecumenism. Notice what he seeks to gain by this new ecumenism identified with the charismatic movement: "If we were to renounce our past sectarian mentality and embrace our communities by using our sanctuaries for non-denominational Sunday services, people would think very differently about our schools and churches. We would experience a dialogue with non-Adventist Christians that would not only benefit us but would open many non-Adventist minds to the value and meaning of the Sabbath. It may be that God raised us up as a people for such a time as this."[15]

Our author recognizes that the "spiritual ecumenicity" he is calling for will require Adventists to "give up their own identities." But he does not seem to mind, since the "intercessory prayer and a shared love for their cities and communities" are more important than our doctrinal distinctives.[16] He is fully aware of the significance of what he is advocating:

"I believe that the consequences of this decision [alliance with the charismatic renewal movement for "intercessory prayer"] will determine the future course of Adventism to a great degree." But he explains that the kind of reformation he is calling for is warranted because Adventist eschatology, which warns against unbiblical alliances,[17] "has been built on an unsound foundation, and that it has ultimately done us more harm than good." In his opinion, Adventism's remnant theology, which is "more firmly ingrained in the Adventist psyche because of Ellen White's powerful endorsement," leads to "ethnocentrism," "xenophobia," and "paranoia."[18]

Consequently, he calls upon the church to outgrow the vice of isolationism and parochial Christianity and embrace the virtues of an inclusive Christianity which will respond to the needs of our cities and communities. Although he admits that it is "difficult for people who were born and raised believing that they were God's Remnant Church, God's special chosen people, to embrace an ecumenical spirit of any kind," he proceeds to suggest that we must "stop thinking just of ourselves as 'God's chosen *people'* and start recognizing the existence and ministry of 'God's chosen *peoples.'* It is a call to move from an ethnocentric remnant theology to a spirit of religious affirmation which acknowledges that the 'kingdom of God on earth' transcends every religious movement of humankind, and rejoices that the future kingdom will include 'many mansions'."[19]

Some Suggested Strategies. Believing that it is "churches and movements that are willing to lose their lives, or *give up their own identities,* for the kingdom of God that will find their lives and be used by God to bring the greatest blessings to humanity," he suggests some "practical things" Adventists can do "to contribute to this goal." Among these are:

"1. We can cease to think or speak of ourselves as the remnant church and see ourselves as a part of God's larger remnant. 2. We can take advantage of the special opportunity we have to attend other churches (since they meet on a different day) to befriend them, learn from them, share with them, and affirm the good things we see in them. 3. Each of us can make a special effort to maintain active membership in at least one non-Adventist community service organization to combat our natural tendency to isolationism. 4. We can involve ourselves in interdenominational bible study and/or [charismatic] intercessory prayer groups to broaden our own spiritual perspectives. 5. We can come to see Christ, not as the possession of Adventism or even of Christianity, but as the universal God and Saviour He is. Such a Christ is much more appealing to non-Christians than the Christ of parochial Christianity."[20]

Hermeneutical Foundation. Since the author rightly recognizes that "theology is dependent on one's hermeneutical approach to scripture,"[21] it stands to reason that the theological views expressed in *Adventism for a New Generation* are also established on its author's "dynamic," "developmental," and "Christ-centered view of inspiration."[22] He develops this new approach to the Scriptures because he believes that "the Seventh-day Adventist church has never fully outgrown the Fundamentalist view of Inspiration that it grew up with in the nineteenth century"—a view of inspiration he characterizes as "a literal, rigid, propositional, or 'proof text' interpretation of Scripture."[23]

In making the above assertion, he is simply singing the popular refrain from the chorus of "New Generation" scholars who argue unjustifiably that the plain reading of Scripture historically adopted by Seventh-day Adventists (the "proof text method," to use the overworked expression) is somehow defective.[24] He admits that the new views regarding biblical authority and interpretation being circulated by the "New Generation" scholars are the result of "a broader understanding of the nature of inspiration that has come through Adventism's exposure to higher education and the application of the historical-critical method to both Scripture and the writings of Ellen White."[25]

Reformation or Deformation? Readers should clearly understand that the above author is not alone in holding this vision of an *Adventism for a New Generation.* He is one of the few who, instead of spreading his views quietly, has had the courage to publicize them in print. One influential Adventist educator, in endorsing the book, states that it is "one of those books that demand attention and thought. .... *I recommend this book to pastors, educators and thought leaders who want a thorough analysis of what 'might be' if we fully commit our mission to the work of God.*"[26]

Besides the endorsers of this work, a number of other Adventist thought-leaders, scholars, and church administrators are also demanding revisions in our historic Adventist doctrines to make them "more relevant to this generation."[27] While such ideas are prevalent, the most vocal proponents (at least those currently in denominational employment) seldom publish their revisionist views. Thus the theological views expressed in *Adventism for a New Generation* must be seen as only the tip of a theological iceberg.

But are the calls for reformation within Adventism really designed to restore the biblical truths held by our pioneers? Are the different approaches to Scripture, and the different versions of Adventism they spawn, suggestive of a return to authentic Seventh-day Adventism (if we can talk about "authentic" Adventism at all), or are these aberrations of Adventism and hence, evidence of an identity crisis?[28]

What really does it mean when today we hear about renewal and intercessory prayer, wonderful works for our "cities and communities," replacing the vice of ethnocentric remnant theology with the virtues of "God's larger remnant"? Are the disdain for the works of our pioneers, the giving up of the pillars of our faith, and the desire to align our church with the charismatic movement indications of real reformation within the church? Or are they, rather, a departure from the faith—a distortion of the biblical truths of Adventism?

Could the major cracks we see in the theological foundation of our faith be signs of an impending crisis? Is it possible that "books of a new order"—the flurry of books and articles being published, endorsed, and distributed—in our day are vital warnings of an end-time deception—a deception that will closely parallel the "alpha" that took place in the days of Ellen White?[29]

End-Time Deception? In the wake of the Kellogg crisis in the early 1900s, Ellen White penned the following insightful scenario of what Satan sought to do in her day as well as in ours:

"The enemy of souls has sought to bring in the supposition that a great reformation was to take place among Seventh-day Adventists, and that this reformation would consist in giving up the doctrines which stand as the pillars of our faith, and engaging in a process of reorganization. Were this reformation to take place, what would result? The principles of truth that God in His wisdom has given to the remnant church, would be discarded. Our religion would be changed. The fundamental principles that have sustained the work for the last fifty years would be accounted as error. A new organization would be established. Books of a new order would be written. A system of intellectual philosophy would be introduced. The founders of this system would go into the cities, and do a wonderful work. The Sabbath of course, would be lightly regarded, as also the God who created it. Nothing would be allowed to stand in the way of the new movement. The leaders would teach that virtue is better than vice, but God being removed, they would place their dependence on human power, which, without God, is worthless. Their foundation would be built on the sand, and storm and tempest would sweep away the structure" (*Selected Messages,* 1:204-205).

In our final chapter we shall call attention to the implications of the above statement. At the moment, however, we must note the striking parallels between the above statement and the suggestions being made by advocates of the so-called *Adventism for a New Generation:*

(1) a repudiation of the doctrinal pillars of our faith;

(2) a quest for re-organization and new organizations (is this a reference to congregationalism and ecumenical alliances?);

(3) a disdain for the historic principles (Adventist pioneers' alleged "literal," "rigid," and "proof-text" method of interpretation, and the supposed "ethnocentric," "xenophobic," and "paranoic" theology of the remnant?);

(4) the introduction of intellectual philosophy (the "dynamic," "developmental," and "Christ-centered view of inspiration," and the sophisticated revision of Adventist theology to make it intellectually acceptable to the "New Generation"?);

(5) the wonderful work in the cities (the charismatic "intercessory prayer" for renewal of our "cities and communities"?);

(6) the disregard of the Sabbath (even while professing "to open many non-Adventist minds to the value and meaning of the Sabbath"?);

(7) nothing stands in the way of this new movement (perhaps, the defiant and rebellious spirit that says "I'll go my own way regardless of what the world church thinks"?);

(8) the exaltation of virtue above vice on the basis of *secular and humanistic principles,* since God is left out, and the leaders depend on their own power (echoes of "justice," "compassion," "fairness," "equality," "moral imperative," "acceptance," "love," etc.?); and,

(9) the futility of building on a foundation of sand (the lethal bankruptcy of constructing one's theological house on a foundation other than the Scriptures?).

Are we living in the days of a gathering storm, a storm which will soon sweep away any theological structure built upon the sand? If so, is this the time to encourage the *liberal left* to revise our understanding of apocalyptic books like Daniel, Revelation, and *The Great Controversy*? Probably we are now in a better position to appreciate the full implications of the series of questions we quoted in Chapter One:

"Aren't we triumphalistic in seeing ourselves as the one true church? Hasn't the Sabbath/Sunday issue, so relevant when *The Great Controversy* was written, become obsolete in today's secular society? Haven't Adventists erred in focusing on the pope while neglecting to take a stand against oppressive dictators of the 20th century? Shouldn't we concentrate on the modern 'beasts' of ethnic hatred, oppression of minorities, and abuse of the eco-system? *Perhaps apocalyptic, with its sensationalism, represents an immature stage of Christianity. Perhaps we should replace it with the gospel of love, acceptance, and forgiveness.*"[30]

Where will the Adventist church be if we replace its historic doctrines—the three angels' messages or the "everlasting gospel" (Rev 14:6-14), as we commonly refer to them—with a gospel of mere "love, acceptance and forgiveness"? Can people preach such a gospel with certainty and conviction? Will such a church grow?

The Problem of Church Growth

Certainly, the Seventh-day Adventist church is thriving worldwide—particularly in the non-industrialized parts of the world. But Adventism is baptizing more people in the developing world not because the "very minimal way of life" in these areas conditions people to accept "anything that offers them a glimmer of hope for something better." On the contrary, people in developing countries do not just accept "anything" that offers hope—such as the kinds of fables or myths that liberal scholarship presents as "objective truths." People join churches in which biblical truth is proclaimed with certainty, not with equivocation or tentativeness.

Therefore, it is a gross over-simplification to conclude that Adventism in some parts of the world is growing because "a person living in a mud hut somewhere is going to feel pretty happy about the possibility of living in mansions in heaven."[31] True happiness is not measured by whether a person lives in a mud hut or a mansion. Instead, Jesus said, "If ye know these things, happy are ye if ye do them" (John 13:17). Loving obedience to Christ is a major secret of church growth. For, *when Jesus lives in the heart, living in a hut offers more joy than the "joy" of more—earthly mansions, possessions, position, power, etc.*

A more accurate reason why churches are growing in certain parts of the world is that the believers, teachers, evangelists, pastors, and leaders in these places still uphold the Bible's full inspiration, absolute trustworthiness, and final authority in all issues of doctrine and lifestyle.[32] But a theological house constructed upon shifting sand cannot stand; neither can it attract people who are seeking a church home as a place of refuge.

This is what is at stake in the quarrel between higher criticism and the historic Adventist plain reading of Scripture. It is this issue that has divided North American scholars between liberals and conservatives. It is this issue that has divided theological faculties. And if more and more students, church members, and leaders adopt the defective methodology of higher criticism, it becomes more likely that the worldwide church will be polarized theologically, not culturally. In other words, if the trend continues, what will divide "the church of the West" from "the rest of the church" will be their respective attitudes toward Scripture's authority and interpretation.

One writer recently stumbled onto this truth: "The vote refusing the NAD permission to ordain its women is the real 'tip of the iceberg,' the iceberg being the clash between *scriptural literalism,* a view largely held in the developing world—Africa and much of South America and Inter-America, and a *principle-based approach* to Scripture followed in areas where the church has matured for a century and a half."[33]

Perception or Deception?

Our church faces a hermeneutical crisis—a crisis that threatens to divide our worldwide family by undermining the very basis of our unique identity and mission. Challenging our biblically-established doctrines is no indication of spiritual maturity or scholarly enlightenment. Rather, it could signal the end-time departure from the faith which the Bible writers and Ellen G. White prophesied (2 Tim 4:3-4; Amos 8:11-12; cf. *Selected Messages,* 1:204-205).

We have shown that those who reject the historic Adventist approach in favor of the contemporary liberal approaches will ultimately deny the full authority of the Bible. When this happens, they will be faced with two choices: "the authority of the church expressed through its [liberal] theologians and/or administrators, and the assumed authority of the Spirit expressed through charismatic renewal. In the former, the theological or administrative elite determine for the church what parts of the Bible it may take as authoritative Scripture. In the latter, religious experience and excitement, rather than the objective written Word of God, determine the faith. The first leads to a Catholic understanding of the nature of the church, the second to a Pentecostal understanding."[34]

Bible-believing Adventists need to be aware of what is at stake in this new papalism of the scholar, administrator, or "charismatic" interpreter. "Satan is constantly endeavoring to attract attention to man in the place of God. He leads the people to look to bishops, to pastors, to professors of theology, as their guides, instead of searching the Scriptures to learn their duty for themselves. Then, by controlling the minds of these leaders, he can influence the multitudes according to his will" (*The Great Controversy,* p. 595).

Thus, the reading of Scripture through the hermeneutical lenses of the historical-critical method is not evidence of true insight or clear *perception* but rather an omen of blindness or *deception.* Ellen White anticipated our times when she wrote:

"In our day, as of old, the vital truths of God's word are set aside for human theories and speculations. Many professed ministers of the gospel do not accept the whole Bible as the inspired word. One wise man rejects one portion; another questions another part. They set up their judgment as superior to the Word; and the Scripture which they do teach rests upon their own authority. Its divine authenticity is destroyed. Thus seeds of infidelity are sown broadcast; for the people become confused and know not what to believe. . . . Christ rebuked these practices in His day. He taught that the word of God was to be understood by all. He pointed to the Scriptures as of unquestionable authority, and we should do the same. The Bible is to be presented as the word of the infinite God, as the end of all controversy and the foundation of all faith" (*Christ's Object Lessons*, p. 39).

Let us not be misled by fancy labels that sound good—labels like: "historic method," "principle approach," "contextual approach," "casebook approach," "progressive approach," "dynamic approach," "developmental approach," "matured approach," "Christ-centered approach," etc. Neither should we be misled by the suggestion that because "a majority of our scholars" hold a particular view, that view must be right. Like the Bereans of old, we must *search the Scriptures* to see whether the views they hold are biblically sound. And having ascertained the truth for ourselves, whenever new views are urged upon us we must reply in the words of Martin Luther: "Unless I am convinced by the plain testimony of Scripture, I shall not recant."

Since the Bible is the only dependable source of knowledge about our Savior Jesus Christ and His plan of salvation, we should heed this inspired counsel: "Brethren, cling to your Bible, as it reads, and stop your criticisms in regard to its validity, and obey the Word, and not one of you will be lost" (*Selected Messages*, 1:18).

In the above statement we find the two hermeneutical options facing the church: taking the Bible "as it reads" (the historic Adventist plain reading of Scripture) and "criticisms" (liberalism's historical-*critical* methods). The choice we make will result in either clear *perception* or blind *deception* regarding the biblical message.

The relevance of the above counsel will become clearer in the next chapter, "Contending for the Word." But as we conclude the current chapter we would echo Ellen White's plea: "Brethren, cling to your Bible, as it reads, and stop your criticisms in regard to its validity, and obey the Word, and not one of you will be lost" (*Selected Messages*, 1:18).

NOTES

1. George R. Knight, "Proving More Than Intended," *Ministry,* March 1996, p. 28. See also our comment on p. 79, note 5.

2. Reinder Bruinsma, *Seventh-day Adventist Attitudes Toward Roman Catholicism 1844-1965* (Berrien Springs, Mich.: Andrews University Press, 1994), pp. 295, 301-302.

3. Steven G. Daily, *Adventism for a New Generation* (Portland/Clackamas, Ore.: Better Living Publishers, 1993). Endorsements of his book by nine "Christian thought-leaders" are found on the back cover (see note 26). The author is listed in *Adventist Today* as an editorial advisor.

4. Ibid., pp. 314, 202.

5. Ibid., pp. 200, 194.

6. Ibid., p. 20. He writes elsewhere: "When God's people catch a vision of what it really means to keep the Sabbath, they will occasionally or regularly take part of a Sabbath day . . . by visiting,

helping, *or voluntarily cleaning whatever that person's needs call for"* (ibid., p. 148). Cf. pp. 140-148, where he describes how, week after week each Sabbath, he led students in the Adventist university to clean the streets, paint houses and lay foundations.

7. Ibid., p. 36.

8. Ibid., pp. 77-78, 47.

9. Ibid., pp. 296-297.

10. Ibid., p. 297.

11. Ibid., p. 298.

12. Ibid., p. 298.

13. Ibid., pp. 312-313. Daily writes: "Such an ecumenical movement will restore integrity to the word *church.* This movement is directly connected to the 'Charismatic renewal' that is impacting mainline churches, and is based primarily on the shared faith, hope, and love of ministers and church members from various denominations who have come together in a spirit of intercession to pray for their respective cities. This kind of intercessory prayer ministry is very developed in some cities and virtually non-existent in others. But no one can deny that it is the spoken will of Christ (John 17:21). My prayer is that Adventism will be on the cutting edge of this movement, rather than occupying its usual position at the end of the tail" (ibid., p. 313).

14. Ibid., pp. 312-313, 172-173.

15. Ibid., p. 313.

16. Ibid., pp. 315, 314. Daily approvingly cites a charismatic work: "In his spiritually-anointed book, *The House of the Lord,* Francis Frangipane calls upon all Christians, including Adventists, *to quit debating their differences* and to focus on the essentials of Christ, the Holy Spirit, intercessory prayer and a shared love for their cities and communities. . . . It is the churches and movements that are willing to lose their lives, or give up their own identities, for the kingdom of God that will find their lives and be used by God to bring the greatest blessings to humanity. When we are willing to let go of our own future, our own security, our own tendency to engage in self-preservation, we will be ready to receive the remnant promise" (ibid., pp. 314-315).

17. For a Seventh-day Adventist assessment of the ecumenical movement, see Bert B. Beach, *Ecumenism: Boon or Bane?* (Washington, D.C.: Review and Herald, 1974), 283-292.

18. *Adventism for a New Generation,* pp. 315-316.

19. Ibid., p. 314.

20. Ibid., pp. 315-316, emphasis supplied.

21. Steven Daily, "The Irony of Adventism: The Role of Ellen White and Other Adventist Women in Nineteenth Century America," (D.Min. project, School of Theology at Claremont, 1985), p. 316.

22. *Adventism for a New Generation,* pp. 77-78.

23. See the discussion of "inspiration" in his "Towards An Adventist Theology of Liberation," a paper presented to the Association of Adventist Women and the Association of Adventist Forums in Loma Linda, California, on March 18, 1984, and reproduced as appendix B in his "The Irony of Adventism: The Role of Ellen White and Other Adventist Women in Nineteenth Century America," pp. 327, 317. He acknowledges that his views on "inspiration" and "hermeneutics" are informed by the neo-orthodox scholar Krister Stendahl and the feminist theologian Elizabeth Schüssler-Fiorenza (ibid., pp. 315-318).

24. Refer to our chapter 4 for a detailed discussion. Notice that a similar statement has come from a group who identify themselves as "Evangelical Adventists": "While early Adventists were clearly committed to scripture, they did not understand how to interpret it. They often used a proof-text method of biblical interpretation to defend their distinctive beliefs and consequently missed the overall, uniting purpose of scripture as a revelation of God's salvation" (M. Rader, D. van Denburgh, and L. Christoffel, "Evangelical Adventism: Clinging to the Cross," *Adventist Today,* January/February, 1994, p. 16). The origin of Evangelical Adventism goes back to the crisis occasioned by Desmond Ford and to the paper *Evangelica,* which was published in the years after Glacier View Conference in 1980.

25. Steven Daily, "The Irony of Adventism: The Role of Ellen White and Other Adventist Women in Nineteenth Century America," p. 327. Elsewhere he asserts that the "historical research" of men

like Ronald Numbers, Walter Rea, and Don McAdams "has completely revolutionized the church's understanding of Ellen White's inspiration." See his "How Readest Thou: The Higher Criticism Debate in Protestant America And Its Relationship to Seventh-day Adventism and the Writings of Ellen White, 1885-1925" (M.A. Thesis, Loma Linda University, 1982), p. 132; cf. pp. 133-135.

26.   The statement is attributed to V. Bailey Gillespie, coordinator of *Valuegenesis* Research Project. The nine recommendations for *Adventism for a New Generation,* found on the back cover of the volume, range from qualified approval to enthusiastic recommendation. Besides Gillespie, the other endorsers are: F. Lynn Mallery (a conference president); William Loveless (senior pastor of an Adventist university church); Gary B. Swanson (editor of *Collegiate Quarterly*); Desmond Ford (evangelist of *Good News Unlimited*); Ted Wick (the Director of Youth Ministries of a Division), Don Hawley (author of *Set Free*), and Randal Wisbey (director of the Youth Resource Center at an Adventist university). Significantly, Tony Campolo, a leading Evangelical scholar, endorses *Adventism for a New Generation* in these words: "Throughout the book I felt the author was reaching out to people like me and telling us that he wants to be our brother in Christ and to join hands with us in the ongoing work of missions and evangelism. . . . *It is the best book I have read explaining Seventh-day Adventism*" (emphasis supplied).

27.   Reinder Bruinsma, *Seventh-day Adventist Attitudes Toward Roman Catholicism 1844-1965,* pp. 295, 301-302. See also, Rolf J. Pöhler, "Change in Seventh-day Adventist Theology: A Study of the Problem of Doctrinal Development" (Th.D. dissertation, Andrews University, 1995). Jack Provonsha, *A Remnant in Crisis* (Hagerstown, Md.: Review and Herald, 1995); Alden Thompson, *Inspiration: Hard Questions Honest Answers* (Hagerstown, Md.: Review and Herald, 1991); Kai J. Arasola, *The End of Historicism: Millerite Hermeneutic of Time Prophecies in the Old Testament* (Uppsala: Kai J. Arasola, 1990); Gerhard van Wyk, "A Practical Theological Perspective on Adventist Theology and Contextualization," *Journal of Adventist Thought in Africa* 1/1 (November 1995):132-149.

28.   Within the context of what William Johnsson's book title captures as "The Fragmenting of Adventism" (Pacific Press, 1995), *Adventist Today* (January-February, 1993) has also presented "A Gathering of Adventism" comprised of "mainstream," "historic," "evangelical," and "progressive" Adventisms. Even *Christianity Today,* the largest Evangelical magazine in the U.S.A., identifies some distinct factions within Adventism—traditionalist, evangelical, liberal, and charismatic—and suggests that these are indications of "an identity crisis" in the church (Kenneth Samples, "The Recent Truth about Seventh-day Adventism," *Christianity Today,* February 5, 1990, pp. 18-19).

29.   Readers will greatly benefit from Lewis R. Walton's recent *Omega II: God's Church at the Brink* (Glenville, Calif.: [Lewis R. Walton], 1995).

30.   Beatrice Neall, "Apocalyptic—Who Needs It?" *Spectrum* 23/1 (May 1993):46, emphasis supplied.

31.   Frank Knittel, "Observations of a President, Pastor, Entrepreneur," *Adventist Today,* November-December, 1995, p. 11. Knittel was responding to ethicist Jim Walter's question, "Why do you think it is that Adventism baptizes so many converts in the underdeveloped world, and so few in developed nations?" His full response is: "In the underdeveloped world the people have a very minimal way of life. Anything that offers them a glimmer of hope for something better is attractive. A person living in a mud hut somewhere is going to feel pretty happy about the possibility of living in mansions in heaven"! Is he suggesting that people living in the "underdeveloped world" will fall for "anything"? Or that "happiness" can be measured by whether a person lives in a "hut" or an earthly "mansion"?

32.   It is not without significance that Dean M. Kelley's book, *Why Conservative Churches Are Growing* (New York: Harper and Row, 1972), documents that the churches which grow are those with conservative tenor.

33.   Jim Walters, "General Conference Delegates Say NO on Women's Ordination," *Adventist Today,* July-August, 1995, p. 13, emphasis supplied.

34.   C. Raymond Holmes, "The Future of Adventist Bible Interpretation," *Adventists Affirm* 5/1 (Spring 1991):31.

Chapter Six

Contending for the Word

In the previous chapter we showed how some Seventh-day Adventists are *departing from the Word*. But this deviation from the Word cannot be fully understood unless it is seen in its total cosmic framework. As we suggested at the end of that chapter, skepticism towards the full inspiration, trustworthiness, and the sole authority of Scripture is a vital phase in the enemy's end-time strategy to lead God's people away from the pillars of their faith and especially from the Spirit of Prophecy.

The Enemy's Plan. "'It is Satan's plan to weaken the faith of God's people in the *Testimonies*,' 'Satan knows how to make his attacks. He works upon minds to excite jealousy and dissatisfaction toward those at the head of the work. The gifts are next questioned; then, of course, they have but little weight, and instruction given through vision is disregarded.' 'Next follows skepticism in regard to the vital points of our faith, the pillars of our position, *then doubt as to the Holy Scriptures*, and then the downward march to perdition. When the *Testimonies*, which were once believed, are doubted and given up, Satan knows the deceived ones will not stop at this; and he redoubles his efforts till he launches them into open rebellion, which becomes incurable and ends in destruction'" (*Testimonies for the Church*, 5:672, emphasis supplied).

Disregard of the Bible. "The agencies which will unite against truth and righteousness in this contest are now actively at work. God's holy word, which has been handed down to us at such a cost of suffering and blood, is but little valued. The Bible is within the reach of all, but there are few who really accept it as the guide of life. Infidelity prevails to an alarming extent, not in the world merely, but in the church. Many have come to deny doctrines which are the very pillars of the Christian faith. The great facts of creation as presented by the inspired writers, the fall of man, the atonement, and the perpetuity of the law of God, are practically rejected, either wholly or in part, by a large share of the professedly Christian world. Thousands who pride themselves upon their wisdom and independence regard it an evidence of weakness to place implicit confidence in the Bible; they think it a proof of superior talent and learning to cavil at the Scriptures and to spiritualize and explain away their most important truths. Many ministers are teaching their people, and many professors and teachers are instructing their students, that the law of God has been changed or abrogated; and those who regard its requirements as still valid, to be literally obeyed, are thought to be deserving only of ridicule or contempt" (*The Great Controversy,* pp. 582-583).

The Need to Contend for the Faith

Inspired Warnings. The apostle Paul warned: "Now the Spirit speaketh expressly, that in the latter times some shall depart from the faith, giving heed to seducing spirits, and doctrines of devils; speaking lies in hypocrisy; having their conscience seared with a hot iron" (1 Tim 4:1, 2). Ellen G. White had this text in mind when she explained the reason for her published writings.

She wrote: "I am instructed that the Lord, by His infinite power, has preserved the right hand of His messenger for more than half a century, in order that the truth may be written out as He bids me write it for publication, in periodicals and books. Why?— *Because if it were not thus written out, when the pioneers in the faith shall die, there would be many, new in the faith, who would sometimes accept as messages of truth teachings that contain erroneous sentiments and dangerous fallacies. Sometimes that which men teach as 'special light' is in reality specious error, which, as tares sown among the wheat, will spring up and produce a baleful harvest. And errors of this sort will be entertained by some until the close of this earth's history"* (*This Day with God,* p. 126, emphasis supplied).

Given the strange winds of doctrine blowing in our day, can we doubt that our generation could be witnessing the predicted end-time departure from the faith? Skepticism abounds with regard to vital pillars of our faith; doubts are created about the Holy Scriptures; our critics despise the historic plain reading of Scripture as a "literal," "rigid," "proof-text" or "Fundamentalist" method; "books of a new order" are being published and distributed; doctrinal tares are being broadcast by voice and by pen. And at a time when we most need the *Testimonies,* we are being told that Mrs. White's messages were culturally conditioned; if relevant at all, they are suitable only for devotional purposes. These prevailing conditions demand a courageous, resolute response.

Contending for the Word. The admonition of Jude, the brother of our Lord Jesus Christ, is particularly applicable to our times: "Dear friends, although I was very eager to write to you about the salvation we share, I felt I had to write and urge you to *contend for the faith* that was once for all entrusted to the saints. For certain men whose condemnation was written about long ago have secretly slipped in among you. They are godless men, who change the grace of our God into a license for immorality and deny Jesus Christ our only Sovereign and Lord" (Jude 3, 4 NIV).

Ellen White stated in a similar context: "My message to you is: No longer consent to listen without protest to the perversion of truth. Unmask the pretentious sophistries which, if received, will lead ministers and physicians and medical missionary workers to ignore the truth. Every one is now to stand on his guard. God calls upon men and women to take their stand under the blood-stained banner of Prince Emmanuel. I have been instructed to warn our people; for many are in danger of receiving theories and sophistries that undermine the foundation pillars of the faith" (*Selected Messages,* 1:196-197).

She asked: "What are God's servants doing to raise the barrier of a 'Thus saith the Lord' against this evil? The enemy's agents are working unceasingly to prevail against the truth.[1] *Where are the faithful guardians of the Lord's flocks? Where are His watchmen? Are they standing on the high tower, giving the danger signal, or are they allowing the peril to pass unheeded?"* (ibid., p. 194, emphasis supplied).

Responding to the Call. The late Enoch de Oliveira (1924-1992), a church administrator from Brazil, clearly understood what was at stake in the hermeneutical crisis. Prior to his retirement, he served as president of the South American Division (1975-1980) and vice-president of the General Conference (1980-1990) during a period that saw major theological turmoil in the church. One of his lasting contributions to the worldwide Seventh-day Adventist church was his great courage in *contending for the Word* against the inroads of theological liberalism.

The insightful address that follows, "A Trojan Horse Within the Church," was the keynote sermon Elder Oliveira delivered at the International Convention of the Adventist Theological Society held in Indianapolis, June 28-30, 1990, just prior to the General Conference session. Although conditions in the church now may differ somewhat from those in 1990, this sermon aptly summarizes the concerns undergirding this book. It may also be read as Oliveira's farewell message to the worldwide church; two years after delivering this message, he was laid to his rest.[2]

"A Trojan Horse Within the Church"[3]

In one of his famous epics, Homer describes the clever device the Greeks employed to conquer the city of Troy during the Trojan war.

To enable the Greeks to enter the legendary city by stealth, the master carpenter, Epeius, built a huge hollow wooden horse. According to Homer, 100,000 soldiers besieged Troy. The ten-year siege ended when the Greeks concealed some soldiers in the horse and then left it behind as they pretended to withdraw.

Despite the warning of Laocoön, Sinon persuaded the Trojans to move the horse inside the city walls. At night the Greek army returned and the soldiers who had hidden inside the horse opened the city gates to their comrades. In this way Troy was invaded successfully and destroyed.

Although the war between the Greeks and the city of Troy is generally considered a historical fact, the episode dealing with the Trojan horse has been considered a mythological tale. Nonetheless, from this epic we can derive some timely illustrations that are applicable to the situation our church finds itself in today.

For many years the Seventh-day Adventist church succeeded in bravely and tenaciously resisting the fearful assaults of the enemy. The walls of the "holy city" remained impregnable. But in his determination to conquer and destroy God's church, the prince of this world has undertaken to employ clever and deadly secret weapons.

"There is nothing that the great deceiver fears so much," wrote Ellen G. White, "as that we shall become acquainted with his devices" (*The Great Controversy*, p. 516).

After many attempts to conquer the "city of God" by applying the same kind of deceitful action employed by the Greeks, the great adversary has been able to obtain his ends by surreptitiously introducing the Trojan horse of liberalism within the walls of Zion.

Now that liberalism has become operative within our church, we perceive how vulnerable we can be to the assaults of Satan. As a church we have been inclined to believe that our greatest danger of being defeated by the powers of evil would come from without. While we may be able to perceive clearly from the walls of Zion what Satan is doing to conquer and destroy the church, we do not seem able to do much about standing firmly against the evils that are developing insidiously within our midst. Ellen White warns: "We have more to fear from within than from without" (*Selected Messages*, 1:122).

Liberals Are Not Bad People

Those who are promoting liberalism in our ranks are not "bad" people. They are committed believers. Many of them exhibit the beauty of Christian virtues in their lives. Most of them love the church. They would like to share the faith and certainties of our forefathers, but in the honesty of their hearts, they do not have them. They are unable to see the uniqueness of our message, the distinctiveness of our identity, the eschatological dimension of our hope, or the urgency of our mission. Representing a wide spectrum of religious thought, they attempt to reinterpret traditional theological Seventh-day Adventist thinking by dressing some of our old doctrines in what appear to them to be new and attractive semantic garments.

Why are these people advocating liberal views among us? Why are they so enthusiastically playing the role of apostles of change in our theological system?

First of all, it seems to me, they are eager to discard the "cult" label that has been used so widely to characterize Seventh-day Adventism. They long to see our religious movement become a part of what they consider mainstream Christianity. In their endeavor to attain religious "respectability," they suggest the reinterpretation of some historical views of our theology that they believe are Biblically indefensible.

Although accepting some aspects of our distinctiveness, such as the Sabbath and our health principles, they believe that the time has come for revision in our theological system. In fostering such a revision, some feel uncomfortable with the "remnant" concept as understood by the founders of our message. They believe that all "sectarian mentality" should be rejected as presumptuous and arrogant.

Other liberals, in their endeavor to make our theology more "relevant," question the integrity of the sanctuary doctrine and unite their voices with those of our opponents in this matter. They explain the two-phase ministry of Christ in the heavenly sanctuary as a face-saving device created by Edson, Crosier, and others to bail our pioneers out of the Millerite failure.

There are those who are alarmed about what seems to them to be excessive borrowing by Ellen White of material from a variety of sources. Misguided by distorted ideas about the way inspiration works, they are willing to challenge the validity of her claims, rejecting her prophetic authority.

Some liberals define our eschatology as a by-product of nineteenth-century North American culture and, as such, as deserving of substantial reformulation. They insist that after 145 years of proclamation we can no longer preserve the fervent expectation that permeated the church in its formative years.

Liberal scientists in the church insist that the creation doctrine should be reevaluated in the context of current scientific information and hypotheses.

According to the February 5, 1990 issue of *Christianity Today,* the obsession for change in the Seventh-day Adventist ranks had its beginnings in the 1950s and 1960s, when our students in much larger numbers than before began to attend non-Adventist seminaries and universities seeking advanced degrees. Some of these students, in spite of unfavorable circumstances, were able to preserve their religious experience and came forth strengthened in their convictions. Others, influenced by modern Biblical criticism and liberal theology, reshaped their beliefs.

What Is Being Gained by These Attempts at Change?

What are we gaining from the liberal attempts to make our message more "palatable" to the world? When so many seeds of doubt, uncertainty, and strife are sown, what else can be expected? Liberalism is reaping what it has sown. It sowed unbelief and it is harvesting apostasies.

During the early 1980s, an unprecedented number of ministers and lay people left the church in Australia and New Zealand. During the 1970s our church in those two countries lost one believer for every three who came in. In 1981, after a particularly notable attempt to effect a liberal change, the percentage of loss rose to 46 percent. It peaked at 63 per cent in 1982 and then settled down at approximately 50 percent—a loss of one member for every two believers. (See *Australasian Record,* Oct. 28, 1989.)

We must not remain indifferent to such staggering losses. We must not minimize the tragic consequences of our internal confrontations caused by new theologies. The casualties are thousands of perplexed souls who, spiritually confused, are departing from us, throwing away their confidence in the validity of our message. They have lost the landmarks of our faith and no longer have a clear understanding of what we stand for.

The following set of North American Division statistics reflects the consequences of ongoing theological and other attempts to change our beliefs in the United States and Canada:

Years	Annual Growth Rates
1931-1940	4.4%
1941-1950	3.1%
1951-1960	2.9%
1961-1970	2.8%
1971-1980	3.2%
1981-1988	2.3%

What is the message in these numbers? Oscar Wilde, famous dramatist of the past century, with inimitable irony affirmed that "there are three kinds of lies in the world: common lies, small lies, and statistics." Thus Wilde underlined the fact that statistics may deceive and lead us to wrong conclusions. But even though statistics are susceptible of incorrect interpretation, we dare not minimize their importance in an analysis of the crisis that we face. They can help us understand the gravity of our problems.

It is true that we can be deceived by numbers and conclude that in spite of what seems apparent the North American Division is still growing. But it is not growing. According to reliable sources, 30 to 35 percent of our believers no longer attend church. With this decrease in attendance has come a decrease in offerings. Sharp cutbacks in church budgets have been approved. Enrollment in our schools is declining. Institutions have been closed. We are in the process of trimming down our church's operations and reducing our task forces. The market for our books is shrinking. Denominational periodicals have been merged and yet their circulation has still dropped. We have come to a time of financial restraints, with most conferences cutting back on their ministerial forces. These are inevitable consequences of what has happened in theological areas.

After so many seeds of doubt and uncertainty have been sown within the church by those who are obsessed with the desire to reinterpret our theology, after so many years of theological disputation, what else should we expect? We are witnessing the inevitable harvest of liberalism. When unbelief is sown, the harvest is bound to be apostasy.

After its insidious penetration within the walls of God's city, liberalism in its various shapes and forms has succeeded in opening the gates of the church to the invasion of such other evils as pluralism, secularism, humanism, materialism, futurism, and preterism.

Pluralism

To diffuse the polarization we are facing, some articulate scholars suggest the official adoption of theological pluralism, the acceptance of peaceful coexistence of conflicting, even opposing, views among us.

"On fundamental beliefs, unity; on non-essentials, liberty; in everything, love," is the popular dictum that inspires pluralistic scholars in their appeal for flexibility and openness. But who is going to determine what is essential and what is negotiable? Individuals, independent ministries, theological societies, the annual council, or the church as a whole under the guidance of the Holy Spirit? Would we be able to retain our self understanding as God's last prophetic movement, if we were to fragment our beliefs by including in them divergent schools of thought?

We need theological unity in our preaching and in our publications, but above all, we need unity in the theological departments of our colleges and universities. I submit that no school of theology, under pluralistic influences, shaken by the confrontation of ideas, is able to produce preachers with strong convictions. Without preachers having certainty, there is no power in their preaching.

The successful spread of the gospel over the Mediterranean world in the days of the apostles threatened Christian unity. People of widely divergent backgrounds were baptized, bringing into the church some of the popular religious concepts of the age. Thus, there was a real danger that the teachings of the church would be affected by syncretism. Aware of this danger, Paul exhorted the Ephesians to maintain unity. See Eph 4:4-6.

Addressing "the churches of Galatia," the apostle expressed his regret for the way the Galatians, under pluralistic influences, changed their minds and turned away from the grace of Christ to a "different" gospel (Gal 1:6). Was Paul being narrow-minded in his appeal for unity? After all, those Jewish-Christians certainly preached salvation through Christ. They never denied, as far as we know, that it was necessary to believe in Jesus as Messiah and Saviour. Why then was Paul so vehement in his opposition to this Jewish-Christian preaching? Because the Judaizers insidiously distorted the gospel of Christ, throwing the believers into a state of mental and spiritual confusion. At the real risk of being labeled intransigent, Paul exhorted the Galatians to pay no attention to those messengers who, claiming ecclesiastical authority, were disrupting the peace and unity that had existed among the saints.

Let's Learn from Methodist Experience

Methodism in our day is known for its wide latitude of beliefs. Its clergy have freedom to subscribe to different schools of Bible interpretation. Attempts to define basic Methodist doctrine have met much opposition, and Methodist theology has become surprisingly divorced from its own tradition. Persons who want to be accepted as church members are no longer required to endorse any specific creed. To the question, "What do Methodists believe," ministers and laity respond by saying that they believe in Jesus.

Today the Methodist Church is in a steep numerical decline. "In the 1965-1975 period the United Methodist Church lost over one million members," says C. Peter Wagner, *Leading Your Church to Growth*, p. 32. And who is responsible for this sharp defection? The exodus that the Methodists are facing is not to be blamed on outside forces. The real blame lies within their church. If the Methodist Church were attacked by enemies from outside, if it were suffering persecution as a result of its endeavors to evangelize the world, there would be hope. But the world does not persecute a church that seems to stand for nothing. The Methodist Church is declining as a result of its failure to preserve its own religious heritage.

Can we learn some profitable lessons from its perplexing experience?

Preterism, Historical Criticism, and Futurism

A segment of the Seventh-day Adventist scholarly community no longer accepts the principles of prophetic interpretation that made our church what it is.

In the books of Daniel and Revelation, our pioneers found our time and our mission. Applying the historicist method of prophetic interpretation, which had been used by the majority of Christians over the centuries and which earned the subsequent endorsement of Ellen G. White, our forefathers were able to unfold the history of the long conflict between Christ and Satan. They were able to look upon themselves as an integral part of the cosmic program.

Today, however, we sense a gradual rejection of the historicist approach and a growing acceptance of the Counter Reformation schools of prophetic interpretation. Furthermore, historical-criticism does not allow for true long-range prediction. As a result, in some quarters our message has been changed and has lost its distinctiveness and its power.

Moving the fulfillment of the long-term prophecies to the end of the age (the futurist view), or relegating their significance to the distant past (the preterist view), or denying true long-term prophecy (the historical-critical view), makes the prophecies of Daniel and Revelation irrelevant and transforms the Advent-ist movement into just another denomination without power and special prophetic message.

Secularism

Another intruder that is expanding its presence within the walls of God's city is the trend known as "secularism," often defined as the organization of life as if God did not exist. Its growing influence is producing a decline in attendance, reduced commitment to Christian ideals, and an increasing tendency to view the church—any church—as obsolete and irrelevant. Professional growth and prestige, business and profits, economic status and academic attainments are overestimated, while Christian virtues are neglected, or relegated to second place.

According to Norman Blaike, American Christians today can be divided into two groups, the "supernaturalists" and the "secularists." The "supernaturalists," Blaike observes, are generally to the right theologically, while the "secularists" are to the left. The "supernaturalists," he states, prize Christian virtues, such as devotion, piety, and church commitments, while "secularists" admire tolerance, success, efficiency, and academic achievements. (See N. W. H. Blaike, "Altruism in the Professions: The Case of the Clergy," *Australia and New Zealand Journal of Sociology,* 10 [1974]:87.)

The process of secularization is affecting not only believers but also institutions. According to George Marsden, Duke University historian, the religious character of many erstwhile Christian institutions has been eclipsed with "nobody noticing and nobody seeming to mind" (*Time,* May 22, 1989).

In the past two decades we have seen Seventh-day Adventist institutions affected by substantial changes that have not all been on the plus side. Surreptitiously, secularism makes inroads that tend to eclipse the religious character of these institutions. Religious services are still held in their chapels, but they are more a form than a spiritual force.

Theological liberalism makes an immense contribution to this insidious secularism of believers and institutions by its rejection of an authoritative church, an authoritative Bible, and an authoritative body of truth. It is more than willing to accommodate religion to the spirit of the times.

Other Evils

Other evils, such as exaggerated academic freedom, the historical-critical approach to Scripture, and theistic evolution (with its very long chronology) are making their contribution to the undermining of confidence in basic beliefs and leading congregations to spiritual disaster.

It is impossible to prevent the teaching of aberrant views within the church, when the concept of academic freedom without sound confessional responsibility is accepted. Defenders of academic freedom in our midst state that we are not a creedal denomination and so every believer should be free to endorse different theological views. But we understand that if an individual is a Seventh-day Adventist, he or she should subscribe to our Fundamental Beliefs in their entirety. Otherwise, he or she ceases to be a Seventh-day Adventist.

I still remember the strong opposition manifested by some Adventist scholars when the historical-critical methodology was condemned officially by the General Conference on the basis that this method, by definition, excludes our belief in the transcendence of the Scriptures.[4]

I believe, however, that the church has the unquestionable right to decide which approach should be used by our scholars and preachers. This is our only safeguard to protect our religious heritage, which subscribes to the Reformation principle that the Bible is the infallible Word of God and its own interpreter. Theistic evolution (or progressive creationism) is a concept accepted by a growing number of scientists in our ranks. It involves the subordination and accommodation of the Scriptures to the Darwinian view of gradual evolution. Those who endorse this school of thought no longer regard key portions of the Bible as reliable sources of historical information. In taking this position they place scientific hypotheses above Scripture, making science a judge of the Word of God.

The Fifth Column

The Spanish Civil War (1936-1939) left a million dead. When the conflict seemed to be reaching its climax, General Emilio Mola commanded four columns moving toward the capital of the country. But in addition to his four columns he was counting on a fifth column, one that had entered Madrid behind its defenses, to deliver the city to him when the decisive moment arrived.

Among the lessons that history teaches us, we find the fall of empires and institutions that succumbed to internal forces. The historian Gibbon (1737-1796) ascribes the fall even of Rome to internal, not external, causes. He mentions the fourteenth-century Italian poet, Petrarch, who described the fall of Rome as follows: "Behold the remains of Rome, the shadow of its early greatness! Neither time nor the barbarians can glory in having brought about this stupendous destruction: it was accomplished by its own citizens, the most illustrious of her children."

Many civilizations have been defeated by the internal sabotage of fifth columnists. History warns us what can take place in the church. External opposition is not our worst enemy. Instead, the insidious deteriorating influences introduced by Satan, our great adversary, do the most harm.

What has been the greatest defeat suffered by the Christian church? Was it the loss of life as a result of violence, martyrdom, and torture? No. The church's greatest defeat took place when it accepted the favor of the Roman Empire and lost its purity and fervor. When the church left the catacombs, it adjusted to the splendor of the world. Satan's fifth columnists—his Trojan horse—weakened the church internally, paving the way for dilution of faith and the establishment of pseudo-Christianity.

Conclusion

The picture I have presented of the Seventh-day Adventist church can be considered bleak and dark. But in my closing remarks, I would like to present a brighter side. In spite of the problems we face today, we have many reasons to believe in the triumph of our message as long as we stay faithful to the Bible. A revival will come and our eyes will see powerful miracles of evangelism.

Our message and movement deserve to be characterized by a triumphant spirit. They are not based on "cunningly devised fables" but on the unshakable foundation of "the sure word of prophecy."

"The church may appear as about to fall, but it does not fall. It remains, while the sinners in Zion will be sifted out—the chaff separated from the precious wheat" (*Selected Messages,* 2:380).

The conviction that God guides this movement allows us to declare, without a shadow of doubt, that the fire on Seventh-day Adventist altars will never go out. The determination to win the world to Christ will motivate us in our united evangelistic program. The world will be lighted with the glory of our proclamation of the Advent hope.

NOTES

1. Ellen White has given a detailed, compelling account of the enemy's strategies in *Testimonies to Ministers,* pp. 472-475; cf. *Special Testimonies,* Series B, No. 2, pp. 5-59.

2. The *Adventist Review,* May 7, 1992, p. 6, reported his death: "Enoch Oliveira, 68, who served as a General Conference vice president from 1980 to 1990, died in Curitiba, Parana [Brazil], on April 10 [1992] after a long bout with cancer. Oliveira's ministry spanned more than 40 years. After graduating from Brazil College in 1945, Oliveira started the pastoral ministry in Curitiba, Parana. He later served as ministerial secretary of the South American Division, and as executive secretary from 1970 to 1975. In 1975 Oliveira became the first South American native to serve as president of that division. A prolific author and speaker, Oliveira penned three books, *God Is at the Helm, Year 2000—Anguish or Hope,* and *Good Morning, Lord.*"

3. Enoch de Oliveira, "A Trojan Horse Within the Church," *Journal of the Adventist Theological Society* 2/1 (1991):6-17.

4. For a detailed discussion of this issue, see chapter 4.

What is the place of the Bible in an age of theological pluralism? Are there mistakes and contradictions in the Bible? What about new Bible translations? How should we handle the alleged inconsistences in the Bible? What principles should we use to interpret the Bible?

III. RESPONSE TO THE CRISIS

Chapter Seven

Upholding the Word[1]

In our day we see an indifference, even a reluctance, on the part of some Christians to allow the Bible to address contemporary issues of faith and practice. Thus, the Bible is believed to be silent on almost every question—abortion, homosexuality, women's ordination,[2] polygamy, war, divorce and remarriage, etc. This attitude is a symptom of the theological uncertainty infecting much of Christendom.

Reflecting upon the situation in Protestant churches, a well-respected evangelical scholar remarked, "The outside observer sees us as staggering on from gimmick to gimmick and stunt to stunt like so many drunks in a fog, not knowing at all where we are or which way we should be going. Preaching is hazy; heads are muddled; hearts fret; doubts drain our strength; uncertainty paralyzes action." Moreover, Bible-believing Christians are told that "the wish to be certain is mere weakness of the flesh, a sign of spiritual immaturity."[3]

The technical name for this state of affairs is "theological pluralism." And while its advocates celebrate the "diversity" of theological views as a mark of open-mindedness, the Bible writers call it an end-time loss of faith in the Bible and its God (2 Tim 4:3-4; cf. Isa 5:21). Such erosion of the Bible's authority leads Christians to choose and accept only those parts of the Bible palatable to their taste. When this happens, the Bible is taken merely as an *inspiring booklet,* rather than an *inspired Book.*

How and why did this happen? How is it playing out in the churches? How is it affecting the attitude of Christians on issues of faith and practice? And how can Christians continue *upholding the Word* in an age of theological pluralism?

The Silence of the Bible

Over two decades ago, James D. Smart observed with great concern "the growing silence of the Scriptures" in the preaching and teaching of the church and in the consciousness of Christian people, "a silence that is perceptible even among those who are most insistent upon their devotion to the Scriptures."

Smart described a conspiracy among the various liberal and conservative factions of Christianity to reduce the Bible to a subordinate status in the church. He argued that because an open attack upon the whole Bible, or even upon a portion of it (e.g., the Old Testament), would undoubtedly have met with almost universal resistance, their strategy was to work "unobtrusively, not by any concerted plan of any faction but as the result of factors that are at work unconsciously in all of us." If successful, the conspiracy would create a situation in which most Christians would "awaken one day to find ourselves a church almost totally alienated from the Scriptures." Smart found the scheme so dangerous that he felt compelled in his book "to sound an alarm."[4]

Although Bible-believing Christians cannot agree with Smart's own liberal position on biblical authority, yet his observation on the growing silence of the Bible has merit. Until the eighteenth-century Enlightenment, the overwhelming majority of Christians affirmed faith in the full inspiration, trustworthiness, and dependability of the entire Bible as the Word of God. Since the rise of rationalism, however, various attempts have been made to silence the authority of the Bible on issues of faith and life. These have taken several forms: from (1) outright denial of the uniqueness of God's word, through (2) hesitancy to accept its teaching because of its supposed ambiguities, inconsistencies, or irrelevance to contemporary issues, to (3) reinterpretation of its teaching to accommodate unbiblical views and lifestyles.

Although some of the most creative theological minds of the century contributed to undermining faith in the Scriptures, the "conspiracy" to silence the Bible was not recently hatched by some liberals or conservatives, as Smart suggests. Actually, silencing the Bible has been Satan's master strategy all through history.

Satan's Master Strategy

Genesis 3:1-6 not only tells of the human race's fall but also describes the strategy Satan followed. Approaching Eve in the guise of a serpent, he employed a two-fold scheme to undermine the Word of God. First, he asked, "Did God really say that . . . ?" thus raising doubts about the *nature* of God's Word. This is no different from the contemporary skepticism over the inspiration of the contents of the entire Bible.

Second, Satan moved from the nature of God's Word to a methodological issue—the question of interpretation. In effect he argued, "Let's even assume that God actually said something to you. Do you think that He really *means* what He said?" This question takes different forms today: Does the Bible really teach that Christians should not lie, steal, kill, or break the Sabbath under *any* circumstances? Does the Word of God really forbid homosexuality, polygamy, abortion, the use of alcohol, or the wearing of jewelry?

In other words, the Genesis account of the fall highlights two major reasons for the erosion of biblical authority: (1) uncertainty over the *nature* of the Word of God (inspiration) and (2) uncertainty over how it should be *understood* (interpretation or hermeneutics). Mistaken views in these areas set the stage for theological pluralism. Notice how the crisis came to Adam and Eve.

The Lord explicitly stated that they would "surely die" if they disobeyed His Word. Satan countered: "You will not surely die." The two statements are contradictory and lead to different destinations. But contemporary pluralistic scholars, following the lead of Satan, maintain that both contradictory statements are true. They even pride themselves on believing that this kind of pluralism of thought is a mark of "open-mindedness"—the very lie that Satan told, when he said to Adam and Eve, "Your eyes shall be opened. . . ."

Because theologians are the architects of theological pluralism, and because it is they who have laid the foundation for the erosion of biblical authority in the various churches, we will briefly summarize the confusing voices of scholarship regarding the exact nature of the Bible's inspiration and how the Bible should be understood.

Scholars and the Word of God

Bible-believing Christians have always held that the entire Scripture, consisting of the sixty-six books of the Old and New Testaments, *is* the authoritative word of God. They believe that the Holy Spirit so guided the Bible writers that even though they employed their own words to communicate the message, what they finally put down in writing is a trustworthy and dependable account of God's message (2 Pet 1:20-21; 2 Tim 3:16). The written Word is, therefore, not merely the words of fallible men, but the Word of the living God which should be accepted, believed, and obeyed (1 Thess 2:13). But this historic Christian belief is being challenged in several ways.

Over a century ago, B. B. Warfield, one of the leading scholars who brought the issue of biblical inspiration to the forefront of discussion, quipped that "wherever five 'advanced thinkers' assemble, at least six theories as to inspiration are likely to be ventilated."[5] Conflicting positions on inspiration have led to a plurality in methods of Bible interpretation. This plurality in turn has led to the reduction of the Bible's authority, as is evident in the subtle, even ambiguous, manner in which the Bible has been described. A few examples will illustrate this shrinking authority of the Bible from an objective *Book* to a subjective *booklet*.

New Views on the Word of God. For instance, some scholars, following the influential Swiss theologian Karl Barth, hold that the Bible only *contains* the Word of God or that it only only *becomes* the Word of God to individuals when it grips their hearts. In this view, unless the Bible "becomes" the word of God to the interpreter or reader, it is only the word of fallible human beings. This belief, known as neo-orthodoxy, might well be described as the *"potential* Word of God" position.

Other scholars teach that not every part of the Bible is inspired. In their estimation some sections reflect the mistaken opinions of the Bible writers. Not accepting the Bible in its entirety as inspired, they use higher critical methods to determine which parts are accurate or true and what, if anything, some portions of the Bible can teach us about the beliefs and history of the times.

These theologians would see the Bible as either a *partial* Word of God (if the alleged mistakes in the Bible are counted as substantial), or they would treat the Bible as *primarily* the Word of God (if the alleged inaccuracies are deemed few). But in either case, based on their theories of inspiration and interpretation, these scholars reject the Bible as entirely God's authoritative Word, dependable and trustworthy in all of its teachings. They accept only the portions of Scripture that "make sense" to them or which support positions they already hold. In so doing, they reduce the Bible from an inspired Book to an inspiring booklet—the latter referring to those portions they consider worthy of God's inspiring activity.

Catchy Phrases. Theologians use well-crafted phrases to express their revised ideas of biblical authority. For example, one English theologian has suggested the phrase *"Scripture as a whole"* instead of *"the whole Scripture"*; another person proposed the expression, *"biblical authorization"* rather than *"biblical authority"*; other scholars believe that the Scriptures provide only a *"biblical direction"* (or trajectory, flow, or plot, as in a play) and not necessarily a *"biblical directive."* One ecumenical document described the Bible as possessing a *"normative priority,"* but not in the sense of *"normative supremacy."*[6] John Shelby Spong, the Episcopal bishop of Newark, understands the Bible as *"a historic narrative of the journey of our religious forbears,"* not *"a literal road map to reality."*[7] None of the above subtle phrases ascribes full authority or normative role to the whole Bible as the Word of God.

Some otherwise Bible-believing scholars are finding these new ideas on the Bible appealing. For instance, one prominent evangelical scholar suggested that when Christians approach the Bible, they must "look to it with an expectation of finding God's sure word in it." He urged readers of the Bible to "listen in faith *for* the Word of God in these human words . . . in spite of all its [the Bible's human] limitations."[8] The implication is that the Bible is not the Word of God but only contains the Word of God.

This view has found liturgical expression in some churches where the traditional expression before the reading of the Scriptures, "Let us listen *to* the Word of God," has been replaced by the statement, "Let us listen *for* the word of God." Another spin-off of this approach is found in some schools of missiology and contextual theology which attempt to isolate the cultural and supracultural elements from Scripture. Thus, one evangelical theologian asserts that the Bible is an *inspired classic casebook,* a collection of case studies portraying and interpreting instances of divine-human encounter;[9] or, as one Adventist scholar promotes, the Bible is a *casebook,* as distinguished from a *codebook.*[10]

Impact on the Bible

Each of the above discordant notes within scholarly circles is a sophisticated challenge to the historic Christian view of the inspiration and authority of the Bible. And each of them employs, for the study of the Scriptures, some modified version of the historical-critical method of interpretation—a method which masquerades as "scientific" but which in actuality is a pagan ideology.[11] When scholars pass the Bible through this critical shredding machine, what remains is a Bible bruised, battered, and torn to pieces.

Fragmented Text. Roman Catholic scholar Sandra M. Schneiders' evaluation of the historical-critical approach to the Bible may be equally applicable to most of the contemporary approaches to the Word of God. She noted that over the last century, "scholars seemed to be caught in an infinite historical regress, tracing the ever more remote explanation of the ever more fragmented text into an ever receding antiquity that was ever less relevant to the concerns of the contemporary believer."[12]

Spiritual Emptiness. According to one knowledgeable Adventist scholar, "These methods raise all sorts of questions about how we got the text but say nothing about the truths it contains. It is like a hungry man who sits down to banquet and only dissects the food, probing down to the plate, cogitating on how each item may have arrived on the dish, but who eats nothing and leaves empty."[13]

Loss of Faith. As a result of the doubts being raised on many Bible passages, 1) preachers no longer preach with conviction on any subject; 2) teachers are tentative in their teaching of Bible doctrine; 3) leaders hesitate to make decisions on the basis of the Bible; and 4) lay people are discouraged from reading, studying, and meditating upon the Word of God. Saddest of all, the ensuing famine for the Word of God (see Amos 8:11-12) has led many to lose their faith in Jesus Christ, the One to whom all Scripture points (John 5:39; Luke 24:25-27).

This failure to find Jesus Christ can best be appreciated if we return to the earlier analogy of the person who sits down to a banquet: "The starving man sits down to the banquet once more. This time he does not probe into the different items on the plate, nor does he try to speculate on how these items got onto the plate, nor does he try to figure out the cook's intention in choosing the items and why he arranged them as they are. Rather, he comes to the food to see what he can add, by way of thinking, to make the food come alive, to give it meaning. He realizes that he is a co-cook and must apply his human reason to give the real meaning to this scrumptious feast. He comes to force onto this cooking his cultural ideas of cooking. After much thought he believes that he has added significantly to the meaning of the food. With that he gets up and leaves— empty once more. He may claim to be liberated by the process, but he remains unfed. Why? *He ignored the cook who handed him the plate.*"[14]

Ellen G. White anticipated this sad situation: "The work of 'higher criticism,' in dissecting, conjecturing, reconstructing, is destroying faith in the Bible as a divine revelation; it is robbing God's word of power to control, uplift and inspire human lives" (*Education,* p. 227). The tragedy is that theological pluralism hails this spiritual blindness as a sign of open-mindedness and scholarly enlightenment!

Impact on the Churches

The doubts which scholars have created regarding the Word of God have seriously undermined the confidence of average church members in the Bible. Somehow, they have come to believe that the Bible is so full of problems that only the learned scholars can understand its true meaning. This belief in the alleged obscurity of the Bible is precisely what Roman Catholicism advanced to argue for the infallibility of the pope. If ordinary church members cannot understand the Bible, they need an infallible pope to interpret it for them.

Papalism of Scholars. Therefore, to believe in the obscurity of the Bible is to accept a new form of papalism—the infallibility of scholars, to whom believers must go for biblical answers. The sixteenth-century reformers rightly rejected this position on the grounds that papalism replaces the Holy Spirit, Christ's appointed Teacher of the church (John 16:13ff.), with a fallible human being. To put it differently, this new papalism of scholars denies that the Holy Spirit is always available to help anyone who is humbly seeking to understand His inspired Word.

Bible-believing Christians need to be aware of what is at stake in this new papalism. "Satan is constantly endeavoring to attract attention to man in the place of God. He leads the people to look to bishops, to pastors, to professors of theology, as their guides, instead of searching the Scriptures to learn their duty for themselves. Then, by controlling the minds of these leaders, he can influence the multitudes according to his will" (*The Great Controversy,* p. 595).

Regrettably, uncertainty over the Bible's authority has trickled down to almost every level of the church's life. We see this subtle shift from the inspired Book to an inspiring booklet being played out in many ways:

Practice of Laymembers. Besides the fact that not many people spend time these days studying and meditating on the Word of God, a casual glance will reveal that fewer and fewer of our church members even bring their Bibles to church; when they do, they rarely open them. One reason may be that the Bibles are seldom used in the churches. For instance, during the Sabbath school Bible study hour, many teachers read more from the lesson quarterly than from the Bible itself. Not too long ago, an editor of the *Adventist Review* observed: "Too often I find that what passes for Bible study in many Sabbath school classes is little more than a rehash of familiar sayings, personal opinion, and Ellen White quotations. It isn't *Bible* study, but simply comments *about* the Bible. . . . Our 'lesson study' has the guise of Bible study, but it isn't. It is more a study of the Sabbath school lesson quarterly than the Bible."[15]

Also, during Sabbath school time, when the activities for the day are running late, the Bible study period of the Sabbath school often is reduced to make time for the seemingly "more important" programs. In some instances, the weekly Sabbath school Bible study lessons are ignored, the leaders choosing instead to use the time for "more relevant contemporary issues." These things reveal our attitudes toward the place of the Bible, not only in our private devotional lives but also in our corporate church life.

Practice of Ministers. In many minds, worship means listening to a sermon. But sometimes the preachers are not much help in leading us to the Bible. In fact, they also have contributed to this growing silence of the Bible, whenever their "preaching" consists of little more than an assemblage of what they have read from some magazine, author, or newspaper, or of some "new light" from the prophets of TV talk-show programs. Some preachers who attempt preaching from the Bible create their own "folk canon," limiting their preaching to only a few books or sections of the Bible and a few favorite topics. Can you remember the last time you heard a sermon preached from books such as Leviticus, Chronicles, Obadiah,

Habakkuk, Zechariah, James, Philemon, Jude, or Revelation? Are these books less inspired than the others?

In an effort to appear relevant and up-to-date, some preachers would rather preach about therapy or healing than about repentance and costly discipleship. The consequence is that many contemporary sermons—better described as speeches or lectures, or at best sermonettes—hardly call attention to the "blessed hope" of the second coming or to the assurance of the pre-advent (investigative) judgment. And why should members study the Bible if the ministers don't preach from it?

Practice of Musicians. The theological content of music in most Christian churches reveals this subtle shift from Book to booklet. Many of the songs that were sung in our own Adventist churches years ago were actually filled with Bible content or themes. Familiar hymns like "Lift up the Trumpet," "We Know Not the Hour," "Guide Me, O Thou Great Jehovah," "The Judgment Has Set," etc., are fitting examples.

In much of our contemporary practice, however, we hear more sentimental New Age music in which Jesus is re-cast as a buddy or a boyfriend, God is increasingly portrayed as an indulgent Father who will tolerate anything His spoiled children do or want, and the Holy Spirit is reduced to one's inner self (to use the language from Hindu mystical religion), or even treated as a cosmic pill to give people a spiritual "high."

Since much contemporary Christian music does not seem to be grounded in sound biblical teaching,[16] it is not surprising that what ought to be an effective vehicle for the proclamation of the everlasting gospel has become the occasion for the display of individual talent, often evoking applause as a response. Is this a reason why congregational hymn singing is fading out in some places?

Practice of Church Leaders. The growing silence of the Bible is also perceptible at the various levels of the church's decision-making bodies. In some instances, when issues of doctrine and practice come up for discussion, pragmatic considerations and the authority of the "vote" tend to hold sway over prayerful and thoughtful consideration of Bible principles.[17] It has become convenient to say, "The Bible is silent," in order to avoid dealing with difficult ethical and theological issues.

Thus, when theological problems arise which threaten to jeopardize God's truth and honor, some find it more expedient to wish them away with inaction or to let the individual members or world fields do as they please than to demand a plain "Thus saith the Lord." The courage of Bible-based convictions is greatly needed in many places.

The Challenge Facing Adventists

The above discussion has highlighted the growing silence of the Bible in Christian churches. In spite of the increase of pluralism resulting from the erosion of biblical authority, Seventh-day Adventists must not move with the flow of current trends. "To the law and to the testimony: if they speak not according to this word, it is because there is no light in them" (Isa 8:20).

What then should the Seventh-day Adventist church do about the pressing theological issues which currently confront her—issues such as ordination of women, baptizing practicing polygamists, embracing homosexual lifestyle, divorce and remarriage, and fighting in the wars of one's tribe or nation? Here are a few suggestions.

1. Subordinate Religious Experience to the Word of God. Increasingly, Christians are questioning everything in the Bible except what agrees with their subjective religious experience (often called "the Holy Spirit's leading"). Thus we hear, "The Spirit has *called* me"; "the Spirit has *assured* me"; "the Spirit has *accepted* me"; and "the Spirit has *blessed* me."

Experience surely is important in Christianity (1 John 1:1-3). The real issue, however, is whether experience should have priority over Scripture. The Bible testifies that as important as even a Spirit-inspired experience may be, the Holy Scriptures are more sure than any experience.

In Chapter Five we called attention to the apostle Peter's manner of addressing this issue in 2 Peter 1:16-21. In verses 16-18 Peter rejected the claim that the Christian message is a myth with no objective basis in a factual historical event. As proof, he cited the apostles' experiential knowledge—"we were eyewitnesses . . . we heard . . . we were with Him." However, Peter continued in verse 19 by saying that there is something "more sure" than experience: the prophetic word, the divinely-inspired, authoritative Scriptures (vv. 20-21).

Peter's approach is the very opposite of our pluralistic generation's. In our case, we accept the Bible because it confirms our experience; the experience is the norm. But the apostle argues that his sanctified experience is trustworthy because it is confirmed by the Scriptures! Jesus did something very similar. In explaining His death and resurrection (Luke 24:25-27), Jesus could have appealed to real experiences—resurrected saints, angels appearing at the tomb, etc. Instead, He pointed His disciples to "Moses and all the prophets," something "more sure" than experiences. The men from Emmaus confirmed this, testifying that what caused their hearts to "burn within" them (v. 32) was Jesus' opening of the Scriptures to them.

Ellen White explained why faith must be established on the Word of God, not one's subjective experience or feeling: "Genuine faith is founded on the Scriptures; but Satan uses so many devices to wrest the Scriptures and bring in error, that great care is needed if one would know what they really do teach. It is one of the great delusions of this time to dwell much upon feeling, and to claim honesty while ignoring the plain utterances of the word of God because that word does not coincide with feeling. . . . Feeling may be chaff, but the word of God is the wheat. And 'what,' says the prophet, 'is the chaff to the wheat?'" (*Review and Herald,* November 25, 1884).

2. Recognize that Majority Votes Don't Establish Truth. The quest for political freedom and democracy has also led increasingly to people demanding a say in matters affecting their lives. Not surprisingly, some within the church are insisting that Christian doctrine and lifestyle should also be defined by the will of the people, through referenda, public opinion polls, surveys, etc.; they seek theology of public opinion, not theology of biblical revelation.

Despite the values of democracy, Bible-believing Christians need to remind themselves that Christ is the Head of the church; therefore the decisions of the church must be ratified not by a mere referendum of its members, but by the authority of the Bible. Leon Morris's helpful distinction between a church and a democracy is pertinent: "In a democracy there is no authority but that which arises from within, the will of the people. In a church there is no authority but that which comes from outside, the will of God. Democracy is effective when the people are energetic and help themselves, the church when God acts and redeems men."[18]

3. Govern Ethical Sensitivity by the Bible. Our generation is painfully aware of injustice and bigotry in our world—racism, sexism, anti-Semitism, apartheid, etc. Because people in the past have used the Bible to justify these oppressive acts or structures, some biblical scholars attempt to atone for such prejudice and bigotry by cutting out from the Bible, for all practical purposes, the sections that offend their ethical sensitivities on equality, fairness, justice, compassion, etc.

Usually the Old Testament is the target of fierce attack because of the alleged "horror stories" it contains or for its presumed male-centeredness (androcentricity), which supposedly legitimized a "patriarchal structure" and an anti-women bias.[19] Consequently, some theologians point to societies which have moved beyond racial segregation to integration. On that analogy, they urge the Christian church to revise its alleged doctrine of "gender segregation" to allow for gender integration ("inclusiveness"). What they are actually advocating, though, is the celebration of the values of a unisex society—a community in which gender barriers in roles, clothing, human sexuality, etc., are eliminated.[20]

The way to accomplish this is to adopt what one Adventist scholar referred to as a "hermeneutic of compassion," a method which makes it possible for Christians to ignore, reject, or reinterpret those "non-Christian" parts of the Bible which offend their ethical feelings. One extreme example of this effort is the campaign to get rid of the "sexist" or male-oriented language in the Bible, and to replace it with gender-inclusive expressions which blur distinctions between male and female: "Lord God" becomes "Sovereign God," "heavenly Father" becomes "heavenly Parent," "Son of God" becomes "Child of God,"[21] and the God of Abraham, Isaac and Jacob becomes "the goddess Sophia."[22]

This is an old heresy (Marcionism) dressed up in modern clothing. John Bright's response is pertinent: "I find it most interesting and not a little odd that although the Old Testament on occasion offends our Christian feelings, it did not apparently offend Christ's 'Christian feelings'! Could it really be that we are ethically and religiously more sensitive than he? Or is it perhaps that we do not view the Old Testament—and its God—as he did?"[23]

4. Have Courage to Stand for Biblical Convictions. Probably the most basic reason for the subtle shift of attitude from the Bible as an inspired Book to its perception as an inspiring booklet is the strong pressure on Christians to conform to the contemporary drifts of new opinions.

"New" has become the operative word on every label; without it, products and ideas cannot sell. (This reflects the evolutionary theory's view of upward progress.) Who has not heard about the "New Age Religion" with its "New Theology" and "New Morality" for the coming "New World Order"? Is it any wonder then, to find "New" Testament Christians who have experienced the "new birth" and have become "new creatures" expressing in their "new tongues" their dislike for the "Old" Testament and the "old" paths?

Response to "New Truths." What then should Bible-believing Christians say in response to the old heresies being recycled as new truths (or as one Adventist scholar ingeniously calls them, "present" truths) for today's pluralistic age?

First, what is new is not always true. Sometimes the "new" is something which "has been already, in the ages before us" (Eccl 1:9, 10); in other cases the "old" is preferable to the "new" because it is right (Isa 58:12; Jer 6:16). Peter Taylor Forsyth wrote, "I am sure no new theology can really be theology, whatever its novelty, unless it express[es] and develop[s] the old faith which made those theologies that are now old the mightiest things of the age when they were new."[24] In other words, new truths should never contradict old truths (Isa 8:19, 20).

Second, Christians must have the moral courage to move against popular tides of unbiblical opinions. This is neither easy nor palatable, since those who do so are often labeled and disdained by their peers as uninformed, obscurantist, pre-scientific, intolerant (according to the canons of pluralism), or even fundamentalist.

In a lecture given in Wycliffe Hall at Oxford University, British scholar Gordon J. Wenham aptly described the situation: "I suspect that if either you [a student] or your lecturers discover during your study that you are a Sabellian montanist or semipelagian gnostic [these were christological heresies in the early church], it will not cause over-much excitement. Such deviants are common place today and in this pluralistic society are usually accepted without much fuss. However should you be diagnosed as a fundamentalist your fate may be very different. In the modern theology faculty fundamentalism is the great heresy. It is regarded as nearly as dangerous as the HIV virus and is treated with similar fervour but with rather less tact and sympathy."[25]

Regrettably, Christians who seek the applause of the world rather than the commendation of God find it more expedient to conform to society's unbiblical norms than to endure sophisticated intimidation by their peers. And when they conform, the surest way they maintain an appearance of Christianity is to *adopt a hermeneutic that explains away unpopular biblical positions in a popular new light.*

Though the temptation to make the distinctive teachings of the Bible compatible with the contemporary culture is strong, the Bible warns us against conforming to the world's ideas. "Be not conformed to this world" (Rom 12:1); "Love not the world, neither the things that are in the world" (1 John 2:15-17). Martin Luther King, Jr., observed, "We are called to be people of conviction, not conformity; of moral nobility, not social respectability. We are commanded to live differently and according to a higher loyalty."[26]

Daniel E. Pilarczyk, the archbishop of Cincinnati, raised a pertinent question: "If the church is singing the same tune as everyone else, then who needs the church?"[27] If Jeremiah were living in our day, he would ask the same question that he posed to his contemporaries: "Now why go to Egypt to drink water from the Shihor? And why go to Assyria to drink water from the River?" (Jer 2:18 NIV).

Conclusion

We started this chapter by calling attention to the uncertainty of some Christian churches over such contemporary issues as abortion, homosexuality, polygamy, women's ordination, divorce and remarriage, fighting in wars, etc. We suggested that this reluctance is a symptom of the theological pluralism infecting much of Christendom and which has had a devastating impact on the life and mission of the church. What is at stake is the nature of the Bible (the exact nature of its inspiration) and the approach to the Bible (the appropriate method for its interpretation).

The Bible and the Bible Only. Today the Seventh-day Adventist church also faces these foundational issues as it grapples with the question of ordaining women as elders and pastors as well as baptizing practicing polygamists. In deciding which direction to go on these issues, the church should ensure that these questions not be settled according to the cultural preferences of each local region of the worldwide Seventh-day Adventist church. Since the problems are theological rather than sociological, only the Holy Scriptures can have the final say on the issues at hand. Moreover, in both instances those ordained or baptized must be accepted whole-heartedly by every Seventh-day Adventist believer; for in a worldwide church such as we have, ordination and baptism in one division of the world field are automatically valid for another and should remain that way.

As the church prayerfully considers such questions, it needs to remember the statement by Ellen G. White: "God will have a people upon the earth to maintain *the Bible, and the Bible only,* as the standard of all doctrines and the basis of all reforms. The opinions of learned men, the deductions of science, the creeds or decisions of ecclesiastical councils, as numerous and discordant as are the churches which they represent, the voice of the majority—not one nor all of these should be regarded as evidence for or against any point of religious faith. Before accepting any doctrine or precept, *we should demand a plain 'Thus saith the Lord' in its support"* (*The Great Controversy,* p. 595, emphasis supplied).

Promise for Bible Students. Ellen White assured us: "If all would make the Bible their study, we should see a people who were better developed, who were capable of thinking more deeply, who would manifest greater intelligence than those who have earnestly studied the sciences and histories of the world, apart from the Bible. The Bible gives the true seeker for truth an advanced mental discipline, and he comes from contemplation of divine things with his faculties enriched; self is humbled, while God and his revealed truth are exalted" (*Bible Echo and Signs of the Times,* October 1, 1892).

This promise is not reserved for the proponents of the so-called "principle-approach" who claim to possess a "high level of abstract thinking." Instead, it applies to all God's end-time people, those who seek to live by "the Bible and the Bible only," who are making a diligent effort to uphold the plain reading or literal understanding of the Bible.

But in order to *uphold the Word* and not distort it, we must have a clear understanding of how some are *liberating the Word*. This we shall take up in the next chapter.

NOTES

1. A modified version of this chapter is found in the author's "The Bible: Inspired Book or Inspiring Booklet?" *Adventists Affirm* 9/1 (Spring 1995):20-29.

2. The issue of women's ordination is a case in point. Until recently Seventh-day Adventist proponents of women's ordination had often argued that the Bible was "silent" or "neither for nor against" the ordination of women as elders/pastors. Thus, they presented the issue as a "cultural" problem to be settled by administrative policy. However, since the 1995 General Conference session at Utrecht, some have argued that women's ordination is a "moral imperative"—suggesting that the issue is *theological* after all, even as opponents have insisted all along. For more on this, see Samuel Koranteng-Pipim's unpublished article, "Women's Ordination: The Evolving Arguments" (1996), available at the Adventist Heritage Center of the James White Library, Andrews University. Now that both proponents and opponents of women's ordination claim the Bible to be on their side, the hermeneutical questions raised in chapter 5, part II, can be discussed candidly.

3. James I. Packer, *God Has Spoken* (Grand Rapids, Mich.: Baker, 1979), pp. 19, 20.

4. James D. Smart, *The Strange Silence of the Bible in the Church: A Study in Hermeneutics* (Philadelphia: Westminster Press, 1970), pp. 15-16.

5. B. B. Warfield, *The Inspiration and Authority of the Bible* (Philadelphia: Presbyterian & Reformed Publishing, 1948), p. 105. Benjamin Jowett's century-old statement regarding conflicting views of inspiration is still applicable today: "The word inspiration has received more numerous gradations and distinctions of meaning than perhaps any other in the whole of theology. There is an inspiration of superintendence and an inspiration of suggestion; an inspiration that would have been consistent with the Apostle or Evangelist falling into error, [and] an inspiration which would have prevented him from erring; verbal organic inspiration by which the inspired person is the passive utterer of Divine word, and an inspiration which acts through the character of the sacred writer; there is an inspiration which absolutely communicates the fact to be revealed or statement to be made, and an inspiration which does not supersede the ordinary knowledge of human event; there is an inspiration which demands infallibility in matters of doctrine, but allows for mistakes in fact. Lastly there is a view of inspiration which recognizes only its supernatural and prophetic character, and a view of inspiration which regards the apostles and evangelists as equally inspired in their writings and their lives, and in both receiving the guidance of the Spirit of truth in a manner not different in kind but only in degree from ordinary Christians" (Benjamin Jowett, "On the Interpretation of Scripture," in *Essays and Review,* n. ed. [London: John W. Parker and Son, 1860], p. 345).

6. Nils Ehrenstrom and Gunther Gassman, *Confessions in Dialogue: A Survey of Bilateral Conversations among World Confessional Families 1959-1974* (Geneva: World Council of Churches, 1975), p. 150.

7. John Shelby Spong, *Rescuing the Bible from Fundamentalism* (San Francisco: HarperSanFrancisco, 1991), p. 33.

8. Clark Pinnock, *Tracking the Maze* (San Francisco: Harper and Row, 1990), pp. 174, 175, emphasis supplied.

9. Charles Kraft, *Christianity in Culture: A Study in Dynamic Biblical Theologizing in Cross-Cultural Perspective* (Maryknoll, N.Y.: Orbis, 1979), pp. 201, 301, 398.

10. Alden Thompson, "God's Word: Casebook or Codebook?" *Ministry,* July 1991, pp. 6-10. Because this view has been popularized in some quarters of the Seventh-day Adventist church, a

helpful analysis and evaluation has been provided in Frank Holbrook and Leo Van Dolson, eds., *Issues in Revelation and Inspiration* (Berrien Springs, Mich.: Adventist Theological Society Publications, 1992).

11. This characterization comes from Eta Linnemann, *Historical Criticism of the Bible: Methodology or Ideology?* (Grand Rapids, Mich.: Baker, 1990). On this method of interpretation, see Appendix C for the "Methods of Bible Study Committee Report," approved by the Annual Council of 1986.

12. Sandra M. Schneiders, "Does the Bible Have a Postmodern Message?" in *Postmodern Theology: Christian Faith in a Pluralistic World,* ed. Frederic B. Burnham (San Francisco: Harper and Row, 1989), pp. 60-61.

13. Norman R. Gulley, "Reader-Response Theories in Postmodern Hermeneutics: A Challenge to Evangelical Theology," in *The Challenge of Postmodernism: An Evangelical Engagement,* ed. David S. Dockery (Wheaton, Ill.: Victor Books, 1995), p. 216.

14. Ibid., p. 226, emphasis supplied. The above author employed this analogy in connection with the "emptiness" of the postmodern reader-response theories of interpretation.

15. Myron Widmer, "Biblical Wimps, or Giants?" *Adventist Review,* September 12, 1991, p. 4.

16. For a helpful discussion of the relationship between worldviews and music, see Wolfgang H. M. Stefani, "The Concept of God and Sacred Music: An Intercultural Exploration of Divine Transcendence/Immanence As a Stylistic Determinant for Worship Music with Paradigmatic Implications for the Contemporary Christian Context," (Ph.D. Dissertation, Andrews University, 1993).

17. The church's handling of the abortion and women's ordination issues provides two cases in point. For an eye-opening discussion of how financial and pragmatic considerations impacted upon the church's current views on abortion and theology of (the ordained) ministry, see George B. Gainer, "Abortion: History of Adventist Guidelines," *Ministry,* August 1991, pp. 11-17, and Bert B. Haloviak, "The Internal Revenue Service and the Redefinition of Adventist Ministry," *Adventist Today,* May-June 1996, pp. 12-15.

18. Leon Morris, *I Believe in Revelation* (Grand Rapids, Mich.: Eerdmans, 1977), p. 75. For a discussion of the extent and limitations of church authority, see Samuel Koranteng-Pipim, *Searching the Scriptures: Women's Ordination and the Call to Biblical Fidelity* (Berrien Springs, Mich.: Adventists Affirm, 1995), pp. 19-21, 89-90.

19. On this, see Gerhard F. Hasel, "Biblical Authority and Feminist Interpretation," *Adventists Affirm* 3/2 (Fall 1989): 12-23.

20. See Samuele Bacchiocchi, "Recovering Harmonious Gender Distinctions," *Adventists Affirm* 9/1 (Spring 1995):61-66.

21. Cf. Wayne Grudem's 22-page article, "What's Wrong with Gender-Neutral Bible Translations? A Critique of the *New Revised Standard Version,*" available through The Council on Biblical Manhood and Womanhood (CBMW), P. O. Box 317, Wheaton, IL 60189 or E-mail: CBMWHendo@aol.com.

22. See Elizabeth Achtemeier, "Why God Is Not Mother: A Response to Feminist God-talk in the Church," *Christianity Today,* August 16, 1993, pp. 16-23. For a shocking account of how this feminist "re-imagining" of God is being actively promoted in Christian churches, see James R. Edwards, "Earthquake in the Mainline," *Christianity Today,* November 14, 1994, pp. 38-43.

23. John Bright, *The Authority of the Old Testament* (Nashville: Abingdon Press, 1967), p. 77ff.

24. Quoted in Kenneth Hamilton, *What's New in Religion* (Grand Rapids, Mich.: Eerdmans, 1968), p. 6.

25. Gordon J. Wenham, "The Place of Biblical Criticism in Theological Study," *Themelios* 14/3 (1989):84. Bible-believing Christians should not be intimidated by any pejorative labels, which are calculated to induce them to accept some "progressive" ideas (theological codeword for deviations from Scripture).

26. Martin Luther King, Jr., *Strength to Love* (Glasgow: Wm Collins Sons & Co., 1986), p. 18.

27. *Time,* November 5, 1990, p. 83.

Chapter Eight

Liberating the Word

The Bible was originally given in ancient Middle-Eastern cultures, in languages foreign to most people today. Bible-believing Christians have always maintained that in order for the Scriptures to function as the "liberating Word of God," there is a need for "liberating the Word" from its ancient historical, cultural, and grammatical context. But they also insist that this process of "liberating the Word" through translation, printing, and interpretation should not involve imposing today's ideological concerns upon inspired Scripture.

Historical-critical scholarship, on the other hand, believes that in order for the inspired Word to be liberating, the Bible must first be "liberated" from its alleged *inherent shortcomings*. To make the Bible "relevant," they diminish Scripture's authority from *the liberating Word,* through the process of *liberating the Word,* to what liberal scholarship considers as *the liberated Word.*[1] Thus, in "liberating the Word," different liberal groups introduce several distortions into the Bible's message.

Attempts to Liberate the Word. For example, *classical liberal theology* tries to "liberate the Word" from its alleged historical, scientific, theological, and ethical mistakes; *social gospel theology* seeks to "liberate the Word" from its alleged abstract doctrinal interpretations to today's concrete social and political contexts; *feminist theology* wants to "liberate the Word" from its alleged patriarchal worldview, sexist language, and patriarchal God-talk; *gay (homosexual) theology* attempts to "liberate the Word" from its alleged homophobic bias so that it will show compassion and understanding; *liberation theology, black theology,* and *third-world theologies* endeavor to "liberate the Word" from the one-sided, white middle-class, privatized interpretation that has enslaved, colonized, and exploited the poor, the people of color, and the marginalized; and *experiential theology* undertakes to "liberate the Word" from dry, wooden, and lifeless interpretation void of the Holy Spirit.[2]

In view of the different ideological agendas that come into play in the process of *liberating the Word,* our generation is witnessing some of the grossest abuses of the Word imaginable. The distortion of the Word at the hands of church members, teachers, pastors, and scholars raises serious doubts about their claim to uphold the Word as the inspired, trustworthy, and authoritative revelation of God's will for humanity.

Even though *Receiving the Word* is concerned with how historical-critical interpreters have distorted the Word, we need to discuss other possible distortions of the Word from the moment the Bible writers penned their original messages (the inspired *autographs*), through the transmission and translation of the text, to its contemporary interpretation.

The Inspired Writers of "the Liberating Word": No Distortions of the Word

We have noted earlier that even though the Bible was written in an imperfect human language, imperfect in the sense that "infinite ideas cannot be perfectly embodied in finite vehicles of thought" (*Selected Messages,* 1:22), God supernaturally guided the inspired writers of Scripture in such a way that they communicated God's message in an accurate and trustworthy manner. When, therefore, the Bible writers describe something touching upon science, history, geography, etc., as actually taking place, we are to believe it as trustworthy. Thus, there was *no distortion of the Word* when the Bible writers wrote their messages.

The Holy Spirit guided them, not allowing their personal or cultural prejudices to distort the God-given message. Rejecting any suggestion that their messages were "culturally conditioned," the apostle Peter wrote: "Knowing this first, that no prophecy of the scripture is of any private interpretation. *For the prophecy came not in old time by the will of man; but holy men of God spake as they were moved by the Holy Ghost*" (2 Pet 1:20-21). "For we have not followed cunningly devised fables, when we made known unto you the power and coming of our Lord Jesus Christ, but were eyewitnesses of his majesty" (2 Pet 1:16; cf. 1 Cor 2:10-13).

Scripture's Trustworthiness. Ellen G. White affirmed the trustworthiness of the Bible's historical accounts, since the Holy Spirit "guided the pens of the sacred historians" in such a manner that "the Bible is the most instructive and comprehensive history that has ever been given to the world. . . . Here we have a truthful history of the human race, one that is unmarred by human prejudice or human pride" (*Gospel Workers,* p. 286; *Fundamentals of Christian Education,* pp. 84-85; cf. *Education,* p. 173).

There are no distortions in the biographies and history of God's favored people for, in the words of Ellen White, "this history the unerring pen of inspiration must trace with exact fidelity" (*Testimonies for the Church,* 4:370). Whereas uninspired historians are unable to record history without bias, the inspired writers "did not testify to falsehoods to prevent the pages of sacred history being clouded by the record of human frailties and faults. The scribes of God wrote as they were dictated by the Holy Spirit, having no control of the work themselves. They penned the literal truth, and stern, forbidding facts are revealed for reasons that our finite minds cannot fully comprehend" (ibid., p. 9).

Even the Bible's science is authentic. "Its sacred pages contain the only authentic account of the creation. . . . There is harmony between nature and Christianity; for both have the same Author. The book of nature and the book of revelation indicate the working of the same divine mind" (*Fundamentals of Christian Education,* pp. 84-85).

"Inferences erroneously drawn from facts observed in nature have, how-ever, led to supposed conflict between science and revelation; and in the effort to restore harmony, interpretations of Scripture have been adopted that under-mine and destroy the force of the Word of God." Ellen White rejected natural-istic evolution and the long ages of geology. "Geology has been thought to contradict the literal interpretation of the Mosaic record of the creation. Mil-lions of years, it is claimed, were required for the evolution of the earth from chaos; and in order to accommodate the Bible to this supposed revelation of science, the days of creation are assumed to have been vast, indefinite periods, covering thousands or even millions of years. Such a conclusion is wholly un-called for. The Bible record is in harmony with itself and with the teaching of nature" (*Education,* pp. 128-129).

Thus, any distortion in the Bible's message would *not* come from the Bible writers themselves who were guided in their writing of Scripture. We should not expect distortions in the Word as it came from the hands of the Bible writ-ers. Any distortions will have to come, not from the original copies (the *auto-graphs* which no longer exist), but rather from either copyists and translators as they transmitted the sacred texts or from contemporary interpreters in their effort to understand the inspired message.

Copyists' and Translators' "Liberating the Word": Minor Distortions of the Word

While no distortions came from the hand of the original Bible writers, some alterations and *minor distortions* have crept into the Word during the process of transmission and translation.[3] This section will attempt to show the nature of these minor distortions at the hand of copyists and translators.

The Old Testament section of our Bibles is a translation of manuscripts that were originally written in Hebrew, with a few portions of Ezra (4:8-6:18; 7:12-26), Daniel (2:4-7:28) and a single verse in Jeremiah (10:11) written in Aramaic. Aramaic is a sister language to Hebrew, just as Swedish is to Norwegian. The New Testament section of our Bibles is a translation from manuscripts originally written in Greek. Since we do not have authentic autographs from the hands of the Bible writers themselves, our Bibles represent, at best, hand-written copies of the original writings (*manuscripts*). Most likely, they are made from copies of copies, or maybe copies of copies of copies. And for most church members, these copies are available only as *translations*.

Remarkable Accuracy. In an earlier chapter, *Trusting the Word,* we noted how very accurately the manuscripts of both the Old and New Testaments were copied and transmitted. But whenever the inspired texts of Scripture are copied or translated into other languages there is always the possibility that some alterations and minor distortions of the Word will take place. Ellen White confirmed this possibility, suggesting that there may have been occasional errors or even deliberate text manipulations by some copyists (*Selected Messages,* 1:16; *Early Writings,* pp. 220-221).[4]

However, scholars generally agree that these transmission errors can be identified by the discipline known as *textual criticism,* sometimes called *lower criticism* to distinguish it from the higher criticism of liberal scholars. By analyzing and evaluating the various ancient manuscripts, this scholarly discipline seeks to ascertain which reading of a passage is closest to the original.

Distortions by Copyists

Old Testament Manuscripts (MSS). The Jews did a magnificent job in copying the Old Testament manuscripts. Until the temple was destroyed in A.D. 70, the Jews kept standard copies of the Scriptures in the temple in Jerusalem, just as we keep standard weights and measurements in museums. In order that all copies of the Old Testament would conform to the standard copy in the temple, strict rules were followed.

As we noted in Chapter Two, the Massoretes, the group of Jews who around A.D. 700 invented a system for writing Hebrew vowels, drew up tables, one for each book of the Bible, showing how many times a particular letter appeared in that book. No word or letter could be written from memory. After a scribe had finished his work of copying out a book, he had to count the letters in it and compare his scores with those in the standard table. If his did not tally with the standard score, his newly copied manuscript was to be discarded entirely and the task begun again. This process ensured remarkable accuracy.

But human nature being what it is, one wonders if a scribe would scrap a whole book if he fell short by one or two letters in his count. One can expect some deliberate textual manipulations in such instances. Some minor distortions may also have occurred unintentionally.

Nature of Old Testament Errors. Problems occurred when a change of vowels resulted in a change of meaning. Let's illustrate with the English word **LEAD**. Prior to the invention of written vowels for Hebrew around A.D. 700, if there were a word LEAD, this word would have been spelled in Hebrew as **LD**. Now, *lead* can have at least two meanings. There is one meaning in the sentence "lead me home," and another in "heavy as lead." If different vowels are attached to these two consonants, one can come up with words like *lead, lid, lad, led, laid, lied, load, loud, old.* In deciding what word **LD** should be, the context of a passage is helpful. But sometimes, the context can go either way. For example, "**LD** me home" can be rendered "*lead* me home," "*led* me home," "*laid* me home," or even "*load* me home"! Assuming we try the other sentence "heavy as **LD**" one can translate it as "heavy as *lead*," "heavy as [a] *lad*," or "heavy as [a] *load*." One can imagine other different ways **LD** can be read.

Fortunately, written Hebrew does not depend as heavily on vowels as English does. The Massoretes, fluent in Hebrew, had very little difficulty reading without written vowels—just as Israelis today read their newspapers without vowels.

Also, since a number of Hebrew letters resemble other letters closely, a copyist could make scribal mistakes. For example, we find the names *Hadadezer* (2 Sam 8:3) and *Hadarezer* (1 Chron 18:3) referring to the same person. The difference here is the Hebrew letter "d" (ד) being mistaken for the letter "r" (ר). We can understand a copyist's blunder when we realize: (i) how much alike some words look in the Hebrew—e.g., *Zabdi* (זבדי, Josh 7:1) and *Zimri* (זמרי, 1 Chron 2:6); or (ii) how easy it is for letters to be transposed, as we do when we write "thier" instead of "their"; in the Old Testament, we find, for example, instead of *Hasrah*, the name of a person, we have *Harhas*; instead of *kebes*, the word for a lamb, we have *keseb*; instead of *algum*, the name of a tree, we have *almug*; instead of *Timnath-heres*, the name of the city where Joshua was buried, we have *Timnath-serah.*

The above examples illustrate the distortions that have arisen during the transmission of the Old Testament manuscripts.

Remarkable Accuracy. However, in spite of problems like these, the Old Testament manuscripts exhibit remarkable accuracy. Until the discovery of the

Dead Sea Scrolls in 1947, the oldest known Hebrew manuscripts had been copied around the tenth century A.D. The Dead Sea Scrolls, however, were hidden away in caves just before A.D. 70, when the Romans invaded Palestine. Many of them were already one or two hundred years old at the time.

Doubts about the reliability of the tenth-century manuscripts were dispelled when they were compared with the Dead Sea Scrolls, a thousand years older. One leading authority remarks: "The new evidence confirms what we had already good reason to believe—that the Jewish scribes of the early Christian centuries copied and recopied the text of the Hebrew Bible with the utmost fidelity."[5] In all likelihood our Old Testament is remarkably similar to the Old Testament Bible Jesus used.

New Testament Manuscripts. The copyists of the New Testament did not match those of the Old in terms of high standards. This does not mean that the manuscripts of the New Testament are bad, but only that the quality controls in place for the Old Testament were not there. A few of the copyists' distortions will illustrate this point.[6]

Nature of New Testament Errors. If a New Testament copyist was writing down what was being read to him by another, he might hear something incorrectly and therefore make a mistake. For instance, the manuscript variants in Romans 5:1 may result from a copyist hearing *echomen* ("we have") instead of *echōmen* ("let us have"). Similarly, because the pronunciation of *ou* and *u* is often indistinguishable, we may understand why there are variants in Revelation 1:5. Thus, whereas the King James Version (KJV) reads "and *washed* us," based on a manuscript that reads *lousanti,* other versions, such as the New International Version (NIV), on the basis of other manuscripts that read *lusanti,* have "and *freed* us."

Again, similarity in pronunciation may explain the discrepancies in the manuscripts of 1 John 1:4. Did the apostle John write his letter so that "*our* joy" may be complete (NIV, RSV) or in order that "*your* joy" may be full (KJV)? The Greek pronouns *hemeis* ("we") and *humeis* ("you"), when inflected to express possession ("our" and "your," respectively), were pronounced very much alike, a fact reflected in variant manuscripts.

On the other hand, if instead of listening to a reader, a scribe was reading and copying a manuscript by himself, several kinds of inadvertent errors could occur. One of them happens when there are similar endings of lines or words (the technical name for this kind of copyist error is *homoeoteleuton*). A scribe copies what he sees, but when his eyes return to the parent manuscript, he mistakenly skips to the second of these similar items, leaving out some material; or he might copy the same line twice when his eyes skip back to the earlier occurrence.

Other errors include intentional changes, either for the copyist's own personal or theological reasons, or when he thought he was correcting the mistakes of a preceding scribe, whom he believed may have made some mistakes in grammar, vocabulary, or spelling. Ellen White noted: "I saw that God had especially guarded the Bible; yet when copies of it were few, learned men had in some instances changed the words, thinking that they were making it more plain, when in reality they were mystifying that which was plain, by causing it to lean to their established views, which were governed by tradition" (*Early Writings,* pp. 220-221).

Sometimes, a scribe had several manuscripts from which he made his copy. If he discovered that the manuscripts read differently, he made a judgment by either choosing one reading and leaving the other, or in some cases, putting the two together to make a conflated reading. Thus, if a manuscript has "church of God" in Acts 20:28, and others have "church of the Lord," a later copyist, who wants to provide readers with the benefit of the two readings, may conflate the two to produce "church of the Lord and God."

Reasons for New Testament Errors. Generally, the New Testament copyists were not as rigorous in their work as were the scribes of the Old Testament writings. Unlike the well-trained Jewish scribes who copied the Old Testament so meticulously, the early Christian believers often came from the lower classes and lacked the professional skill of the scribe. Consequently, the few who could read and write produced copies of the inspired autographs with little or no proofreading.

Moreover, persecution and confiscations of their sacred books often led them to copy the texts hastily. Heretical groups also made their own copies, sometimes deleting portions and mutilating others. Only after emperor Constantine (A.D. 274/80-337) was converted to Christianity were there enough freedom and resources for Christians carefully to copy and proofread manuscripts. Because most of the New Testament manuscripts that exist today came from this Byzantine period, they are referred to collectively as the *Byzantine text.*

Compensating for Disadvantages. The disadvantages of the New Testament manuscripts, however, are offset by their numbers. There are far more New Testament than Old Testament manuscripts from which one can make comparisons. About 5,000 separate manuscripts of the Greek New Testament exist in the different museums and libraries around the world. While some are only fragments, about 50 contain the entire New Testament.

Besides, many early copies were translated into other languages. Some 6,000 Latin manuscripts have survived, plus about 1,000 other manuscripts in languages such as Syriac, Coptic, Armenian, Georgian, Ethiopic, and Gothic. Further, large parts of the New Testament are quoted in early Christian writings.[7]

The sheer quantity and reliability of the New Testament manuscripts far exceed any other historical material that has survived from antiquity.[8]

Remarkable Accuracy. When one recognizes the conditions under which the New Testament manuscripts were copied and the fact that the copyists did not have the advantages of printing presses and computer spell-checkers, it is remarkable to find among the existing manuscripts a 99.9% accuracy. Even where there are variations, most concern specific *words* where the scribes made copying mistakes. So accurate are the New Testament manuscripts that someone has estimated that if all the uncertain words in a five-hundred page Greek Testament were assembled, they would occupy only four-tenths of a single page![9] That is, the uncertain words from the different existing manuscripts are only about 0.08% of a 500-page book.

Even here, this insignificant percentage is possible only by assuming that the ending of Mark (16:9-20) and the passage about the woman taken in adultery (John 7:53-8:11) were not part of the autographs. But if one accepts these passages as part of the original text (they appear in some 99% of Greek manuscripts, and they are attested in numerous places in the writings of Ellen G. White[10]), the purity of the New Testament manuscripts is even higher.[11]

Though variations may allow us to speak only of a high degree of *relative accuracy* of the texts, the differences are so minor that no viable variant affects any major Christian doctrine. One knowledgeable scholar states: "What is at stake is a purity of text of such a substantial nature that nothing we believe to be doctrinally true, and nothing we are commanded to do, is in any way jeopardized by the variants. This is true of *any* textual tradition [family of texts]."[12]

Divine Guidance in Transmission Process. Such remarkable accuracy is possible only if the Holy Spirit guided the transmission process. Ellen White confirmed that even though scribes may have made some copying mistakes, God Himself guarded the transmission process so that the Bible is God's trustworthy book. "This Holy Book has withstood the assaults of Satan, who has united with evil men to make everything of divine character shrouded in clouds and darkness. But the Lord has preserved this Holy Book by His own miraculous power *in its present shape*" (*Selected Messages,* 1:15, emphasis supplied).

Probably the Lord kept the original manuscripts from us so that we would not make shrines or idols of them. But as further manuscripts are found buried in ruins or in forgotten monasteries, and as computer technology is refined to analyze existing various manuscripts, we may yet establish even more reliable texts than the 99.9% accurate texts from which most of our present Bibles have been translated.

The minor nature of the alterations and distortions that have occurred in the transmission of the inspired Bible messages suggests that whenever Bible students study their Hebrew and Greek Bibles, they can count on these texts to convey the message God inspired thousands of years ago. The example of Jesus and the apostles in treating copies of the Old Testament as "Scripture" (Greek *graphe*) teaches us to do the same.

Although the autographs no longer existed, Christ read from "Scripture" (*graphe*) in the synagogue at Nazareth (Luke 4:21); Paul read from "Scripture" (*graphe*) in the synagogue in Thessalonica (Acts 17:2); the Ethiopian eunuch was reading "Scripture" (*graphe*) when Philip met him (Acts 8:32-33); and the apostle Paul writes that the "Scriptures" (*graphe*) that were being used by believers in his day are all inspired (2 Tim 3:16). These copies were not the autographs; no doubt they contained some scribal errors. Yet the Bible calls the copies "Scripture" (*graphe*).

Therefore, Bible students who are able to read and understand copies of the Hebrew and Greek Bibles can be quite sure that they are studying essentially the same Old Testament Hebrew text that Jesus used and the New Testament Greek text that the Spirit of Christ inspired the apostles to write. In the words of Ellen White, "The Bible is the most ancient and the most comprehensive history that men possess. It came fresh from the fountain of eternal truth, *and throughout the ages a divine hand has preserved its purity"* (*Education,* p. 173, emphasis supplied).

Distortions from Translators

Since very few of us can read and understand the Bible's original languages, we must rely on translations. But every translation of the Bible is an interpretation. In order for the inspired message to be understood, the translator must put the biblical message in a form that will produce the same effect on the contemporary reader as it did on the original recipients of the inspired message.

In some cases, a literal, word-for-word translation (called *formal* or *complete equivalence*[13]), in which the grammatical structure of the original language is reproduced as much as possible in the receiving language, may be hard to understand. In order for the text to be clearer, one must rephrase the message without losing the original intent (this is referred to as *dynamic equivalence*). However, those who do oral translations for speakers will readily admit that, despite their best intentions, there are occasional distortions in the message. These *translation losses* and *translation distortions* may not necessarily be the fault of the translators.[14]

Kinds of Translation Distortions. While the distortions of the Word that were introduced by copyists of the ancient biblical manuscripts were minor (less than 0.1%), Bible *translations* or *paraphrases* introduce their own kinds of distortions in the message of the inspired writers. Not infrequently, these errors stem from how translators embark upon their task. Translators introduce two major kinds of errors.

First, some translation errors result from the assumptions the translators bring with them. For example, errors may creep into the biblical message if translators are driven by some hidden or explicit theological or ideological agenda. One can point to the *New World Translation* (the Jehovah's Witnesses' Bible) as a translation driven by the anti-Trinitarian theology of a religious group. Another example is the National Council of Churches' gender-inclusive Bible, the *New Revised Standard Version* [NRSV], which, despite some strengths, is driven by a desire to rid the Bible of the alleged gender-bias of the Bible writers. The same can be said of certain other translations in which references to the "right hand" of God have been replaced with "the mighty hand" of God, in an apparent effort not to offend left-handed people![15]

Second, distortions in translations occur if translators use faulty, questionable, or too few Greek and Hebrew manuscripts as the basis for their translations, or if they do their work without much input from a wide range of people. This point puts in better perspective the debate about the *King James Version* (KJV) vis-a-vis modern translations.

The King James Version. Our popular *King James Version* Bible is based on the work of the foremost sixteenth-century Renaissance Dutch scholar, Desiderius Erasmus (1469-1536). To produce a copy of the New Testament text for publication on the newly established movable-type printing press, Erasmus went to Basel, Switzerland, where, upon examining a number of Greek manuscripts in its libraries, he selected a half-dozen of them as good representatives. After nine months of work, he produced an edited version from the chosen Greek manuscripts.

Although Erasmus himself acknowledged that his work was "done headlong rather than edited," his Greek New Testament became the standard, almost the sole printed Greek text from the sixteenth century to the nineteenth. It is often known as "the Received Text" (Latin, *Textus Receptus*), a title given to it almost 100 years after Erasmus's death in publisher Elzevir's second edition of the work (1633). This Greek text, which later became the basis of the *King James Version* of the Bible, "is not the 'received text' in the sense that it has been received from God *as over against* other Greek manuscripts. Rather, it is the 'received text' in the sense that it was the standard one at the time of the Elzevirs."[16]

However, since the nineteenth century, when scholars began to discover other manuscripts, many translations of the Bible have been made. Unlike the *King James Version,* most of the recent translations did not use only a half-dozen Greek manuscripts, but rather hundreds of early manuscripts; their Greek texts required not nine months of work, but rather years of labor; not one person, but dozens and scores of scholars have collaborated in producing the current standard Greek New Testament texts.

While there are variations, the differences between "the Received Text" of the *King James Version* and the present standard Greek texts are so minor that there is practically very little difference between the two. As explained earlier, if the uncertain words in a five-hundred page Greek Testament were assembled, they would occupy only four-tenths of a single page! Therefore, while the controversy over the merits and demerits of the King James Version cannot be dismissed lightly, neither should the issue be over-exaggerated. The degree of uncertainty raised by the various Greek texts is far less than the distortions introduced by contemporary interpreters.[17]

Usefulness of Different Versions. Just as the Holy Spirit guided in the copying and re-copying of the ancient texts, one can also expect the Spirit to speak through the different translations—whether King James Version, New International Version, Revised Standard Version, New World Translation, Living Bible, Clear Word, etc.

Every translation is an imperfect human attempt to communicate, in contemporary language, God's message which the prophets and apostles first communicated in Hebrew, Aramaic, and Greek. Each Bible translation has its own strengths and weaknesses. One can overcome most of the translation distortions simply by using different Bible versions in studying the Scriptures.[18] In the next chapter we shall offer suggestions on how to select appropriate Bible versions.

Those who are distressed by the proliferation of Bible versions will benefit from an insightful statement found in the preface of some of the earliest editions of the *King James Version:*

"We do not deny, nay we affirm and avow, that the very meanest translation of the Bible in English set forth by men of our profession . . . containeth the word of God, nay is the word of God: As the King's speech, which he uttered in Parliament, being translated into French, Dutch, Italian, and Latin, is still the King's speech, though it be not interpreted by every translator with the like grace, nor peradventure so fitly for phrase, nor so expressly for sense, everywhere . . . [there is] no cause therefore why the word translated should be denied to be the word, or forbidden to be current, notwithstanding that some imperfections and blemishes may be noted in the setting forth of it."[19]

Translations are Also Scripture. In fact, when the New Testament writers quoted from the Old Testament, they seem to have used Greek translations of the Hebrew Scriptures (the *Septuagint*, abbreviated LXX).[20] If translations of the Hebrew Bible into Greek, however imperfect the translation may have been, are treated by the New Testament writers as "Scripture" (*graphe*), contemporary Bible students can also treat whatever versions of the Bible they have—whether English, Swahili, Chinese, Russian, Yoruba, French, Spanish, etc.—as God's inspired message to them.

Bible students need not be overly concerned about *distortions of the Word* at the hands of copyists or translators. Ellen White speaks to this issue when she wrote:

"Some look to us gravely and say, 'Don't you think there might have been some mistake *in the copyist or in the translators?*' This is all probable, and the mind that is so narrow that it will hesitate and stumble over this possibility or probability would be just as ready to stumble over the mysteries of the Inspired Word, because their feeble minds cannot see through the purposes of God. Yes, they would just as easily stumble over plain facts that the common mind will accept, and discern the Divine, and to which God's utterance is plain and beautiful, full of marrow and fatness. *All the mistakes will not cause trouble to one soul, or cause any feet to stumble,* that would not manufacture difficulties from the plainest revealed truth" (*Selected Messages,* 1:16, emphasis supplied).

Bible students must be more concerned about the distortions of the Word that result when they themselves grossly misinterpret the inspired Word.

Contemporary Interpreters Produce "the Liberated Word": Gross Distortions of the Word

The minor distortions of the Word by copyists and translators can be corrected and controlled by comparing their work with available manuscripts and other versions of the Bible. However, with interpreters (or *exegetes*) there is a greater likelihood of a gross abuse of the Word. This is because interpreters (church members, teachers, or preachers) may have no controls to regulate their interpretations.

The grossest distortions of the Word occur at the level of interpretation. This is because interpreters tend to approach the Word with their own agenda, seeking to "liberate the Word." Such distortions happen at the two major levels of interpretation: (i) at the popular churchly level, and (ii) at the scholarly academic level.

Popular Distortion: Relevance as Interpretation

One common kind of biblical distortion takes place at the popular level, when Bible students (church members and pastors) confuse interpretation with relevance or meaningfulness. Here, instead of first ascertaining what a text originally meant and then, using valid principles, applying the meaning to contemporary needs, Bible students seek to read into the text what they believe the text means to them.

Thus, they impose upon the scriptural passage their own meanings or opinions, transforming biblical exposition into a proof-text imposition. In other words, *exegesis* (reading *out* of the text meaning that is already there) becomes *eisegesis* (reading *into* the text meaning that is not there). This error is very subtle.

To illustrate how Scripture is distorted when believers attempt to apply the Bible to their lives without regard to what the Scripture really means, we shall look at two familiar areas of church life where such distortion often takes place.

Distortion by Bible Students. At a typical Bible study, whether Sabbath School class or small group meeting at the home, someone reads a short verse or passage. The leader then asks: "What does this passage mean to you?" to which several respond with whatever thoughts come to their minds. Very few, if any, have had the time to study the passage ahead of time. Since the leader seeks to encourage everyone, he affirms each one by expressing delight in their spiritual insights. What may not be readily obvious to many is that Bible study has been transformed to a pooling of the ignorance and opinions of people *about* the Bible!

The problem with this popular approach to Scripture is that it identifies relevance as interpretation. Notice that the leader really asked the wrong question. The Bible passage read was first directed to a particular individual or groups of individuals at a certain time and place, by a certain inspired writer or speaker, for a specific purpose. Instead of asking "What does the passage mean *to you?*" is it not first important to ask: "What does the text *mean?*"

Popular distortions of Scripture can be ridiculous. Recently, I read the following account: "I watched in horror a couple of years ago as a guest on a charismatic television network explained the 'biblical basis' of his ministry of 'possibility thinking.' 'My ministry is based entirely on my life verse, Matthew 19:26, *With God all things are possible.* God gave me that verse because I was born in 1926.'

"Obviously intrigued by that method of obtaining a 'life verse,' the talk show host grabbed a Bible and began thumbing through excitedly. 'I was born in 1934,' he said. 'My life verse would be Matthew 19:34. What does it say?' Then he discovered that Matthew 19 has only thirty verses. Undeterred, he flipped to Luke 19 and read verse 34: *And they said, the Lord hath need of him* (KJV).

"Thrilled, he exclaimed, 'Oh, the Lord has need of me! The Lord has need of me! What a wonderful life verse! I've never had a life verse before, but now the Lord has given me one! Thank you, Jesus! Hallelujah!' The studio audience began to applaud.

"At that moment, however, the talk show host's wife, who had also turned to Luke 19, said, 'Wait a minute! You can't use this. This verse is talking about a *donkey!*'"[21]

Such distortions are not limited to charismatics. The story aptly illustrates the willy-nilly way some church members approach Scripture. Seeking for something that seems applicable to whatever trial or need they are facing, some Bible students use Scripture in this manner. While God can speak through donkeys and even stones, studying the Bible in this way is not how to ascertain "a word from the Lord."

Distortion by Bible Teachers and Preachers. Some pastors, preachers, and teachers are also guilty of this "the Lord gave me this verse" abuse of Scriptures, though they may often give the appearance of being faithful to the Word. But just as some believers distort the Word by seeking the contemporary meaning of the Bible without regard to its historical, cultural, and grammatical meaning, so also do these pastors, preachers, and teachers use the Bible merely as a launching pad to recycle their opinions. What often parades as biblical teaching and preaching in today's churches is more of form, rhetoric, and antics than of substance.

To give the impression that they are explaining the Bible, these teachers and preachers may sprinkle a few Greek and Hebrew words on some selected Bible texts, and having performed this ceremonial rite, they launch into: (i) moralistic advice or pep-talks on some techniques of modern psychological therapy, (ii) a rousing speech on politics or some other ideological fad, (iii) a pursuit of comedy, theatrics or even occultic exorcisms of alleged demonic oppression, (iv) creative or moving stories to tickle the ears, or (v) recycled public opinions or the opinions of experts.

All this is done in the name of "relevance" or of meeting the needs of church members, with the teachers and preachers thinking that such gimmicks and high-sounding human words will revitalize the church and cause it to grow. Meanwhile, the world and the church languish in a great famine for the unadulterated Word of God (cf. Amos 8:11-12).

A *Los Angeles Times Magazine* article illustrated the results of this famine. A Protestant church in Southern California distributes flyers advertising their church as "God's Country Goodtime Hour," with a bold promise: "Line dancing following worship." The reporter wrote: "The pastor is dancing, too, decked out in Wrangler boots and Levis." She continued: "Members listen to sermons whose topics include the pastor's '70 Ford pickup, and Christian sex (rated R for 'relevance, respect, and relationship . . . and more fun than it sounds'). After service, they dance to a band called—what else?—Honkytonk Angels. Attendance has been steadily rising."[22]

The apostle Paul had the solution to today's problem: "I charge thee therefore before God, and the Lord Jesus Christ, who shall judge the quick and the dead at his appearing and his kingdom. *Preach the word;* be instant in season, out of season; reprove, rebuke, exhort with all longsuffering and doctrine. For the time will come when they will not endure sound doctrine; but after their own lusts shall they heap to themselves teachers, having itching ears; And they shall turn away their ears from the truth, and shall be turned unto fables. But watch thou in all things, endure afflictions, do the work of an evangelist, make full proof of thy ministry" (2 Tim 4:1-5, emphasis supplied).

Diminishing Popular Distortions. Sound principles of Bible interpretation (hermeneutics) can reduce some of the distortions of the Word. By studying the Bible in its historical, grammatical and literary context, comparing Scripture with Scripture, we can come to a better understanding of what a text meant to its original readers. Only as we understand what a text *meant* to its writer and original recipients can we be in a position to know what it *means* for us today.

In the next chapter we shall show that "rightly dividing the Word" means avoiding spiritualizing or allegorizing the Bible in the name of relevance or meaningfulness. We must first ascertain the historical-grammatical meaning of Scripture, and from there proceed to draw valid principles for contemporary application.

Scholarly Distortion: Evaluation as Interpretation

The scholars' most common form of scriptural distortion is viewing interpretation as *evaluation.* Rather than simply seeking to understand what the Bible writer said or wrote, such scholars think that they must declare whether a given passage is truthful, ethical, or factually accurate.

Scholars thus impose upon the Bible passage their own assumptions or presuppositions regarding what constitutes truthfulness, right and wrong, or factual accuracy, and on these assumptions they reconstruct the Bible, distorting biblical exposition into an ideological imposition.

In other words, in the scholarly approach (the historical-critical method), what should have been a sound *exegesis* (reading *out* of the biblical text what is already there) is reduced to a dubious *eisegesis* (reading *into* the biblical text what is not there). In this respect, both the scholarly approach and the popular approach are expressions of the proof-text method. They differ only in kind and degree.

To understand how scholars are manufacturing difficulties from the plainest revealed truths of Scripture, imposing their unbiblical assumptions on Scripture, we shall need to take a look at their attitude toward the Bible and the kinds of doubts they raise concerning its inspired message.

The Critical Scholars and the Bible

In the Seventh-day Adventist church, just as in other Bible-believing conservative churches, criticism of the Bible is carried out by moderate liberals. As we explained in Chapter Three, moderate liberalism or accommodationism is old-fashioned liberalism in new and respectable garb: "The only significant difference between the new Liberalism and the old seems to be that the former lays more stress than did the latter on the importance of *believing* the more or less mangled Bible that comes out of the critical mincing-machine."[23]

Unlike the classical or radical liberals whose loud critical voices are heard from time to time in Christian churches, accommodationists are not so radical or vocal in their rejection of some portions of the Bible. This is why they appeal to many Christians as earnest, "progressive," and "open-minded" Christians.

They argue eloquently that the Bible is not as simplistic or ordinary as the radical liberals want people to believe; neither is it wholly trustworthy and dependable as the Bible-believing Christians want to maintain. But accommodationists are closer to radical liberals than to Bible-believing conservatives in their views on biblical authority and interpretation.

Biblical Authority. Even though they claim to make the Bible central in their Christian faith and practice, accommodationists do not take the Bible as the final word on any issue. The Bible only opens possibilities for its readers, but the determination of what to believe and practice is the individual's responsibility. The Bible, they claim, does not have answers for every issue; more often it raises questions.

One non-Adventist accommodationist writer stated: "There is a natural and understandable human desire to have some authority available to us that would answer all questions. What God has given us, instead, is a Word which prompts more questions than it answers. In Scripture, God has uttered for us not the last word but the first—a Word designed to set us off on a pilgrimage, in pursuit of that life that he has willed for us to have."[24]

When this author writes that "in Scripture, God has uttered for us not the last word but the first," he is stating subtly that the Bible is not the sole or normative authority for the Christian. In this view, Scripture has only a "primary authority" over experience and empirical data.

Biblical Interpretation. Besides their different views on scriptural authority, critical scholars also differ from Bible-believing scholars in their method of Bible interpretation. Accommodationists claim to find in the Bible some intrinsic problems such as errors, contradictions, irrelevance, and even immorality. The preferred terms for the alleged contradictions and errors in the Bible are "diversities," "differences," and "disturbing details."

According to moderate liberals, such problems should not disturb mature Christians, since the "discrepancies" or "inaccuracies" inherent in Scriptures are "minor" in comparison to the Bible's great themes of salvation. Accommodationists explain that just as I consider my wife to be a good loving wife despite her occasional mistakes, so also the Bible is a good book, despite its occasional inaccuracies.

If Scripture is not absolutely trustworthy and dependable, how are we to determine when the Bible is not presenting the truth? Accommodationist scholars answer this question by appealing to the "assured results" of modern (liberal) scholarship. In other words, they exalt the findings of historical-critical methodology as the norm by which we can accept or reject certain portions of the Bible.

But the accommodationist is faced with a dilemma. He wants to be true to the Bible and to critical methodology at the same time. He wants the acceptance of Bible-believing conservative Christians, and at the same time, he seeks the respect of liberal theologians. In the end, he is not truly accepted by either camp.

A Look at Some Bible Difficulties

In order to understand the nature of Scripture's alleged discrepancies, we must look briefly at some of the assumptions behind accommodationists' claims of error.[25] As we did with the quail problem in Chapter One, in Chapter Ten we shall deal with many of them.

The Bible and Modern Science. The Bible's worldview, we are told, conflicts with some aspects of modern science. Consequently Christians can no longer accept those portions of Scripture founded on this "pre-scientific" worldview.

These questions are often posed: (1) Can well-meaning Christians still accept a literal six-day creation when modern science has "clearly and persuasively" shown that the theory of evolution is more acceptable than divine creation? (2) Since the earth revolves around the sun and not vice versa, how could the sun have stood still in Joshua's day? (3) How do we prove the Bible's assertion in Leviticus 11:6 and Deuteronomy 14:7 that hares chew the cud? (4) How can the circular "sea of cast metal" in Solomon's temple (2 Chron 4:1-2) have a diameter of 10 cubits and yet have a circumference of 30 cubits, when we know from simple mathematics that the circumference should be about 31.42 cubits (circumference = π x diameter, i.e., 3.142 x 10)?

The Bible and Ancient History. Moderate liberals argue that the way in which the Bible writers wrote their accounts of ancient historical events is no different from the manner in which historians of every generation report theirs. Even in our age of computers, satellites, fax machines, and internet communication systems, it is often difficult to ascertain fully the facts surrounding an event. It is very difficult to explain, for example, what *really* happened during the Gulf War and the *real* reason behind it. Because people may forget, misunderstand, misinterpret, and even distort events, some suggest that the Bible's historical accounts suffer the same problems as other histories.

Questions often raised include: (1) Was there ever a *worldwide* flood in the days of Noah, as recorded in Genesis 6-8? (2) Did the number of people who left Egypt during the exodus reach 600,000 men (about 2 million people, if women and children are included)? (3) Did Caesar Augustus order an empire-wide census while Quirinius was governor over Syria (Luke 2:1-2)?

The Bible and Predictive Prophecy. Critical scholars suggest that whatever Scripture presents as a prophetic prediction of the future is no prediction after all, since the "open view of God" in liberal theology does not allow for a God who knows the future. Therefore, Bible prophecies are dismissed as descriptions of what has already happened presented in the guise of a prophecy of what will happen (this is known technically as *vaticinium ex eventu*). This view also assumes that there can be no miraculous manifestations, including God's ability to foretell the future; therefore, wherever there are clear evidences of fulfilled prophecies, the prophecies must have been written after the events actually took place.

Questions associated with this view affect how we date some books of the Bible and how their prophecies are to be interpreted. For example: Are the five books of Moses to be dated to the time of Moses or to a later date such as the 10th century B.C. (the time of David and Solomon), the 9th century (the time of Elijah and Elisha), or the 8th, 7th or 6th centuries or later (pre-exilic, exilic or even post-exilic times)? Did Daniel the prophet really live and prophesy in the 6th century B.C. (the time of Babylon) as the Bible says, or did someone else write the Book of Daniel in the 2nd century B.C. (during the time of Greece), making up "prophecies" to fit past events?

The Bible and Ethical Morality. Some scholars find certain Bible accounts ethically repugnant to their individual feelings and moral judgments. It is ironic that our generation, thriving on violence and lewdness in popular magazines and television, should be repulsed by certain accounts in the Bible.

Examples often cited include:

(1) The morally offensive character and acts of Old Testament *figures*. Examples include the lies, cover-ups, immorality, adultery, murder, etc., of Abraham, Jacob, David, Solomon, and others—people on the Bible's honor roll (Heb 11).

(2) The morally offensive character and acts of *God*. These include statements in the Bible in which God is represented as partial, fickle, hateful, vengeful, and otherwise morally unworthy; God's apparent complicity in the she-bear attack on a group of boys (2 Kings 2:23-25); God's command to Israel to "go and smite Amalek, and utterly destroy all that they have; do not spare them, but kill both man and woman, infant and suckling, ox and sheep, camel and ass" (1 Sam 15:3); God's endorsement of executions of people with other religions (e.g., Baal worship, witchcraft, sorcery, astrology, etc.), other days of worship than His seventh-day Sabbath (Ex 22:18, 20; Ex 35:2; Num 15:32-36; Deut 13:1-10), alternate lifestyles like homosexuality, sex between consenting adults—within or without the marriage relationship (Lev 20:10-21; Deut 22:20-22), problem children—whether they be incorrigible, delinquent, or disobedient (Deut 17:12; 21:18-21; Ex 21:15; Lev 20:9; Prov 20:20), etc.[26]

The Bible's Own Alleged Internal Discrepancies. While the previous cases of alleged errors are ideological in nature, that is to say, the Bible is construed as mistaken on the basis of the accommodationist's presuppositions on science, history, and ethics, the fourth example of "inaccuracies" in the Bible is argued on the basis of alleged self-contradictions in the scriptural text itself.

In a court of law, a lack of confidence in the credibility of a witness can result in dismissing the witness's testimony in important matters. Thus, if it can be shown from the Bible itself that it contains discrepancies, contradictions, and errors, however minor or inconsequential they may be, then one may more easily reject any other part of the Bible, including doctrinal and theological parts.

For example, one can easily dismiss the Bible's condemnation of homosexuality if it can be proved that the Bible is mistaken on some issues and therefore may be mistaken in its condemnation of homosexuality. Similarly, if one can disregard the creation basis of the Bible's teaching of *male* headship, why can't one also ignore the *seventh-day* Sabbath, since it is also rooted in creation?[27]

The kinds of questions raised by the Bible's alleged internal discrepancies include: Where was Jacob finally buried? Was it at Shechem, in the tomb of Abraham (Acts 7:16) or at Hebron (Gen 50:13; cf. 23:19)? Who is telling the truth regarding the motivation, the exact number, the personalities, and costs involved in David's census? Is it 2 Samuel 24 or 1 Chronicles 21?

Further, which of the four gospel writers should be trusted when there are apparent discrepancies between their accounts? For example, which genealogy of Christ is correct, Matthew 1 or Luke 3? How many demoniacs met Jesus at Gadara— one (Mark 5:2 and Luke 8:27) or two (Matt 8:28)? How many blind men were healed in Jesus' encounter with Bartimaeus—one (Mark 10:46 and Luke 18:35) or two (Matt 20:30)? Did Jesus instruct his disciples to take a staff on their preaching mission (Mark 6:8) or did he specifically prohibit the taking of a staff (Matt 10:9-10; Luke 9:3)? How many times did the cock crow (Matt 26:74; Luke 22:60; John 18:27; Mark 14:72)? How many angels were at Christ's tomb on the resurrection morning—one (Matt 28:5 and Mark 16:5) or two (Luke 24:4 and John 20:12)?

In a later chapter we shall *wrestle with the Word* regarding some of these alleged errors or contradictions of the Bible. Before doing so, however, we shall first highlight some implications these so-called discrepancies may have for the authority and reliability of Scriptures. For if these questions are valid, they suggest that the Bible writers were not always truthful or accurate in what they wrote.

Implications of Alleged Discrepancies

Charles Wesley, one of the founders of Methodism, drew out the implications of the alleged biblical discrepancies:

> The Bible must be the invention either of good men or angels, bad men or devils, or of God. Therefore:
>
> 1. It could not be the invention of good men or angels, for they neither would nor could make a book, and tell lies all the time they were writing it, saying, "Thus saith the Lord," when it was their own invention.
>
> 2. It could not be the invention of bad men or devils, for they would not make a book which commands all duty, forbids all sin, and condemns their souls to hell to all eternity.
>
> 3. Therefore, I draw this conclusion, that the Bible must be given by divine inspiration.[28]

But if the alleged discrepancies are valid, Bible-believing Christians will have to address their implications for Scripture's inspiration, trustworthiness, and authority.

The Question of Divine Accommodation. Does God accommodate Himself to popular opinion, even opinions that are in error? Does God in Scripture ever make an incidental affirmation of a "fact" that was untrue? Some scholars think so. They argue that even though God or Jesus was aware of the truth of certain minor historical, scientific, or geographical facts, (a) for the sake of the people at that time whose knowledge of those truths was limited, and (b) for the sake of effectively communicating His ethical and theological teachings to them, He deliberately accommodated His message to the needs of the people, sometimes by adopting mistaken views prevalent in those days.

This view is not only contrary to Scripture's own testimony, it raises many theological questions:

1. If this view of divine accommodation is right, that is to say, if God intentionally affirmed incidental falsehoods in order to present greater truths, then God is guilty of telling "white lies." But the Bible teaches that it is "impossible for God to lie" (Heb 6:18); God "cannot lie" (Titus 1:2); "thy word is truth" (John 17:17; cf. 10:35).

2. If such a view of accommodation is correct, it raises moral problems for Christians since they are called to imitate the character of God (Lev 11:44; Eph 5:1).

3. If this position on accommodation is right, it denies the Bible writers' unanimous affirmation of the truthfulness of *every* statement in Scripture—not some, or most (Ps 12:6; 18:30; 119:96; Prov 30:5; Matt 22:44-45; Luke 24:25; John 10:35; Acts 3:18; 24:14; Rom 15:4; 2 Tim 3:16-17; etc.).

4. If such a view of divine accommodation is valid, it is contrary to Jesus' claim that "He who sent me is true, and I declare to the world what I have heard from Him" (John 8:26, 38).

5. Finally, adopting this view of divine accommodation is contrary to the practice of Jesus, who refused to accommodate Himself to the mistaken views current in his day. His statements, "You have heard that it was said of old. . . . But I say unto you" (Matt 5; cf. John 8:24, 44), illustrate this fact. For this reason, Jesus took contrary positions on divorce, oath-taking, and traditions regarding food (Matt 19:9; 23:16-22; 15:11-20). If Jesus, the Incarnate Word, deliberately accommodated Himself to mistaken views of His day, He was a liar and therefore a sinner. But the Bible says that He "did no sin, neither was guile found in his mouth" (1 Pet 2:22).

The Problem of "Mistakes" or "Errors." By errors, we are *not* referring to those that may have crept into the text as a result of transmission (e.g. occasional or apparent discrepancies due to copyist glosses, slips, misspellings, additions, etc.) and which can be corrected by comparing the various manuscripts.

The question at hand has to do with "errors" alleged to have originated with the Bible writers themselves at the time they wrote their accounts. For example, was Moses mistaken when he wrote of a literal six-day creation, a literal Adam and Eve, a literal universal flood, a miraculous Exodus consisting of over 600,000 males, etc.? Was Matthew deceived or mistaken about the virgin birth or about the crucifixion and the bodily resurrection of Jesus? Was Paul misguided when he condemned homosexuality because he lacked knowledge of an alleged genetic basis for homosexuality? These are the kinds of "errors" we have in mind.

Are the details (however minor) in the Bible accurate and trustworthy, or are they mere theological statements, void of any factual certainty? How do we define what constitutes an "error" in Scripture? Does an interpreter possess superior wisdom and spiritual insight to determine the "mistakes," "contradictions," or "errors" of the Bible? What if the person's judgment is wrong? What if that individual condemns as "mistaken" what is correct and endorses as correct what is erroneous?

Bible-believing Christians accept the biblical command: "Trust in the Lord with all thine heart; and lean not unto thine own understanding. In all thy ways acknowledge him, and he shall direct thy paths" (Prov 3:5, 6).

Therefore, when Bible-believers perceive difficulties in Scripture, rather than judging the Bible to be "contradictory," they question their own assumptions. As they study prayerfully, they ask God to shed more light on the difficult passages. God has done so in the past.

For example, through the painstaking studies of the Adventist scholar Edwin Thiele, the world came to recognize that there are no contradictions in the chronology of the Hebrew Kings; through the discovery of scientists, He proved that rabbits (Lev 11) chew the cud; through archaeologists He showed the trustworthiness of historical details of the Old Testament.[29]

The decision to suspend judgment as they wrestle with difficult biblical texts is one of the reasons why Bible-believing scholars study the Bible so earnestly. It would be easier for them simply to declare unresolved difficulties as errors, thereby avoiding the challenge of seeking biblical solutions.

Saving Acts vs. Factual Statements. As we pointed out in Chapter Five, Part III, some scholars suggest that we can accept the Exodus miracle but that the *exact number* of people involved in the Exodus is not that crucial; they claim that there was a miraculous flood in Noah's day but that it was less than a *universal* event. In effect, these scholars suggest that in Scripture some things are "essential" and others are "debatable." Their model for biblical inspiration allows for human imperfections in the "lesser matters" of Scriptures.[30]

Can we make a distinction between theological statements of God's saving acts and their accompanying historical descriptions? Is there a dichotomy between true doctrine and true science? For example, can we separate the theology of creation (the "who" of creation) from the scientific issues (the "how" and the "how long" of creation)? Can we separate the miracles of the exodus from the actual number of people who left Egypt and the biblical dating of that event? On what basis do we accept one and not the other?

Bible writers make no such distinction between saving acts and the historicity of the details. Some 400-500 years after the events of Moses' day, later Old Testament writers reaffirmed their historicity (see, for example, Ps 105; 106; Isa 28:21; 1 Kings 16:34).

The New Testament writers, more than a thousand years after the events, trusted even the smallest details of the Old Testament narratives. They wrote about detailed aspects in the Old Testament accounts of Abraham, Rebecca, and the history of Israel (Acts 13:17-23; Rom 4:10, 19; 9:10-12; 1 Cor 10:1-11). They gave a detailed description of the Old Testament sanctuary (Heb 9:1-5, 19-21), the manner of creation (Heb 11:3), the particulars of the lives of Abel, Enoch, Noah, Abraham, Moses, Rahab and others (Heb 11; 7:2; James 2:25), Esau (Heb 12:16-17), the saving of eight persons during the universal flood (1 Pet 3:20; 2 Pet 2:5; 3:5, 6), and the talking of Balaam's donkey (2 Pet 2:16), etc.

Moreover, Jesus, our example, accepted the full trustworthiness of the Old Testament accounts, making no distinction between history and theology. For example, He believed in the historicity of Adam and Eve, Cain and Abel, Noah's universal flood, and Jonah's story (Matt 19:4, 5; 23:35; 24:38, 39; 12:40).

On the basis of the Scriptures, Bible-believing scholars make no dichotomy between so-called "essential" and "debatable" aspects of Old Testament saving acts. *They do not claim to be more Christlike than Christ, or more apostolic than the apostles, in their use of Scripture.* Like their Savior, they accept every historical detail—chronology, numbers, events and people—as a matter of faith and practice.[31]

Diminishing Scholarly Distortions

We have mentioned that moderate liberals' distortions of the Word arise from their viewing *evaluation* as part of interpretation of the biblical text. By imposing their ideological assumptions on the Bible, such scholars reject as unreliable, mistaken, or erroneous the parts of Scripture which do not conform to their presuppositions.

In a later chapter, *Receiving the Word* will address some of the problem passages which historical-critical scholars often cite as untrustworthy. Here, however, we shall state some key principles for Bible-believing Adventists to remember whenever they are confronted with apparent errors, contradictions, or mistakes in the Bible.

The following principles are based on the fact that the Bible is both human and divine. This mysterious union finds a fitting analogy in the Person of Jesus Christ at his incarnation. Just as Christ was fully divine even in His humanity, so Scripture is of divine origin though written by human hands.[32] This truth should caution us against hastily ascribing mistakes or contradictions to the Bible writers.

1. A Divine Document. As a divine document the Bible shares in the unquestionable, supreme, and infallible authority of God. In the words of Ellen G. White, Christ "pointed to the Scriptures as of unquestionable authority, and we should do the same. The Bible is to be presented as the word of the infinite God, as the end of all controversy and the foundation of all faith."[33] "God and heaven alone are infallible. . . . Man is fallible, but God's Word is infallible."[34] Therefore the Bible is "an unerring counselor, and infallible guide" and the "perfect guide under all circumstances of life";[35] "an unerring guide," "the one unerring guide," "the unerring standard," "an unerring light," "that unerring test," and "the unerring counsel of God."[36]

Because the Bible shares in the unerring character of God, we should not question the truth of any of its parts or pick flaws with what may seem to be mistakes, inconsistencies, or errors. Neither should we criticize nor ridicule the Scriptures.[37] "We should reverence God's word. For the printed volume we should show respect, never putting it to common uses, or handling it carelessly."[38]

2. A Human Document. As a human document the Bible reflects the individuality of its human writers. "God has been pleased to communicate His truth to the world by human agencies, and He Himself, by His Holy Spirit, qualified men and enabled them to do this work. He guided the mind in the selection of what to speak and what to write (*The Great Controversy,* p. vi).

"In our Bible, we might ask, Why need Matthew, Mark, Luke, and John in the Gospels, why need the Acts of the Apostles, and the variety of writers in the Epistles, go over the same thing? The Lord gave His word in just the way He wanted it to come. He gave it through different writers, each having his own individuality, though going over the same history. Their testimonies are brought together in one Book, and are like the testimonies in a social meeting [testimony service]. They do not represent things in just the same style. Each has an experience of his own, and this diversity broadens and deepens the knowledge that is brought out to meet the necessities of varied minds. The thoughts expressed have not a set uniformity, as if cast in an iron mold, making the very hearing monotonous. In such uniformity there would be a loss of grace" (*Selected Messages,* 1:21-22).

Rather than looking for alleged contradictions in the parallel accounts (e.g., the different ways the Gospel writers presented their accounts), we must look for underlying harmony. "The Creator of all ideas may impress different minds with the same thought, but each may express it in a different way, *yet without contradiction.* The fact that this difference exists should not perplex or confuse us. It is seldom that two persons will view and express truth in the very same way. Each dwells on particular points which his constitution and education have fitted him to appreciate. The sunlight falling upon the different objects gives those objects a different hue" (*Selected Messages,* 1:22, emphasis supplied).

3. A Trustworthy Document. In a trustworthy document, unresolved difficulties should challenge interpreters' assumptions, attitudes, and approaches. Since the Bible is reliable and trustworthy, and since there is an underlying harmony in all of its parts, whenever there appears to be a contradiction or mistake in the Scriptures, Bible-believing students should seriously examine their own presuppositions, attitudes, and approach to Scripture.

Conclusion

This chapter has briefly discussed why and how the authority of the Bible is often diminished from *the liberating Word* (at the hands of the inspired writers), through the process of *liberating the Word* (by copyists and translators who seek to make the Bible accessible to average people), to *the liberated Word* (at the hands of interpreters). While there was no distortion of the Word when the Bible writers communicated their inspired messages, and while minor distortions of the Word developed during the time of transmission (i.e., copying and translation), the grossest distortions of the Word occur at the hand of interpreters.

This raises the question: How can Christians today, who have received the Word as inspired, trustworthy, and their sole authoritative norm, ensure that the Bible in their hands will truly function as the liberating Word of God? The answer lies in *rightly dividing the Word.* To this issue we turn our attention in the next chapter.

NOTES

1. These expressions come from the feminist scholar Letty M. Russell, "Introduction: Liberating the Word," in *Feminist Interpretation of the Bible,* ed. Letty M. Russell (Philadelphia, Pa: Westminster

Press, 1985), pp. 11-18. We will employ the terms in the titles for the three major sections of this chapter, but with a different meaning from what Russell originally meant by them.

2. See Norman R. Gulley, "Reader-Response Theories in Postmodern Hermeneutics: A Challenge to Evangelical Theology," in *The Challenge of Postmodernism: An Evangelical Engagement,* ed. David S. Dockery (Wheaton, Ill.: Victor Books, 1995), pp. 219-224. In chapter 11 we will briefly discuss the methodologies of liberation and feminist theologies.

3. Kathleen McCan called my attention to a slight distinction between an "alteration" and a "distortion." An alteration occurs when there is a change in an original document. Sometimes the alteration (or changing) of a single word of a sender's message does not change the essential meaning (e.g., "Thus saith the Lord" and "Thus speaketh the Lord" convey the same exact meaning). Other times an alteration effects a slightly different meaning than that which was originally intended (e.g., the insertion of a comma by translators of Luke 23:43 has Jesus as saying, "Verily I say unto thee, today shalt thou be with me in paradise"). While the essential message of Jesus, His assurance to the thief on the cross, is preserved, the timing of when the thief would be with Jesus introduces a (slightly) different meaning to the words of Jesus. Still, some alterations involve a deliberate distortion (e.g., the translation of John 1:1 in the Jehovah's Witnesses' *New World Translation* inserts the single letter word "a" before God: "In the beginning was the Word and the Word was with God and the Word was a god"). In short, while there were no distortions from the original Bible writers, some alterations and minor distortions have been introduced in the Word during the copying and translation process.

4. Ernst Würthwein, an authority in textual criticism, offered some reasons for transmission errors: "We know how easily errors can occur in copying a text. By accident a word may be missed or repeated, groups of words may be inadvertently transposed or replaced by similar or synonymous words, and if the handwriting is difficult to read, an element of guesswork may enter. Many errors may be due to carelessness, especially if the copyist is a professional scribe who works rapidly and becomes casual, and further may not be familiar with the subject of the text he is copying. But even the scribe who approaches his text with interest and devotion may introduce corruptions. He may find an expression in his exemplar which in his view reflects an earlier scribe's misunderstanding of the author, and in his concern for the meaning of the text he naturally corrects it, just as we would correct a typographical error in a printed book. But his correction itself could very well reflect his own misunderstanding! It is not only the casual or absentminded scribe who introduces errors, but the conscientious scribe as well. The next stage in the process is obvious. A scribe copying a faulty manuscript—and no manuscript is without errors—will deal with his predecessor's errors either by guesswork or with ingenuity, with the result a series of intended improvements leading away from the original text" (see Ernst Würthwein, *The Text of the Old Testament,* trans. Errol F. Rhodes [Grand Rapids, Mich.: Eerdmans, 1979], p. xvii).

5. F. F. Bruce, *Second Thoughts on the Dead Sea Scrolls* (Grand Rapids, Mich.: Eerdmans, 1964), p. 61.

6. Causes of error in New Testament manuscripts are discussed in some detail in Bruce M. Metzger, *The Text of the New Testament: Its Transmission, Corruption, and Restoration,* 2nd ed. (New York: Oxford University, 1968), pp. 186ff.; Jack Finegan, *Encountering New Testament Manuscripts: A Working Introduction to Textual Criticism* (Grand Rapids, Mich.: Eerdmans, 1974); D. A. Carson, *The King James Version: A Plea for Realism* (Grand Rapids, Mich.: Baker, 1979), pp. 21-24; Carson's work is an excellent resource for students, pastors, and lay people who seek to understand some of the principles of biblical textual criticism. We are indebted to the above works for the discussion in the following paragraphs.

7. Lee J. Gugliotto, *Handbook for Bible Study* (Hagerstown, Md.: Review and Herald, 1995), pp. 313-346.

8. F. F. Bruce, *The New Testament Documents: Are They Reliable?* 5th rev. ed. (Grand Rapids, Mich.: Eerdmans, 1984), pp. 15-17. In comparing the quality and quantity of the 5,000 Greek New Testament manuscripts with other ancient historical material, Bruce, the classicist turned biblical scholar, wrote: "Perhaps we can appreciate how wealthy the New Testament is in manuscript attestation if we compare the textual material for other ancient historical works. For Caesar's *Gallic War*

(composed between 58 and 50 B.C.) there are several extant MSS [manuscripts], but only nine or ten are good, and the oldest is some 900 years later than Caesar's day. Of the 142 books of the Roman History of Livy (59 B.C.-A.D. 17) only thirty-five survive; these are known to us from not more than twenty MSS of any consequence, only one of which, and that containing fragments of Books iii-vi, is as old as the fourth century. Of the fourteen books of the *Histories* of Tacitus (c. A.D. 100) only four and a half survive; of the sixteen books of his *Annals,* ten survive in full and two in part. The text of these extant portions of his two great historical works depends entirely on two MSS, one of the ninth century and one of the eleventh. The extant MSS of his minor works (*Dialogus de Oratoribus, Agricola, Germania*) all descend from a codex of the tenth century. The History of Thucydides (c. 460-400 B.C.) is known to us from eight MSS, the earliest belonging to c. A.D. 900, and a few papyrus scraps, belonging to about the beginning of the Christian era. The same is true of the History of Herodotus (c. 488-428 B.C.). Yet no classical scholar would listen to an argument that the authenticity of Herodotus or Thucydides is in doubt because the earliest MSS of their works which are of any use to us are over 1,300 years later than the originals" (ibid., pp. 16-17).

9. The estimate comes from Edward W. Goodrick, the author of *Do It Yourself Hebrew and Greek,* a textbook for biblical Hebrew and Greek. See his book, *Is My Bible the Inspired Word of God?* (Portland, Ore.: Multnomah Press, 1988), p. 57. This latter work is extraordinarily comprehensive, even in its simplicity and brevity. Cf. Brooke Foss Westcott and Fenton John Anthony Hort, *The New Testament in the Original Greek,* rev. American ed., 2 vols. (New York: Harper, 1887), 2:2.

10. For a detailed listing of such occurrences in the writings of Ellen G. White, see volume 5 of the *Seventh-day Adventist Bible Commentary* (Washington, D.C.: Review and Herald, 1956), pp. 660, 983, 994.

11. Since some manuscripts omit or place in brackets the texts of John 7:53-8:11 and Mark 16:9-20, textual scholars, whether liberal or conservative, disagree over whether or not these are part of the apostolic autographs. Their disagreements relate to the rules they apply in their work of textual analysis. This much, though, can be said: "It is true that the longer ending of Mark 16:9-20 is found in 99 percent of the Greek manuscripts as well as the rest of the tradition, enjoying over a period of centuries practically an official sanction as a genuine part of the gospel of Mark. But in Codex Vaticanus (**B**) as well as in Codex Sinaiticus (ℵ) the gospel of Mark ends at Mark 16:8, as it did also in numerous other manuscripts according to the statements of Eusebius of Caesarea and Jerome" (Kurt Aland and Barbara Aland, *The Text of the New Testament,* trans. Erroll F. Rhodes [Grand Rapids, Mich.: Eerdmans, 1987], p. 287). For a discussion of some rules of textual criticism, and how they are applied to some selected texts of the New Testament, see ibid., pp. 275-311.

12. D. A. Carson, *The King James Version Debate: A Plea for Realism* (Grand Rapids, Mich.: Baker, 1979), p. 56.

13. The Preface to the New King James Version explains, "This principle of complete equivalence seeks to preserve *all* of the information in the text, while presenting it in good literary form. Dynamic equivalence, a recent procedure in Bible translation, commonly results in paraphrasing where a more literal rendering is needed to reflect a specific and vital sense."

14. See General Conference Committee on Problems in Bible Translation, *Problems in Bible Translation* (Washington, D.C.: Review and Herald, 1954).

15. For detailed evaluation of the strengths and weaknesses of the major English translations, see Jack P. Lewis, *The English Bible from KJV to NIV: A History and Evaluation* (Grand Rapids, Mich.: Baker, 1991); cf. Sakae Kubo and Walter Specht, *So Many Versions: Twentieth Century English Versions of the Bible* (Grand Rapids, Mich.: Zondervan, 1975); C. Raymond Holmes, *The Tip of An Iceberg* (Berrien Springs, Mich.: Adventists Affirm and Pointer Publications, 1994), pp. 95-98; see also Wayne Grudem's 22-page article, "What's Wrong with Gender-Neutral Bible Translations? A Critique of the *New Revised Standard Version,*" available through The Council on Biblical Manhood and Womanhood (CBMW), P. O. Box 317, Wheaton, IL 60189 or E-mail: CBMWHendo@aol.com.

16. Carson, *The King James Version Debate,* p. 36.

17. For a work advocating the merits of the King James Version (KJV), see Benjamin G. Wilkinson, *Our Authorized Bible Vindicated* (Washington, D.C.: n.p., 1930); *Answers to Objections to "Our*

Authorized Bible" (Payson, Ariz.: Leaves of Autumn Books, 1989). A moderating voice in the KJV debate is James R. White's *The King James Only Controversy: Can You Trust the Modern Transla-tions?* (Minneapolis, Minn.: Bethany House, 1995); cf. D. A. Carson, *The King James Version De-bate: A Plea for Realism;* Jack P. Lewis, *The English Bible From KJV to NIV: A History and Evalua-tion,* pp. 401-404. For a brief but excellent summary of the arguments for and against the Greek manuscripts behind the KJV Bible, see the preface to the recently published *The New Geneva Study Bible [KJV],* ed. R. C. Sproul (Nashville, Tenn.: Thomas Nelson, 1995), pp. x-xiii.

18. Those who need guidance in choosing English Bible versions would benefit greatly from Jack P. Lewis, *The English Bible from KJV to NIV: A History and Evaluation*; Sakae Kubo and Walter Specht, *So Many Versions: Twentieth Century English Versions of the Bible.*

19. A helpful discussion can be found in Arthur S. Maxwell's *Your Bible and You* (Washington, D.C.: Review and Herald, n.d.), pp. 37-44 (i.e. chapter 4, titled, "Which Version is Best?").

20. See for example, Matt 21:42 and Mark 12:10-12 (cf. LXX, Ps 117:22-23 [Eng. Ps 118:22-23]), John 13:18 (cf. LXX, Ps 40:9 [Eng. 41:9]), Rom 4:3 (cf. LXX Gen 15:6), Rom 9:17 (cf. LXX, Ex 9:16), Rom 11:3-4 (cf. LXX, 1 Kings 19:10, 14, 18); Gal 3:8 (cf. LXX, Gen 12:3); Gal 4:30 (cf. LXX, Gen 21:10); 1 Tim 5:18 (cf. LXX, Deut 25:4); James 2:8 (cf. LXX, Lev 19:18); James 4:6 (cf. LXX, Pro 3:34); 1 Pet 2:6 (cf. LXX, Isa 28:16); Luke 4:18-19, 21 (cf. LXX, Isa 61:1-2); Acts 8:32-33 (cf. LXX, Isa 53:7-8). See Gleason L. Archer and G. C. Chirichigno, *Old Testament Quotations in the New Testament: A Complete Survey* (Chicago, Ill.: Moody Press, 1983).

21. John F. MacArthur, Jr., *Charismatic Chaos* (Grand Rapids, Mich.: Zondervan, 1992), p. 102.

22. Judy Raphael, "God and Country," *Los Angeles Times Magazine,* November 6, 1994, p. 14.

23. James I. Packer, *'Fundamentalism' and the Word of God* (Grand Rapids, Mich.: Eerdmans, 1958), p. 153.

24. William Countryman, *Biblical Authority or Biblical Tyranny?: Scripture and the Christian Pilgrimage* (Philadelphia: Fortress Press, 1981), p. 10.

25. Although a number of scholars have raised the same problems, I cite and adapt from the following works as representative: William Contryman, pp. 13-24, Dewey Beegle, *Scripture, Tradi-tion and Infallibility* (Grand Rapids, Mich.: Eerdmans, 1973), pp. 175-197; Stephen T. Davies, *The Debate about the Bible: Inerrancy versus Infallibility* (Philadelphia: Westminster Press, 1977), pp. 95-107; William LaSor, "Life Under Tension—Fuller Theological Seminary and the Battle for the Bible," in *The Authority of Scripture at Fuller* (Pasadena, Calif.: Fuller Theological Seminary Alumni, *Theology, News and Notes,* Special Issue, 1976), pp. 5-10, 23-28; David L. Edwards and John Stott, *Evangelical Essentials: A Liberal-Evangelical Dialogue* (Downers Grove, Ill.: InterVarsity Press, 1988), pp. 79-82; Alden Thompson, *Inspiration: Hard Questions, Honest Answers* (Hagerstown, Md.: Review and Herald, 1991), pp. 137-264.

26. The best summary of these problems is given by William Brenton Green, Jr., "The Ethics of the Old Testament: The Objections to Old Testament Ethics," *Princeton Theological Review* 28 (1929):313-366, reprinted in *Classical Evangelical Essays in Old Testament Interpretation,* compiled and edited by W. C. Kaiser, Jr. (Grand Rapids, Mich.: Baker, 1972), pp. 207-235, and Walter C. Kaiser, Jr., *Toward Old Testament Ethics* (Grand Rapids: Zondervan, 1983), pp. 247-304.

27. For more on this, see chapter 5, part 2, where we discuss the key hermeneutical issues regard-ing the role of women in the home and church, alongside the biblical understanding of the Seventh-day Adventist pioneers. Cf. Willard M. Swartley, *Slavery, Sabbath, War, and Women: Case Issues in Biblical Interpretation* (Scottdale, Pa.: Herald Press, 1983), pp. 152-234.

28. Quoted in Robert W. Burtner and Robert E. Chiles, *A Compendium of Wesley's Theology,* p. 20.

29. Edwin Thiele, *A Chronology of the Hebrew Kings* (Grand Rapids, Mich.: Zondervan, 1977). Regarding the questions raised about rabbits chewing the cud, studies comparing cows and rabbits have concluded that "it is difficult to deny that rabbits are ruminants" (Jules Carles, "The Rabbit's Secret," *CNRS Research* 5 [1977]:37). For a brief summary and bibliography of scientific studies on the issue, see Leonard R. Brand, "Do Rabbits Chew the Cud?" *Origins* 4/2 (1977):102-104; cf. *Fauna and Flora of the Bible* (London: United Bible Societies, 1972), p. 39. For how archaeological discov-

eries have confirmed the Bible, see, for example, Siegfried H. Horn, *The Spade Confirms the Book* (Washington, D.C.: Review and Herald, 1980).

30. See for instance, Thompson, *Inspiration,* pp. 202, 222, 229, 248, 249; Jeane Haerich, "Genesis Revisited," in *The Welcome Table: Setting A Place for Ordained Women,* ed. Patricia A. Habada and Rebecca Frost Brillhart (Langley Park, Md.: TEAMPress, 1995), pp. 99-101; cf. George Knight, *Anticipating the Advent: A Brief History of Seventh-day Adventists* (Boise, Id.: Pacific Press, 1993), pp. 106-107.

31. The foregoing analysis is adapted from Samuel Koranteng-Pipim, "An Analysis and Evaluation of Alden Thompson's Casebook/Codebook Approach to the Bible," in *Issues in Revelation and Inspiration,* ed. Frank Holbrook and Leo Van Dolson (Berrien Springs, Mich.: Adventist Theological Society Publications, 1992), pp. 49-51.

32. *Selected Messages,* 1:21; *The Great Controversy,* p. vi; *Testimonies for the Church,* 5:747.

33. *Christ's Object Lessons,* pp. 39-40; cf. *The Desire of Ages,* p. 253.

34. *Selected Messages,* 1:37, 416.

35. *Fundamentals of Christian Education,* p. 100.

36. *The Acts of the Apostles,* p. 506; *Testimonies for the Church,* 5:389; *The Ministry of Healing,* p. 462; *Testimonies for the Church,* pp. 247, 192; 4:441.

37. *Selected Messages,* 1:17-18.

38. *Education,* p. 244.

Chapter Nine

Rightly Dividing the Word

One major reason for today's gross distortion of the Word is that students, teachers, preachers, and leaders handle the Scriptures in a careless manner.

Lamenting this lackadaisical recklessness toward Scripture, one non-Adventist author wrote: "Imagine the practical implications if teachers of mathematics or chemistry were as slapdash as some who handle the Word of God. Would you want to be served by a pharmacist, for example, who used the 'best guess' method of filling prescriptions? Or would you take your business to an architect who worked mostly with approximations? Or would you allow a surgeon to operate on you with a table knife instead of a scalpel? The sad truth is that society would quickly grind to a halt if most professions approached their work the way many Bible teachers do."[1]

Against this background of recklessness toward the Word, the charge of the apostle Paul to Timothy becomes particularly relevant. "Study to shew thyself approved unto God, a workman that needeth not to be ashamed, *rightly dividing the word of truth*" (2 Tim 2:15). Rightly dividing the Word demands that in interpreting the Scriptures, the Bible student must: (1) not depart from the Word; (2) not doubt the Word; (3) adopt the right presuppositions and attitudes toward the Word; and (4) uphold the plain reading of Scripture.

These four requirements arise from Scripture itself, which is why they are found in the 1986 "Methods of Bible Study" document (see Appendix C). In this chapter of *Receiving the Word,* we shall flesh out these guidelines by citing some relevant passages from the writings of Ellen G. White.

Do Not Depart from the Word

In order to divide the Word rightly, the Bible student must first accept the Word wholeheartedly as the inspired, trustworthy, and solely authoritative norm for the Christian. Regrettably, many in our day are reluctant to do so. But Bible-believing Seventh-day Adventists have not been left in the dark about how Satan is working to lead people away from the truth. Deceiving Bible students, teachers, preachers, and scholars is part of Satan's end-time strategy to cut people away from their only source of authoritative knowledge.

"In these days of delusion, every one who is established in the truth will have to contend for the faith once delivered to the saints. Every variety of error will be brought out in the mysterious working of Satan, which would, if it were possible, deceive the very elect, and turn them from the truth" (*Selected Messages,* 2:98).

Ellen White proceeded to identify four major kinds of deception that Satan will introduce in order to lead Christians away from their trust and reliance in the Bible: deception from learned persons, deception through ignorance and folly, deception from false dreams and visions, and deception subtly disguised as truth (see *Selected Messages,* 2:98-100).[2]

In view of these deceptions, Christians must always insist upon the Bible as more authoritative than the opinions of human beings, whether educated or not, and regardless of whether these human opinions are attended by supernatural phenomena or disguised in angelic garments.

Rightly dividing the Word demands an uncompromising insistence upon the Word as the one non-negotiable basis of all theological discussions. Not even the decisions of church committees, the majority vote of church members, or results from public opinion polls should be exalted above the plain teaching of Scripture.

We are told: "God will have a people upon the earth to maintain *the Bible, and the Bible only,* as the standard of all doctrines and the basis of all reforms. The opinions of learned men, the deductions of science, the creeds or decisions of ecclesiastical councils, as numerous and discordant as are the churches which they represent, the voice of the majority—not one nor all of these should be regarded as evidence for or against any point of religious faith. Before accepting any doctrine or precept, *we should demand a plain 'Thus saith the Lord' in its support"* (*The Great Controversy,* p. 595, emphasis supplied).

Do Not Doubt the Word

The second step in *rightly dividing the Word* is not to doubt the Word. There are two major reasons why Christians must not doubt the Word.

First, the Bible is the most authoritative guide for Christian doctrine and conduct. "All Scripture is given by inspiration of God, and is profitable for doctrine, for reproof, for correction, for instruction in righteousness: that the man of God may be perfect, throughly furnished unto all good works" (2 Tim 3:16, 17).

Receiving the Word has a profound impact on the Bible student. Ellen White explains: "No other book is so potent to elevate the thoughts, to give vigor to the faculties, as the broad, ennobling truths of the Bible. If God's Word were studied as it should be, men would have a breadth of mind, a nobility of character, and a stability of purpose rarely seen in these times" (*Steps to Christ,* p. 90).

Second, God desires to help every Bible student rightly to understand and apply its truths. Through the ministry of the Holy Spirit and the guidance of heavenly angels, those who study the Bible are to be led "to feel the importance of those things easy to be understood" and they are to be prevented "from wresting truths difficult of comprehension." God's ultimate desire is that interpreters of His written Word will "be charmed with its beauty, admonished by its warnings, or animated and strengthened by its promises" (*The Great Controversy*, pp. 599, 600).

In view of the importance of the Word in the Christian's life and the willingness of God to help believers understand its message, Bible students must always trust the Word. When there seems to be cause to doubt the Word, Christians must be mindful of the various factors that can contribute to their doubts:

1. Some Doubts about the Bible are Due to Wrong Assumptions. "All do not understand expressions and statements alike. Some understand the statements of the Scriptures to suit their own particular minds and cases. Prepossessions, prejudices, and passions have a strong influence to darken the understanding" (*Selected Messages*, 1:20). "The Lord designs that our opinions shall be put to the test, that we may see the necessity of closely examining the living oracles to see whether or not we are in the faith" (*Review and Herald*, December 20, 1892).

"You are not to take your ideas to the Bible, and make your opinions a center around which truth is to revolve. You are to lay aside your ideas at the door of investigation, and with humble, subdued hearts, with self hid in Christ, with earnest prayer, you are to seek wisdom for God" (*Fundamentals of Christian Education*, p. 308).

"There are men who strive to be original, who are wise above what is written; therefore, their wisdom is foolishness. They discover wonderful things in advance, ideas which reveal that they are far behind in the comprehension of the divine will and purposes of God. In seeking to make plain or to unravel mysteries hid from ages from mortal man, they are like a man floundering about in the mud, unable to extricate himself and yet telling others how to get out of the muddy sea they themselves are in. This is a fit representation of the men who set themselves to correct the errors of the Bible. No man can improve the Bible by suggesting what the Lord meant to say or ought to have said" (*Selected Messages*, 1:16).

2. Some Doubts about the Bible are Due to Human Pride and Arrogance. "Those who think to make the supposed difficulties of Scripture plain, in measuring by their finite rule that which is inspired and that which is not inspired, had better cover their faces, as Elijah when the still small voice spoke to him; for they are in the presence of God and holy angels, who for ages have communicated to men light and knowledge, telling them what to do and what not to do, unfolding before them scenes of thrilling interest, waymark by waymark in symbols and signs and illustrations" (*Selected Messages,* 1:17).

"The ingenuity of men has been exercised for ages to measure the Word of God by their finite minds and limited comprehension. If the Lord, the Author of the living oracles, would throw back the curtain and reveal His wisdom and His glory before them, they would shrink into nothingness and exclaim as did Isaiah, 'I am a man of unclean lips, and I dwell in the midst of a people of unclean lips' (Isa. 6:5)." (*Selected Messages,* 1:18; cf. *Seventh-day Adventist Bible Commentary,* 7:919-920).

"It is sometimes the case that men of intellectual ability, improved by education and culture, fail to comprehend certain passages of Scripture, while others who are uneducated, whose understanding seems weak and whose minds are undisciplined, will grasp the meaning, finding strength and comfort in that which the former declare to be mysterious or pass by as unimportant. Why is this? It has been explained to me that the latter class do not rely upon their own understanding. They go to the Source of light, the One who has inspired the Scriptures, and with humility of heart ask God for wisdom, and they receive it. There are mines of truth yet to be discovered by the earnest seeker" (*Testimonies for the Church,* 5:704).

"Christ represented the truth as treasure hid in a field. It does not lie right upon the surface; we must dig for it. But our success in finding it does not depend so much on our intellectual ability as on our humility of heart and the faith which will lay hold upon divine aid" (ibid.).

3. Some Doubts about the Bible are Due to Superficial Reading. "As several [Bible] writers present a subject under varied aspects and relations, there may appear, to the superficial, careless, or prejudiced reader, to be discrepancy or contradiction, where the thoughtful, reverent student, with clearer insight, discerns the underlying harmony" (*The Great Controversy,* p. vi).

"The truths of the Bible are as pearls hidden. They must be searched, dug out by painstaking effort. Those who take only a surface view of the Scriptures will, with their superficial knowledge, which they think is very deep, talk of the contradictions of the Bible, and question the authority of the Scriptures. But those whose hearts are in harmony with truth and duty will search the Scriptures with a heart prepared to receive divine impressions. The illuminated soul sees a spiritual unity, one grand golden thread running through the whole, but it requires patience, thought, and prayer to trace out the precious golden thread" (*Selected Messages,* 1:20).

"Without the guidance of the Holy Spirit we shall be continually liable to wrest the Scriptures or to misinterpret them. There is much reading of the Bible that is without profit and in many cases is a positive injury. When the Word of God is opened without reverence and without prayer; when the thoughts and affections are not fixed upon God or in harmony with His will, the mind is clouded with doubt; and in the very study of the Bible, skepticism strengthens. The enemy takes control of the thoughts, and he suggests interpretations that are not correct" (*Testimonies for the Church,* 5:704, 705).

4. Some Doubts about the Bible are Instigated by Satan. "Men arise who think they find something to criticize in God's Word. They lay it bare before others as evidence of superior wisdom. These men are, many of them, smart men, learned men, they have eloquence and talent, the whole lifework [of whom] is to unsettle minds in regard to the inspiration of the Scriptures. They influence many to see as they do. And the same work is passed on from one to another, just as Satan designed it should be" (*Selected Messages,* 1:17).

"Man can be exalted only by laying hold of the merits of a crucified and risen Savior. The finest intellect, the most exalted position, will not secure heaven. Satan had the highest education that could be obtained. This education he received under the greatest of all teachers. When men talk of higher criticism, when they pass their judgment upon the word of God, call their attention to the fact that they have forgotten who was the first and wisest critic. He has had thousands of years of practical experience. He it is who teaches the so-called higher critics of the world today. God will punish all those who, as higher critics, exalt themselves, and criticize God's Holy word" (*Review and Herald,* March 16, 1897).

Adopt the Right Presuppositions and Attitudes toward the Word

To *rightly divide the Word,* Seventh-day Adventist students of the Bible must adopt the right presuppositions and attitudes consistent with the nature of the Bible as God's holy, inspired and trustworthy Word. The following are some key assumptions and attitudes that can aid the interpreter:

1. The Bible. The Bible is God's inspired Word. The Holy Spirit inspired the human writers with thoughts, ideas, and objective information and guided them in communicating the message. Thus, in the written Word, just as in the Incarnate Word, Jesus Christ, there exists an indivisible union of human and divine elements, neither of which should be emphasized to the neglect of the other (2 Pet 1:21; cf. *The Great Controversy,* pp. v, vi).

Although written in an ancient Near Eastern/Mediterranean setting, the Bible transcends its cultural backgrounds. Since human nature is essentially the same, and since God's expectations of human beings do not change, irrespective of their culture and time, the Bible speaks to all cultural, racial, and situational contexts of all ages. The message of Scripture, the written Word, is therefore no more culturally conditioned than is the message of Jesus Christ, the Incarnate Word, who lived in the same culture and proclaimed God's eternal message to the entire human race.

Because the Bible is not culturally conditioned, the accounts in Scripture— including the Bible's history, science, miracles, chronologies, prophecies, etc.— must be trusted as authentic and reliable.

2. The Human Interpreter. Since human beings are finite and sinful, they cannot on their own arrive at a saving knowledge of truth without the Holy Spirit's guidance. Thus, while human reason is to be employed to the fullest, confidence in one's natural mental powers actually blocks spiritual understanding. Reason must never be king; it must always be the servant within the context and under the authority of God's Word.

As a sinner, every interpreter comes to Scripture with certain individual, cultural, and religious biases or prejudices (what scholars refer to as "preunderstandings"). These preconceived ideas or blind spots tend to obstruct the correct understanding of the Word. The way to surmount them is through the Spirit's twofold work of regeneration and sanctification, during which the mental powers of the believer are redirected and renewed day by day to conform to the true biblical worldview. Interpreters receive this divine help by approaching Scripture in humble dependence upon the Holy Spirit.

3. The Holy Spirit's Guidance. The attitude of submission does not mean that the interpreter must abdicate the powers of reason or private judgment. Instead, submission ensures that these powers will be sanctified through the Spirit's work of illumination (John 14:26; 16:13, 14; 1 Cor 2:10-14; 1 John 2:27).

One way by which an interpreter expresses humility and submissiveness before God is by prayer. Bible students must pray before and after reading the written Word. Through prayer they are connected with the mind of the Holy Spirit, the real Author of inspired Scripture.

To benefit fully from the Spirit's illumination, the interpreter must be willing to submit to the teachings of Scripture. Psalm 119:34 is a model prayer that illustrates the correct attitude for approaching the Scriptures: "Give me understanding, that I may keep thy law and observe it with my whole heart." Christians must not only distrust themselves and their thoughts, they must also be willing to obey whatever the Bible teaches them.

"Many a portion of Scripture which learned men pronounce a mystery, or pass over as unimportant, is full of comfort and instruction to him who has been taught in the school of Christ. One reason why many theologians have no clearer understanding of God's Word is, they close their eyes to truths which they do not wish to practice. An understanding of Bible truth depends not so much on the power of intellect brought to the search as on the singleness of purpose, the earnest longing after righteousness" (*The Great Controversy,* p. 599).

"Whenever men are not seeking, in word and deed, to be in harmony with God, then, however learned they may be, they are liable to err in their understanding of Scripture, and it is not safe to trust to their explanations. When we are truly seeking to do God's will, the Holy Spirit takes the precepts of His word and makes them the principles of the life, writing them on the tablets of the soul. And it is only those who are following the light already given that can hope to receive the further illumination of the Spirit" (*Testimonies for the Church,* 5:705).

4. Other Considerations. Following are some important considerations before one actually starts to study the Scriptures.

(a) Select an appropriate Bible version. Where one cannot read the original languages in which the Bible was given, one must choose a Bible translation. Select a Bible version that is faithful to the meaning contained in Hebrew or Greek, giving preference to translations done by a broad group of scholars rather than by an individual, a small group, or a particular denomination.

Also, remember that there are two major approaches adopted by Bible translators. On one side are literal, "formal-equivalent" versions which attempt to offer word-for-word, clause-for-clause, sentence-for-sentence translation of the original language. The *King James Version* and the *New American Standard Bible* (NASB) are examples of this approach. As far as possible, this approach preserves the original wording of the Bible, even though it may sometimes be difficult to understand or awkward to read.

On the other side are paraphrases and "dynamic equivalent" versions, such as the *Living Bible* and the *Clear Word,* which employ contemporary expressions to present the same kind of impact the Bible had on its original hearers. While this approach makes the Bible "come alive," it often loses many of the nuances of the original language, and it is much more likely to reflect the translator's biases. In using paraphrases, Bible students must be aware of their dangers. The preface of the *Living Bible* contains this important statement:

"There are dangers in paraphrases, as well as values. For whenever the author's exact words are not translated from the original languages, there is a possibility that the translator, however honest, may be giving the English reader something that the original writer did not mean to say. This is because a paraphrase is guided not only by the translator's skill in simplifying but also by the clarity of his understanding of what the author meant and by his theology. For when the Greek or Hebrew is not clear, then the theology of the translator is his guide, along with his sense of logic, unless perchance the translation is allowed to stand without any clear meaning at all. The theological lodestar in this book has been a rigid evangelical position."

The author of *The Clear Word* Bible made the same point in his preface: "This is not a new translation but a paraphrase of the Scriptures. *It is not intended for in-depth study or for public reading in churches.* Those who are better qualified have given readers of the Holy Scriptures excellent translations for such purposes and undoubtedly will continue to do so as additional manuscripts come to light."[3]

Thus, the two approaches to Bible translations—word-for-word and paraphrases—have their strengths and weaknesses. Between the two extremes are versions which seek to enjoy the best of both worlds, such as the *Revised Standard Version,* which lies closer to the word-for-word approach, and the *New International Version,* leaning toward the dynamic equivalence side.

With so many Bible versions in English, it is important to choose carefully the version in which to study the Bible. Two helpful guides to selecting English Bibles are the books *So Many Versions* and *The English Bible from KJV to NIV.*[4]

Serious Bible students may want to adopt a suggestion that some have found useful: Use at least four Bible versions: (1) the *King James Version,* with its majestic language and hallowed associations; (2) a word-for-word version (e.g. the *New American Standard Bible*); (3) a paraphrase (e.g., *The Clear Word* Bible or *The Living Bible*); and (4) one from the middle (e.g., the *Revised Standard Version* or the *New International Version*). While concentrating on one version for reading and memorizing, it is best to compare the various versions regularly. The best Bible version, however, is still the original Hebrew and Greek.

(b) Choose a plan of Bible study. To avoid the dangers of illegitimate proof-texting (see Chapter One of this book), the interpreter must settle on a definite plan. One can adopt, for example, a book-by-book study, a topical study (e.g., salvation, second coming, the Sabbath, hope, etc.), a biographical study (such as the life of Joseph, Hannah, Elijah, Daniel, Peter, John, Mary, etc.), or a word study (e.g. peace, love, sin, etc.). Following a definite plan in studying the Scriptures can help avoid the haphazard and aimless approaches of the proof-text method.

A plan of Bible study should include *how* to study Scriptures for maximum benefit. "There is but little benefit derived from a hasty reading of the Scriptures. One may read the whole Bible through, and yet fail to see its beauty or to comprehend its deep and hidden meaning. One passage studied until its significance is clear to the mind, and its relation to the plan of salvation is evident, is of more value than the perusal of many chapters with no definite purpose in view and no positive instruction gained. Keep your Bible with you. As you have opportunity, read it; fix the texts in your memory. Even while you are walking the streets, you may read a passage, and meditate upon it, thus fixing it in the mind" (*Steps to Christ,* p. 90).

(c) Make a commitment to "sola scriptura." Upholding *sola scriptura* (the sole authority of Scripture) means believing and obeying all that Scripture sets forth, letting Scripture judge and control every thought and practice—including biblical interpretation. Against Scripture, there is no appeal, for "the scripture cannot be broken" (John 10:35).

In upholding the sole authority of Scripture, we acknowledge that it is both *sufficient* (i.e., it contains all that the church needs to know for guidance in the way of salvation and for the work of ministry) and *clear* (i.e., it can be understood from within itself, by comparing one passage of Scripture with another) (2 Tim 3:16-17). This means that Scripture does not need to be supplemented by an external source (human reason, experience, tradition). Neither is it to be interpreted in the light of some outside source (e.g., ecclesiastical tradition, philosophy, science, extrabiblical religion, psychology, etc.), as though the authority of such a source were equal to or above that of Scripture. Rather, the sufficiency and clarity of Scripture affirm the Protestant Reformation principle that Scripture must remain its own interpreter.

Both the sufficiency and clarity of Scripture imply that the Spirit, as the infallible interpreter, can enable every sincere seeker of truth to know God's will (John 7:17). This does not mean that no difficulties will be found in the Bible, but only that because the Holy Spirit attends the Word, every Christian—scholar and non-scholar—can understand the substance of the Bible's message by comparing Scripture with Scripture.

Uphold Adventism's Plain Reading of Scripture

Against the methods of higher criticism, Seventh-day Adventists have traditionally followed the sixteenth century Protestant Reformers in seeking the plain meaning of Scripture. This approach seeks to discover the historical, grammatical, literary meaning of Scripture, and on the basis of what the text meant to its original recipients, the interpreter makes a responsible application to contemporary needs. As we showed in Chapter One, this approach to the plain meaning of Scripture is *not* a proof-text method, contrary to what proponents of the historical-critical method want people to believe.[5]

The traditional Adventist approach to Scripture is opposed to the modern liberal approaches known collectively as the historical-critical method. The difference between these two conflicting approaches does not lie merely in the names, but rather in their underlying assumptions. For this reason, merely changing the name from "historical-critical method" to "historical method," "principle approach," "contextual approach," "casebook approach," "matured approach," "progressive approach," "Christ-centered," "developmental," or some other term cannot make the method acceptable.

Inasmuch as the Rio de Janeiro document ("Methods of Bible Study") that was approved at the 1986 Annual Council in Brazil is in harmony with the plain teachings of Scripture, we recommend its guidelines to Bible-believing Adventists who seek to do serious and faithful study of the Bible (see Appendix C). The following ten principles are implied in the Adventist approach. Think of them as Adventism's *Hermeneutical Decalogue:*[6]

1. The Literal Principle. Interpreting the Scriptures literally means we must understand the Bible in its *plain, obvious,* and *normal* sense. We must not allegorize or spiritualize it away in order to find some hidden, mystical, deeper, or secret meaning. The literal or plain meaning of Scripture should not be confused with a "literalistic" interpretation, which fails to recognize figures of speech like parables, symbols, similes, and hyperboles in the Bible.

The literal principle recognizes different kinds of literature in the Bible, each known technically as a *genre.* Genres are of two kinds. First, some genres describe compositions of a Bible book: *gospel* (e.g., Matthew, Mark, Luke, and John), *epistle* (e.g., the letters to the Corinthians and Galatians), *narrative* (e.g., Genesis), *prophecy/preaching* (e.g. Isaiah), *wisdom* (e.g., Proverbs and Ecclesiastes), *apocalyptic* (e.g., Daniel, Revelation), etc.

Embedded within each genre composition is a second kind of genre. This includes: *history, parable, poetry, metaphors, symbols, or allegory.*

The genre of a text affects how it is interpreted. The interpretation of a poetic text (e.g. the Psalms) would be different from that of a narrative (e.g. Acts). Interpreting a wisdom book such as Proverbs may not require a historical context to understand the universal application as would a book like Philemon. Similarly, if a text is a parable, the details—people, events, times, and places—may not be historical. But even though parables may be hypothetical, metaphorical, or simply stories drawn from everyday occurrences, spiritual truths that are illustrated by the parables always do have literal meaning. The same can be said of symbolic language in Daniel, Ezekiel, Zechariah, and Revelation. Though symbols and figures are used, by careful study one can ascertain the literal truth they communicate. *The literal principle therefore suggests that one must look for the plain, obvious, clear, normal meaning of Scripture, even in the figures of speech that are employed.*

Thus, we must clearly understand the use of *simile* (e.g., "He [a righteous man] is *like* a tree planted by the rivers of water" [Ps 1:3]; the Lord's anointed Messenger "shall sit *as* a refiner and purifier of silver" [Mal 3:3]); *metaphor* (e.g., Jesus said of Herod, "Go ye, and tell that fox . . ." [Luke 13:32]); *hyperbole* (e.g., "I am weary with my groaning; all the night make I my bed to swim [in tears]; I water my couch with my tears" [Ps 6:6]); *figures of speech* or *idiomatic expressions* (e.g., "the mountains and the hills shall break forth before you into singing, and all the trees of the field shall clap their hands" [Isa 55:12]); *paradox* (e.g., "the last shall be the first, and the first last" [Matt 20:16]); *allegory* (e.g., Paul's allegorical use of the story of Sarah and Hagar [Gal 4:22-31]); *typology* (e.g., the earthly sanctuary, priesthood, kingship, and the experience of Old Testament Israel [1 Cor 10:1-13; Rom 5:12-21; 1 Pet 3:18-22; Ex 25:40; Heb 8 and 9]); etc.[7]

2. Grammatical Principle. *This principle requires an interpreter to pay close attention to words, wordings, and context of any given text.*[8] Words like "love," "fear," or "hear" sometimes translate more than one Hebrew or Greek word and in some cases may have more than one meaning. This should not be a problem to interpreters. After all, even in the English language, depending on the context, the word *love* may express fondness ("I love ice cream"), preference ("I love Toyota cars"), endearment ("I love my child, wife, husband, mother, etc."), religious devotion ("I love Jesus"), or even sex ("They made love to one another").

The *grammatical principle* requires the interpreter to understand the meaning of words in their immediate context as well as in the larger context of the Bible. Failure to do so results in reading meanings into the Bible—such as when some homosexual theologians suggest that when the Bible says David *loved* Jonathan, it refers to a homosexual relationship.

Importance of Words. Words are important for two reasons. First, even though the Bible writers employed their own words in writing Scripture, they were divinely guided in the choice of those words (see 2 Sam 23:2-3; 1 Chron 28:19; Jer 26:2; 36:2; Eze 2:2; 11:5; Micah 3:8; John 6:63; 1 Cor 2:13; Rev 22:19; cf. Ex 4:10-16; cf. 7:1-2).

As we noted in Chapter Two, the Spirit's guidance of the inspired writers in expressing their God-given thoughts and ideas in their own words is known technically as *verbal (propositional) inspiration.* We should not confuse this with *mechanical (dictation) inspiration,* a mistaken theory which claims that the Holy Spirit dictated each word of Scripture.

Ellen G. White wrote concerning her experience: "I am just as dependent upon the Spirit in *relating* or *writing* the vision as in having the vision." Again:

"Although I am as dependent upon the Spirit of the Lord in *writing* my views as I am in receiving them, yet the words I employ in describing what I have seen are my own, unless they be those spoken to me by an angel, which I always enclose in marks of quotation" (*Selected Messages,* 3:48, 49, emphasis supplied). Thus, words are important.

Second, while we may use words carelessly in our private communications, such as in our private letters or school notes, words are particularly important when authoritative documents are being written. Since we pay attention to words and wording in making our wills, in signing business agreements, and in enacting laws in Parliament or Congress, why should we expect to do any less for the words in the most important document human beings have—the Bible?

Thus, even whether a word is in the singular or plural, or in the present tense or past tense, is extremely important. The apostle Paul used a single word in the singular as the basis for his argument showing that Jesus is the mediator of the covenant (Gal 3:16; cf. John 10:34-36). On another occasion Jesus argued his Deity on the basis of the present tense (John 8:57-58).

Importance of Wording. Also, the way a text is *worded*—the arrangement and positions of words in sentences—may communicate important ideas such as emphasis or connection. For example, beginning a sentence with "therefore," "because," "nevertheless," or "wherefore" may suggest a link with the previous sentence. As in English we tend to use *italics* and punctuation marks (e.g. the exclamation sign [!]) for emphasis, we need to watch for other signs of emphasis in the Bible writings.

To illustrate the importance of wording and punctuation, consider the difference a little comma made at a wedding. Just after the pastor had pronounced the couple husband and wife, a special delivery person rushed in with a telegram from the bride's closest friend, who had been unable to arrive on time because of a flight delay. From the airport she sought to send a telegram that read: "PASTOR, AFTER PRONOUNCING MARY AND JOHN HUSBAND AND WIFE, READ FIRST JOHN 4:18 AS MY SPECIAL MESSAGE TO MARY."

Now 1 John 4:18 reads: "There is no fear in love; but perfect love casteth out fear." But in her haste, the bride's girl-friend made a little mistake (just a comma), and instead sent this telegram: "PASTOR, AFTER PRONOUNCING MARY AND JOHN HUSBAND AND WIFE, READ FIRST, JOHN 4:18 AS MY SPECIAL MESSAGE TO MARY."

Delighted by this timely message, the pastor opened to John 4:18 and read aloud: "For thou has had five husbands; and he whom thou now hast is not thy husband. . . ."

Are the rules of grammar important? Ask Mary. The point of this story is that we must pay close attention to such things as the Bible writers' words, wordings, idioms, and the style they employed in quoting sources in the Old

Testament. In the Bible, the position of a word in a sentence sometimes indicates emphasis. Thus, Bible students, especially those using the Hebrew and Greek, need to respect how the Bible writers worded their messages. In putting into practice the grammatical principle of interpretation, Bible students may use helpful tools like dictionaries in English, Greek, and Hebrew, and Bible concordances, which list every word in the Bible and where that word appears.

Importance of context. Interpreters must give careful consideration to a text's immediate *context*—the verses before and after a given passage, making up its logical unit or paragraph. For as we mentioned in Chapter One in discussing the proof-text method, a text taken out of its context (whether historical, literary or grammatical) is a pretext.

In determining context, one must remember that today's chapter and verse divisions in our Bibles, while useful in assisting readers to locate particular passages, were not part of the original. Neither Moses nor Paul, for example, divided their books into chapters and verses. The *chapters* in our current Bibles originated with Stephen Langton, who introduced them into the Latin Bible at the beginning of the thirteenth century. *Verse* divisions in the Old Testament come from Rabbi Isaac Nathan around A.D. 1440, and New Testament verse divisions from Robert Stephanus in A.D. 1551.[9] So, one must not necessarily be restricted by chapter and verse divisions in deciding the context of a text.

3. Historical Principle. *Interpreting the Bible historically calls for a grasp of the cultural, political, and religious setting in which a passage was written.* It involves an understanding of the political situation (slavery, exile, persecution, etc.), the religious developments (e.g., the spiritual condition of Old Testament Israel in the days of the judges was different from the condition in the days of King Josiah), and the cultural backgrounds. With the aid of Bible concordances, one can come to a reasonable understanding of the historical and cultural background *from the Bible itself.*

Bible dictionaries, handbooks, and commentaries may be useful, although one must be extremely careful in selecting these scholarly tools. Many academic resources are based on speculative *reconstructions.*

Understanding the historical background enables today's interpreters to put themselves "in the shoes" of those who received the Bible messages originally. For example, when reading the Sermon on the Mount (Matthew 5-7), "Let us in imagination go back to that scene, and, as we sit with the disciples on the mountainside, enter into the thoughts and feelings that filled their hearts. Understanding what the words of Jesus meant to those who heard them, we may discern in them a new vividness and beauty, and may also gather for ourselves their deeper lessons" (*Thoughts from the Mount of Blessing,* p. 1).

4. Canonical Principle. *The canonical principle recognizes that the information we need to understand the Bible is found in the canon of Scripture itself; thus Scripture is to be its own interpreter.* This is a valid Reformation principle (often known as the "analogy of Scripture") which Seventh-day Adventists historically have upheld.

The canonical principle rejects the widespread contemporary practice of scholars. Instead of allowing the entire sixty-six books of the Bible to be the *only* context for understanding biblical history and culture, they tend to read the Bible in the light of ancient cultures of Bible times, and even in the light of some modern cultures. They believe that these extra-biblical data hold the key to the meaning of Scripture.

For example, such scholars deny that Moses actually got the pattern of his sanctuary from what God revealed to him (Ex 25:40), saying instead that he borrowed the idea from some ancient Canaanite culture. Also, though Paul grounds his doctrine of male-female relationships in creation and in the fall (1 Tim 2:11ff.; 1 Cor 11:3, 9, 11; 14:34-35), some would rather believe that his arguments were occasioned by the cultural conditions of his day (e.g., the worship of the goddess Artemis or Diana, Gnostic philosophy, etc.).[10] Moreover, in deciding whether tongues (Greek *glossa*) in 1 Corinthians 12-14 should be understood as speaking real languages or some unintelligible ecstatic utterances, some scholars are more influenced by contemporary religious manifestations (Christian and non-Christian) than by the testimony of Scripture itself (Acts 2; 10:44-47; 11:15-17; 19:1-7).[11] In these examples, cultural practices—past and present—become the ultimate norm in interpretation, not *sola scriptura*.

Whenever we fail to allow Scripture to interpret itself, instead depending on a few elite scholars to tell us what may have been the actual background of a particular passage, we are making fallible human speculation, tradition, experience, or custom the norm of authority. In effect, such scholarly speculations deny that Scripture is sufficient and clear. Ellen White rejected this approach: "Men need not the dim light of tradition and custom to make the Scriptures comprehensible. It is just as sensible to suppose that the sun, shining in the heavens at noon-day, needs the glimmerings of the torchlight of earth to increase its glory. In the Bible every duty is made plain, every lesson is comprehensible" (*Fundamentals of Christian Education,* p. 391).

The Protestant principle that Scripture is its own interpreter discredits the popular belief that every person or theologian is his own interpreter. If every person is his own interpreter, one can easily misinterpret a lack of consensus among theologians on issues such as women's ordination, homosexuality, and speaking in tongues as a lack of agreement among the inspired writers themselves—implying that the authority of theologians is on an equal level with that of the inspired Bible writers. On the other hand, upholding the principle that Scripture interprets itself suggests that when Bible students lack consensus, they must prayerfully continue searching the Scriptures until God sheds further light on the issue.

Ellen White repeatedly emphasized, "Make the Bible its own expositor, bringing together all that is said concerning a given subject at different times and under varied circumstances" (*Child Guidance,* p. 511). "I saw that the Word of God, as a whole, is a perfect chain, one portion linking into and explaining another" (*Early Writings,* p. 221). We must submit to "the Bible as the word of God, the only sufficient, infallible rule," which "must be its own interpreter" (*The Great Controversy,* p. 173). "Scripture interprets scripture, one passage being the key to other passages" (*Evangelism,* p. 581). "The Bible is its own expositor. Scripture is to be compared with scripture" (*Education,* p. 190).

Thus, when the canonical principle asserts that we must interpret Scripture in the light of Scripture, the implications are that: (1) the information needed to understand a given passage of the Bible can be found in the pages of Scripture itself, and (2) an obscure or difficult text must always be interpreted in the light of a clear text dealing with the same subject in another part of Scripture.

5. Consistent Principle. *This principle of interpretation asserts that since the sixty-six books of the Bible are ultimately the product of one Divine mind, the Bible is consistent with itself, with no part contradicting another.* This principle, also known as "the unity of Scripture," was taught by the sixteenth-century Protestant Reformers and our nineteenth-century Adventist pioneers.

This principle means that if "we hold an interpretation of one passage that does not square with something in another passage, one of the passages is being interpreted incorrectly—or possibly both of them."[12]

The consistent principle of interpretation grows out of the canonical principle of comparing Scripture with Scripture. One verse traditionally used to illustrate this principle is Isaiah 28:9-10: "Whom shall he teach knowledge? and whom shall he make to understand doctrine? them that are weaned from the milk, and drawn from the breasts. *For precept must be upon precept, precept upon precept; line upon line, line upon line; here a little and there a little*" (cf. v. 13).

Higher critical scholarship has attacked this principle of interpretation, for two major reasons. First, some have misused the practice, recklessly pulling a text out of its original historical context. Second, historical-critical scholars believe that there is no unity in the Bible, an essentially human document with little, if any, input from God.

Because liberal scholarship talks about "the diversity of Scripture" rather than the Bible's unity, its followers dismiss anyone who insists upon comparing Scripture with Scripture as practicing a "proof-text" or "key-text" approach.

Ironically, those who disparage the principle of comparing Scripture with Scripture find it valuable to compare Scripture with extra-biblical materials they seems to consider more reliable than the Bible itself!

The consistency principle is extremely important for interpreting parallel accounts in Scripture—some of which present differences in detail (e.g., 2 Sam 24 and 1 Chron 21; 2 Kings 18-20 and 2 Chron 32; Matt 21:33-44, Mark 12:1-11 and Luke 20:9-18). In studying passages of this kind, the interpreter must make sure that the parallels refer to the same historical events. For example, just as contemporary preachers and speakers often present the same messages on different occasions to different audiences and with different wording, so Jesus may have spoken some of His parables at different times, to different groups, and with different wording and emphasis. Even when the gospel writers record the same events, each Bible writer may emphasize different aspects of the events and in some cases may choose not to mention some details (see *Selected Messages,* 1:21, 22; *The Great Controversy,* p. vi).

In other instances some dissimilarities may be due to minor errors of copyists (*Selected Messages,* 1:16). Scholars can detect these by comparing various manuscripts. But sometimes our present knowledge does not allow us to reconcile apparent discrepancies. In such cases, rather than hastily declaring the differences to be contradictions or errors, the interpreter must suspend judgment until more information and better evidence are available to resolve the apparent discrepancy.

The consistent principle of interpretation holds that any interpreter "who says that the Bible contradicts itself because it appears so to him displays his ignorance either of the enormous competence of its author [God] or, in comparison, of his own abysmal ignorance and displays an overconfidence which borders on arrogance."[13]

6. Christological Principle. *Interpreting Scripture christologically means that the Bible student must recognize Jesus Christ as the subject matter of Scripture, since everything in Scripture bears witness of Him.* Jesus Christ Himself said: "Search the scriptures; for in them ye think ye have eternal life: *and they are they which testify of me*" (John 5:39). Christ is not just the center, He is the focus of Scripture.

One seventeenth-century English Puritan aptly summarized the christological principle: "Keep still Jesus Christ in your eye, in the perusal of the Scriptures, as the end, scope and substance thereof: what are the whole Scriptures, but as it were the spiritual swaddling clothes of the holy child Jesus? 1. Christ is the truth and substance of all the types and shadows. 2. Christ is the substance and matter of the Covenant of Grace, and all administrations thereof; under the Old Testament Christ is veiled, under the New Covenant revealed. 3. Christ is the centre and meeting place of all the promises; for in him the promises of God are yea and Amen. 4. Christ is the thing signified, sealed and exhibited in the Sacraments [ordinances] of the Old and New Testament. 5. Scripture genealogies use to lead us on to the true line of Christ. 6. Scripture chronologies are to discover to us the times and seasons of Christ. 7. Scripture-laws are our schoolmasters to bring us to Christ, the moral by correcting, the ceremonial by directing. 8. Scripture-gospel is Christ's light, whereby we hear and follow him; Christ's cords of love, whereby we are drawn into sweet union and communion with him; yea it is the very power of God unto salvation unto all them that believe in Christ Jesus; and therefore think of Christ as the very substance, marrow, soul and scope of the whole Scriptures."[14]

Thus the whole of the Bible prophesied, typified, and prefigured Jesus Christ. "The Old Testament sheds light upon the New, and the New upon the Old. Each is a revelation of the glory of God in Christ. Christ as manifested to the patriarchs, as symbolized in the sacrificial service, as portrayed in the law, and as revealed by the prophets is the riches of the Old Testament. Christ in His life, His death, and His resurrection; Christ as He is manifested by the Holy Spirit, is the treasure of the New. Both Old and New present truths that will continually reveal new depths of meaning to the earnest seeker" (*Counsels to Parents, Teachers, and Students,* pp. 462, 463).

This is why it is reported of Jesus that, on the road to Emmaus with two believers after His resurrection, "beginning at Moses and all the prophets, he expounded unto them in all the scriptures the things concerning himself" (Luke 24:27, cf. 44-49). Can we imagine the heart-warming experience that will be ours if we make Jesus the focus of our daily lives, especially as we seek to find Him each time we study and meditate upon the Scriptures (cf. Luke 24:32)?

Ellen G. White described the reward of such an exercise: "Memory's hall should be hung with sacred pictures, with views of Jesus, with lessons of His truth, with revealings of His matchless charms. If memory's hall were thus furnished, we would not look upon our lot as intolerable. We would not talk of the faults of others. Our souls would be full of Jesus and His love. We would not desire to dictate to the Lord the way that He should lead. We would love God supremely and our neighbor as ourselves. When the joy of the Lord is in the soul, you will not be able to repress it; you will want to tell others of the treasure you have found; you will speak of Jesus and His matchless charms. We should devote all to Him. Our minds should be educated to dwell upon those things that will glorify God; and if our mental powers are dedicated to God, our talents will improve, and we shall have more and more ability to render to the Master. We shall become channels of light to others" (*In Heavenly Places,* p. 123; cf. *The Ministry of Healing,* p. 514).

7. Cosmic Principle. As an essential aspect of the christological principle, *Seventh-day Adventist interpreters of Scripture must see the events recorded in the Bible within the larger context of the great controversy between Christ and Satan.*[15]

Ellen G. White made this principle the key emphasis of her writings: "The central theme of the Bible, the theme about which every other in the whole book clusters, is the redemption plan, the restoration in the human soul of the image of God. From the first intimation of hope in the sentence pronounced in Eden to that last glorious promise of the Revelation, 'They shall see His face; and His name shall be in their foreheads' (Revelation 22:4), the burden of every book and every passage of the Bible is the unfolding of this wondrous theme— man's uplifting—the power of God, 'which giveth us the victory through our Lord Jesus Christ.' 1 Corinthians 15:57. He who grasps this thought has before him an infinite field for study. He has the key that will unlock to him the whole treasure house of God's word" (*Education*, pp. 125, 126).

"The Bible is its own expositor. Scripture is to be compared with scripture. The student should learn to view the word as a whole and to see the relation of its parts. He should gain a knowledge of its grand central theme—of God's original purpose for the world, of the rise of the great controversy, and of the work of redemption. He should understand the nature of the two principles that are contending for the supremacy, and should learn to trace their working through the records of history and prophecy to the great consummation. He should see how this controversy enters into every phase of human experience; how in every act of life he himself reveals the one or the other of the two antagonistic motives; and how, whether he will or not, he is even now deciding upon which side of the controversy he will be found" (*Counsels to Parents, Teachers, and Students*, pp. 462).

8. Practical Principle. *Interpreting the Bible practically suggests that once the meaning of a text has been ascertained, it must be applied to the life of the interpreter* (2 Tim 3:16-17). The Bible is a practical book that addresses us in our concrete situation. It speaks to us as we stand before God guilty, helpless, confused, in need of pardoning and sustaining grace.

Thus, the plain reading of Scripture does not stop at what a text *meant* to the original readers, or what it reveals about Jesus. It also speaks to us in our relationships with others. This phase of interpretation is often called *application*.

For example, in studying Bible characters, the history of Israel, and the early church, we must avoid their mistakes and emulate their examples when they were consciously following the Lord. Ellen G. White wrote: "Those who question why the word of God brings out the sins of His people . . . should consider that it was all written for their instruction, that they may *avoid the evils recorded and imitate only the righteousness of those who served the Lord"* (*Testimonies for the Church,* 4:12).

We must apply the truths of Scripture to every aspect of our being, including our minds, our wills, our motivating drives, and our condition.

When applying Bible truths to our *minds,* we must say: "In the light of what we have discovered, we must not think in certain ways; if we have been doing so, we must stop." Second, we must apply the Bible's truths to our *wills,* so that we can state: "The truth presented shows us that we must not behave thus-and-so; if we have started, we must quit immediately. Instead, we must behave in such and such a manner." Third, biblical application must be made to our *motivating drives,* so that if we have been living the way we should, we have every good reason to continue, or to change our ways, if we are not living in that way. Finally, we must apply Scripture to our *conditions.* Here the logical question we must ask is: "How do we stand in relation to the truth presented? Have we faced it, taken it to heart, measured and judged ourselves by it? How do we stand in relation to the God who speaks it to us?"[16]

9. Communicative Principle. *The communicative or sharing principle calls for sharing what one has discovered in studying the Scriptures.*[17] This can take several forms. For example, the sharing can be done through a sermon, Bible study, testimony, witnessing, classroom lecture, evangelistic effort, or apologetic writing. This principle calls upon the interpreter to submit his findings to the correction, confirmation, and edification of his fellow believers. Comparing one's interpretation with that of others within the worshiping community, submitting it to their scrutiny and correction, is one way to reduce the effects of one's blind spots.

While the Holy Spirit guides individual believers in their understanding of Scripture, the Bible tells us that a more complete knowledge of God comes when one studies the Word in partnership "with all the saints" (Eph 3:18). God gives spiritual understanding through the Christian community. Responsible interpretation therefore demands that the Bible student compare his understanding with the discoveries of other believers, from the first century through the sixteenth-century Protestant Reformers, the eighteenth-century Puritans and Methodists, the nineteenth-century Adventist pioneers, and twentieth-century Bible-believing scholars.

This principle recognizes that we are not the only ones the Holy Spirit has been teaching. Others, in earlier generations and in our own, have also been enlightened by the Spirit, and we stand to benefit from their discoveries and mistakes. By studying the Bible in partnership with other members of the church, the believer recognizes that God has entrusted different gifts to different members of the church for the edification of the entire body (1 Cor 12). Within this context of spiritual gifts the church must recognize those who are endowed with such gifts as teaching, knowledge, wisdom, and discernment of spirits. The roles of theologians, and elders/pastors (those who are "apt to teach") also become particularly significant. In a worldwide church such as ours, these gifts are essential to our united understanding of the Bible.

Reluctance to study the Bible "with all the saints" leads to "Lone Ranger-ism" in interpreting Scripture—the spirit that says, "I'll go my own way without regard to what the community of believers thinks." Studying the Scriptures "with all the saints" serves as a check on our tendency to believe that we alone are guided by the Holy Spirit.

"God has not passed His people by and chosen one solitary man here and another there as the only ones worthy to be entrusted with His truth. He does not give one man new light contrary to the established faith of the body. In every reform men have arisen making this claim. . . . Let none be self-confident, as though God had given them special light above their brethren. Christ is represented as dwelling in His people. Believers are represented as 'built upon the foundation of the apostles and prophets, Jesus Christ Himself being the chief Cornerstone; in whom all the building fitly framed together groweth unto an holy temple in the Lord: in whom ye also are builded together for an habitation of God through the Spirit' [Eph 2:20-22]" (*Testimonies for the Church,* 5:291, 292).

Furthermore, the Spirit's design that believers study His word "with all the saints" delivers us from the tyranny of being tied to our own thoughts and our naive cultural conceits. It enables us to recognize that the Holy Spirit is not active only in a few regions of the world, or at the study of only a few scholars and church members, but that He is also leading other believers (experts and non-scholars, without regard to gender, race or social status) to a clear understanding of God's will in His written Word. It is as Christians study the Bible together and share the Word with each other, not as solitary individuals or as groups of individuals from particular regions of the world, that they are given understanding most fully.[18]

10. Confirmative Principle. For Bible-believing Seventh-day Adventists, there is one other principle that flows out of the communicative principle: *this principle suggests that one must compare all interpretations to the insights of Ellen G. White.*

Every Christian denomination respects the interpretative insights of leading figures in their respective traditions. Lutherans pay attention to the works of Martin Luther, Calvinists look to John Calvin, Methodists value the works of John Wesley, and liberals measure their views against liberal giants. Thus, Seventh-day Adventists should not be embarrassed to take seriously the works of Ellen G. White. Though Ellen White never studied Hebrew or Greek, and though she had no Ph.D. in theology, her insights into Bible truth cannot be dismissed lightly or even patronized as the private opinions of a nineteenth-century "devotional writer."

In fact, given their belief that Ellen White received the prophetic gift, Seventh-day Adventists must value her theological insights more highly than any uninspired authority or expert, whether church leader or scholar. Without exhausting or preempting the task of serious biblical interpretation or exegesis, her expositions on any given Bible passage offer inspired guidance to the meaning of the passage (see *Evangelism*, p. 256; *The Great Controversy*, pp. 193, 595; *Testimonies for the Church*, 5:665, 682, 707, 708; *Counsels to Writers and Editors*, pp. 33-35).

She herself described her two-fold function in the church as follows: "God has, in that Word [the Bible], promised to give visions in the *'last days'*; not for a new rule of faith, but for the comfort of His people, and to correct those who err from the Bible truth" (*Early Writings*, p. 78). The light God gave her, she explains, "has been given to correct specious error and to specify what is truth" (*Selected Messages*, 3:32).

Notice that the writings of Ellen White are not to establish a new rule of faith apart from the Bible. Rather, they have been given the church to "comfort" God's people (when they are in the right path), to "correct" them (when they err from the truth) and to "specify" what is truth (when they are not sure). With so many confusing, conflicting voices involved in biblical interpretation, can anyone doubt the importance and urgency of the Spirit of Prophecy in the hermeneutical enterprise?

Summary of Principles. The *hermeneutical decalogue* outlined in this section essentially captures the historic plain reading approach of Bible-believing Adventists, the historical-grammatical method found in the "Methods of Bible Study" report (see Appendix C). Because such an approach to Scripture deals a blow to liberalism's higher criticism (the historical-critical method), we should expect that scholars who favor the latter approach will strongly oppose the "Methods of Bible Study" report, or at least that they will quietly ignore it.[19]

Conclusion

The best way to summarize the thrust of this chapter of *Receiving the Word* is to quote a statement from Ellen G. White: "As our physical life is sustained by food, so our spiritual life is sustained by the word of God. And every soul is to receive life from God's word for himself. As we must eat for ourselves in order to receive nourishment, so we must *receive the word* for ourselves. We are not to obtain it merely through the medium of another's mind. We should carefully study the Bible, asking God for the aid of the Holy Spirit, that we may understand His word. We should take one verse, and concentrate the mind on the task of ascertaining the thought which God has put in that verse for us. We should dwell upon the thought until it becomes our own, and we know 'what saith the Lord'" (*The Desire of Ages,* p. 390, emphasis supplied).

Rightly dividing the Word requires that we take the following steps outlined in the above statement:

(1) Make a commitment to study the Bible carefully;

(2) Pray for the Holy Spirit's enlightenment for correct understanding;

(3) Choose a verse (or a small section) at a time;

(4) Concentrate the thought (i.e., prayerfully reflect or meditate) on God's message;

(5) Find out what the passage means to you in your concrete situation;

(6) Having discovered "what saith the Lord," put it into practice.

These are some implications of *receiving the Word* and *rightly dividing it.* This does not mean we shall find no difficulties in the Bible. The Bible itself tells us we shall. But employing the principles of interpretation discussed in this chapter and summarized in the 1986 report "Methods of Bible Study," we shall be able to resolve some of the Bible difficulties. In the next chapter, we shall employ these principles in *wrestling with the Word.*

NOTES

1. John MacArthur, Jr. *Our Sufficiency in Christ* (Dallas, Texas: Word Publishing, 1991), p. 129.

2. Following are the relevant statements from *Selected Messages,* 2:98-100.

Deception from learned persons: "There will be human wisdom to meet—the wisdom of learned men, who, as were the Pharisees, are teachers of the law of God, but do not obey the law themselves" (p. 98).

Deception through ignorance and folly: "There will be human ignorance and folly to meet in disconnected theories arrayed in new and fantastic dress—theories that it will be all the more difficult to meet because there is no reason in them" (p. 98).

Deception from false dreams and visions: "There will be false dreams and false visions, which have some truth, but lead away from the original faith. The Lord has given men a rule by which to detect them: 'To the law and to the testimony: if they speak not according to this word, it is because there is no light in them' (Isa. 8:20). If they belittle the law of God, if thy pay no heed to His will as revealed in the testimonies of His Spirit, they are deceivers. They are controlled by impulse and impressions, which they believe to be from the Holy Spirit, and consider more reliable than the Inspired Word. They claim that every thought and feeling is an impression of the Spirit; and when they are reasoned with out of the Scriptures, they declare that they have something more reliable. But while they think that they are led by the Spirit of God, they are in reality following an imagination wrought upon by Satan" (pp. 98, 99).

Deception subtly disguised as truth: "Satan will work in a most subtle manner to introduce human inventions clothed with angel garments. But the light from the Word is shining amid the moral darkness; and the Bible will never be superseded by miraculous manifestations. The truth must be studied, it must be searched for as hidden treasure. Wonderful illuminations will not be given aside from the Word, or to take the place of it. Cling to the Word, receive the ingrafted Word, which will make men wise unto salvation" (p. 100).

3.   Jack J. Blanco, *The Clear Word* (Hagerstown, Md.: Review and Herald, 1994), p. vii, emphasis supplied. Regrettably, readers of Bible paraphrases often overlook these judicious cautions. Because of the inherent dangers of Bible paraphrases some have also questioned their use in personal devotions.

4.   Sakae Kubo and Walter Specht, *So Many Versions: Twentieth Century English Versions of the Bible* (Grand Rapids, Mich.: Zondervan, 1975); Jack P. Lewis, *The English Bible from KJV to NIV: A History and Evaluation* (Grand Rapids, Mich.: Baker, 1991). In these two works, one will find a detailed evaluation of the strengths and weaknesses of the major English translations.

5.   In recent times some Adventist scholars have mistakenly identified the historical-grammatical method as essentially built on "fundamentalist proof-text principles and conclusions." For more on this see chapter 4 where we discuss this issue in the context of the "quarrel over the Word."

6.   The arrangement of the principles under ten sections is this author's own. Others may prefer discussing the historical-grammatical method differently. While the ten principles may overlap somewhat, each is implied in the "Methods of Bible Study" Report. Because we have organized our discussion under ten hermeneutical principles, we have borrowed the phrase "hermeneutical decalogue" from Richard M. Davidson's excellent article, "Interpreting Scripture: An Hermeneutical 'Decalogue'," *Journal of the Adventist Theological Society* 4/2 (1993):95-114. Our hermeneutical decalogue differs in arrangement and specific details from Davidson's, even though there is considerable correspondence of thought.

7.   For more on this, see Lee J. Gugliotto, *Handbook for Bible Study* (Hagerstown, Md.: Review and Herald, 1995), pp. 49-71, 261-289; Richard M. Davidson, *Typology in Scripture: A Study of Hermeneutical TYPOS Structures* (Berrien Springs, Mich.: Andrews University Press, 1981).

8.   See Gugliotto, *Handbook for Bible Study*, pp. 33-48; 173-214.

9.   Bruce M. Metzger, *Manuscripts of the Greek Bible: An Introduction to Paleography* (New York: Oxford University Press, 1981), pp. 40-42.

10.   No credible scholar should attempt to discuss this issue without interacting with the series of grammatical, linguistic, exegetical, hermeneutical, and theological essays in the book *Women in the Church: A Fresh Analysis of 1 Timothy 2:9-15*, ed. Andreas J. Köstenberger, Thomas R. Schreiner, and H. Scott Baldwin (Grand Rapids, Mich.: Baker, 1995). This volume, the most comprehensive work to date on the issue of the male-female relationship in the home and church, challenges the ideological dogmatism and exegetical speculation of those opposing the biblical doctrine of headship responsibility.

11.   An excellent treatment of the subject from a Bible-believing perspective is Gerhard F. Hasel's *Speaking In Tongues: Biblical Speaking in Tongues and Contemporary Glossolalia* (Berrien Springs, Mich.: Adventist Theological Society Publications, 1991). This detailed and well-researched book challenges the present-day reinterpretation of "speaking in tongues."

12.   John F. MacArthur, Jr., *Charismatic Chaos* (Grand Rapids, Mich.: Zondervan, 1992), p. 113.

13.   Edward W. Goodrick, *Is My Bible the Inspired Word of God?* (Portland, Ore.: Multnomah, 1988), p. 88.

14.   Isaac Ambrose, *Works* (1701), p. 201, quoted in James I. Packer, *A Quest for Godliness: The Puritan Vision of the Christian Life* (Wheaton, Ill.: Crossway Books, 1990), p. 103.

15.   On the importance of the "great controversy" theme in the Christian worldview, see Samuel Koranteng-Pipim, "Contemporary Culture and Christian Lifestyle: A Clash of Worldviews," *Journal of the Adventist Theological Society* 4/1 (Spring 1993):143-147.

16.   Paraphrased from James I. Packer's "Speaking for God," in Richard Allen Bodey, ed., *Inside the Sermon* (Grand Rapids, Mich.: Baker, 1990), p. 190.

17. Gerhard Maier refers to this phase of interpretation as "communicative interpretation" (see Gerhard Maier, *Biblical Hermeneutics* [Wheaton, Ill.: Crossway, 1994], pp. 402-409).

18. For more on this, see Samuel Koranteng-Pipim, "The Spirit of Rebellion: Another Look at Post-Utrecht Ordinations in Some SDA Congregations," unpublished article (Berrien Springs, Mich., February 1996), available at the Adventist Heritage Center, James White Library, Andrews University. Cf. *Searching the Scriptures: Women's Ordination and the Call to Biblical Fidelity* (Berrien Springs, Mich.: Adventists Affirm Publications, 1995), pp. 41-44; C. Raymond Holmes, "Post-Utrecht: Conscience and the Ecclesiastical Crisis," *Adventists Affirm* 10/1 (Spring 1996):44-49, 56.

19. See chapter 4 for a detailed discussion of the relationship of Adventist scholars to the "Methods of Bible Study" report. See also George W. Reid, "Another Look at Adventist Methods of Bible Interpretation," *Adventists Affirm* 10/1 (Spring 1996):50-56; C. Mervyn Maxwell, "'Take the Bible as It Is,'" *Adventists Affirm* 10/1 (Spring 1996):26-35.

Chapter Ten

Wrestling With the Word

As we explained in Chapter Three, the three theological factions—radical liberals, moderate liberals (accommodationists), and Bible-believing conservatives—claim to take the authority of the Bible very seriously. The quarrel in the Christian church over biblical authority and interpretation arises over how to handle the difficulties in Scripture.

All three contestants claim that in the face of biblical difficulties they allow the Bible to speak for itself; but letting "the Bible speak for itself" apparently means different things to liberals and accommodationists than it does to Bible-believing conservatives. The real issue boils down to assumptions that are shaping Christians' attempts at *wrestling with the Word.*

Attitudes Toward Bible Difficulties. Bible-believing Christians take seriously the Bible's claim to truthfulness. But when liberals and accommodationists come across difficulties in the Bible, they do three things: (1) they declare the problems to be inaccuracies, contradictions or errors. Then, to account for the alleged mistakes or contradictions in the Bible, (2) they redefine the meaning of inspiration or the nature of the Bible to allow for the possibility of mistakes or inaccuracies, and (3) they adopt various versions of the higher critical methodology to interpret the scriptural difficulties.

Yet it seems that liberals or accommodationists do not always agree on what constitutes a discrepancy or contradiction! Neither are they in accord over the nature of the Bible's inspiration and the appropriate method of Bible interpretation, except to agree that the Bible is not fully inspired, trustworthy, and authoritative. This situation has led to the confusion of voices in the churches on almost every theological subject.

So we shall devote this chapter to some of the Bible difficulties historical-critical scholars often bring up. Using the principles discussed in the previous chapter, "Rightly Dividing the Word," we shall engage in *wrestling with the Word.* We shall take a closer look at other "quail problems" (see Chapter One) that Bible-believing Christians often must deal with. But first, let us offer some principles for handling Bible difficulties.

Handle Bible Difficulties Carefully

The Bible Contains Difficulties. While *receiving the Word* as the inspired, trustworthy, and authoritative revelation of God's will for humanity, Bible-believing Christians recognize that the Bible contains unresolved difficulties. In fact, the Bible itself teaches this. In 2 Peter 3:15, 16, we read: "Our beloved brother Paul also according to the wisdom given unto him hath written unto you; as also in all his epistles, speaking in them of these things; *in which are some things hard to be understood,* which they that are unlearned wrest, as they do also the other scriptures, unto their own destruction."

Notice three things from the above text: (1) there are some difficult things in the Bible; (2) the "unlearned and unstable" deal with these Bible difficulties in illegitimate ways—they "wrest" (twist or distort) the difficulties; (3) the distortion of these "things hard to be understood" results in the "destruction" of such individuals and possibly those who follow them.

If mishandling the Bible can cost one's salvation, it is important for Bible-believing Christians to know how to handle Scripture's difficulties.

Guidelines for Resolving Bible Difficulties. More than half a century ago, R. A. Torrey, one time dean of the Bible Institute of Los Angeles, spoke for many Bible-believers on this issue. In the following abstract from a sermon, Torrey gives seven important guidelines for Christians facing Bible difficulties. These suggestions parallel Ellen White's insightful discussion of the same issue in *Steps to Christ* (pp. 105 to 113). Torrey wrote:

"First of all, let me say, *Let us deal with any Difficulty and every Difficulty we meet in the Bible with perfect honesty.* Whenever you find a Difficulty in the Bible, frankly acknowledge it, do not try to obscure it, do not try to dodge it, do not evade it. Evasion never pays. Be honest through and through; perfect honesty and frankness always win out in the long run. . . . If you are really convinced that the Bible is the Word of God, you can far better afford to wait for an honest solution of a Difficulty than you can afford to attempt a solution that is evasive and unsatisfactory. Let us hate all manner of evasion and lying. A 'pious lie' is the most impious and the most destructive of all lies.

"In the second place, *Let us deal with any Difficulty we meet in the Bible with that humility that becomes all persons of such limited understanding as we are.* Recognize the limitations of your own mind and knowledge, and do not for a moment imagine that there is no solution just because you have found none. There is, in all probability, a very simple solution, even when you can find no solution at all.

"In the third place, *Let us deal with every Difficulty we meet in the Bible with indomitable determination.* Make up your mind that you will find the solution, if you possibly can, no matter what amount of time and study and hard thinking it may require. The Difficulties in the Bible are our Heavenly Father's challenge to us to set our brains to work, and to keep them at work until we have solved the puzzle. Do not give up searching for a solution because you cannot find one in five minutes or ten minutes or ten days. Ponder over it and work over it for days if necessary. The work will do you more good than the solution does. There is a solution somewhere and you will find it, if you will only search for it long enough and hard enough. . . .

"In the fourth place, *Deal with every Difficulty you find in the Bible with perfect fearlessness.* Oh! there are so many students of the Bible who have horrid skeletons and frightful ghosts in the closets of their Bible thinking. There are passages here and there at which they are afraid to look. . . .

"Do not be frightened when you find a Difficulty, no matter how unanswerable or how inexplicable or how unsurmountable it may appear at first sight. Thousands of men have found just such Difficulties before you were born. Not only that, but they have seen this same Difficulty that now frightens you. These Difficulties were all seen hundreds of years ago, and still the Old Book stands. The Bible that has already stood eighteen centuries of rigid examination, and also of incessant and awful assault, is not likely to go down before your discoveries, or even before the discharge of any 'modern,' 'scholarly,' 'critical' guns (in which they certainly use neither smokeless nor noiseless powder) nor before the poison gases of 'Modern Criticism' either, which is usually found to be only 'hot air' after all. To one who is at all familiar with the history of 'critical' attacks on the Bible, the childlike confidence of these self-sufficient 'modern' (destructive) 'critics,' who think they are going to annihilate the Bible at last, is both amazing and amusing. . . .

"In the fifth place, *Let us deal with the Difficulties we find in the Bible with undiscouraged and untiring patience.* Do not be discouraged in the least, if some Difficulty that you discover, or that someone else fires at you, does not disappear at the first hour's consideration of it, or in a day. Have you never had problems in other lines of study that you could not solve even in a year? If not, you have never done any deep studying along any line. If some Difficulty persistently defies your very hardest efforts to solve it, lay it aside for a while and ponder other things. Very likely, when you come back to it, it will have disappeared, and you will wonder how you were ever perplexed by it. . . .

"In the sixth place, and this is of tremendous importance, *Deal with all Bible Difficulties Scripturally.* If you find an apparently staggering Difficulty in one part of the Bible, look for some other passage of Scripture to throw light upon it and solve it. The best solvent of Bible Difficulties is found in the Bible itself. Nothing explains Scripture like Scripture. That is one of the countless practical proofs of the Divine origin of the Bible, that 'all Scripture is God breathed.' . . . The entrance of God's words had given light; it had given understanding unto the simple (Ps. 119:130).

"In the seventh and last place, *Deal with every Difficulty prayerfully.* It is simply wonderful how Difficulties dissolve when one looks at them on his knees. It is an easy way to 'dissolve doubts' and explain 'dark sentences.' Daniel found it so many centuries and chiliads ago (Dan. 5:12, cf. Dan. 6:10). There is a glorious alchemy about prayer that transforms the darkest and most bewildering Difficulties into clear shining and illuminating truth, that transforms 'stones of stumbling' into the many jeweled walls of the New Jerusalem, with its endless day and 'no night there.' It is well, as you read your Bible, not only to pray, 'Open thou my eyes, that I may behold wondrous things out of thy law' [Ps. 119:18] but, also, 'Open thou my eyes that I may see through the rough oyster shell of seeming difficulty to the glorious pearl of lustrous truth within.' Not only does God, in answer to prayer, open our eyes 'to behold wondrous things' out of His law, but He also opens our eyes to look through a Difficulty that before we prayed seemed impenetrable. One great reason why so many 'Modern Bible Scholars' have learned to be destructive critics is because they have forgotten how to pray."[1]

Promise of Divine Illumination. We conclude from the foregoing that students of the Bible have always recognized that some portions of the Bible are more difficult than others. Not only does the Bible itself say so (Heb 5:12-14, 2 Pet 3:15, 16), but it also tells us how to deal with these difficulties. Just as the Bible writers "enquired and searched diligently" those things they could not understand (1 Pet 1:10-11; cf. 1 Cor 2:11; Dan 8 and 9), so should Bible-believers begin the study of the Word with prayer: "Open thou mine eyes, that I may behold wondrous things out of thy law" (Ps 119:18).

If Christians diligently *search* the Scriptures (John 5:39; Acts 17:11), God has promised: "Yea, if thou criest after knowledge, and liftest up thy voice for understanding; if thou seekest her as silver, and searchest for her as for hid treasures; then shalt thou understand the fear of the Lord, and find the knowledge of God" (Prov 2:3-5; cf. Eph 1:17).

We shall now apply the above guidelines and those discussed in the previous chapter to some of liberalism's most "disturbing" problems, praying that God sheds further light on His inspired Word.

Wrestling with Some "Disturbing" Problems

Admittedly, in this chapter we are not able to deal individually with all the questions raised by radical and moderate liberals. But at least we can attempt to show that there are alternative approaches to the alleged difficulties. Let us look at a few Old and New Testament passages often cited as evidence of the Bible's own internal discrepancies. At the end of this section we shall suggest some resources dealing with other kinds of Bible difficulties.

Proverbs 26:4, 5. Scholars often cite these two verses as a striking instance of apparently contradictory proverbs. The passages read:

"Answer not a fool according to his folly, lest you be like him yourself" (v. 4).
"Answer a fool according to his folly, lest he be wise in his own eyes" (v. 5).

Are these two verses contradictory? If these were really inconsistent, would they have been placed side by side? A careful reading of the texts suggests that both proverbs are sounding a caution to those who are dealing with unreasonable people. The argument runs somewhat like this: Sometimes your answer to a fool can make you look like a fool; at other times, your answer will help him; therefore be careful how you answer a fool.

These proverbs bring out the dilemma that always faces those who seek to reason with the unreasonable ("fools"). The experience of the Apostle Paul illustrates this dilemma. In 2 Corinthians 11:16, he says: "Let no man think me a fool; if otherwise, yet as a fool receive me, that I may boast myself a little." Yet in the next chapter (12:11), he writes: "I am become a fool in glorying; ye have compelled me: for I ought to have been commended of you: for in nothing am I behind the very chiefest apostles, though I be nothing." Between 2 Corinthians 11:16 and 12:11, Paul found himself speaking as a fool, yet he knew that if he did not do so his audience would have been confirmed in their foolish opinions. It is the same kind of issue that the two proverbs are dealing with; there is no inconsistency between verses 4 and 5 of Proverbs 26.

Deuteronomy 23:1-3. Scholars cite the first three verses of Deuteronomy 23 as three disturbing examples of "minor" discrepancies in Scripture. By comparing each of these verses with certain other biblical passages they try to show that the exclusions of "eunuchs" (v. 1) "bastards" (v. 2) and "Ammonites and Moabites" (v. 3) "from the assembly of the Lord" were later overruled in Isaiah 56:3-5, Judges 11:1, 9-10, 29, and Ruth 4:10-17, respectively. Is it really so?

(1) Deuteronomy 23:1 excludes "from the assembly of the Lord" men whose reproductive organs were mutilated. No reason is given. It may be that such a condition was an affront to the gift of procreation; such mutilation could also have been a practice in pagan religions. Whatever the reason, we can infer from Deuteronomy 14:1, 2 that this exclusion of eunuchs was a specific application

of the command to the Israelites not to mutilate themselves deliberately, because they were "an holy" and "peculiar people unto himself [the Lord God], above all the nations that are upon the earth." As a holy people, the Israelites were not to practice self-mutilation, the way the idol worshiping nations around them were doing. Doing so would represent apostasy from the true God of Israel.

But in Isaiah 56:3-5 the prophet proclaims that "eunuchs" who were faithful to God keeping His "sabbaths" and "covenants," might find an honored place in God's family before those who were sound in body but who broke His covenant. Doesn't this contradict Deuteronomy 23:1?

If we follow higher-critical scholars in rejecting the long-standing Adventist belief that there is a harmony in the Bible's various parts, we might infer a contradiction. But if we recognize the Bible as the product of a divine Author, and thus, as trustworthy and harmonious in its teachings, then we can resolve the apparent difficulty by comparing Scripture with Scripture.

Perhaps the eunuchs spoken of in Isaiah 56, having previously gone the way of their pagan neighbors, had returned and renewed their relationship with the true God. Under the circumstances, God takes them back and extends His blessing to such people (cf. Eze 18:20-32). In fact, the New Testament shows that an Ethiopian eunuch experienced this salvation.

Thus, Deuteronomy 23:1 and Isaiah 56:3-5, when taken together, teach us that irrespective of past background, if we seek a covenant relationship with God, He will accept us (Isa 1:18). There is no contradiction between the two passages.

(2) In Deuteronomy 23:2, "bastards" are also excluded from the assembly of the Lord. In Judges 11, however, "the Spirit of the Lord came upon" Jephthah the Gileadite, a "son of a harlot." Apparently because in English today, a "bastard" typically refers to someone born out of wedlock, some assume that the word "bastard" in Deuteronomy includes the "son of a harlot" in Judges.

The alleged contradiction between Deuteronomy 23:2 and Judges 11 is another classic example of liberal *eisegesis,* reading into the text what is not there by imposing meanings upon the biblical text.

The root word translated "bastard" in Deuteronomy (*mamzer*) is uncertain in meaning. The only other place that the word appears is in Zechariah 9:6. Rabbinic tradition holds that it refers to a person "born of incest," a "non-Israelite," or a "stranger of unknown ancestry" who holds to a foreign religion. If this is indeed the case, Jephthah does not fit the definition of a "bastard" in Deuteronomy 23:2. But since Bible-believers do not take tradition (past or present) as their final authority, and since the meaning of *mamzer* is presently uncertain, it is only fair to withhold judgment on this passage until all available light is shed on the exact meaning of the Hebrew word translated as "bastard."

(3) In Deuteronomy 23:3, the Ammonites and Moabites "even to the tenth generation" are excluded from the assembly of the Lord. But in a different section of Scripture we learn that Ruth, "the Moabitess," becomes the wife of Boaz and the ancestor of David (Ruth 4) and therefore of Jesus.

Was the exclusion in Deuteronomy 23:3 overruled in Ruth 4? Does this apparent "inconsistency" justify the liberal claim that in this "obvious contradiction," God is teaching Christians to trust Him rather than an imperfect human Bible, or that He is able to make something good (the roots of the Messiah) from the cultural prejudice of the writer of Deuteronomy? It does not appear so.

Though the text is not explicit, it is very possible that like others in Scripture, this command in Deuteronomy 23:3 is conditional, contingent upon the faith response of the people of Moab and Ammon. For the purpose of argument, however, let us assume that the command is not conditional. What light does Scripture shed on this issue?

The Ammonites and Moabites were the descendants of incestuous relationships between Lot and his two daughters (Gen 19:30-38). The Bible does not give a reason for this exclusion, even though we know that there had been hostility between these two nations and Israel (Judges 11:4-33; 1 Sam 11:1-11; 2 Sam 10, etc.). We also know from the Scriptures that at the time of the exodus, Israel did not conquer the Ammonites (Deut 2:19, 37; Judges 11:15) and that both the Ammonites and the Moabites refused to offer hospitality to the Israelites (Deut 23:4; cf. Num 22-24). How does the exclusion of the Ammonites and Moabites from the assembly of the Lord "even to the tenth generation" relate to Ruth "the Moabitess"?

From the time of Moses to the time of Ruth was about 300 years. Is this period of time equivalent to "ten generations"? The answer depends on the span of a generation. If we understand a "generation" as equivalent to the average age at which persons "beget" (or "generate") their firstborn, we learn from the Bible that, after the flood (Gen 11:10-24), the usual age at which a man became a father (i.e., "begat" children) was around 30 years. Ten generations would therefore be about 300 years, the period between Moses and Ruth!

In each of the three "disturbing" examples from Deuteronomy 23, the Bible itself gives us the key. A careful investigation of the Scriptures may offer even better solutions to some of the most troublesome problems.

2 Samuel 24 and 1 Chronicles 21. These two accounts of David's census are often cited as *the* classic examples of "obvious contradictions" in parallel biblical passages. The four questions usually raised in connection with these two accounts are:

286 Receiving the Word

(1) Who ordered David's census? *God* (2 Sam) or *Satan* (1 Chron)?

(2) How many persons were numbered? *1,300,000* (2 Sam) or *1,570,000* (1 Chron)?

(3) At whose threshing floor was the angel of the Lord seen? *Araunah's* (2 Sam) or *Ornan's* (1 Chron)?

(4) How much money was paid? *50 shekels of silver* (2 Sam) or *600 shekels of gold* (1 Chron)?

Without attempting to trivialize the importance of biblical details, we offer some explanations for the seemingly inconsistent accounts.

(1) Who ordered David's census? The "Who" of the census can be explained by referring to God's *permissive* will in the affairs of the world. Examples can be multiplied in the Bible; God's permission to Satan to afflict Job, the hardening of Pharaoh's heart, the choice of Saul as king of Israel, etc.

In the parallel accounts in 2 Samuel 24 and 1 Chronicles 21, (i) David was responsible in the sense that he *chose* to displease God by having the census, even against the objections of Joab; he later confessed his sin (2 Sam 24:10, 17; cf. 1 Chron 21:8, 17); (ii) Satan, the adversary of God and His people, was also responsible in the sense that he was the one who *incited* David; (iii) God was responsible in the sense that He *permitted* Satan to incite David.

(2) How many people were numbered? A casual reading of the two parallel passages will reveal some apparent inconsistencies. The account in 2 Samuel reports that there were 800,000 armed men in Israel and 500,000 in Judah (totaling *1,300,000*); the passage in 1 Chronicles gives 1,100,000 in "all Israel" and 470,000 in Judah (totaling *1,570,000*). Not only are the total numbers different, but the underlying figures for Israel and Judah are also different. How do we account for this difference?

The Bible makes it clear that (i) this census that took Joab 10 months to conduct was *not complete,* apparently because of the plagues that had set in (1 Chron 27:24). (ii) We are also told that he did not number the tribes of Levi and Benjamin (1 Chron 21:6). (iii) The figure of Chronicles with 1,100,000 for "*all* Israel" is larger than Samuel's 800,000, apparently because Samuel does not include the 288,000-strong standing army of David (1 Chron 27:1-15). Note that there is no *all* before "Israel" in Samuel's account. Adding the 288,000 to the 1,300,000 total of Samuel's account yields *1,588,000,* against Chronicle's *1,570,000.* Interestingly, the Chronicles total is the smaller; this same book says that Joab did not complete the census.

The point is that we need not ascribe "inconsistency" or "error" to the two accounts. Indicators in the texts as well as the explicit statement of the Bible itself testify that the numbers given are not complete.

(3) At whose threshing floor did the angel of the Lord appear? The names given in the two parallel accounts, "Araunah the Jebusite" and "Ornan the Jebusite," may refer to the same person. First, in the Bible, persons sometimes possess two different names (such as Abram/Abraham, Jacob/Israel, Jethro/Reuel, Simon/Peter, Saul/Paul). Second, we need not be surprised that Araunah could be the same as Ornan. The original Hebrew alphabet consisted of consonants only. Vowel signs were not introduced until more than a thousand years after Malachi, the last book of the Old Testament, was completed.

Thus, the Hebrew root letters for the name *Araunah* appear to have been *'rn* and those for *Ornan* likewise *'rn*. The differences in vowels and ending may be due simply to the varying pronunciations of the Jebusite's name at the time the accounts were recorded. The point is that these two apparently different names are linguistically related, derived from the same root.

(4) How much did David pay? The two parallel accounts provide us with an answer. In 2 Samuel 24:24 we are told: "So David bought the *threshing floor* and the *oxen* for *50 shekels of silver.*" In 1 Chronicles 21:15, "So David paid Ornan *600 shekels gold* by weight for the *site.*" Are there any inconsistencies? Apparently not.

The Chronicles account tells of the cost of the *site;* this might be the entire site of which the *threshing floor* was only a part. If so, we can understand why the *site* cost 600 shekels of gold and the *threshing floor* only 50 shekels of silver. We do not, therefore, need to ascribe inconsistency to the two accounts.

Approximations and Imprecisions As Alleged Errors

Errors charged to Bible writers by liberal scholars are often the result of approximations or imprecision on the part of the Bible writers. We will cite a few examples.

The Alleged Mathematical Error in 2 Chronicles 4:1-2. How can the circular "sea of cast metal" in Solomon's temple (2 Chron 4:1-2) have a diameter of 10 cubits and yet have a circumference of 30 cubits, when we know from simple mathematics that the circumference should be about 31.42 cubits (Circumference = π x Diameter, i.e., 3.142 x 10)? The implication of this question is that, if the Bible writers could not be exact in this simple mathematical problem, how can these inspired writers be trusted with complicated computations of time prophecies (such as the 2300 years of Daniel 8:14) and other numbers dealing with biblical chronology or genealogies?

What the critics fail to realize is that the Bible writer did not tell us whether the 30 cubits figure given for the circumference of the basin is an *approximate* figure or an *exact* one. While it is true that Circumference = π x Diameter, the value of π can never be an exact figure. In other words, since π is an infinite non-repeating decimal (3.14159265+), any approximation of π, either as 3.0, 3.1, 3.14, 3.142, 3.1416, 3.14159, or 3.141593, etc., is technically in error. Thus, *whatever* figure the Bible writer uses to compute the circumference could be declared an error by the critics. It is obvious that in the case of the laver in Solomon's temple, the Bible writer could only have given an approximation of the circumference (taking π as 3.0), just as all scientists today will have to approximate if they are to compute the circumference of a circle whose diameter is 10 units.

But if the critics want us to be really picky, there is another way we can look at this alleged mistake. Notice that all the Bible states is that Solomon "made the Sea of cast metal, circular in shape, measuring ten cubits *from rim to rim* and five cubits high. It took a line of thirty cubits *to measure around it.*" What does "from rim to rim" refer to? Is it the inner diameter of the basin or the outer one? Could it be that when he was referring to the diameter of 10 cubits he had in mind the *outer* diameter but when he mentioned the 30 cubits circumference he had in mind the *inner* diameter? Why not? A school-child can remind the critical scholars that the circular basin, just like a salad bowl in mama's kitchen, has a thickness!

Our effort in going through this rather ridiculous exercise is to point out that we should not ascribe "ignorance" or "mistake" to the writer of Chronicles when we are not told whether he intended his mathematical figures to provide an exact scientific calibration or an approximate measure of the size of the basin. Those who charge the writer of Chronicles with error because he was not "mathematically precise" are also betraying their ignorance of basic laws of engineering and physics. The fact is that while mathematicians can calculate the exact measurement of a design in brass, it is always difficult for those in the workshop to shape a metallic object to the exact specifications. The workshop engineers always do their measurements to within a certain degree of error. And they also factor in the impact of temperature changes to allow for expansion and contraction of the brass metal being used to construct the object. The point is that the critics may need to reconsider the basis of their skepticism.

The Alleged Error of Botanical Classification. Again critics charge the Bible with error when it allegedly makes a wrong classification of plants. In 1 Kings 4:33, Solomon is said to have spoken of trees, "from the cedar tree that is in Lebanon even unto the hyssop that springeth out of the wall." This is supposedly an instance of an inspired writer following a "primitive" system of botanical classification according to size of plants, instead of following our modern "scientific" system that is based on the structure of the flower. Critics attribute the same kind of "error" to Jesus, who stated that the mustard seed "is the least of all seeds: but when it is grown, it is the greatest among herbs and becometh a tree, so that the birds of the air come and lodge in the branches thereof" (Matt 13:32). The question in this case is: Is the mustard seed really the "least [smallest] of all seeds"?

The Bible-believing scholar asks: What makes one form of botanical classification (plants, seeds, etc.) better than another? What determines whether, for example, one person's classification of shoes according to size is better than another's classification according to gender (ladies' versus mens'), age (children's versus adults'), color (red, black, brown), material (leather, rubber, etc.), or even origin (Italian, Brazilian, Zambian, etc.)?

All classifications deal with an ordering system or pattern which serves the specific purpose of the information or fact(s) being communicated. Is our classification of shoes (or cars, clothes, apples, etc.) any different from the Bible characters' classification of plants and seeds? Who decides whether one form of classification is "primitive" (because it is based on external appearance using the naked eye) and the other "scientific" (using microscopes or dissection, etc.)?

In the case of the mustard seed, should we fault Jesus for declaring it to be "the least of all seeds"? Since there are *microscopic* seeds too small to be seen with the naked eye and far smaller than the mustard seed, are we to conclude that in non-salvation issues Christ was careless in handling truth? Rather than Jesus having made a "mistake," it is the scholars themselves who are to be faulted for adopting a scientific definition of seed (*sperma*) that is foreign to the context of Matthew 13:32. Liberal scholarship ascribes "error" (however unintentional) to Jesus Christ only because it fails to recognize (1) the historical-cultural context, (2) the literary-grammatical context and (3) the canonical context—three principles we discussed in the previous chapter.

If historical-critical scholars had not imposed their ideologies on the Bible, they might have recognized these three contexts. (1) In an agricultural community such as Christ's audience, "seed" (*sperma*) in this setting would have meant anything farmers plant in the ground to grow (not "a fertilized and ripened plant ovule containing an embryo capable of germinating to produce a new plant," as one modern dictionary defines it). (2) In the verses *before* and *after* Matthew 13:32, the word seed refers to that which a man takes and *sows in the field* (vv. 24, 27, 37). (3) This meaning of seed in Christ's statement also appears in other sections of the New Testament canon (comparing Scripture with Scripture).

We may thus conclude that in Matthew 13:32, Jesus does not even make an incidental affirmation of factual error, neither does He "accommodate" the truth because of the "limited scientific knowledge" of his hearers. All Jesus was conveying in His parable is that "the mustard seed is such a tiny seed among the seeds you grow on the farm, yet when it grows it becomes one of the largest garden plants." The *New International Version* captures this understanding: "Though it is the smallest of *all your seeds,* yet when it grows, it is the largest of garden plants and becomes a tree, so that the birds of the air come and perch in its branches."

Alleged Error in Hosea 6:6. The prophet Hosea reports God as saying: "For I desired mercy, and not sacrifice; and the knowledge of God more than burnt offerings." According to the critics this statement is another indication of blatant error. They ask: "If God doesn't want sacrifice and burnt offering, why did He command the children of Israel to offer sacrifices and burnt offerings to Him? Why did He ask Abraham to sacrifice his son as a burnt offering Him? And why did He allow His Son to be sacrificed on the cross?" In the opinion of the scholars, either God doesn't want sacrifice, in which case Jesus did not have to die as atonement for our sins, or God wants sacrifice but He denies it, which implies that God sometimes allows some forms of lying, as He Himself apparently does in the above verse.

Once again these skeptical questions and the spurious theologies they spawn are exotic ways by which historical-critical scholars advertise their ignorance. They seem to forget that the Bible was written by Hebrews, not by Americans, Europeans, or Africans. And since the Scriptures were written in Hebrew, Aramaic, and Greek, they occasionally express some thoughts in *idioms* that may be foreign to us.

The statement in Hosea 6:6 is an example of a Hebrew idiom, which the Bible itself explains. In the book of Deuteronomy, forty years after God had made His covenant with one generation of Israelites, Moses spoke to the sons and grandsons of that generation: "The Lord made not this covenant with our fathers but with us, even us, who are all of us here alive this day" (Deut 5:3).

The fact is, however, that God actually *did* make a covenant with their fathers at Mt. Sinai. In Deuteronomy 5:3 Moses employed a Hebrew idiom. What he was saying was this: "God did not *only* make a covenant with our fathers, but *also* with us." An understanding of this idiomatic expression by Moses leads us to understand Hosea 6:6 ("I desired mercy, and not sacrifice") to mean: "I desired *not only* sacrifice, but *also* mercy."

Therefore, the alleged contradiction or error found in Hosea 6:6 arises out of the failure of some modern scholars to appreciate idioms in the Hebrew language. It may also be an indication of the cultural arrogance that leads today's critics to think that the expressions in their language are superior to those of the Bible writers.

These alleged errors—ascribed to Bible writers because they employed approximations (the circumference of the laver), another type of classification (of plants and seeds), and a particular idiomatic expression (God desires mercy, not sacrifice)—are variations of the "cultural conditioning" argument we identified in Part II of Chapter Five. Our response here is the same: "the barbarian blindly asserts the primacy of his own temporal and cultural provincialism in judging and understanding and interpreting all that occurs, and the *learned* barbarian does precisely the same thing, but adds footnotes."[2]

The 600,000 Figure at the Exodus

This is probably one of the key "rational difficulties" often cited by critical scholars. If this figure is an "exaggeration" of the actual number who left Egypt, why cannot other figures cited by Bible writers be equally suspect? For example, if this figure is unreliable, how can one reckon biblical genealogies or estimate that the age of the earth is "about 6,000 years"?

The Bible states that those who left Egypt at the exodus were 600,000 men, besides women and children (Ex 12:37). Adding children and women will yield a figure close to two million. In the course of the Israelites' journey, other censuses were taken that place the number in the same range.[3]

Traditionally, scholars have questioned the accuracy of the two million number, saying that it would have been impossible for such a large number of people to leave Egypt in a single night, be sustained logistically in the barren desert, cross the Jordan in a day, march around the small 10-acre city of Jericho, etc. Consequently, they have come up with all kinds of approaches to reduce this large number of people in the exodus. Some have explained the large numbers recorded in the Bible as due to "corruptions" in the text, such as transmission errors, even though the present text shows no evidence of such. Others have suggested that the numbers are symbolic or even represent the population of a later period.[4]

One Adventist scholar adds his voice to the popular conjecture that the word *'eleph,* translated "thousand," should be translated by its other meanings: *family division* (e.g., Josh 22:14); *clan* (e.g., 1 Sam 23:23; Micah 5:2), *captain* (Jer 13:21) or even *ruler* (as in Matt 2:6, quoting Micah 5:2). In this way the 600,000 men (Ex 12:37) will mean 600 family divisions, or 600 clans, or 600 captains or rulers—an explanation that makes the alleged "ambiguity" in the numbers seem more reasonable to "analytical" minds.[5]

There is a problem, however: how does one translate 603,550 men? What do you do with the 550? It is really fascinating to observe how creative scholars can be. They answer that 603,550 men is simply 603 clans consisting of 550 men! Thus the 601,730 men at the third census (Num 26:51) is simply 601 clans with 730 men.

But there are three main lines of evidence from Scripture itself by means of which Bible-believers may legitimately reject these critical reconstructions.[6]

In the first place, whenever the Bible employs *'eleph* as a number ("thousand"), it is often associated with *me'oth,* the word for "hundreds" as the next lower unit. For example, in Exodus 12:37 *me'oth* ("hundreds") is in close association with *'eleph* ("thousand"). Now, in Numbers 1:21, the number of males in the tribe of Reuben is cited literally as "six and forty thousand and five hundreds" [46,500]. In order for the critics to translate *'eleph* as "clans" or "family divisions," they have to translate the verse in two ways—either that the Reubenites "were forty and six clans *and five hundred"* (i.e., a total of 546 clans, a figure the critics themselves will not accept); or that there "were forty and six clans and five hundred *men"* (an untenable liberal *eis*egesis since it requires the scholars to introduce the word "men," a word that is not originally in the text).

Second, a comparison of the figures given for the first and second census recorded in the book of Numbers (Num 2:1-32; 26:1-51) show that Moses understood *'eleph* to be "thousand"—not "clans" or "divisions." Here is how the Bible computes the numbers of the various tribes:

Tribe	First census	Second census
Reuben	46,500	43,730
Simeon	59,300	22,200
Gad	45,650	40,500
Judah	74,600	76,500
Issachar	54,400	64,300
Zebulun	57,400	60,500
Ephraim	40,500	32,500
Manasseh	32,200	52,700
Benjamin	35,400	45,600
Dan	62,700	64,400
Asher	41,500	53,400
Naphtali	53,400	45,400
TOTAL	**603,550**	**601,730**

The Bible gives both the figures and the totals, and the result is mathematically correct.

Now if we follow the suggestion that instead of counting Reuben's number in the first census as 46,500, we understand the *'eleph*s as 46 "clans" amounting to 550 men, we run into some major problems. Adding all the tribes' "clans" (that is, 46 + 59 + 45 + 74 + 54 + 57 + 40 + 32 + 35 + 62 + 41 + 53) should yield *603 'eleph*s or "clans," according to the total given in Numbers 2:32. But it does not! Instead, we get *598 'eleph*s, suggesting that something is wrong with this proposed critical approach. Similarly, if we follow the critics' suggested solution, the second census figures will yield only *596 'elephs* instead of the expected *601* of Numbers 26:51. The problem is further compounded if we attempt to add the figures in the *me'oth* or "hundreds" columns.

Third, in Exodus 38:25-28 (cf. 30:12), the Bible itself states that there came a time during the exodus when each male was asked to pay a tax of half a shekel. Scripture records the total amount of money collected from the half-shekel tax as 100 talents 1,775 shekels, i.e. 301,775 shekels. This works out to the exact amount of money to be expected from 603,550 men, each taxed a half-shekel; in other words, 1/2 x 603,550 = 301,775! This close matching of men and money (*"about* six-hundred thousand men," Ex 12:37) is possible only if *'eleph* is understood to mean "thousand"—not clan. This third reason is the most compelling argument dismissing the critical reconstruction of the biblical numbers.

The point is: The Bible states that the number of people during the exodus was approximately 600,000 males (two million, allowing for women and children). There is no reason to dismiss the biblical figures just because our "rational minds" have difficulty accepting the explicit unambiguous claims of the Bible.

Our conclusion, on the basis of the Bible's own internal keys (the sum raised from the tabernacle tax, and the unambiguous computation of the census figures) is that the word *'eleph* in these figures should be translated as "thousands" and not as "clans" or "family divisions." Hence the approximate figure of 600,000 males (or a total of about 2 million people, women and children included) was the actual number of people involved in the exodus. Once again, Ellen White was far ahead of the scholars when she stated that those who "had come forth from Egypt" during the exodus were "millions" (*Patriarchs and Prophets,* p. 410).

Alleged Error of New Testament Writers Quoting the Old Testament "Wrongly"

Higher critical scholarship sometimes asks: "How can we trust the New Testament writers when they cannot even quote the Old Testament correctly?" The thrust of this rhetorical question is that since the New Testament writers allegedly quoted the Old Testament wrongly, the Holy Spirit evidently did not guide the accuracy of Scripture. This implies that the Bible has some portions that are not inspired, and in this way it is no different from pagan religious literature in which there is a mixture of truth and error. For other liberal scholars, the allegation that the New Testament writers used the Old Testament "freely" (i.e. misused it) suggests that modern scholars, "led by the Spirit," should also be allowed to use the Scriptures "freely."

Two examples are often cited as indications of alleged wrong quotations of the Old Testament. Before examining them, we will note that those who make these charges fail to recognize that the Jewish writers did not follow the same literary standards employed today.

For example, they did not have quotation marks to distinguish a *direct quotation* (e.g., John wrote, "God is love") from an *indirect quotation* (e.g., "John has said that God is love"). They did not follow our standard of shortening a long quotation with an ellipsis (as in "Remember the Sabbath day to keep it holy . . . the seventh day is the Sabbath"). Unlike the practice in our day of using square brackets (e.g., "The seventh-day [i.e., Saturday] is the Sabbath"), there is no way we can tell when the New Testament writers slipped in their own comments in a quotation from the Old Testament. They did not have footnote or endnote references by which to identify quotations from various sources. And there is no way we can tell whether they were making direct quotes or mere paraphrases or allusions (e.g., "The Lord is my shepherd and I shall have no need to worry about what to eat, drink, or wear"). In the last example, unless it is known that we are simply paraphrasing or alluding to Psalm 23:1 and Matthew 6:31, someone may fault us for "wrongly quoting" either David or Matthew. With this background, we shall now consider two New Testament examples critics have often interpreted as mistaken quotations.[7]

Mark's Alleged Error in Quoting Isaiah "Wrongly." In introducing John the Baptist as the forerunner of Jesus Christ, the Gospel writer Mark states: "As it is written in Isaiah the prophet, 'Behold, I send my messenger before thy face, who shall prepare thy way; the voice of one crying in the wilderness: Prepare the way of the Lord, make his paths straight—'" (Mark 1:2, 3).

Mark actually quotes from two Old Testament sources. First, he quotes from Malachi 3:1 ("Behold I send my messenger to prepare the way before me"), and only after that does he keep his promise by quoting Isaiah 40:3 ("A voice cries: 'In the wilderness prepare the way of the Lord, make straight in the desert a highway for our God'"). Why does Mark "mistakenly" attribute his quote to Isaiah?

Mark's allegedly wrong citation is actually the result of some twentieth-century scholars' insistence that the first century Jewish writer must follow modern literary standards. In our day, we may simply say something to this effect: "As far as John the Baptist is concerned, you know what Isaiah the prophet (and, by the way, the later prophet Malachi also) has said: 'Behold, I send . . .'." Mark, however, does not follow our modern conventions. The original recipients of Mark's Gospel understood his point. In citing his sources, he gives credit to Isaiah, either because that was the major thrust of his argument, or because he was citing the major prophet Isaiah as a representative of the Old Testament prophets who prophesied about John in this manner.

Matthew's Alleged Error in Quoting "Wrongly." The same point can be made of the alleged error of Matthew (27:9) in attributing a quotation from the prophet Zechariah to the prophet Jeremiah (cf. Zech 11:12, 13; Jer 19:1-13; 32:6-9). To critics, this is a "classic example" of an inspired writer (Matthew) having a lapse of memory, indicating that we cannot always take them seriously.

Bible-believing scholars have responded with three possible explanations. First, the "error" can be explained as creeping into the text during the transmission process. The idea here is that a copyist may have inadvertently written the name of Jeremiah in place of Zechariah. Perhaps, though there are more convincing solutions.

A second explanation takes into account the prevalent practice in Judaism to name a body of works produced by two or more writers after the most prominent in the group. This is analogous to politicians using the names London and Moscow in reference to the cities and people of the United Kingdom and Russia. Thus, since Jeremiah is believed to be the more notable of the two prophets, Matthew may have attributed the quotation to "the prophet Jeremiah."

Assuming this is the case, does an instance of imprecision or approximation merit the label "error"? Who decides whether one kind of language or description is better than another? Should it be scholars in Washington and Paris, or those in Accra and Buenos Aires? This is the old question of the alleged intellectual supremacy of Athens over Jerusalem, philosophy over biblical revelation.

But while the second argument may be likely, it does not allow the entire sixty-six books of the Bible to be the *only* context to understand Scripture. It reads the Bible in the light of cultural practices in ancient times, not internal evidence in Scripture. This calls for a more biblically-grounded argument.

The third explanation is much more likely. There are indications in the New Testament text under consideration that Matthew quoted from both Zechariah and Jeremiah, but attributed the quote to the more notable Old Testament prophet (Jeremiah). Matthew (27:9) quotes from Zechariah when he states the *amount* paid to Judas for betraying Christ: ". . . the handsome price at which they priced me! So I took the thirty pieces of silver and threw them into the house of the Lord to the potter" (cf. Zech 11:13). But Matthew continues by specifying the *field* of the potter, of which Zechariah makes no mention. Since the context of Matthew 27:6-9 is about the chief priests of Jerusalem purchasing a *burial plot* using Judas's bribe money, the inspired writer Matthew understood the significance of this in the light of what Jeremiah had written.

Notice that Jeremiah also spoke of a burial plot near Jerusalem (Jer 19:2, 11), as well as about the purchase of a field for a specified number of shekels (Jer 32:9). Thus, Matthew was conflating statements from Zechariah (the actual *cost* of Christ's betrayal) and Jeremiah (what the betrayal money was used for, namely, to buy a burial *field*). Since Matthew quoted more than one Old Testament author, he does what other New Testament writers do in instances of this kind, that is, they cite only the more notable one. Thus, just as Mark (1:2-3) conflates a quotation from Malachi 3:1 and Isaiah 40:3 but attributes it only to Isaiah, so in Matthew 27:9 the inspired writer cites only Jeremiah, even though he had conflated both Zechariah and Jeremiah.

This is an instance where the Bible writers employed their own conventions in citing sources. Can we fault them as mistaken because they do not follow our present system of referencing sources, a system that is ever changing, even in our own time?

Apparent Contradictions in Parallel Gospel Accounts

Of the many allegations of contradictions or errors which historical-critical scholars offer, the differences between the four Gospels are most cited as evidence that the Bible writers are not trustworthy, since they do not seem to agree on certain points in their recording of the same events.

Yet even if the Gospel writers recorded the stories exactly the same in every tiny detail, the critics would still not trust them. They would conclude that the Bible writers collaborated in a fishy scheme to remove all possible discrepancies. The point is that, because the historical-critical method is established on skepticism, under no circumstance would its followers trust everything they read in Scripture.[8]

In any case we still have to ask, What should the Bible student do in the face of apparent contradictions in parallel accounts in the Gospels? For example, how many demoniacs met Jesus at Gadara—one (Mark 5:2; Luke 8:27) or two (Matt 8:28)? How many blind men were healed near Jericho—one (Mark 10:46; Luke 18:35) or two (Matt 20:30)? How many angels were at Christ's tomb—one (Matt 28:5; Mark 16:5) or two (Luke 24:4; John 20:12)? We cannot dismiss these questions as minor or inconsequential errors in matters of history; the credibility and reliability of the Bible as God's inspired and trustworthy revelation is at stake.

One knowledgeable scholar compared the issue of the Bible writers' credibility to what happens at court trials: "In a court of law, particularly in a criminal case, the trustworthiness of a witness is of prime importance. The cross-examining attorney will make every effort to prove that the witness cannot be believed, that he is not a truthful person. The attorney may put various kinds of questions to the witness in an endeavor to trip him up in a discrepancy, thus showing the jury that in one statement or the other the witness must be lying or confused. Even though the discrepancy may pertain to a matter not directly germane to the case, the jury's confidence in the witness's general credibility is necessarily shaken, and they may reasonably reject his testimony relating to other, more important matters."[9]

Thus, if critics can show that the Bible writers are not trustworthy in even inconsequential historical accounts, can we trust their testimony in the weightier aspects of doctrine or salvation? Let us consider four examples.[10]

The Number of Demoniacs Healed. According to Matthew, there were two demoniacs who came to Jesus, while Mark and Luke say that one approached Him. This is not an instance of contradiction. It would have been a contradiction if Mark and Luke had stated that there was *only* one demoniac. But they did not say so. In order for the texts to be contradictory, the critical scholars would need to change the text, in which case the problem would not rest with the Bible, but with the critics.

Besides, in order to claim contradiction, the critical scholars have to ignore a fundamental mathematical law: *wherever there are two, there is always one. No exceptions.* Matthew tells us that there were two demoniacs. Apparently, Mark and Luke mention one because he was the more prominent of the two.

The Number of Angels at Jesus' Tomb. Matthew (28:5) and Mark (16:5) refer to one angel at the tomb, while Luke (24:4) and John (20:12) indicate that there were two angels. Is this a discrepancy? Only if we assume that Matthew and Mark claim that there was *only* one angel, and only if we ignore the fundamental mathematical law that "wherever there are two, there is always one." The situation is similar to the case of the demoniacs. We learn from two of the gospel accounts that there were two angels. Since there were two angels, a gospel writer may choose to focus on one. The fact that two of the writers focused on one angel does not mean there was only one angel. The critics have to read something into the text to say that Matthew and Mark allowed for *only* one angel.

Luke records that at the first approach of the women to the empty tomb, two angels appeared to them. Matthew focuses only on one angel because, apparently, it was he who caused the earthquake, rolled the stone door, frightened the guards, and *spoke* (he "said to the women, 'Do not be afraid'"). John (20:11) indicates that Mary Magdalene came back to the tomb a second time, after Peter and John had been there. It was then that Mary "saw two angels" and spoke to them as they sat by the tomb. Thus, there were two angels involved, although one was more prominent.

The Blind Men of Jericho. Here again, even though Matthew (20:29-34) records two men healed while Mark (10:46-52) and Luke (18:35-43) speak of one, there is no contradiction. Mark did not say there was *only* one blind man; and as we have pointed out, wherever there are two, there is always one. Mark identifies one by name (Bartimaeus) and gives his father's name (Timaeus), which suggests that he is concentrating on one of the blind men who was well-known to him. Is it not natural, for example, that if two people receive a Nobel prize and one of them is a personal acquaintance or from your home town, you will tend to focus on the one you know?

Note that in the three examples above, each Gospel writer focused on aspects of the events which he found most striking or meaningful. This is no different from the way we see things in the Bible; though we may be reading the same passage, our different individual dispositions, backgrounds, and experiences enable us to see different aspects of the same truth. Even the way we express these truths (the vocabulary, expressions, etc.) will be different. But we all gain a better appreciation of the truth when we share our perspectives. Such is the case with the varying accounts of the Gospel writers.

Ellen White made this point clearly: "Written in different ages, by men who differed widely in rank and occupation, and in mental and spiritual endowments, the books of the Bible present a wide contrast in style, as well as a diversity in the nature of the subjects unfolded. Different forms of expression are employed by different writers; often the same truth is more strikingly presented by one than by another. And as several writers present a subject under varied aspects and relations, there may appear, to the superficial, careless, or prejudiced reader, to be discrepancy or contradiction, where the thoughtful, reverent student, with clearer insight, discerns the underlying harmony" (*The Great Controversy*, p. vi).

The Inscription on the Cross of Christ. Critical scholars often cite the different accounts of the inscription on Jesus' cross as a case of "obvious discrepancy." How do we explain the differences in wording?

Matthew 27:37:   *This is Jesus the king of the Jews*
Mark 15:26:   *The king of the Jews*
Luke 23:38:   *This is the king of the Jews*
John 19:19:   *Jesus of Nazareth the king of the Jews*

The explanation is not too difficult to find when we let the Bible speak for itself. Three kinds of explanations are possible. First, according to John, the notice was written in three languages—Hebrew, Greek and Latin (John 19:20). There is no indication in the Gospels to suggest that the wording was the same in all three languages. It is quite possible that one writer was giving us an exact copy of the Greek inscription while the others provided translations of the Hebrew or the Latin version, or even perhaps a mixture of them both.

Second, there were no punctuation marks in Bible times, no quotation marks, brackets, commas, etc. This can create problems for the modern reader who seeks to judge the Bible writers by modern literary standards. Let us illustrate this with an example:

1. *Direct Quotation:* Pilate's inscription read: "Jesus of Nazareth, the King of the Jews."
2. *Indirect Quotation:* Pilate wrote that Jesus was the King of the Jews.

It must be clear to the reader that even though the two sentences above are "quotations" of Pilate, the use of quotation marks and a colon in the first example makes it easier for us to know the extent of Pilate's exact words, even though both sentences convey Pilate's message inscribed on the cross. This may shed some light on the alleged contradictions in the accounts of the gospel writers regarding the inscription on the cross.

Finally, it is possible that each Gospel writer only gives part of the complete statement as follows:

Matthew 27:37:   "This is Jesus [*of Nazareth*] the king of the Jews"
Mark 15:26:   "[*This is Jesus of Nazareth*] the king of the Jews"
Luke 23:38:   "This is [*Jesus of Nazareth*] the king of the Jews"
John 19:19:   "[*This is*] Jesus of Nazareth the king of the Jews"

It stands to reason that the whole statement may have been *"This is Jesus of Nazareth the king of the Jews."* In this case each of the Gospel writers gives the essential part of the message ("the king of the Jews"), but no Gospel gives the whole inscription. The important thing to remember, even in this possible scenario, is that none of the Gospel writers contradicted the other. Their accounts are diverse and mutually complementary, but not contradictory.

Ellen White is on target again: "As presented through different individuals, the truth is brought out in its varied aspects. One writer is more strongly impressed with one phase of the subject; he grasps those points that harmonize with his experience or with his power of perception and appreciation; another seizes upon a different phase; and each, under the guidance of the Holy Spirit, presents what is most forcibly impressed upon his own mind—a different aspect of the truth in each, *but a perfect harmony through all.* And the truths thus revealed unite to form a perfect whole, adapted to meet the wants of men in all the circumstances and experiences of life" (*The Great Controversy,* p. vi, emphasis supplied).

What we have attempted to show in this chapter is that the alleged "inconsistencies" which critical scholars claim to have found in Scripture are either misunderstandings of the text or the result of wrong assumptions. If this is so, the efforts in some Adventist ranks to construct new theories of Scripture inspiration and interpretation are misdirected and misleading.

Other Areas

The responses given here to these "difficult" passages are not intended to be the final word on the questions. What we have simply sought to do is to suggest that there are other ways of looking at these age-old problems masquerading in some minds as "disturbing discrepancies." Whatever solutions may be offered for any biblical difficulty, Bible-believers must insist that the Scriptures remain the final authority. Perhaps this exercise will convince us to suspend judgment rather than declaring difficult passages of Scripture as "contradictions" or "errors." The Bible should always reprove and correct us, not vice versa (2 Tim 3:16, 17).

Admittedly, the examples cited in this chapter do not exhaust the difficulties that some readers may confront in studying the Scriptures. Because our concern has been with the Bible's own alleged internal discrepancies, we have not dealt with problems relating to modern science, ancient history, predictive prophecy, and ethical morality. Readers who want to pursue these areas may consult the works cited in the note.[11]

We have also not dealt with the oft-repeated scholarly *myth* that the Old Testament "accommodated" or tolerated (some say encouraged) polygamy, divorce and remarriage, slavery, and "patriarchy," practices later allegedly corrected by the "Spirit's leading." Some have already challenged these assertions.[12] Another critical issue not dealt with in this book is the issue of war and non-violence in the Bible. We hope to take this up in a future work.

Insightful Statements. Meanwhile, as we continue *wrestling with the Word,* we would call attention to this insightful statement by Ellen G. White: "Many, especially those who are young in the Christian life, are at times troubled with the suggestions of skepticism. There are in the Bible many things which they cannot explain, or even understand, and Satan employs these to shake their faith in the Scriptures as a revelation from God. . . . The difficulties of Scripture have been urged by skeptics as an argument against the Bible; but so far from this, they constitute a strong evidence of its divine inspiration. If it contained no account of God but that which we could easily comprehend; if His greatness and majesty could be grasped by finite minds, then the Bible would not bear the unmistakable credentials of divine authority. The very grandeur and mystery of the themes presented, should inspire faith in it as the Word of God" (*Steps to Christ,* pp. 105, 107).

Conclusion

It is fitting to close this chapter with timely counsel from Adventism's *foremost* Bible interpreter:

"There are many things apparently difficult or obscure, which God will make plain and simple to those who thus seek an understanding of them. But without the guidance of the Holy Spirit we shall be continually liable to wrest the Scriptures or to misinterpret them. There is much reading of the Bible that is without profit, and in many cases a positive injury. When the Word of God is opened without reverence and without prayer; when the thoughts and affections are not fixed upon God, or in harmony with His will, the mind is clouded with doubt; and in the very study of the Bible, skepticism strengthens. The enemy takes control of the thoughts, and he suggests interpretations that are not correct. Whenever men are not in word and deed seeking to be in harmony with God, then, however learned they may be, they are liable to err in their understanding of Scripture, and it is not safe to trust to their explanations. Those who look to the Scriptures to find discrepancies, have not spiritual insight. With distorted vision they will see many causes for doubt and unbelief in things that are really plain and simple."[13]

On the other hand there is abundant reward for Bible-believing Christians who approach the Scriptures with humility of heart and a desire to obey God's revealed will. Through the illumination of the Spirit, "God intends that even in this life the truths of His Word shall be ever unfolding to His people. . . . God desires man to exercise his reasoning powers; and the study of the Bible will strengthen and elevate the mind as no other study can. Yet we are to beware of deifying reason, which is subject to the weakness and infirmity of humanity. If we would not have the Scriptures clouded to our understanding, so that the plainest truths shall not be comprehended, we must have the simplicity and faith of a little child, ready to learn, while beseeching the aid of the Holy Spirit. A sense of the power and wisdom of God, and of our inability to comprehend His greatness, should inspire us with humility, and we should open His Word, as we would enter His presence, with holy awe. When we come to the Bible, reason must acknowledge an authority superior to itself, and heart and intellect must bow to the great I AM. . . . And all who come in this spirit to the study of the Bible, will find abundant evidence that it is God's Word, and they may gain an understanding of its truths that will make them wise unto salvation" (*Steps to Christ,* pp. 109, 111).

Such will be the attitude of all those who seek to honor the inspired and authoritative Word of God. Because they have seen the bankruptcy of liberalism's skepticism towards the Bible, they reject any use of the historical-critical method. Testimonies of such scholars will be encouraging to us in our struggles with Bible difficulties. In the next chapter, we shall hear courageous individuals *testifying about the Word.*

NOTES

1. R. A. Torrey, *Is the Bible the Inerrant Word of God?* (New York: George H. Doran Company, 1922), pp. 66-75.

2. Roland M. Frye, "A Literary Perspective for the Criticism of the Gospels," in Donald G. Miller and Dikran Y. Hadidian, eds., *Jesus and Man's Hope,* vol. 2 (Pittsburgh: Pittsburgh Theological Seminary, 1971), p. 198, emphasis supplied.

3. The first census, involving all the people over 20 years, was commanded by God for the purpose of taxing them half a shekel each for the building of the tabernacle (Ex 30:11-16; 38:25f.). The number then was 603,550. The same number was obtained in a second census (Num 1:1-54) some nine months after the first census; in this second instance the purpose was to determine the number of people eligible for war. There was a third census, totalling 601,730 (Num 26:51) taken nearly forty years later, for the purpose of distributing the land of Canaan. What is clear is that the number of people from the time of their departure from Egypt to the time of their arrival in the promised land was over 600,000 males, or about 2 million in all (cf. Num 2:32; 11:21).

4. Many faithful Bible readers, however, have taken these numbers at face value. Their faith rests in the assurance that "our God is able" (Dan 3:17). They argue that if God was able to rescue the Israelites from the hands of the Egyptian forces, if He was able to part the Red Sea, to provide manna to feed them and water from the rock, and if He was able to shelter them by day and night with His presence in the pillar of cloud and fire (Ps 105, 106), would it have been difficult for Him to deliver some 600,000 men from Egypt? Their faith response is unequivocally, "There is nothing too hard for the Lord." This may sound childish to some; but even a small figure of 20,000 would easily have perished from hunger and thirst in that wilderness just as quickly as 600,000 men. Why do we have to believe in a "miracle" with a reduced number and not exercise the same faith in a "miracle" with a large number, just as the Bible says?

5. See Alden Thompson, *Inspiration,* pp. 221-225. For a response to this "casebook approach" to Scriptures, see Frank Holbrook and Leo Van Dolson, eds., *Issues in Revelation and Inspiration,* pp. 54-60, 173-199.

6. Randall W. Younker, "A Few Thoughts on Alden Thompson's Chapter: Numbers, Genealogies, Dates," in *Issues in Revelation and Inspiration,* pp. 173-199, offers an excellent critique of other kinds of liberal reconstructions.

7. For a detailed discussion of this issue, see Roger Nicole, "The Old Testament Quotations in the New Testament With Reference to the Doctrine of Plenary Inspiration," in *Evangelicals and Inerrancy: Selections from the "Journal of the Evangelical Theological Society,"* ed. Ronald Youngblood (Nashville, Tenn.: Thomas Nelson, 1984), pp. 1-12; S. Lewis Johnson, Jr., *The Old Testament in the New: An Argument for Biblical Inspiration* (Grand Rapids, Mich.: Zondervan, 1980); Richard Davidson, "Revelation/Inspiration in the Old Testament: A Critique of Alden Thompson's 'Incarnational' Model," in *Issues in Revelation and Inspiration,* ed. Frank Holbrook and Leo Van Dolson (Berrien Springs, Mich.: Adventist Theological Society Publications, 1992), pp. 127-131; Allan Hayward, *God's Truth!* (London: Marshall, Morgan and Scott, 1973), pp. 185-188; Samuel Koranteng-Pipim, "Paul's Use of Deut. 25:4 in 1 Cor. 9:9ff.: Its Implications for Biblical Inspiration and Hermeneutics" (1989), unpublished term paper, available at the Adventist Heritage Center of the James White Library, Andrews University.

8. Refer to the "principle of criticism"—the third naturalistic foundation of the historical-critical method—in chapter 3.

9. Gleason L. Archer, "Alleged Errors and Discrepancies in the Original Manuscripts of the Bible," in *Inerrancy,* ed. Norman Geisler (Grand Rapids, Mich.: Zondervan, 1980), p. 59.

10. In the discussion that follows, we are indebted to Norman Geisler and Thomas Howe, *When Critics Ask: A Popular Handbook on Bible Difficulties* (Wheaton, Ill.: Victor Books, 1992). This 600-page volume is essentially an encyclopedia that offers alternatives to liberal interpretations of Bible difficulties.

11. William H. Shea's "Interpreting History" in his *Daniel 1-7: Prophecy As History* [The Abundant Life Bible Amplifier] (Boise, Id.: Pacific Press, 1996), pp. 33-48; cf. his "The Interpretation of Prophecy" in his *Daniel 7-12: Prophecies of the End Time* [The Abundant Life Bible Amplifier] (Boise, Id.: Pacific Press, 1996), pp. 33-46. Norman Geisler and Thomas Howe, *When Critics Ask* (see note 10 above); John W. Haley, *Alleged Discrepancies of the Bible* (Pittsburgh, Pa.: Whitaker House, [1887?]); Gleason L. Archer, "Alleged Errors and Discrepancies in the Original Manuscripts of the Bible," in Norman Geisler, ed., *Inerrancy* (Grand Rapids, Mich.: Zondervan, 1980), pp. 57-82; see also his *Encyclopedia of Bible Difficulties* (Grand Rapids, Mich.: Zondervan, 1982); H. E. Guillebaud, *Some Moral Difficulties of the Bible* (London: Intervarsity, 1949); Angel M. Rodriguez, "Those Troublesome Psalms," *Perspective Digest* 1/1 (1996):16-21, 67-73; Alan Hayward, *God's Truth!* (London: Marshall, Morgan and Scott, 1973); Edwin Thiele, *A Chronology of the Hebrew Kings* (Grand Rapids, Mich.: Zondervan, 1977); Walter C. Kaiser, *Hard Sayings of the Old Testament* (Downers Grove, Ill.: InterVarsity Press, 1988); Siegfried H. Horn, *The Spade Confirms the Book* (Washington, D.C.: Review and Herald, 1980); Gerhard F. Hasel, *Biblical Interpretation Today* (Washington, D.C.: Biblical Research Institute, 1985); see also his *Understanding the Living Word of God* (Mountain View, Calif.: Pacific Press, 1980); Noel Weeks, *The Sufficiency of Scripture* (Carlisle, Pa.: Banner of Truth Trust, 1988); Frank Holbrook and Leo Van Dolson, eds., *Issues in Revelation and Inspiration* (Berrien Springs, Mich.: Adventist Theological Society Publications, 1992). For an excellent critique of some of the major assumptions underlying the alleged discrepancies in New Testament passages, see David R. Hall, *The Seven Pillories of Wisdom* (Macon, Ga.: Mercer University Press, 1990); cf. Eta Linnemann, *Is There a Synoptic Problem?: Rethinking the Literary Dependence of the First Three Gospels,* trans. by Robert W. Yarbrough (Grand Rapids, Mich.: Baker, 1992).

12. Readers will benefit from the following works which challenge the above "accommodation" hypotheses: Ronald A. G. du Preez, "Polygamy in the Bible with Implications for Seventh-day Adventist Missiology" (D. Min. project dissertation, Andrews University, 1993); J. Carl Laney, "Deuteronomy 24:1-4 and the Issue of Divorce," *Bibliotheca Sacra* 149 (Jan-Mar 1992):3-15; Theodore D. Weld, *The Bible Against Slavery: Or, An Inquiry into the Genius of the Mosaic System, and the*

Teachings of the Old Testament on the Subject of Human Rights (Pittsburgh: United Presbyterian Board of Publication, 1864); cf. Dale B. Martin, *Slavery As Salvation: The Metaphor of Slavery in Pauline Christianity* (New Haven: Yale University Press, 1990). These works offer biblical evidence showing that God at no time tolerated polygamy, divorce and remarriage, and slavery as morally legitimate practices for His people. On the issue of patriarchy, Guenther Haas, "Patriarchy as An Evil that God Tolerated: Analysis and Implications for the Authority of Scripture," *Journal of the Evangelical Theological Society,* September 1995, pp. 321-326, has challenged the notion that male headship (in the home and church) is an evil practice that God tolerated.

13. *Steps to Christ,* pp. 110-111. Ellen G. White was more than a "devotional writer." In fact, the chapter in *Steps to Christ* from which the quotation comes, titled "What to Do with Doubt" (pp. 105-113), is one of the best treatises on how to deal with Bible difficulties.

Chapter Eleven

Testifying About the Word

Though skeptical approaches to Scripture abound among scholars, many in the academic community do not follow those approaches but take a reverent, believing attitude toward Scripture. Some, even among world-class scholars who have been intimately acquainted with such issues as this book raises, have converted from skepticism to faith. Their experiences with liberalism's higher criticism may be instructive to those in our ranks who are tempted to employ the historical-critical method or who may already be infatuated with it.

Since both classical and moderate liberals are sowing doubts concerning the Word (see Chapter Three), we shall listen first to the testimonies of some former representatives of both groups. Then, as a model for Bible-believing scholars in an increasingly liberal environment, this chapter, "Testifying About the Word," will close with the testimony of a noted Bible-believing conservative scholar.

But since every road has a destination, as a prelude to these testimonies we shall briefly point out the *ultimate destination* of those travelling on the hermeneutical road of theological liberalism. By showing how modern higher criticism bankrupts Christian theology and leads away from faith in God, the Bible's Author, we may enable the reader better to detect winds of liberalism wherever they may blow.

Liberalism: The Critical Voices Within

Theology as taught in most seminaries and universities today is based on theological liberalism's historical-critical method. Many scholarly commentaries, articles, and books reflect this method, and it also filters down to the pulpits. Unfortunately, church members, students, and leaders—those who are most affected by it—are not always clearly aware of it.

Liberalism is not a school of thought in the sense of reflecting a uniform set of beliefs. Rather, it is a frame of mind that seeks to adapt religious ideas to modern culture. One scholar defined it well, saying that in liberalism, "a God without wrath brought men without sin into a kingdom without judgment through the ministrations of a Christ without a cross."[1]

Essential Characteristics of Liberalism

Moderates/accommodationists who are still aboard the historical-critical train must be aware that this train will ultimately lead them to the same destination as the radical liberals. We shall highlight five elements that indicate when riders of this train have finally arrived at the destination anticipated by its liberal engineers.

An Immanent Worldview. Ultimately the liberal worldview has no supernatural realm. God is within nature rather than beyond it, working through natural processes (e.g. evolution) rather than through radical discontinuities with it (e.g. special six-day creation). In theological talk, this worldview is called *immanence;* both pantheism and the New Age philosophy are versions of the immanent worldview.

In this worldview, there can be no true supernatural miracles such as the Bible teaches. Therefore when liberal scholars use the term "miracle," we must understand that they mean something completely different. In fact, Friedrich Schleiermacher (1768-1834), the acknowledged father of modern liberalism, *redefined* miracles this way: "Miracle is simply the religious name for event. Every event, even the most natural and usual, becomes a miracle as soon as the religious view of it can be the dominant."[2]

Thus when liberals write about the "miracle" of Jesus' virgin birth, they understand this birth as a "miracle" only because every birth is a miracle in itself. In other words, since every birth is a unique and distinctive event, Jesus' birth is also unique, hence a "miracle."

This is a typical liberal approach: take a biblical term (inspiration, incarnation, resurrection, Sabbath, sanctuary, atonement, etc.), empty the term of its biblical meaning, and then inject it with a liberal meaning. In this way, unsuspecting church members will not readily see the difference.

An "Inspiring" View of the Bible. When liberals say that they believe in the "inspiration" of the Bible (or Ellen White), they often actually mean that the Bible is inspired in the same way that Shakespeare is inspired. The Bible, liberals argue, though a fallible human product, is an inspiring document just like any other outstanding work—whether it be music by Beethoven, a speech by Martin Luther King, Jr., a sermon by Spurgeon, a lecture by Ghandhi, a ministry like that of Mother Theresa, or leadership by Joan of Arc. God can still use a fallible human work to unfold "truth" and effect a "dynamic, living revelation" of Himself.

For liberals, the Bible is culturally conditioned. It is a fallible human record of the writers' religious experiences rather than a divine revelation of truth and reality. Consequently, the Bible is not the authoritative norm on which Christians ought to base all their doctrines or practices. The statement of Gordon Kaufman, describing the demise of biblical authority, may well represent the views of many liberals: "The Bible no longer has unique authority for Western man. It has become a great but archaic monument in our midst. It is a reminder of where we once were—but no longer are. It contains glorious literature, important historical documents, exalted ethical teachings, but it is no longer the word of God."[3]

Without an authoritative biblical norm, human reason and experience constitute liberalism's highest norms. Because reason and experience may differ from person to person and culture to culture, liberalism proposes that a pluralism of ideas or doctrines offers the best hope of arriving at truth.

This means that, in the church, everyone must be permitted to believe and teach whatever they please, even if contrary to the teachings of the Bible. After all, liberals argue, even in the Bible there is "diversity" in the teachings of the Bible writers. The liberal mantra is: "Paul became a Jew to the Jews and a Greek to Greeks." On this basis they argue that the church should allow pluralism in doctrine and practice—as long as no one is hurt.[4]

Divinity of Human Beings. According to liberal theology, human beings are not intrinsically evil as the Bible teaches; they are naturally good. This view is based on the evolutionary idea of human progress. According to the father of modern liberalism, "sin is so little an essential part of the being of man that we can never regard it as anything else than a disturbance of nature."[5] Many liberals would maintain that all human beings possess a divine God-consciousness within them, which they themselves can develop, without any need of a radical transformation by grace from outside.

Since human nature is essentially good, liberal scholars tend not to talk about human sinfulness (the consequence of Adam's fall and our individual choices) or conversion (the radical change in our nature), but a psychological "nurturing" (gradual development of one's potential).

They also teach that the fundamental human problem is not sin but the environment surrounding us—whether it is our genes, natural environment, or socio-political realities. If we can change the order of society, we will reach utopia, experiencing "God's kingdom on earth." This has led to an uncritical embracing of different versions of liberation theology (e.g., Western social gospel theologies, Latin American, African, Asian, feministic, gay and lesbian liberation theologies).

This is why liberals are more interested in social or political activities than in evangelism. Why evangelize when everybody has the truth or when no one can be sure of what truth is, anyway? and when everyone is good already? For liberals, God is active not only in the church, but also in political activity and other social movements.[6] Thus in liberalism, there is no place for a second coming of Jesus, a new heaven, or divine judgment. Human beings can create their own utopia on earth. They do not need a God from outside to reward or punish.

The Man Jesus Christ. Christianity teaches that though divine, Jesus became human; God became man. But in liberalism, Jesus Christ was a man who became God. He is not the preexistent Son of God; He was a good man who developed his God-consciousness to the highest degree, and therefore became God.[7] Since all human beings possess the same God-consciousness within them, they also can become God. This is essentially Satan's first theology lecture in the garden of Eden.

Liberals also hold that the substitutionary death of Jesus on the cross was not an atonement for the world's sins, but rather, it is an example of self-sacrificing, philanthropic love. They maintain that the notion that the blood of Jesus was shed for the sins of others is a primitive idea, offensive to today's "enlightened" thought and "matured" or "progressive" ethical sensitivities.

Ideology over Methodology. Biblical Christianity calls upon believers to accept the totality of Scripture and to submit humbly to its teachings. But liberalism, for ideological reasons, refuses to surrender to the full authority of the Bible. Thus, in practice, liberal interpretation of Scripture is not faithful biblical methodology but a battle for the supremacy of conflicting secular ideologies.

The title of Eta Linnemann's book, *Historical Criticism of the Bible: Methodology or Ideology?*, alludes to this point.[8] Another scholar asserts it more explicitly, arguing that, in the view of many contemporary theologians, the continuing authority of the Bible for today's world depends upon how we address two related issues: "the ideological *use* of Scripture, which is, if you will, an exterior problem; and the ideological *content* of Scripture, which is intrinsic to the text."[9]

Theologies of Liberation. The various theologies of liberation provide an example of ideological *use* of Scripture. They claim that powerful groups (e.g., the rich, white Anglo-Saxons, heterosexuals, and males) have employed the Bible to legitimize exploiting, dominating, and enslaving the socially powerless classes (e.g., the poor and marginalized, people of color, females, and homosexuals), and they profess to deliver the Bible into the hands of the oppressed as a resource for liberation, thus "correcting" the abuse. Such an ideological hermeneutic uses the biblical data selectively, choosing only those sections it can interpret to justify liberation from society's oppressive structures.

To succeed in their reinterpretation of the Bible, many theologies of liberation—e.g., the social gospel, Latin American, Black, African, Asian, feminist, and gay and lesbian liberation theologies—adopt the historical-critical approach to Scripture. As Linnemann explains, the method's basic objective is to conduct biblical research as if there were no God.[10] Denying the traditional understanding of the Bible's inspiration in favor of "dynamic revelation" or "dynamic truth," theologians of liberation dismiss as culturally conditioned any teaching in the Bible that runs contrary to their secular ideology. Ultimately, human reason and subjective experience become the final norm for liberal scholars.

Feminist Theology. Of the various brands of liberation theology, twentieth-century feminist theology is notable for accusing Scripture *itself* of oppressive ideological content. For this reason, it poses one of the greatest threats to biblical Christianity. One scholar has accurately explained that whereas other liberation theologies claim the Scriptures have been *used* to legitimize oppression (hence the need by liberation theologians to "liberate" the Word from its white, Anglo-Saxon abusers), feminism perceives the Bible itself as both a *producer* and *product* of female oppression—that is, some of the Bible's *content* is itself oppressive! She aptly summarized the view of feminist theologians:

"The Bible was written in a patriarchal society by the people, mostly men, whom the system kept on top. It embodies the androcentric, that is, male-centered, presuppositions of that social world, and it legitimizes the patriarchal, that is male-dominant, social structures that held that world together. Its language is overwhelmingly male-oriented, both in its reference to God and in reference to people. In short, the Bible is a book written by men in order to tell *their* story for *their* advantage. As such, it confronts both women and justice-inspired men with an enormous problem. It is not at all certain that the Bible can survive this challenge, that it can retain the allegiance of people called to justice and freedom in a postmodern world."[11]

Holding that Scripture contains oppressive material against women, feminist interpreters not only pick and choose from the Bible (as their other liberation theology counterparts do), but they are also *suspicious* of the biblical text. Using the two principles of selectivity and skepticism, feminist interpreters insist that as they approach Scripture, "our ideology takes precedence over the ideology of the [biblical] literature."[12] This attitude of both doubt and scorn toward the Bible's message is an essential hallmark of the feminist hermeneutic.

Feminism's threat to Christianity stems, in part, from the fact that its influence is more widespread than is often realized. Mary A. Kassian's eye-opening book, *The Feminist Gospel: The Movement to Unite Feminism With the Church* (a "must read" for all Bible-believing Seventh-day Adventists—lay people, pastors, and scholars),[13] convincingly shows that besides shaping contemporary discussions of male and female roles in the home and the church, feminist philosophy also finds expression in various denominations through their women's task forces, in colleges and universities through women's studies courses, in churches through women's ministries, in seminaries through feminist theologies, and in worship expression through inclusive language in hymns and Bible translations and through feminist rituals in liturgies. Few realize, however, that behind most of the preoccupations of the various women's groups, studies, and ministries lurks an agenda which seeks to reinterpret the Christian faith and lifestyle.

Could this ideological agenda, and the desire to obliterate gender role differentiations, be the underlying reason why, despite her favorable disposition towards legitimate women's causes and ministries, Ellen G. White cautioned against the feminist movement of the 19th century, known then as the "woman's rights movement"? She warned that "those who feel called out to join the movement in favor of woman's rights and the so-called dress reform might as well sever all connection with the third angel's message. The spirit which attends the one cannot be in harmony with the other. The Scriptures are plain upon the relations and rights of men and women" (*Testimonies for the Church,* 1:421).[14]

In short, liberalism has substituted a religion of immanence for the Christian faith. Instead of the Messiah Jesus, liberals have a religious hero or martyr; instead of creation from nothing (*ex nihilo*), they have evolution; instead of an eschatology in which God Himself intervenes in human history, they have the philosophy of human progress and utopianism; instead of the absolute authority of the Bible, they have relativism and pluralism of ideas; and instead of a faithful biblical methodology, they have profane secular ideologies.[15]

Bankruptcy of Liberalism and Its Method. Following the example of their Savior, Bible-believing Christians reject the liberal position on the Bible and the atheistic assumptions upon which the historical-critical method of interpretation is based. Recognizing these so-called "scientific" methods as nothing more than false human structures, "hollow and deceptive philosophy, which depends on human tradition" (Col 2:8 NIV) and "every pretension that sets itself up against the knowledge of God" (2 Cor 10:5 NIV), true Christians respond, "How can you believe if you accept praise from one another, yet make no effort to obtain the praise that comes from the only God?" (John 5:44 NIV).

One respected scholar summarized the baneful effect of liberal theology this way: "It raises a doubt about every single biblical passage, as to whether it truly embodies revelation or not. And it destroys the reverent, receptive, self-distrusting attitude of approach to the Bible, without which it cannot be known to be 'God's Word written'."[16] He explained that the loss of the historic conviction that the Bible in its entirety is God's word has undermined preaching, undercut Biblical teaching, weakened the faith of believers, discouraged lay Bible reading, and saddest of all, has hidden Christ from the view of many Christians.[17]

Ellen G. White had liberals in mind when she wrote: "Men are teaching for doctrine the commandments of men; and their assertions are taken as truth. The people have received man-made theories. So the gospel is perverted, and the Scripture misapplied. As in the days of Christ, the light of truth is pushed into the back-ground. Men's theories and suppositions are honored before the word of the Lord God of hosts. The truth is counteracted by error. The word of God is wrested, divided and distorted by higher criticism. Jesus is acknowledged, only to be betrayed by a kiss" (*Bible Echo and Signs of the Times,* February 1, 1897).

Recognizing the dangers involved, Ellen White urged believers, "Brethren, cling to your Bible, as it reads, and stop your criticisms in regard to its validity, and obey the Word, and not one of you will be lost" (*Selected Messages,* 1:18).

Further, she urged: "The life of God, which gives life to the world, is in His word. It was by His word that Jesus healed disease and cast out demons. And by His word He stilled the sea and raised the dead; and the people bore witness that His word was with power. He spoke the word of God, as He had spoken it to all the prophets and teachers of the Old Testament. The whole Bible is a manifestation of Christ. It is our only source of power. Do not rely upon any human agency for your wisdom. Take the Lord at His word, believing you do receive the things you ask of Him" (*Manuscript Releases,* 11:29).

Testimony of A Former Liberal Scholar

Liberalism is incompatible with the biblical faith. Wherever it is accepted, it devastates the faith of its recipients. It reduces the Bible to a dead letter, unable to bring life and meaning to the hearts of people. Many Christians who have been infatuated by this kind of theology have had to resort to secular psychology, sociology, socialism, and other "isms" in their attempt to find meaning.

The most scathing criticism of liberalism's historical-critical theology comes from the German New Testament scholar, Dr. Eta Linnemann, once among liberalism's ablest defenders. Listen to the testimony of this Lutheran scholar as she explains why she gave up liberal theology:

"'Why do you say "No!" to historical-critical theology?' I have been confronted with this question, and I wish to state at the outset: My 'No!' to historical-critical theology stems from my 'Yes!' to my wonderful Lord and Savior Jesus Christ and to the glorious redemption he accomplished for me on Golgotha.

"As a student of Rudolf Bultmann and Ernst Fuchs, as well as of Friedrich Gogarten and Gerhard Ebeling, I had the best professors which historical-critical theology could offer to me. And I did not do too badly in other respects, either. My first book turned out to be a best-seller. I became professor of theology and religious education . . . [and] was inducted into the Society of New Testament Studies. I had the satisfaction of an increasing degree of recognition from my colleagues.

"Intellectually comfortable with historical-critical theology, I was deeply convinced that I was rendering a service to God with my theological work and contributing to the proclamation of the gospel. Then, however, on the basis of various observations, discoveries, and a resulting self-awareness, I was forced to concede two things I did not wish: (1) no 'truth' could emerge from this 'scientific work on the biblical text,' and (2) such labor does not serve the proclamation of the gospel. . . .

"Today I realize that historical-critical theology's monopolistic character and world-wide influence is a sign of God's judgment (Rom. 1:18-32). God predicted this in his Word: 'For the time will come when men will not put up with sound doctrine. Instead, to suit their own desires, they will gather around them a great number of teachers to say what their itching ears want to hear' (2 Tim. 4:3). He also promised to send a 'powerful delusion so that they will believe the lie' (2 Thess. 2:11). *God is not dead, nor has He resigned. He reigns, and He is already executing judgment on those who declare him dead or assert that He is a false god who does nothing, either good or evil.*

"Today I know that I owe those initial insights to the beginning effects of God's grace. . . . Finally God himself spoke to my heart by means of a Christian brother's words. By God's grace and love I entrusted my life to Jesus.

"He immediately took my life into his saving grasp and began to transform it radically.

"I became aware of what folly it is, given what God is doing today, to maintain that the miracles reported in the New Testament never took place. Suddenly it was clear to me that my teaching was a case of the blind leading the blind. I repented for the way I had misled my students. . . .

"By God's grace I experienced Jesus as the one whose name is above all names. I was permitted to realize that Jesus *is* God's Son, born of a virgin. He *is* the Messiah and the Son of Man; such titles were not merely conferred on Him as the result of human deliberation. I recognized, first mentally, but then in a vital, experiential way, that Holy Scripture is inspired.

"Not because of human talk but because of the testimony of the Holy Spirit in my heart, I have clear knowledge that my former perverse teaching was sin. At the same time I am happy and thankful that this sin is forgiven me because Jesus bore it on the cross.

"That is why I say 'No!' to historical-critical theology. I regard everything that I taught and wrote before I entrusted my life to Jesus as refuse [garbage]. I wish to use this opportunity to mention that I have pitched my two books . . . along with my contributions to journals, anthologies, and *Festschriften*. Whatever of these writings I had in my possession I threw into the trash with my own hands in 1978. I ask you sincerely to do the same thing with any of them you may have on your own bookshelf."[18]

This is the testimony of retired professor, Dr. Eta Linnemann, dated July 5, 1985. It was my privilege to listen to this famed Christian scholar as she gave the testimony of her conversion from liberalism to Christianity to members of the Adventist Theological Society, and later to the students and faculty of the Seventh-day Adventist Theological Seminary at Andrews University.[19]

Tragically, many scholars, unlike Dr. Linnemann, are not willing to say a complete "No" to historical-critical theology. To them liberal theories have attained the status of idols to which they feel forced to bow. Scholars who choose to move against these popular liberal tides are often termed "hopelessly uninformed," "blinded by a combination of ego needs and naivete," "narrow minded," "anti-intellectual," "pre-scientific," and "fundamentalistic."[20]

The fear of being so labeled and the pressure for recognition as "open-minded," "progressive," or "enlightened" scholars has led some otherwise splendid Christian scholars to adopt these pagan theories of the Bible. These scholars we have identified as accommodationists or moderate liberals. If radical liberals are "the critical voices" in the church, accommodationists/moderate liberals are "the confusing voices."

Accommodationism: The Confusing Voices Within

Accommodationism is old-fashioned liberalism in new and respectable garb. As we explained in Chapter Three, "The only significant difference between the new Liberalism and the old seems to be that the former lays more stress than did the latter on the importance of *believing* the more or less mangled Bible that comes out of the critical mincing-machine."[21]

Accommodationism's evangelistic strategy seeks to make Christianity more palatable to secular (naturalistic) minds. But in doing so it jettisons some portions of Scripture as non-essential.

This strategy is seriously flawed. It makes human reason sit in judgment over Scripture and, using its own criteria, decide what is necessary and what is not. By making human judgment the arbiter of divine truth, accommodationism fails to recognize the limitations of human reason. By choosing not to "totally subject human reasoning to the higher authority of the Bible," as an Adventist scholar once wrote to me, the accommodationist may expect to question every-thing in the Bible that does not agree with his or her rational deductions. And because the spiritual diet served by such pick-and-choose theologians is so de-ficient in nutritional value, they are tempted to chase after vitamin supplements from the pharmacies of science, philosophy, sociology, psychology, and other extra-biblical sources.

Testimony of a Former Accommodationist Theologian

The experience of Dr. Thomas C. Oden, Methodist minister and professor of theology and ethics at Drew University, may well illustrate that of scholars who flatter themselves that by accommodating Bible truth to every new fad in science, psychology, sociology, etc., they can attract unbelievers to Christian-ity. This is how he begins the chronicle of his pilgrimage:[22]

"I will describe a particular individual, an ordained theologian whom I have known for a long time and whose career until recently can only be described as that of a 'movement person.' If I appear to go into needless detail about this person, it is nonetheless useful to learn of the specifics of what I mean by an addictive accommodationism. In his pursuit of movements, his overall pattern was diligently to learn from them, to throw himself into them, and then eventually to baptize them insofar as they showed any remote kinship with Christianity, and then to turn to another movement." Oden was describing his own experience.

In the desire to make Christian theology an "amiable accommodation to modernity," Oden found himself involved in many different movements. His list includes the ecumenical movement, the civil rights movement, the anti-war movement during the Vietnam era, the pre-NOW women's rights movement, the existentialist movement, the demythologization movement (writing his doc-toral dissertation on its chief theorist), the client-centered therapy movement, the Gestalt therapy movement, the "third force" movement in humanistic psy-chology, and the T-Group movement.

Oden concludes sadly, however, that after long years of being a wandering theologian, "I now experience the afterburn of 'movement' existence, of mes-sianic pretensions, of self-congratulatory idealism. . . . The shocker is not merely that I rode so many bandwagons, but that I thought I was doing Christian teach-ing a marvelous favor by it and at times considered this accommodation the very substance of the Christian teaching office. While Christian teaching must not rule out any investigations of truth or active involvement to embody it, it should be wary lest it reduce Christian doctrine to these movements, and it should be better prepared to discern which movements are more or less an expression of Christ's ministry to the world."

Although he has not yet fully arrived at the destination of *sola scriptura* (the sole authority of Scripture), it is to Thomas Oden's credit that after his long years in the far country of accommodationist theology, like the prodigal son he has finally made the decision to go back to his father's house.[23]

Oden's traveler's story upon his return home is instructive for anyone currently wandering in the far country: "Meanwhile, in the period before the reversal, my intellectual dialogue remained embarrassingly constricted almost exclusively to university colleagues and liberal churchmen, the only club I knew. When I later discovered among brilliant Protestant evangelicals a superb quality of exegesis, I wondered why it took so long."

Oden may have discovered what Bible-believing Christians have always known: "The honest way to commend God's revealed truth to an unbelieving generation is not to disguise it as a word of man, and to act as if we could never be sure of it, but had to keep censoring and amending it at the behest of the latest scholarship, and dared not believe it further than historical agnosticism gives us leave; but to preach it in a way which shows the world that we believe it whole-heartedly, and to cry to God to accompany our witness with His Spirit, so that we too may preach 'in demonstration of the Spirit and of power.' The apologetic strategy that would attract converts by the flattery of accommodating the gospel to the 'wisdom' of sinful man was condemned by Paul nineteen centuries ago, and the past hundred years have provided a fresh demonstration of its bankruptcy. The world may call its compromises 'progressive' and 'enlightened' (those are its names for all forms of thought that pander to its conceit); those who produce them will doubtless, by a natural piece of wishful thinking, call them 'bold' and 'courageous,' and perhaps 'realistic' and 'wholesome'; but the Bible condemns them as sterile aberrations. And the Church cannot hope to recover its power till it resolves to turn its back on them."[24]

Regrettably, not a few of Adventist scholars and leaders are still halting between two opinions, the worldview of classical liberalism and that of biblical Christianity.[25] Is it any wonder that in certain quarters of the Adventist church the call to "come out of Babylon" is growing faint? Where are today's Daniels and Nehemiahs?

One of them was in a university of modern Babylon. When this Bible-believing Adventist scholar dared to stand, his courage brought about a change in the way scholars look at the Bible. His testimony, which will follow, should encourage believers within mainstream Adventism to continue being faithful. Against the "critical voices" of radical liberalism and the "confusing voices" of accommodationism/moderate liberalism, they should remain the "cautious voices within."

Bible-believing Conservatism: The Cautious Voices Within

Bible-believing Christians within the mainstream Seventh-day Adventist church maintain that since the Bible is the Word of God, it is absolutely dependable or trustworthy in all of its assertions regarding religious doctrine as well as its incidental statements on science, geography and history. Consequently, they do not pick and choose from the Bible nor make a dichotomy between sections of the Bible that are factual and those that are not. But they do recognize that there are difficulties in the Bible which they must contend with as they "wrestle with the Word" daily.

Whereas liberals and accommodationists treat Bible difficulties as inaccuracies, contradictions, or even errors, Bible-believing Christians, relying on the Holy Spirit, study prayerfully and humbly those things in the Bible that are "hard to be understood." These conservatives suggest that there is a better way of dealing with Bible difficulties without compromising the integrity of Scriptures. The next testimony shows that when Christians are "rightly dividing the Word," God sometimes intervenes to enlighten them.

Testimony of a Bible-Believing Conservative Scholar

The attitude of Bible-believing students towards unresolved difficulties is not only biblical, it is the only way to avoid the kind of pick-and-choose approach that characterizes liberal theology in both its classical and moderate forms. The work of the late Seventh-day Adventist scholar, Dr. Edwin R. Thiele, clarifies this point.

But let me first ask you: Have you ever seriously paid attention to details such as this, "Now it came to pass in the third year of Hoshea son of Elah king of Israel, that Hezekiah the son of Ahaz king of Judah began to reign. Twenty and five years old was he when he began to reign; and he reigned twenty and nine years in Jerusalem. . . . And it came to pass in the fourth year of king Hezekiah, which was the seventh year of Hoshea son of Elah king of Israel, that Shalmaneser king of Assyria came up against Samaria, and besieged it. And at the end of three years they took it: even in the sixth year of Hezekiah, that is the ninth year of Hoshea king of Israel, Samaria was taken" (2 Kings 18:1-2, 9-10)?

Have you tried figuring out how to fit together the regnal (ruling) years of the kings of Israel and those of the kings in Judah in the above passage?

For the casual reader of Scripture, phrases such as "Now in the eighteenth year of king Jeroboam" (1 Kings 15:1) pose no problem and usually attract little notice. To biblical scholars of a few years ago, however, the chronologies of the Hebrew kings did not add up correctly. Baffled by the apparent discrepancies, Edwin R. Thiele set out to unravel the mystery. He described his successful breakthrough in this way:

"'It cannot be done. If the numbers had been correct to begin with, it might have been possible to accomplish in straightening out Hebrew chronology, but the numbers of the kings were not correctly recorded at the beginning, so there is nothing that we can do with them today.'

"The voice was that of my teacher, W. A. Irwin, chairman of the Department of Old Testament at the Oriental Institute, University of Chicago, as he rejected my request to make the chronology of the Hebrew kings the subject of my Master's thesis. In beginning his class discussion of the books of Kings, Professor Irwin had called attention to the constant contradictions and errors in the regnal data. At the close of the class I had spoken to him about the need for something to be done about the problems he had mentioned, which led to my request for this to be the subject for my Master's thesis.

"So I chose another subject. When my Master's work was over and I was beginning work on my doctorate I went again to Professor Irwin to request that the chronology of the Hebrew rulers be the subject of my doctoral dissertation. Again he refused, saying that it was entirely impossible to bring any sort of order to the chaotic state of the chronology of the Hebrew rulers.

"When I spoke to him, Professor George Cameron, my cuneiform teacher, was of the same mind as Professor Irwin. And when I approached Prof. A. T. Olmstead, the renowned Assyriologist and Hebrew scholar, he said that for more than 2,000 years the most able Biblical scholars had been wrestling with this problem and had accomplished nothing. If they could do nothing, neither could I. He added that he himself had been working on the chronology of the Hebrew rulers all his life, without success. There was no use for me to make an attempt.

"But I could not bring myself to believe that the Biblical numbers about the Hebrew rulers were a mass of errors. I believed the difficulty was that those who had been working on the problem did not understand the original chronological methods employed by the early recorders. If these could be brought to light, order would replace the seeming chaos. The subject fascinated me, so I gave it a great deal of attention. In time the major difficulties were resolved. I found the Biblical statements beginning to harmonize."[26]

Thiele's painstaking study resolved the problem of the chronology of the Hebrew kings when he took into account three factors the scholars had missed: (a) the coregency of some kings—i.e., in some instances, two kings (e.g., father and son) might be reigning at the same time; (b) the accession year and non-accession year methods of chronological reckoning of regnal years—i.e. there were different calendars used by Israel and Judah when they computed the regnal years of their kings (just as we have different starting points for calendar years, academic years, and tax years); and (c) the month of the year when a ruler began his regnal year—i.e., depending on which calendar one uses, a particular month can mean a different "year" (e.g., January 1 may refer to a different year depending on whether we are reckoning calendar, academic or tax years).

Thiele's dissertation resulted in the book *The Mysterious Numbers of the Hebrew Kings,* which the University of Chicago Press published in 1951. Professor Irwin himself provided fitting testimony to the soundness of the Bible-believer's attitude toward Bible difficulties. The following are some excerpts from his introduction to Thiele's book:

"The unique feature of Professor Thiele's work is that he has . . . shown that the seeming inconsistencies and mathematical contradictions no more than hinted at above, really are nothing of the sort, but integral elements in a sound and accurate chronological system. . . . The validity of his own findings rests on the simple fact that they work! They take account of all the data provided by the Biblical record, and organize them in a system that is rational, consistent, and precise, and coheres likewise with all that is known of relevant chronology of the entire world of the Bible. . . . He has taken passages commonly regarded as patent disclosures of carelessness, if not of ignorance, on the part of the Hebrew historians, and has shown them to be astonishingly reliable. We have, it is true, come some distance from the radical criticism of half a century ago. In treatment of the text and in appraisal of the historic reliability of the records we are in a much more *cautious mood,* as we have seen at one uncertain point after another our skepticism dissipate under new-found facts. . . . And it is a matter of first-rate importance to learn now that the Books of Kings are reliable in precisely that feature which formerly excited only derision. . . . In a brief statement, then, Professor Thiele's work contributes very significantly both to our respect for the accuracy of the Hebrew historians and to a growing confidence in the soundness of the long process through which generation after generation of scribes handed on the sacred text to succeeding ages. . . . Professor Thiele has made an important contribution to our common quest of truth."[27]

The above statement comes from a scholar who once questioned the accuracy of the Bible's numbers. How encouraging it is to know that the numbers of the Hebrew kings, once regarded as wrong, are actually right and give mathematical support to the historical soundness of the accounts of the Hebrew rulers recorded in the Word of God.

But this was possible only because an obscure Bible-believing *student,* like David meeting Goliath, could not bring himself to believe 2,000 years of scholarly consensus held by his theology *professors*—the view that the Bible's numbers about the Hebrew rulers were a mass of errors.

And this renowned scholar was a Seventh-day Adventist in a liberal institution!

Dr. Thiele's example suggests to today's Bible-believing Adventists that whenever they are confronted with what may appear to be mistakes in the Bible, they should suspend judgment on the problem as they patiently seek to discover an underlying harmony. Ellen G. White stated it this way: "As several [Bible] writers present a subject under varied aspects and relations, there may appear, to the superficial, careless, or prejudiced reader, to be discrepancy or contradiction, *where the thoughtful, reverent student, with clearer insight, discerns the underlying harmony* (*The Great Controversy*, p. vi, emphasis supplied).

The Challenge We Face. But daring to be a Daniel, sometimes even in Israel, is not always easy. In many instances, one is misunderstood, misrepresented, and viciously attacked, even by one's friends. Because it is unpopular for anyone today to *uphold the Word,* and because doing so can result in the loss of recognition, position, and employment, only a few are willing to be "faithful unto the end."

Entrenched liberalism within Bible-believing churches has encouraged the academic community (professors of religion and theology, editors, publishers and institutional heads) flagrantly to disregard established Bible truths. Regrettably, there appears to be a reluctance among church leaders (pastors and administrators, whether elected or appointed) to deal courageously with the heresies of historical-critical theology.[28] But should this be so?

The apostle Paul charges Christians "before God, and the Lord Jesus Christ, who shall judge the quick and the dead at his appearing and his kingdom; Preach the word; be instant in season, out of season; reprove, rebuke, exhort with all longsuffering and doctrine" (2 Tim 4:1-2). As we conclude *Receiving the Word,* we shall illustrate what, in practical terms, is entailed by this solemn charge. We shall explore the implications of a Seventh-day Adventist's commitment to *living by the Word.*

NOTES

1. Alas, I cannot trace the source of this description, although I have always believed that it came from the pen of H. Richard Niebuhr.

2. Friedrich Schleiermacher, *On Speeches to Its Cultural Despisers,* trans. John Oman (London: K. Paul, Trench, Trubner & Co., 1893), p. 88.

3. Gordon Kaufman, "What Shall We Do with the Bible?" *Interpretation* 25 (1971):95-112.

4. One of the best critiques of theological pluralism came from John W. Fowler, executive secretary of the Kentucky-Tennessee Conference, Nashville, Tennessee. See his letter to the editor, "Dealing with Pluralism," *Ministry,* December 1995, p.2.

5. Friedrich Schleiermacher, *The Christian Faith,* English trans. of 2nd German edition, edited by H. R. Mackintosh and J. S. Stewart (Edinburgh: T & T Clark, 1948), p. 385; cf. pp. 275-279.

6. Adventists will benefit from Juan Carlos Viera's "Worldview and Mission," *Ministry,* December 1995, pp. 25-27, in which he shows the impact of liberation theology on the doctrine of the church (ecclessiology), the doctrine of Christ (Christology), and the interpretation of Scripture (hermeneutics).

7. Friedrich Schleiermacher, *The Christian Faith,* pp. 385-389.

8. Eta Linnemann, *Historical Criticism of the Bible: Methodology or Ideology?* translated by Robert W. Yarbrough (Grand Rapids: Baker, 1990).

9. Sandra M. Schneiders, "Does the Bible Have a Postmodern Message?" in *Postmodern Theology: Christian Faith in a Pluralistic World,* ed. Frederic B. Burnham (San Francisco: Harper and Row, 1989), p. 64.

10. See Linnemann, *Historical Criticism of the Bible,* pp. 83-123, for a full explanation and description of how this works in practice.

11. Schneiders, p. 65.

12. Danna Nolan Fewell, "Feminist Reading of the Hebrew Bible: Affirmation, Resistance and Transformation," *Journal for the Study of the Old Testament* 39 (1987):78. Cf. Gerhard F. Hasel, "Biblical Authority and Feminist Interpretation," *Adventists Affirm* (Fall 1989):12-23; cf. C. Raymond Holmes, "Slavery, Sabbath, War, and Women" [review of Willard M. Swartley's *Slavery, Sabbath, War, and Women*] *Adventists Affirm* 3/2 (Fall 1989):55-62.

13. Mary A. Kassian, *The Feminist Gospel: The Movement to Unite Feminism With the Church* (Wheaton, Ill.: Crossway, 1992); cf. James R. Edwards, "Earthquake in the Mainline," *Christianity Today,* November 14, 1994, pp. 38-43; Laurel Damsteegt, "Feminism vs. Adventism: Why the Conflict?" *Adventists Affirm* 3/2 (Fall 1989):33-40; William Oddie, *What Will Happen to God?: Feminism and the Reconstruction of Christian Belief* (San Francisco: Ignatius Press, 1988).

14. A discussion of the difference between Seventh-day Adventism and feminism is provided by Laurel Damsteegt, "Feminism Vs. Adventism: Why the Conflict?" *Adventists Affirm* 3/2 (Fall 1989):33-40. Elsewhere, Damsteegt offers a succinct summary of the difference between today's feminist ministries and the women's ministries of the early Adventist pioneers: "Today, feminist ministries contrast sharply with the Women's Ministry back then [in the days of the pioneers]. Whereas the spirituality of the Adventist sisters was the greatest burden of the first movement, it seems to be assumed in the second; whereas soul-winning was the whole purpose of the first, it does not always seem to be foremost in the second; whereas the first movement stressed the worth and influence of a woman on the domestic scene in the home, such a concept seems nigh-repulsive to many in the second movement; whereas power was equated with the Holy Spirit in the first, one almost senses that it is equated with position in the second" (Laurel Damsteegt, "Shall Women Minister?" *Adventists Affirm* 9/1 [Spring 1995]:14). For a discussion of how "Women's Ministry" was understood in early Seventh-day Adventism, see Damsteegt's "S. M. I. Henry: Pioneer in Women's Ministry," *Adventists Affirm* 9/1 (Spring 1995):17-19, 46; cf. Terri Saelee, "Women of the Spirit," *Adventists Affirm* 9/2 (Fall 1995):60-63.

15. The distinctive features of theological liberalism have been summarized as follows: (1) an adaptation of the essentials of Christian faith to current naturalistic and anthropocentric views; (2) a skeptical view of historic Christian supernaturalism and miracles; (3) a view of the Bible as a fallible human record of the religious thought and experience of people who lived in Bible times, rather than viewing Scriptures as a true divine revelation of God's will; (4) an immanent or pantheistic, sub-Trinitarian idea of God as working chiefly through culture, a denial of Jesus Christ's incarnation and Deity, and an optimistic evolutionary worldview; (5) a confident view of humanity's power to perceive God by reflecting on experience, and thus, the belief that human beings can do true theology without making the Bible the sole authority for knowledge; (6) a denial of the fall, human sinfulness, penal substitutionary atonement, a need for God's sovereign grace in conversion, and a personal second coming of Christ and the establishment of His kingdom. See James I. Packer, "Liberalism and

Conservatism in Theology," in *New Dictionary of Theology* (1988), p. 385; cf. James Richmond, "Liberal Protestantism, Liberal Theology, Liberalism," in Alan Richardson, ed., *A Dictionary of Christian Theology* (Philadelphia, Pa.: Westminster, 1964), pp. 191-194; Robert M. Grant and David Tracy, *A Short History of the Interpretation of the Bible* (Philadelphia, Pa.: Fortress, 1984), pp. 110-118.

16. James I. Packer, *God Has Spoken* (Grand Rapids, Mich.: Zondervan, 1979), p. 21.

17. Ibid., pp. 28-32.

18. Eta Linnemann, *Historical Criticism of the Bible: Methodology or Ideology? Reflections of a Bultmannian Turned Evangelical,* translated by Robert W. Yarbrough (Grand Rapids, Mich.: Baker, 1990), pp. 17-20, emphasis hers.

19. It was not coincidental that she addressed the Adventist audience at a time when the controversial book *Inspiration,* published by a church press, was creating concerns in the church. In addition to her testimony, she made a presentation to the Adventist Theological Society in which she contrasted historical-critical theology with a true biblical theology; see her article, "Historical-Critical and Evangelical Theology," *Journal of the Adventist Theological Society* 5/2 (Autumn 1994):19-36.

20. A recent articulation of this view is John Shelby Spong, *Rescuing the Bible from Fundamentalism: A Bishop Rethinks the Meaning of Scripture* (San Francisco: Harper, 1991), pp. 13-36.

21. James I. Packer, *'Fundamentalism' and the Word of God* (Grand Rapids, Mich.: Baker, 1958), p. 153.

22. Thomas Oden, *After Modernity . . . What?* (Grand Rapids, Mich.: Zondervan, 1990), pp. 26-29.

23. Oden's return journey was in the right direction, but he has not yet come to the point of the sole authority of Scripture. He has currently put more stock in classical interpretation (as in the early church Fathers) than in *sola scriptura.*

24. Packer, *'Fundamentalism' and the Word of God,* pp. 167-168.

25. See the helpful article by Fernando Canale, "Importance of Our Worldview," *Ministry,* December 1995, pp. 12-14; cf. Samuel Koranteng-Pipim, "Contemporary Culture and Christian Lifestyle: A Clash of Worldviews," *Journal of the Adventist Theological Society* 4/1 (Spring 1993):129-150.

26. Edwin R. Thiele, "The Chronology of the Hebrew Kings," *Adventist Review,* May 17, 1984, p. 3.

27. William A. Irwin, "Introduction," in Edwin R. Thiele's *The Mysterious Numbers of the Hebrew Kings* (Grand Rapids, Mich.: Eerdmans, 1965 [first published in 1951, by the University of Chicago Press]), pp. xxi-xxiv, emphasis supplied.

28. In chapter 4 of this book we have examined the internal hermeneutical struggle in the Seventh-day Adventist church, discussing the symbiotic or interactive relationship between the key players—scholars and leaders—in *quarreling over the Word.*

Chapter Twelve

Living by the Word

We have come to the final chapter of *Receiving the Word*. As we explained in "To the Reader," this book was written with the following specific objectives: (1) to create an awareness among Bible-believing Adventists—whether laymembers, students, or leaders—of the nature and implications of liberalism's approach to Scripture so that they may be prepared to respond to it effectively; (2) to offer some answers to our young people—including students of religion and theology—who, because of doubts and skepticism created by some of their pastors and Bible teachers, are confused about important issues regarding the authority and interpretation of the Scriptures; and (3) to invite the convinced and crusading advocates of the contemporary liberal methodologies to reconsider their assumptions and attitudes toward the Word.

We have attempted to explain how the loss of Adventist identity and mission in some parts of the world is related to an erosion of confidence in the Bible as God's inspired, trustworthy Word, the church's sole norm of authority for doctrine and practice. By highlighting the *crisis over the Word* we have identified the *doubts over the Word, quarrels over the Word, departures from the Word,* and attempts to *liberate the Word* as symptoms of the cracks in our theological foundation.

We have also shown that these cracks arise from the use of contemporary liberalism's higher criticism. By calling upon readers to make a commitment to be found *trusting the Word, contending for the Word, upholding the Word, rightly dividing the Word, wrestling with the Word,* and *testifying about the Word,* we have urged Bible-believing Adventists to receive, respect and relay the message of God's inspired, trustworthy, and authoritative Word.

Given the issues raised in this book and their implications for the faith and practice of Seventh-day Adventists, it is appropriate that we conclude by addressing one final question: "How should we then live?" (Eze 33:10).

Living by the Word. Jesus Christ Himself provided the response to the above question: "It is written, Man shall not live by bread alone, but by every word that proceedeth out of the mouth of God" (Matt 4:4). In this first recorded message of Christ after His baptism, Jesus bids His followers imitate His example of *living by the Word*. The importance, urgency, and challenge of living by the Word will be the focus of this chapter.

The Importance of Living by the Word

More than two centuries ago, in 1742, a noted scholar stated how the health of the church depends on its feeding on Scripture: "Scripture is the foundation of the Church: the Church is the guardian of Scripture. When the Church is in strong health, the light of Scripture shines bright; when the Church is sick, Scripture is corroded by neglect; and thus it happens, that the outward form of Scripture and that of the Church, usually seem to exhibit simultaneously either health or else sickness; and as a rule the way in which Scripture is being treated is in exact correspondence with the condition of the Church."[1]

Theological and Biblical Malnutrition. Reflecting upon the relevance of the above statement to our contemporary situation, a well-respected Evangelical scholar wrote: "It is no secret that Christ's Church is not at all in good health in many places of the world. She has been languishing because she has been fed, as the current line has it, 'junk food'; all kinds of artificial preservatives and all sorts of unnatural substitutes have been served up to her. As a result, theological and Biblical malnutrition has afflicted the very generation that has taken such giant steps to make sure its physical health is not damaged by using foods or products that are carcinogenic or otherwise harmful to their physical bodies. Simultaneously a worldwide spiritual famine resulting from the absence of any genuine publication of the Word of God (Amos 8:11) continues to run wild and almost unabated in most quarters of the Church."[2]

Cries for the Word. This diagnosis of the Christian church at large can apply to contemporary Seventh-day Adventism. Ellen White's description of the situation in Protestant churches of her day can summarize what obtains in some parts of our own church today:

"The Bible has been robbed of its power, and the results are seen in a lowering of the tone of spiritual life. In the sermons from many pulpits of today there is not that divine manifestation which awakens the conscience and brings life to the soul. The hearers can not say, 'Did not our heart burn within us, while He talked with us by the way, and while He opened to us the Scriptures?' Luke 24:32. There are many who are crying out for the living God, longing for the divine presence. Philosophical theories or literary essays, however brilliant, cannot satisfy the heart. The assertions and inventions of men are of no value.

Let the word of God speak to the people. Let those who have heard only tradi-tions and human theories and maxims hear the voice of Him whose word can renew the soul unto everlasting life" (*Christ's Object Lessons,* p. 40).

Jesus prescribed a cure for this spiritual malady: "Man shall not live by bread alone, but by every word that proceedeth out of the mouth of God" (Matt 4:4). Heeding His counsel will not only satisfy our spiritual hunger but will also help to prevent the kind of famine for the Word that the prophet Amos predicted: "Behold, the days come, saith the Lord God, that I will send a famine in the land, not a famine of bread, nor a thirst for water, but of hearing the words of the Lord: And they shall wander from sea to sea, and from the north even to the east, they shall run to and fro to seek the word of the Lord, and shall not find it" (Amos 8:11-12).

The Urgency of Living by the Word

Living by the Word is the only means by which we can face Satan's end-time deceptions. As we noted in Chapter One, mainstream Adventism is caught in a crossfire of attacks from the liberal left, which operates within the church structure, and the independent right, which often operates from without by es-tablishing organizations and structures of their own. Applying to our situation Ellen G. White's statement that "we have far more to fear from within than from without" (*Selected Messages,* 1:122), we explained why this book con-centrates on the theological views of entrenched liberalism.[3]

Indeed, in Chapters Five and Six we showed how sophisticated *departing from the Word* could represent Satan's end-time attempt to employ intellectual philosophy to undermine the established doctrines of our faith. Such a situation highlights the urgent need for *living by the Word.*

During Jesus' temptations in the wilderness, the enemy confronted Him with subtle reinterpretations of God's Word, calculated to generate doubts and to deceive. Four thousand years earlier, mother Eve faced the same kind of philosophical speculation on the Word of God when Satan appeared to her in the Garden of Eden. Instead of *living by the Word,* she chose to dally with the enemy's suggestions. In the end, her God-given human mind proved no match for the mind of this fallen angel.

But it was not so with Jesus Christ. When confronted with Satan's intellec-tual philosophy, He refused to yield to the subtle temptation to employ the enemy's higher critical method "without adopting its naturalistic presupposi-tions."[4] Instead, He pointed to the plain reading of Scripture: "It is written, Man shall not live by bread alone, but by every word that proceedeth out of the mouth of God" (Matt 4:4). In this assertion, our Savior prescribed for us the only effective response to the enemy's well-planned strategy to deceive.

In Chapter Five, Part VI, we promised to explore more fully the implications of a significant statement by Ellen G. White. We shall do so here, starting with a review of the statement itself. A closer examination of the enemy's end-time strategy will help us to understand the urgency of *living by the Word*.

End-Time Deception. In the wake of the Kellogg crisis in the early 1900s, Ellen White recorded this insightful scenario of Satan's intentions for the church.[5]

"The enemy of souls has sought to bring in the supposition that a great reformation was to take place among Seventh-day Adventists, and that this reformation would consist in giving up the doctrines which stand as the pillars of our faith, and engaging in a process of reorganization. Were this reformation to take place, what would result? The principles of truth that God in His wisdom has given to the remnant church, would be discarded. Our religion would be changed. The fundamental principles that have sustained the work for the last fifty years would be accounted as error. A new organization would be established. Books of a new order would be written. A system of intellectual philosophy would be introduced. The founders of this system would go into the cities, and do a wonderful work. The Sabbath of course, would be lightly regarded, as also the God who created it. Nothing would be allowed to stand in the way of the new movement. The leaders would teach that virtue is better than vice, but God being removed, they would place their dependence on human power, which, without God, is worthless. Their foundation would be built on the sand, and storm and tempest would sweep away the structure" (*Selected Messages,* 1:204, 205).

A summary of this end-time deception's essential characteristics will reveal whether it has anything to say about constructing "Adventism for a new generation" along the lines of modern liberal scholarship.[6]

1. The Motivation. It would come about as some seek to "reform" the church, probably not fully aware that Satan is behind this "great reformation." Could some of the present day efforts to make the church "more relevant to this generation" be playing into the hands of the enemy of souls?

2. The Nature. The so-called reform would consist in giving up the doctrines of our faith and pursuing a reorganization. Is this what we are witnessing today as our distinctive doctrines are being abandoned for theologies of "love" "compassion" and "acceptance"? We have seen attacks on our worldwide church government, persistent calls for "rebellion," prominent people advocating congregationalism, and power consolidating into a few hands. Are these indications of anything?

3. The Results. Among the results of this deception are the following:

(i) The distinctive doctrines that have identified us as a remnant church would be discarded. Does this include the distinctive S's: (a) Scripture's inspi-

ration, trustworthiness, and sole authority, (b) the Substitutionary atonement of Christ, (c) Salvation by grace alone through faith in Jesus Christ; (d) the Sanctuary message, (e) the Second-coming of Christ, (f) the Sabbath of the fourth commandment, (g) the State of the dead, (h) the Spirit of Prophecy, (i) Stewardship, and (j) Standards regarding food, drink, dress, entertainment, relationships, etc.?

(ii) Our religion would be changed. Does it mean that while retaining the name "Seventh-day Adventist" to describe ourselves and our churches and institutions, our faith would not be recognizable to our pioneers? Is a mutation or metamorphosis being suggested here?

(iii) The fundamental principles that have sustained us in the past would be considered defective—i.e., accounted as error. In addition to those already listed above as distinctive doctrines, do these fundamental principles also include principles of interpretation—the plain reading of Scripture, which "new generation" scholars despise as "literal," "rigid," and a "proof-text" method?

(iv) A new organization would be established. Does this include the patterning of our administrative structure and leadership style along the lines of corporate business or political organizations? Does it say anything about the subtle but persistent campaigns for "women elders"? Is this also an allusion to some of the ecumenical alliances being proposed? Does it include, perhaps, new liturgical structures, such as worship styles with charismatic undertones, including the so-called "celebration churches," and interest in "power-encounters," "deliverance ministries," and speaking in unintelligible ecstatic "tongues"?

(v) Books of new order would be written. Does this include the flurry of books, articles, audio and video productions, etc., being published, promoted, and distributed by our publishing houses, Adventist publications and book centers, though they undermine faith in our biblical doctrines and practices? Can it refer to the subtle dissemination of such ideas in our homes, classrooms, pulpits, and at committee meetings? Does it include the attempts by some to challenge, distort, or revise our Adventist history to accommodate today's ideological agendas?

(vi) A system of intellectual philosophy would be introduced. Is this a reference to the departure from the plain reading of the Bible, reinterpreting it along the lines suggested by speculative philosophies—science, tradition, sociology, psychology, etc.? Is it a warning against the prostitution of human rationality into rationalism? Does it say anything about the so-called "matured," "enlightened," "progressive," "principle," "historic," "dynamic," "casebook," "sophisticated," and "abstract" thinking of our day?

(vii) A wonderful work would be conducted in the cities, in which the Sabbath and the God of the Sabbath are lightly regarded. Is this a reference to

humanistic humanitarian works in our cities and communities? Does this also involve an alliance with the charismatic movement, in which "prayer warriors" join hands to offer "intercessory prayer" to "bind and exorcise the demons and wicked spirits that are tormenting our cities and communities"? Is the reference to the Sabbath being lightly regarded a suggestion that some will make concessions in an attempt to make the Sabbath more "relevant and meaningful" both to the world and to church members? Does this include carelessness regarding Sabbath observance, and perhaps a general lowering of all Adventist standards?

(viii) Nothing would be allowed to stand in the way of the new movement. Could this statement be a hint regarding the stubborn, determined, and adamant spirit of the leaders of this *new movement,* who, in the language of today, will "use any means necessary," fair or foul, to pursue their ideological objectives? Are the "tithe embargoes," the "strategy sessions," and "rebellion" of some congregations symptoms of this new movement?

(ix) While teaching that virtue is better than vice, God is removed and they depend on human power. Is this an allusion to a *claim* to have enlightened views on ethical morality (abortion, women's ordination, homosexuality, pre- and extra-marital sex, divorce and remarriage, race relations, etc.) and ethical values ("love," "justice," "compassion," "kindness," "equality," "acceptance," "fairness," etc.), while actually following a humanistic ethical system, from which "God is removed"? Does the suggestion of "dependence on human power" indicate a theology of self-reliance, one which repudiates the substitutionary atonement of Christ, and salvation (both justification and sanctification) by faith alone?

(x) The theological house built on a foundation of sand would be swept away. Is this the clearest indication that any theological house—however impressive it may look on the inside and outside (the curtains, carpets, painting, electronic gadgets, etc.) and however talented the architects may be—will be swept away by the impending storms if it fails to build on the solid foundations of Bible?[7] Could this then suggest that, instead of going along with this new movement which is building its modern towers of Babel, we must rather dig deep, building on Christ the solid Rock—which requires *living by the Word?*

The Enemy's End-Time Strategy. Notice that it was Satan who masterminded liberalism's skepticism toward the Word so that God's people would be uncertain of their true *identity* as God's end-time remnant and their true *mission* of proclaiming the three angels' messages and preparing a people for Christ's second coming. This loss of identity and mission in some parts of the church is resulting in a paralysis and death of the churches and institutions that have come under the sway of historical-critical theology. Then, in another deceptive attempt to "revive" the churches that he has helped to kill, the enemy is suggesting a "reformation" along the lines of the charismatic movement's "new ecumenism."

What the talented architects of "Adventism for a New Generation" overlook is that they are building their theological house on shifting sand. Unless they build on the solid Rock—Christ, the incarnate Word, and the Bible, the written Word—theirs will be like the house in Jesus' parable: "The rain came down, the streams rose, and the winds blew and beat against that house, and it fell with a great crash" (Matt 7:27 NIV).

Doesn't this prospect of an end-time deception demand that we clearly understand what *living by the Word* entails?

The Challenge of Living by the Word

Through the sacred pages of Scripture, Seventh-day Adventists have found their identity as the remnant church (Rev 12:17; 14:12) and their prophetic mandate to proclaim "the everlasting gospel" (Rev 14:6). In this Book they have discovered the will and eternal character of God and His ethical demands upon the believers who claim to be His special end-time people. As "bread" or "food" (Matt 4:4; Job 23:12), the inspired Word has fed us and provided nourishment for our spiritual growth. Today, however, we are afflicted with "theological and biblical malnutrition." In order to recover from our present ailing condition, we must be willing to take the following steps:

1. We Must *Receive the Word.* There was a time when Adventists were known as the "People of the Book," even "Bookworms"! In our day, however, we have become "tapeworms," chasing the latest audio and video tapes from our self-appointed authorities, be they pastors, professors of theology and science, psychologists, parents, or personal acquaintances. But we are to receive the Word, "not as the word of men, but as it is in truth, the word of God, which effectually worketh also in you who believe" (1 Thess 2:13).

This means that rather than holding up human traditions, opinion polls, subjective experience, the pronouncements of learned men, and the latest research findings in naturalistic science and secular psychology as alternative sources of dependable knowledge, we must always insist upon the Bible and the Bible only as the rule of faith and lifestyle (see *The Great Controversy,* p. 595).

2. We Must *Feed on the Word.* "As we feed on the Word of the Lord we are feasting on the Lord of the Word, and in receiving life from His Word, we are receiving *His* very life"[8] (cf. John 6:32-63). "What food is to the body, Christ must be to the soul. Food cannot benefit us unless we eat it, unless it becomes a part of our being. . . . A theoretical knowledge will do us no good. We must feed upon Him, receive Him into the heart, so that His life becomes our life" (*The Desire of Ages,* p. 389). "He who by faith receives the Word is receiving the very life and character of God" (*Christ's Object Lessons,* p. 38).

Feeding on the Word can make even little children grow "wise unto salvation" (2 Tim 3:15). Therefore, we are not to "think that the Bible will become a tiresome book to the children. Under a wise instructor the work [of educating the young in truths of the Word] will become more and more desirable. It will be to them as the bread of life, and will never grow old. There is in it a freshness and beauty that attract and charm the children and youth. It is like the sun shining upon the earth, giving its brightness and warmth, yet never exhausted. By lessons from the Bible history and doctrine, the children and youth can learn that all other books are inferior to this. They can find here a fountain of mercy and of love" (*Ye Shall Receive Power,* p. 141).

3. We Must *Delight in the Word.* This is by reading, studying, hearing and meditating upon the Scriptures (cf. Ps 119:24, 77, 92, 143, 174). It is not enough merely to read the Bible; we must enjoy it and testify about it. Jeremiah said: "Thy words were found, and I did eat them; and thy word was unto me the joy and rejoicing of mine heart" (Jer 15:16). David testified: "How sweet are thy words unto my taste! Yea, sweeter than honey to my mouth!" (Ps 119:103; cf. 19:10). Such has been the experience of God's people throughout the centuries.

However, "the joy of Bible study is not the fun of collecting esoteric tidbits about Gog and Magog, Tubal-cain and Methuselah, Bible numerics and the beast, and so on; nor is it the pleasure, intense for the tidy-minded, of analyzing our translated text into preachers' pretty patterns, with neatly numbered headings held together by apt alliteration's artful aid. Rather, it is the deep contentment that comes of communing with the living Lord into whose presence the Bible takes us—a joy which only His own true disciples know."[9]

Or as Ellen G. White put it, "The word of the living God is not merely written, but spoken. The Bible is God's voice speaking to us, just as surely as though we could hear it with our ears. If we realized this, with what awe would we open God's word, and with what earnestness would we search its precepts! The reading and contemplation of the Scriptures would be regarded as *an audience with the Infinite One*" (*Testimonies for the Church,* 6:393).

4. We Must *Heed the Word.* In Christ's parable of the two builders (Matt 7:24-27), what distinguished the wise man from the foolish man was the fact that the wise man not only heard the Word, he also heeded its message. We must receive the Word as the "word of the living God, the word that is our life, the word that is to *mold* our *actions,* our *words,* and our *thoughts.* To hold God's word as anything less than this is to reject it" (*Education,* p. 260, emphasis supplied). In the words of an old hymn, we must let "our words be echoed by our ways" (cf. 1 Pet 3:1; James 1:22-24).

5. We Must be *Guided by the Word.* In addition to having our individual lives regulated by the Word, the church, as a corporate body of believers, must also be guided by the Word in every facet of its life. A commitment to be so guided will demand the following:[10]

(i) Instead of making personal and corporate decisions on a pragmatic basis, subjective experience, or majority vote, *church members* and *committees* will seek God's will by seriously searching the Scriptures.

(ii) Rather than allowing pluralistic theology and financial profit to drive our *publishing houses, publications,* and *book centers,* we shall publish and distribute books, periodicals, articles, and editorials that are Bible-centered in content and unifying in effect.

(iii) Instead of allowing the winds of secularism to deflect our schools away from the standards and objectives established by our pioneers, our *educational institutions* and *school boards* will maintain a steady direction by hiring and retaining only teachers and workers whose teachings and influence bolster confidence in our fundamental beliefs and lifestyle.

(iv) Rather than encouraging our *medical institutions* and *offices* to do "what seemeth right in their own eyes," we shall allow the Bible to inform our Adventist philosophy and practice of health and healing.

(v) Instead of permitting sociology (the church growth movement), psychology (the self-esteem movement), politics (both the Christian Left and Right), business (profit and marketing techniques), Hollywood (the entertainment industry), and power-encounters (the signs and wonders movement) to determine our methods of evangelism, our style of worship, and the content of our sermons, *pastors, evangelists,* and *those engaged in pastoral work* will provide biblical messages based on the great themes and truths of Adventism.

(vi) Rather than neglecting the Bible for the views of our self-appointed "thought-leaders" or employing the Bible to support pet ideas or to display individual talent, *elders, Sabbath school teachers* and *musicians* will ground their teaching and music solidly in the Word of God.

(vii) Instead of becoming astute politicians and business executives, *church leaders* will be more spiritually oriented, steeping their minds in the principles of Scripture; our pioneers were not merely church administrators, they were also competent Bible theologians with a single-minded commitment to the truths of God's Word and Christian piety.

(viii) Rather than allowing today's anti-Christian higher criticism which dominates the academic community—in professional societies, meetings, scholarly publications, and recognition—to determine the standards of our scholarship, *theologians* and *Bible teachers* will pursue the highest level of academic excellence that will not surrender the truth; they will also not wait until retirement to honor their theological convictions.

(ix) Instead of selling their souls at the price of academic grades, degrees, recommendations, accolades, and recognition, *religion and theology students* will seek an education from Jesus Christ, the Master Teacher. For "in the presence of such a Teacher, of such opportunity for divine education, what worse than folly is it to seek an education apart from Him—to seek to be wise apart from Wisdom; to be true while rejecting Truth; to seek illumination apart from the Light, and existence without the Life; to turn from the Fountain of living waters, and hew out broken cisterns, that can hold no water" (*Education,* p. 83).

(x) And rather than being gullible regarding the counterfeit elements of faith and lifestyle being disseminated in our classrooms, publications, and churches, *young people,* especially *students* in the secondary schools (academies), colleges, and universities, will demand from their teachers, editors, youth pastors, and leaders a plain "Thus saith the Lord" before accepting any new views. In the language of Ellen G. White, "My message to you is: No longer consent to listen without protest to the perversion of truth. . . . God calls upon men and women to take their stand under the blood-stained banner of Prince Emmanuel. I have been instructed to warn our people; for many are in danger of receiving theories and sophistries that undermine the foundation pillars of the faith" (*Selected Messages,* 1:196-197).

6. We Must Have the Courage to *Stand for the Word.* Our individual spiritual lives depend on the inspired Word. Our identity and mission as a church depend upon it. Consequently, we must not adopt postures of theological neutrality when God's truth and honor are being jeopardized. With the prospect of an end-time deception before us, we shall not be afraid to stand up for the truth—even if we have to lose our privileges, opportunities, positions, sources of livelihood, cherished relationships, yes, even our own lives (see Luke 14:26, 27, 33).

Such is the case in the current crisis over biblical inspiration and interpretation. The on-going quarrel over the Word is not the kind of theological hairsplitting among scholars that can be overcome by mere "tolerance," "love," "understanding," or celebrating "diversity" of ideas. What is really at issue is the futile attempt to make error cohabit with truth. And what is at stake is salvation; for the choice is between the false doctrines of men and the truth as it is in Jesus Christ.

Let's be clear on this: No matter how the crisis is disguised, there are only two real choices confronting Bible-believing Adventists. The choice is *not* between scholarly enlightenment and narrow-minded obscurantism, as some have suggested regarding the "abstract thinking" of the so-called "principle approach" versus the "infantile and immature thinking" of the so-called "literal approach."[11] Rather, in the debate over liberalism's higher criticism, the believer is faced with a choice between two versions of Seventh-day Adventism.

Even here, the choice is *not* between Adventism that is patterned after "the church of the West" and an Adventism that is modeled after "the rest of the church." It is a choice between an Adventism consistent with biblical Christianity and a counterfeit fashioned according to the spirit of our age; between an Adventism resting its faith wholly upon the solid foundation of God's revealed Word and another building on the shifting sand of human opinion.

We have to choose whether to bow to the authority of Jesus Christ as revealed in His inspired Word or whether, on our own authority, to discount and disregard some parts of His Word.

We have to decide whether to submit our thoughts to be transformed by His Word or to cherish the intellectual arrogance that refuses to be enlightened by the Word.

We have to choose whether to be deluded by sophisticated Laodiceanism, which flatters itself that "I am rich and increased with goods, and have need of nothing," or whether to be enlightened by "the Amen, the faithful and true witness," who pleads in His inspired Word, "I counsel thee to buy of me gold tried in the fire, that thou mayest be rich; and white raiment, that thou mayest be clothed, and that the shame of thy nakedness do not appear; and anoint thine eyes with eyesalve, that thou mayest see" (Rev 3:14-22).

In short, we face the same choice that confronted Adam and Eve in the garden of Eden: Shall we trust God and obey His inspired Word, or, in our desire to obtain Satan's "open-mindedness," shall we distrust God and disobey His revealed Word? This is the ultimate choice that faces us in this end-time crisis over the Word.

Bible-believing Adventists need, therefore, to understand clearly that the cracks in the theological foundation of our faith—the skepticism about the sole authority and trustworthiness of Scripture—are the most serious threat that our church has ever faced. This is why the present crisis over biblical authority and interpretation cannot be lightly *dismissed* as non-existent, *ignored* by "administrative ostrich-ism," or *camouflaged* either by rearranging the theological furniture or by installing modern theological gadgets.[12]

"Light and darkness cannot harmonize. Between truth and error there is an irrepressible conflict. To uphold and defend the one is to attack and overthrow the other" (*The Great Controversy,* p. 126).

Once we understand what is at stake and have made a commitment to *stand for the Word,* we must be willing to employ our God-given voices, pens, and votes to speak out boldly and clearly against any attempt to make the Bible captive to the spirit of our age, whether in pulpit, classroom, publication, or church council meeting.

Ellen G. White summed up what standing for the Word entails: "Now is the time for God's people to show themselves true to principle. When the religion of Christ is most held in contempt, when His law is most despised, then should our zeal be the warmest and our courage and firmness the most unflinching. *To stand in defense of truth and righteousness when the majority forsake us, to fight the battles of the Lord when champions are few—this will be our test.* At this time we must gather warmth from the coldness of others, courage from their cowardice, and loyalty from their treason" (*Testimonies for the Church,* 5:136).

A Final Appeal to Live by the Word

The 1995 General Conference session at Utrecht, the Netherlands, may be remembered for highlighting the hermeneutical crisis in the contemporary Seventh-day Adventist church. But there is another important General Conference session—the last session Ellen White ever attended—that Adventists should remember. One dramatic act at this gathering may provide today's church with a way out of its hermeneutical dilemma.[13]

The 1909 General Conference Session. The session took place in Takoma Park, Washington, D.C., in 1909. This was not the first time Mrs. White had attended such an assembly of believers. She had been at the first general gathering of Sabbath-keeping Adventists in 1848 and succeeding Sabbatarian conferences.[14] She had been present with the brethren as they diligently studied the Word and established the doctrinal structure of the church on that Word. Ellen White had also attended almost all of the General Conference sessions from 1863 on, when she was not away in Europe and Australia.

But the 1909 session was special. Delegates from various parts of the world brought detailed and thrilling reports. In her lifetime Ellen White had seen the church grow from a handful of Sabbath-keeping Adventists in New England in 1846 to 83,000 at the close of 1908. Of the total, 59,000 lived in the United States and 24,000 in other parts of the world. The 1908 Statistical Report recorded in the 1909 *General Conference Bulletin* indicates that the total tithe paid into the treasuries of the church in 1908 had grown to $1.1 million. There were nearly 800 ordained ministers and 400 more who held ministerial licenses.

Indeed, the Lord had blessed the labors of the group of believers who saw themselves as the "remnant church," a special people with a special message for a special time.

During the three-and-a-half weeks of the 1909 session, Ellen White met with her brethren from the world field as they discussed plans for global evangelism. She used every speaking opportunity given her to admonish, encourage, and instruct the delegates. While she spoke on health reform and health interests, the principal theme in her messages was evangelistic outreach, with emphasis on both personal and city evangelism.

As the session drew to a close, Mrs. White felt impressed that she would never attend another General Conference session; and she never did. What would be her final message to the world assembly?

A Touching Farewell. It was the last day of the session, Sunday afternoon, June 6. Around 3:00 p.m. the delegates were gathered to listen to her speak on the theme, "Partakers of the Divine Nature." Rather than presenting a well-crafted sermon, she simply *read the Word,* occasionally interspersing a few comments of her own. The Bible texts she read were the entire first chapter of 2 Peter and the first and fourth chapters of 1 Peter—passages that speak about the privileges of the Christian. The *General Conference Bulletin* summarized the thrust of her final message under the title, "A Touching Farewell":

"As the aged speaker referred to her appreciation of the privileges of the General Conference session, and expressed her intense anxiety that the meeting might result in great good to all in attendance, the congregation responded with many hearty 'amens.' And, with trembling lips and a voice touched with deep emotion, she assured the ministers and other workers that God loves them, and Jesus delights to make intercession in their behalf.

"The speaker exhorted every worker to go forth in the strength of the Mighty One of Israel. She declared that while she might never have the privilege of meeting her brethren from abroad in another Conference like this one, yet she would pray for them, and prepare to meet them all in the kingdom of glory."

She then closed her address with these words: "Brethren, we shall separate for a little while, but let us not forget what we have heard at this meeting. Let us go forward in the strength of the Mighty One, considering the joy that is set before us of seeing His face in the kingdom of God and of going out no more forever. Let us remember that we are to be partakers of the divine nature, and that angels of God are right around us, that we need not be overcome by sin. Let us send our petitions to the throne of God in time of temptation, and in faith lay hold of His divine power. I pray God that this may be the experience of each one of us, and that in the great day of God we all may be glorified together" (*Manuscript 49,* 1909).

A Dramatic Act and Final Words. Having thus concluded the last sermon she was to preach at a General Conference session, the 82-year old messenger of the Lord moved away from the desk and headed toward her seat. Suddenly she stopped, turned and came back to the pulpit. Picking up the Bible from which she had earlier read, she opened it, held it out on extended hands that trembled with age, and said, *"Brethren and Sisters, I commend unto you this Book."* Without another word, she closed the Book, and walked from the plat-form.[15]

By this dramatic act and these final words, Ellen White reminded the leaders of the church officially assembled in conference of the vital and preeminent role that the Word of God is to play in the life and mission of the Seventh-day Adventist church. In her very first book, she had also written: *"I recommend to you, dear reader, the Word of God as the rule of your faith and practice"* (*Early Writings,* p. 78). Throughout her life and ministry she exalted that Word. And now, in her last official message to the world body at a General Conference session, she again commended that Word to the church.

The Challenge Before Us. It is almost ninety years since she thus exalted the inspired Book before the church. Since that time the Seventh-day Adventist church has experienced all manner of crises. But it has survived and is still growing, especially in areas of the world where the members, teachers, pastors, evangelists, and leaders still uphold that Word. Faithfulness to the inspired Scriptures has been our strength. It has given power to our preaching and weight to our witness. And in these final days it is our only safeguard against the delusions of Satan.[16]

Regrettably, at a time when the clock of human history is about to strike midnight, at a time when there is urgent need for the Bible to shine brightly as a lamp unto our feet and a light unto our path (Ps 119:105), attempts are being made to obscure this divine Light.

Given this fact, we must ask ourselves: What shall we do with the Book called the Holy Bible? Shall we *receive* it as the Word of the living God, or shall we doubt it?

The apostolic church, the church that proclaimed the first advent of Christ, faced this same question. Scripture testifies in many places concerning them: The believers in Samaria *"received the word* of God" (Acts 8:14); the Gentile believers in Caesarea "also *received the word* of God" (Acts 11:1); the believers of Berea *"received the word* with all readiness of mind" (Acts 17:11); and the believers at Thessalonica *"received the word* in much affliction, with joy of the Holy Ghost" (1 Thess 1:6; cf. 2:13).

God's end-time church, some two thousand years after the era of the apostles, also faces the same question. Will the remnant movement that has been divinely commissioned to "lift up the trumpet and loud let it ring" respond positively? The pioneers of the Seventh-day Adventist movement did so.[17] Will the Adventists of this generation, those who are living at the threshold of the next millennium, emulate their pioneers by *receiving the Word?*

How will the church respond?

More importantly, how will *you* respond to this vital question? How will you answer when you appear before the Lord and He asks, Did you *"receive* with meekness *the engrafted word,* which is able to save your soul"* (James 1:21)?

The Reward of *Receiving the Word.* As you deliberate upon this critical issue of life, let me state one more reason why you must respond positively: *The inspired Word is the only book that has power to change your life.* This is what the apostle Peter meant when he wrote that we are "born again . . . by the word of God" (1 Pet 1:23).

In case you are still in doubt, consider this: "There are men who study philosophy, astronomy, geology, geography, and mathematics; but did you ever hear a man say, 'I was an outcast, a wretched inebriate, a disgrace to my race, and a nuisance in the world, until I began to study mathematics, and learned the multiplication table, and then turned my attention to geology, got me a little hammer, and knocked off the corners of the rocks and then studied the formation of the earth, and since that time I have been happy as the day is long; I feel like singing all the time; my soul is full of triumph and peace; and health and blessing have come to my desolate home once more'? Did you ever hear a man ascribe his redemption and salvation from intemperance and sin and vice to the multiplication table, or the science of mathematics or geology?

"But I can bring you, not one man, or two, or ten, but men by the thousand who will tell you, 'I was wretched; I was lost; I broke my poor old mother's heart; I beggared my family; my wife was heart-stricken and dejected; my children fled from the sound of their father's footsteps; I was ruined, reckless, helpless, homeless, hopeless, until I heard the words of that Book'!

"And he will tell you the very word which fastened on his soul. Maybe it was, 'Come unto Me, all ye that labor and are heavy laden, and I will give you rest;' perhaps it was, 'Behold the Lamb of God which taketh away the sin of the world;' it may have been, 'God so loved the world, that He gave His only begotten Son, that whosoever believeth in Him should not perish, but have everlasting life.' He can tell you the very word that saved his soul. And since that word entered his heart, he will tell you that hope has dawned upon his vision, that joy has inspired his heart, and that his mouth is filled with grateful song. He will tell you that the blush of health has come back to his poor wife's faded cheek; that the old hats have vanished from the windows of his desolate home; that his rags have been exchanged for good clothes; that his children run to meet him when he comes; that there is bread on his table, fire on his hearth, and comfort in his dwelling. He will tell you all that, and he will tell you that this book has wrought the change."[18]

Yes, there is power in the Book, a power that rests on the fact that "all scripture is given by inspiration of God, and is profitable for doctrine, for reproof, for correction, for instruction in righteousness: That the man of God may be perfect, throughly furnished unto all good works" (2 Tim 3:16-17).

Given this fact, will you now *receive the Word* and allow it to change your life? Your decision should not be based on what you have read in this book or any other works attempting to defend the inspired Word against the skepticism of higher-critical scholarship. For although in this volume we have sought to challenge liberal thinking in the hope that you will appreciate more fully how the Bible deserves to be accorded the first and highest authority in your life and, in so doing, be led to love and experience fellowship with its divine Author, the irony is that, our endeavor is destined to be ineffective! Why?

Because "what we most need is the book itself. It is its own best witness and defender. Christians sometimes try to defend the word of God. It seems like half a dozen poodle dogs trying to defend a lion in his cage. The best thing for us to do is to slip the bars and let the lion out, and he will defend himself! And the best thing for us to do is to bring out the word of God, and let 'the sword of the Spirit' prove its own power, as it pierces 'even to the dividing asunder of soul and spirit' [Eph 6:17; Heb 4:12]."[19]

Ellen G. White wrote, "The heart that *receives the Word of God* is not as a pool that evaporates, not like a broken cistern that loses its treasure. It is like the mountain stream fed by unfailing springs, whose cool, sparkling waters leap from rock to rock, refreshing the weary, the thirsty, the heavy laden" (*Christ's Object Lessons,* p. 130, emphasis supplied).

How Will We Respond? As we stand at the verge of the Promised Land, I encourage you to join me in *receiving the Word* with "readiness of mind" (cf. Acts 17:11). When pushed by either the liberal left or the independent right to depart from the Word as fully inspired, trustworthy, and as the one authoritative guide for Christian belief and practice, let us make a commitment that we will "not turn from it to the right or to the left." Instead, let us "meditate on it day and night" and be careful to "do everything written in it" (Josh 1:7-8 NIV).

If we thus *receive the Word,* it will bring peace to our troubled consciences, comfort to our broken hearts, light to our perplexed minds, and strength to our discouraged souls. Only then can we truly sing that familiar song which in years past has brought hope and cheer to many a weary pilgrim:

> Give me the Bible, star of gladness gleaming,
> To cheer the wanderer lone and tempest tossed,
> No storm can hide that peaceful radiance beaming,
> Since Jesus came to seek and save the lost.

> *Chorus:*
> *Give me the Bible—holy message shining,*
> *Thy light shall guide me in the narrow way.*
> *Precept and promise, law and love combining,*
> *'Till night shall vanish in eternal day.*

> Give me the Bible, when my heart is broken,
> When sin and grief have filled my soul with fear;
> Give me the precious words by Jesus spoken,
> Hold up faith's lamp to show my Savior near.

> Give me the Bible, all my steps enlighten,
> Teach me the danger of these realms below;
> That lamp of safety, o'er the gloom shall brighten,
> That light alone the path of peace can show.[20]

NOTES

1. John Albert Bengel, *Gnomon of the New Testament,* ed. Andrew R. Fausset, 5 vols. (Edinburgh: T & T Clark, 1857-1858), 1:7.

2. Walter C. Kaiser Jr., *Toward An Exegetical Theology: Biblical Exegesis for Preaching and Teaching* (Grand Rapids, Mich.: Baker, 1981), pp. 7-8.

3. See chapter 1 for a review of the differences and similarities between the liberal left and the independent right.

4. Refer to our discussion in chapters 1 and 2 of this book.

5. Readers will greatly benefit from Lewis R. Walton's recent *Omega II: God's Church at the Brink* (Glenville, Calif.: [Lewis R. Walton], 1995).

6. See our discussion in chapter 5, part 6, where, within the context of how some are *departing from the Word,* we analyzed the proposals for an "Adventism for a New Generation."

7. Refer to "To the Reader" for a discussion of this.

8. Philip G. Samaan, *Christ's Way to Spiritual Growth* (Hagerstown, Md.: Review and Herald, 1995), pp. 142-143, emphasis his.

9. James I. Packer, *God Has Spoken* (Grand Rapids, Mich.: Baker, 1979), p. 10.

10. The suggestions that follow are adapted from the discussion paper for the 1995 General Conference Session, titled, "The Use of Scripture in the Life of the SDA Church" (see Appendix B); Samuel Koranteng-Pipim, "The Bible: Inspired Book or Inspiring Booklet?" *Adventists Affirm* 9/1 (Spring 1995):20-29; cf. chapter 7 of *Receiving the Word*.

11. See "To the Reader" and chapter 4 of this book.

12. See "To the Reader."

13. The following is based on the *General Conference Bulletin,* 1909, pp. 260, 265, 378; Ellen White's 1909 General Conference session sermon, found in Manuscript 49, 1909; and volume 6 of Arthur White's biography of Ellen White, *Ellen G. White: The Later Elmshaven Years, 1905-1915,* pp. 196, 197.

14. The 1848 Sabbatarian Conferences have been referred to by such expressions as "conferences of the brethren," "conferences of believers," "conferences of Sabbath-keepers," "Sabbath conferences," "1848 Bible Conferences," "weekend conferences of 1848," "Sabbath and Sanctuary Conferences," etc. See Alberto R. Timm, "The Sanctuary and the Three Angels' Messages 1844-1863: Integrating Factors in the Development of Seventh-day Adventist Doctrines" (Ph.D. dissertation, Andrews University, 1995), pp. 89-91, especially p. 89, note 2.

15. Reported by W. A. Spicer, then secretary of the General Conference, in his *The Spirit of Prophecy in the Advent Movement* (Washington, D.C.: Review and Herald, 1937), p. 30. Cf. Arthur L. White, *Ellen G. White: The Later Elmshaven Years, 1905-1915,* p. 197.

16. See "The Scriptures a Safeguard," *The Great Controversy,* pp. 593-602; see also Kathy Usilton, "Depending on the Word," *Adventists Affirm* 10/1 (Spring 1996):57-59, 62; Jacob J. Nortey, "The Bible, Our Surest Guide," *Adventists Affirm* 9/1 (Spring 1995):47-49, 67.

17. C. Mervyn Maxwell has offered an excellent review of the historic Adventist approach to Scripture. See his articles "'Take the Bible as It Is,'" *Adventists Affirm* 10/1 (Spring 1996):26-35; "A Brief History of Adventist Hermeneutics," *Journal of the Adventist Theological Society* 4/2 (1993):209-226; cf. George W. Reid, "Another Look at Adventist Methods of Bible Interpretation," *Adventists Affirm* 10/1 (Spring 1996):50-56. A discussion of recent developments regarding Adventist hermeneutics is found in chapter 4 of this book.

18. H. L. Hastings, *Will the Old Book Stand?* (Washington, D.C.: Review and Herald, 1923), pp. 22, 23.

19. Ibid., p. 23.

20. The words are taken from hymn #272 of the *Seventh-day Adventist Hymnal* (Hagerstown, Md.: Review and Herald, 1985).

How should we understand the Bible's inspiration and authority? How should the Scriptures function in the faith and practice of the church? What hermeneutical principles should govern Adventists interpretation of the Bible?

IV. APPENDICES

The Authority of Scripture

The following document, one of the most insightful produced by the Seventh-day Adventist church in recent times, was a discussion paper at the 1995 General Conference Session. Although the session did not vote on it, we reproduce it here because it is a helpful summary of the concerns addressed in this book.

Introduction

Scripture presents its message as revealed from divine sources. Although expressed in our language by humans, it bears the authentic mark of God. Repeatedly we encounter the expression "the word of the Lord came to me" or its equivalent. Jesus and the New Testament writers accepted the Hebrew Scripture as having unquestioned authority.

We are familiar with Paul's reminder to Timothy, "All scripture is inspired by God and profitable for teaching, for reproof, for correction, and for training in righteousness, that the man of God may be complete, equipped for every good work" (2 Tim. 3:16, 17, RSV). And Peter assures us that prophecy comes not from human sources, but "men moved by the Holy Spirit spoke from God" (2 Peter 1:21, RSV).

Despite such biblical statements, we have arrived at a very different place in the history of the faith.

Contemporary theology of almost any shade is now in crisis. It has become relativistic and hesitating. There is no lack of religious literature, to be sure, but one scarcely hears a sure word that recognizes divine authority. The foundations have been shaken. The major cause of this ferment is as plain as the fact itself: an increasing number of our contemporaries deny the existence of a solid platform on which Christian thinking can be built.

The breach between the Reformation and the Roman Catholic Church, 450 years ago, is narrow when compared with the chasm separating those who affirm and those who deny the existence of an objective divine revelation. In those days each side acknowledged the existence of revealed truth. They differed only in its interpretation. Today there is widespread skepticism as to whether an objective revelation exists at all.

General denial that divine revelation is objectively communicated in historical occurrences and intelligible statements of truth has proved to be destructive for theology. In the present climate, the Bible provides themes for theology, but no norms. Hence theology drifts unchecked, subservient to the reigning philosophical or scientific consensus. Whenever the content of Scripture is displeasing or regarded as irrelevant, it can be bypassed in favor of present experience. The result is the death of true biblical theology. The Bible student is free to bend revealed facts to his or her liking and to relativize the biblical truth, dissolving the biblical message in the acid of human subjectivity.

What Is Normative?

Such trends have not left Seventh-day Adventists unaffected. Today, in place of the time-honored view that Scripture is "the infallible revelation of His [God's] will," "the authoritative revealer of doctrines, and the trustworthy record of God's acts in history" (Fundamental Beliefs, No. 1), some among us have come to claim that the truth of revelation is so wholly other, so far beyond comprehension that no one can really say what it is or what it is not. Christian truths, we are told, are relative rather than absolute and therefore neither universal nor normative.

Sources of Authority

Others no longer seem determined to limit themselves to Scripture in the formulation of their views. Various sources—including Scripture, to be sure—are supposed to contribute information from which theological statements are compiled. What happens in fact is that *one* source comes to be treated as the preferred final authority. It may be reason, science, experience, or some other factor, but it is not often Scripture.

Reason has a commendable function in theological expression. We do not wish to deny its role as the discriminating faculty charged with detecting logical contradictions. But we dispute its ability to inaugurate revealed truth, to function by itself as a source of revealed data. In a sense, reason stands prior to revelation, since revelation must be perceived. But reason itself cannot be that revelation.

Tradition too has a role to play in the exercise of biblical authority. To ignore Christian history is to run the risk of repeating its mistakes. The Holy Spirit has been trying to teach Christians for hundreds of years and Seventh-day Adventists for a century and a half. The Bible is never interpreted in a vacuum, but read in the Christian community. That means that there are traditional ways of interpreting it, even among Adventists, and we cannot ignore them. We must listen to what Christians in the past have discovered, but at the same time we must be aware of the danger of submitting the Bible to human interpretations. What we hear from tradition must not stand on the same level with biblical revelation. Scripture is a critical authority confronting the church; and the church and tradition, including our own, must be guided and corrected by the canon of Scripture.

Science and Scripture

Equally pernicious are the claims of science to supersede biblical revelation. Today biblical assertions of all kinds are in conflict with much of current scientific opinion. Hence miracles are dismissed as violating immutable natural laws, and the existence of angels and demons is held to be erroneous and superstitious.

The biblical doctrine of the seven-day creation is causing increasing controversy between Adventist theologians and scientists. Some representing both groups have at times spoken rashly or prematurely. The danger is that theologians will abandon the historicity and factuality of the biblical account of Creation altogether in order to placate the scientists to whom the realm of nature is thought exclusively to belong.

Can we Adventists truly acknowledge the authority of Scripture if we abandon our belief in the reliability and historical authenticity of the Genesis account that teaches creation out of nothing in seven days? Do we also discard the teachings found in chapters 2 and 3 of the same book?

Enormous issues are involved in the doctrines of Creation and the Fall. Today's neo-Darwinian theories are as much cultural myth as scientific statement—a working hypothesis, not a proven theory. We should continue to be bold enough to say that the biblical statements concerning the origin of the earth by a special creation of God as recorded in the book of Genesis are a trustworthy and dependable account of what in fact did occur.

We recognize a significant interaction between science and Scripture. We need to avoid a dogmatic dismissal of the whole scientific enterprise as perverse speculation. Science in its fact-gathering capacity can serve Scripture well, illuminating the biblical text. But throughout our history, science and the Bible have never been put on the same plane. The Bible is the Word of God. Science is an empirical investigation of the natural world.

Cultural Conditioning and Authority

In the realm of history, objection is sometimes made to the reliability and authority of the Bible on the grounds that there are considerable differences between the ways in which its writers saw things and contemporary views. Cultural relativity, it is contended, makes it impossible for us today to take the Bible seriously. Its pages have meaning only in terms of the cultures in which they were written. Historical data and events were recorded, we are told, in the context of the biblical writers and must therefore be tested today by the criteria of our contemporary culture and historiography.

In general, this feeling represents Western cultural pride in the unspoken assumption that it holds a superior standpoint. It is true that this approach does not necessarily demand that our culture be superior, only that it be different. But are we so marooned on the island of our particular culture that we cannot appreciate what those in other cultures are telling us? Are cultures necessarily mutually incomprehensible? If we must not overlook the force of cultural relativism, neither must we exaggerate it.

This is especially the case with the Bible. A continuous history, an unbroken connection, binds us to those who wrote it. We have accepted it as part of our culture. This means strong continuity exists as well as discontinuity. Furthermore, by speaking to universal human needs the Bible in many ways supersedes all cultures: it speaks to humanity. The champions of cultural relativism often are people of considerable independence of mind who cherish nonconformity, a fact that may do credit to them as persons but damages the credibility of their arguments.

A Case for Investigation

Careful study remains essential, despite the fact that it is all too often put to destructive purposes. The answer to negative study of the Bible is not to ban research but to engage in better research. The God who chose to speak to us through writers living in specific historical, social, cultural, and linguistic contexts has, by that very method of speaking, determined how His Word is to be studied. Our understanding of the Bible cannot grow without sincere, thorough, and devout study of, among other things, the biblical languages, and the background—historical, cultural, political—of the biblical events. We must understand the circumstances in the life of Israel, and later the church, which instigated comment from the prophets and apostles. We need to appreciate the process by which the Holy Spirit produced the writings He caused God's people to gather into the Bible. Biblical scholarship, when it works correctly and accepts Scripture in all its parts—as it is and as God's Word—is not a method imposed upon the Bible from without. It is a method demanded from within.

No one wishes to claim that all problems will be solved or that the answer to every difficulty will be immediately apparent. Yet without wishing to minimize any of them we regard no difficulty as insuperable. Upon careful scrutiny, what has happened so often in archaeology may well occur again: so-called incontrovertible evidence of biblical errors may well be shown to be no evidence at all.

Two Sources of Authority

There are only two ways to find out God's will and to state our doctrinal beliefs clearly: (1) from special or supernatural revelation, which means the data first of all in Scripture and then in the writings of Ellen G. White, and (2) from general revelation, such as nature and human wisdom.

An unequivocal, even crucial emphasis on the inspiration and trustworthiness of Scripture has made an invaluable contribution to the health and strength of the SDA Church. It has helped us resist the error of treating some parts of Scripture as divine word while ignoring or rejecting others. It has led us to treasure all parts of

Scripture as "the infallible revelation of His [God's] will" (Fundamental Beliefs, No. 1), and to seek to apply their teachings to all aspects of our life and thought. To us "they are the standard of character, the test of experience, the authoritative revealer of doctrines, and the trustworthy record of God's acts in history" (*ibid.*).

Is There a Place for Discipline in the Christian Life?

To submit to Scripture is part of our Christian calling. Freedom from Scripture is darkness, not light. If the church allows its truth base to slip away, it will embark upon a search for certainty and it will no longer be the pillar and bulwark of the truth, but essentially a debating society for the discussion of ideas.

A solemn responsibility rests upon God's people to maintain the integrity and the spiritual fervor of the church as it proclaims the everlasting gospel. Its character and life imply commitments that are not optional but must be kept, values to be cherished, and conduct that is normative. Thus questions arise: What demands shall the church make upon its members? What is it to do if one refuses to comply with its demands, or if one's principles of conduct are no longer in harmony with those it has developed? What is it to do if one's beliefs contradict those the church considers itself to hold as of divine origin? Is one to be left to go his or her own way, and to lead others also? Or is the church, local and universal, to confront such members, and if so, at what point and in what measure?

The pervasive contemporary conviction is that every generation's theology is conditioned by its social context and therefore destined to be discarded. It is therefore not surprising that some among us contend that submission to confessional statements of faith defined by the church body is a practice dangerous to the welfare and relevance of God's people. So we are told we should do nothing in the face of doctrinal dissent. Even some leaders, sensing the current distaste for religious contention and the deference to ecumenical cooperation, exhibit an increasing impatience with controversy or disciplinary measures because of their apparent futility. Live and let live!

For others, questions about censure and discipline are settled by the clear biblical mandate of Matthew 18 and other statements in the New Testament epistles. For them, church discipline is a command of Scripture, a matter of obedience. It is not the narrow exercise of a private set of beliefs or a way of ridding the church of sinners, but rather redemptive and educative. Although such discipline was widely practiced in the early church as well as throughout church history, in today's climate of nonjudgmentalism it has appeared increasingly quaint and peculiar, and is often abandoned, even among us.

On the other hand, discipline should not be impersonal or lack a redemptive focus. It must never become a tool for expressing personal animosities.

But the integrity of the church is also at issue here. Church discipline is simply the right of self-preservation. No argument about individual liberty, academic freedom, or popular objection to "heresy trials" can negate the need for any group to preserve its fundamental doctrinal commitments. Unless all beliefs are relative and doctrine purely a matter of personal conviction, then action on the part of the church (i.e., discipline, both educative and remedial) is one of the necessary means of preserving the integrity of truth in the church. The right of the church—even its duty—to preserve the integrity of its doctrinal convictions is to be upheld. The church has the right to a body of doctrine that is a test of fellowship as well as the right to censure or exclude those who affirm some other creed. The clarity of the faith demands this. Any other attitude has a debilitating effect on the mission and spiritual vitality of the church. Nor are we to forget that discipline is part of discipling. To separate the two is not only to tear words from their common root, but to split arbitrarily their organic relationship.

Today, faced with conflict against the unbelief of modernism and with the blindness of those unwilling to listen to the advice of the believers, we need more than ever to understand the nature and purpose of the end-time church. In so doing, we may clarify our personal responsibilities and the unchanging realities of divine revelation. What is the church to be according to God's Word? What are its character, identity, marks, and mission? A revival of our awareness of the unique task that is ours will eventually sharpen questions related to the nature of the church, as it always has throughout Christian history. Those who disparage biblical doctrine must face a practical question: Does honesty permit one to continue in a church committed to the exclusive support and proclamation of specific doctrinal truths? Without an uncompromised regard for the authority of Scripture and our fundamental beliefs, only a shadow of Adventism remains.

Recommendations

1. Conduct major conferences on biblical/Spirit of Prophecy authority and unity of belief with the following objectives: (a) project a vision of the power and authority of Scripture for salvation and victorious living, (b) make pastors and teachers aware of current trends in problematic directions, (c) introduce the above concepts into faculty and pastors' meetings, (d) encourage pastors and teachers to make presentations defending the Bible as authority, and (e) gain support for standard Adventist positions.

2. Take steps to restore the process of church discipline in matters of doctrine as well as practical life through sensitive and decisive action dealing with unfaithfulness in behavior and beliefs, with the intention of educating and healing the church body.

3. Plan for conscious efforts to educate the church on how secular values infiltrate Christian faith and practice.

4. Initiate a world study to identify ways that secular values are displacing biblical values in Seventh-day Adventist faith and life.

5. Publish popularly written books and articles making available to the world church the content of recent Biblical Research Institute documents.

6. Appoint boards who will employ and retain persons clearly in harmony with standard Adventist positions.

Appendix B

The Use of Scripture

Like the document reproduced in Appendix A, this document was also a discussion paper at the 1995 General Conference Session. It sets forth some areas in which Scripture can be brought to bear on the life and mission of the Seventh-day Adventist church.

The Use of Scripture in the Life of the SDA Church

Introduction

Scripture has always played a vital role in the life and thought of the Seventh-day Adventist Church. From its beginnings the church has considered Scripture to be the source of its faith and practice. It has been our guide in our quest to know God and understand His eternal character. It has provided our ethical and moral values as well as our understanding of ourselves and the world around us, and it has served as the determinant of the mission and goal of the church and its institutions.

It is the Bible and the Bible alone that provides the prophetic mandate for our existence as the remnant church and teaches us how to live as sons and daughters of God in the midst of a fallen and corrupt world.

The implications of this fundamental theological posture are far-reaching. The Scripture becomes not just the source of beliefs and practice but also the standard by which the church, its message, its mission, and its institutions are to be evaluated. In fact, they govern the whole life of the church in the sense that they provide the concepts, principles, and values that should guide our personal lives as well.

The all-encompassing function of the Bible is clearly stated in 2 Tim. 3:16, 17. According to this pivotal passage, Scripture was given for doctrine, reproof, correction, and instruction in righteousness. The ultimate objective is "that everyone who belongs to God may be proficient, equipped for every good work" (NRSV).

Clearly the intent of God is that His Word be an intimate part of Christian experience. David writes, "I have laid up thy word in my heart, that I might not sin against thee" (Ps. 119:11, RSV). The Word of God is the source of true wisdom (Ps. 119:98; Deut. 4:6), and Paul writes to Timothy, "From childhood you have been acquainted with the sacred writings which are able to instruct you for salvation" (2 Tim. 3:15, RSV).

Instead of standing as a cold framework of obligations, Scripture provides highly personal guidance designed to benefit every believer. For this reason God directed that His people diligently instruct their children in the Word of God (Deut. 6:7-9). Recovery of the neglected Word of God leads to revival, as in Josiah's time.

One of the theological concepts that has contributed to the centrality of Scripture in Adventist faith and life is the great controversy theme. In the cosmic conflict the goal of evil forces is to distort and suppress the truth of God. God has revealed His truth in the person, work, and teachings of Christ, which have been preserved for us by the Holy Spirit in Scripture. It is, therefore, through this revelation that the church is able to distinguish between truth and error.

Use of Scripture: Present Practice

The basic question is whether the theoretical understanding of the role of Scripture in the life of the church is reflected in the daily life of the church. The immediate answer seems to be Yes, it is. Nevertheless, there are new challenges and tendencies that if not addressed may begin to shift the role of Scripture away from its vital and central place in the life of the church.

Use of Scripture in the Administration of the Church

In the history of the Seventh-day Adventist Church most administrators have been known as deep, careful students of the Word. This was true of the pioneers, and also characterizes many of our leaders today who take time in the midst of heavy schedules to steep themselves in a clear understanding of the principles of Scripture. Nevertheless, because of broad responsibilities assigned to leadership today, some church members feel that church leaders often are more business-oriented than spiritually oriented, and that their knowledge of Scripture is limited. The truthfulness of this perception has never been evaluated empirically.

A growing church places heavy burdens on its leaders and consumes most of their time in administrative matters. One of the serious dangers that administrators face is not finding time in their busy schedules to study the Scriptures. It may be useful to remember that church leaders are also stewards of biblical truth. Hence, they should know the Scriptures well.

Because Christ is the head of the church, it is unthinkable that any human instrument should attempt to take over the direction of the body of Christ. It might help to think of the church primarily as an organism rather than an organization. With that in mind, church leaders are part of God's chain of communication. They need to understand God's will as outlined clearly in Scripture, and do everything within their power to fulfill God's expectations.

A dangerous tendency of the church is to consider that what God wants is determined by a simple majority vote. Throughout our history the Holy Spirit has led individuals as well as committees through prayerful study of Scripture. Does it not make sense today that the church, its members, committees, and leaders should also seek to understand God's will for their decision-making in the same way—by searching Scripture in order to apply its divine principles to our contemporary concerns? Unity is the gift that God gives His people when they find Him. Above all, we must be so tuned to Him and to the revelation of His will that when we adopt an action or a program, the large body of believers will sense God's leading and will rejoice to commit themselves fully to implementing it. Indeed, ours must be a vision delineated by Scripture and fostered by the Spirit.

In this context it would be valid to remind ourselves that an increasing number of laypersons are now members of most administrative boards and committees and are directly involved in the decision-making process. Therefore, it would be equally inappropriate for them to vote their personal convictions educated by personal preference or logic alone instead of informed by a careful study of the Word of God and the real needs of the church.

Seventh-day Adventist church leaders, be they church employees or lay people, have tremendous responsibilities not only to be deep students of the Word themselves, but to foster a back-to-the-Bible movement that will help prepare our members for the great tests we will face in the last great crisis.

Use of Scripture in Adventist Publishing Houses and Publications

Adventist publishing houses have provided the church with a plethora of Bible-centered books that have nurtured the church and increased the knowledge of Scripture among the church members.

Recently some Adventist books have fostered pluralism in some of the essential doctrines of the church. Such publications have contributed to frustration among those members who depend on our publishing houses to help guide them to a clear understanding of the teachings of the Seventh-day Adventist Church.

Adventist leaders have come under fire because some of our publications are perceived as either contradicting each other doctrinally or not taking a clear position on issues that trouble the church. It is well known that our pioneers in their search for truth used our periodicals to express, at times, conflicting views on different subjects. Therefore, difference of opinion in nonessentials is not necessarily bad. Yet the question remains, Do our church periodicals by their editorials and articles reflect the Bible-based stance of Adventism throughout its history? The omission of clear references to the Bible in our periodicals could send a subliminal message to the reader that plays down the importance of Scripture. Editors should make sure that whatever is published is Bible-centered in content and unifying in its effect.

It is a matter of concern that some Adventist Book Centers may be distributing books, written by non-Adventists and by Adventists but not published by our publishing houses, that contradict or reject some of our distinctive doctrines. This does not mean that we should distribute only books published by our publishing houses; it does mean that care be taken in the selection of those books published by non-Adventist publishers.

Members also feel that there is a lack of clearly written, easily understandable materials that provide scriptural answers to the questions they face from so many sides today.

Use of Scripture in the Adventist Educational System

A generalized blanket statement on this topic cannot cover the educational program throughout the world church. Our schools do encourage extended use of Scripture, although some tend to do it more than others. Possibly there are some in the world church that do not have adequate access to Bibles.

A number of anecdotal reports that come to church leaders express alarm over the concern that some of our institutions of higher learning may be drifting away from the standards and objectives established for them by their founders, resulting in what seems to be a secular climate on some campuses, with strange winds of doctrine. There is also a concern that methods of Bible study that undermine the authority of Scripture are, in some cases, being used in religion classes. In some parts of the world this has resulted in the rejection of the historicity of Genesis 1-11. Consequently, the Bible comes to play a minimal role in the students' understanding of the origin of the world.

It has also been noted that some Bible classes seem to be taught only as an academic exercise, omitting relevant application of Scripture for the daily life of the student. These anecdotal perceptions should be discredited or confirmed by a serious study of these issues.

Use of Scripture in Denominational Medical Institutions/Offices

Seventh-day Adventist medical institutions today face extremely serious and challenging ethical issues. It is very difficult to ascertain to what extent the Word of God is playing a central and determinative role in their resolution. Elected leadership and the constituency in general should make sure that Scripture is used in addressing those issues. This implies keeping the constituency informed about the ethical problems and the way the Scripture is being used in dealing with them.

Another area of concern could be the extent to which denominational standards derived from Scripture are being followed in those institutions (e.g., Sabbath-keeping, diet). It should be recognized that the issues are complex and difficult to deal with. Practicing our distinctive beliefs in the hospital setting causes hospital administrators to face a myriad of questions for which solutions are not always easily available. It is of utmost importance that church leaders, with Scripture in hand, join hospital administrators in the search for the answers they need.

However, it is quite clear that the Christian philosophy of healing sustained by Adventists medical institutions is biblically based. The goal is to heal the whole person. That goal is based in the biblical understanding of the person as an indivisible entity.

Use of Scripture in Pastoral Work and Preaching

Seventh-day Adventist church members frequently express their desire to hear more biblical sermons based on the great themes and truths of Adventism, with some members feeling that they are not being spiritually fed on Sabbath. Some of them suggest that the messages they hear from week to week are those that could be preached in any Protestant church. Unfortunately, there may be some basis to this perception. The possible connection between this perception and the ministerial training of the pastors may need to be explored.

Use of Scripture Among Church Members

The use of Scripture among church members does not seem to be uniform throughout the world church. In areas of the world in which members are actively involved in Bible studies and preparing people for baptism, the Bible is being studied much more than in places in which this involvement is absent. We do not describe ourselves as the "people of the Book" as much as we have done in the past.

In a recent study of the use of Scripture among church members, some areas of the world field indicated that more are using the Bible today for devotional purposes than they did in 1980. This is indeed an encouraging sign. Nevertheless, there is a general perception among workers that, in at least some areas of the world church, Bible literacy may have declined among church members. This suggests that possibly they are less active in using the Bible. Could it be that we are using the Bible more for devotion and inspiration than for deep personal study?

Possibly the major concern here would be to know to what extent the principles, values, and teachings of Scripture determine the thinking and behavior of church members. Anecdotal information suggests that in general, church members do follow and are greatly influenced by Scripture. In parts of the world some church members seem to have separated, at least in some areas of their lives, their beliefs from their daily behavior.

Recommendations

1. Develop and implement plans to teach the world membership principles of biblical interpretation.

2. Survey world membership to ascertain to what extent principles, values, and teachings of Scripture determine the thinking and behavior of church members.

3. Develop seminars for church leaders to strengthen their use of Scripture in their administrative decisions.

4. Develop plans to ascertain the influence and impact of Scripture in all aspects of institutional life of SDA schools, colleges, universities, publishing houses, and medical entities, and recommend to appropriate administrative bodies ways to strengthen the use of Scripture in these institutions.

5. Evaluate pastoral education curriculum in SDA colleges and seminaries, and recommend ways to place more emphasis on biblical preaching.

6. Take steps to assure basic doctrinal harmony among publications issuing from SDA publishing houses.

Appendix C

Methods of Bible Study

At the 1986 Annual Council meeting in Rio de Janeiro, Brazil, church leaders representing all the world fields approved the report of the General Conference's "Methods of Bible Study Committee (GCC-A). This carefully worded document was published in the Adventist Review (January 22, 1987), pages 18-20. Generally, all Bible-believing Adventists embrace this report as reflective of the principles of interpretation that have been historically accepted by Seventh-day Adventists. For a discussion of how Adventist scholars have related to this document, see Chapter 4 of this book. The following is the entire text of the "Methods of Bible Study" as it was approved at Rio.

Voted, To approve the Methods of Bible Study Committee (GCC-A) report, which reads as follows:

Bible Study: Presuppositions, Principles, and Methods

1. *Preamble*

This statement is addressed to all members of the Seventh-day Adventist Church with the purpose of providing guidelines on how to study the Bible, both the trained biblical scholar and others.

Seventh-day Adventists recognize and appreciate the contributions of those biblical scholars throughout history who have developed useful and reliable methods of Bible study consistent with the claims and teachings of Scripture. Adventists are committed to the acceptance of biblical truth and are willing to follow it, using all methods of interpretation consistent with what Scripture says of itself. These are outlined in the presuppositions detailed below.

In recent decades the most prominent method in biblical studies has been known as the historical-critical method. Scholars who use this method, as classically formulated, operate on the basis of presuppositions which, prior to studying the biblical text, reject the reliability of accounts of miracles and other supernatural events narrated in the Bible. Even a modified use of this method that retains the principle of criticism which subordinates the Bible to human reason is unacceptable to Adventists.

The historical-critical method minimizes the need for faith in God and obedience to His commandments. In addition, because such a method deemphasizes the divine element in the Bible as an inspired book (including its resultant unity) and depreciates or misunderstands apocalyptic prophecy and the eschatological portions of the Bible, we urge Adventist Bible students to avoid relying on the use of the presuppositions and the resultant deductions associated with the historical-critical method.

By contrast to the historical-critical method and presuppositions, we believe it to be helpful to set forth the principles of Bible study that are consistent with the teachings of the Scriptures themselves, that preserve their unity, and are based upon the premise that the Bible is the word of God. Such an approach will lead us into a satisfying and rewarding experience with God.

2. *Presuppositions Arising From the Claims of Scripture*

a. Origin

1) The Bible is the word of God and is the primary and authoritative means by which He reveals Himself to human beings.

2) The Holy Spirit inspired the Bible writers with thoughts, ideas, and objective information; in turn they expressed these in their own words. Therefore the Scriptures are an indivisible union of human and divine elements, neither of which should be emphasized to the neglect of the other (2 Peter 1:21; cf. *The Great Controversy*, pp. v, vi).

3) All Scripture is inspired by God and came through the work of the Holy Spirit. However, it did not come in a continuous chain of unbroken revelations. As the Holy Spirit communicated truth to the Bible writer, each wrote as he was moved by the Holy Spirit, emphasizing the aspect of the truth which he was led to stress. For this reason the student of the Bible will gain a rounded comprehension on any subject by recognizing that the Bible is its own best interpreter and when studied as a whole it depicts a consistent, harmonious truth (2 Tim. 3:16; Heb. 1:1, 2; cf. *Selected Messages*, book 1, pp. 19, 20; *The Great Controversy*, pp. v, vi).

4) Although it was given to those who lived in an ancient Near Eastern/ Mediterranean context, the Bible transcends its cultural backgrounds to serve as God's word for all cultural, racial, and situational contexts in all ages.

b. Authority

1) The 66 books of the Old and New Testaments are the clear, infallible revelation of God's will and His salvation. The Bible is the word of God, and it alone is the standard by which all teaching and experience must be tested (2 Tim. 3:15-17; Ps. 119:105; Prov. 30:5, 6; Isa. 8:20; John 17:17; 2 Thess. 3:14; Heb. 4:12).

2) Scripture is an authentic, reliable record of history and God's acts in history. It provides the normative theological interpretation of those acts. The su-

pernatural acts revealed in Scripture are historically true. For example, chapters 1-11 of Genesis are a factual account of historical events.

3) The Bible is not like other books. It is an indivisible blend of the divine and the human. Its record of many details of secular history is integral to its overall purpose to convey salvation history. While at times there may be parallel procedures employed by Bible students to determine historical data, the usual techniques of historical research, based as they are on human presuppositions and focused on the human element, are inadequate for interpreting the Scriptures, which are a blend of the divine and the human. Only a method that fully recognizes the indivisible nature of Scripture can avoid a distortion of its message.

4) Human reason is subject to the Bible, not equal to or above it. Presuppositions regarding the Scriptures must be in harmony with the claims of the Scriptures and subject to correction by them (1 Cor. 2:1-6). God intends that human reason be used to its fullest extent, but within the context and under the authority of His Word rather than independent of it.

5) The revelation of God in all nature, when properly understood, is in harmony with the Written Word, and it is to be interpreted in the light of Scripture.

3. *Principles for Approaching the Interpretation of Scripture*

a. The Spirit enables the believer to accept, understand, and apply the Bible to one's own life as he[/she] seeks divine power to render obedience to all scriptural requirements and to appropriate personally all Bible promises. Only those following the light already received can hope to receive further illumination of the Spirit (John 16:13, 14; 1 Cor. 2:10-14).

b. Scripture cannot be correctly interpreted without the aid of the Holy Spirit, for it is the Spirit who enables the believer to understand and apply Scripture. Therefore, any study of the Word should commence with a request for the Spirit's guidance and illumination.

c. Those who come to the study of the Word must do so with faith, in the humble spirit of a learner who seeks to hear what the Bible is saying. They must be willing to submit all presuppositions, opinions and the conclusions of reason to the judgment and correction of the Word itself. With this attitude the Bible student may come directly to the Word, and with careful study may come to an understanding of the essentials of salvation apart from any human explanations, however helpful. The biblical message becomes meaningful to such a person.

d. The investigation of Scripture must be characterized by a sincere desire to discover and obey God's will and word rather than to seek support or evidence for preconceived ideas.

4. Methods of Bible Study

a. Select a Bible version for study that is faithful to the meaning contained in languages in which the Bible originally was written, giving preference to translations done by a broad group of scholars and published by a general publisher above translations sponsored by a particular denomination or narrowly focused group.

Exercise care not to build major doctrinal points on one Bible translation or version. Trained biblical scholars will use the Greek and Hebrew texts, enabling them to examine variant readings of ancient Bible manuscripts, as well.

b. Choose a definite plan of study, avoiding haphazard and aimless approaches. Study plans such as the following are suggested:
>   1) Book-by-book analysis of the message.
>   2) Verse-by-verse method.
>   3) Study that seeks a biblical solution to a specific life-problem, biblical satisfaction for a specific need, or a biblical answer to a specific question.
>   4) Topical study (faith, love, Second Coming, and others).
>   5) Word study.
>   6) Biographical study.

c. Seek to grasp the simple, most obvious meaning of the biblical passage being studied.

d. Seek to discover the underlying major themes of Scripture as found in individual texts, passages, and books. Two basic, related themes run throughout Scripture: (1) the person and work of Jesus Christ; and (2) the great controversy perspective involving the authority of God's Word, the Fall of man, the first and second advents of Christ, the exoneration of God and His law, and the restoration of the divine plan for the universe. These themes are to be drawn from the totality of Scripture and not imposed on it.

e. Recognize that the Bible is its own interpreter and that the meaning of words, texts, and passages is best determined by diligently comparing scripture with scripture.

f. Study the context of the passage under consideration by relating it to the sentences and paragraphs immediately preceding and following it. Try to relate the ideas of the passage to the line of thought of the entire biblical book.

g. As far as possible ascertain the historical circumstances in which the passage was written by the biblical writer under the guidance of the Holy Spirit.

h. Determine the literary type the author is using. Some biblical material is composed of parables, proverbs, allegories, psalms, and apocalyptic prophecies. Since many biblical writers presented much of their material as poetry, it is helpful to use a version of the Bible that presents this material in poetic style, for passages employing imagery are not to be interpreted in the same manner as prose.

i. Recognize that a given biblical text may not conform in every detail to present-day literary categories. Be cautious not to force these categories in interpreting the meaning of the biblical text. It is a human tendency to find what one is looking for, even when the author [writer] did not intend such.

j. Take note of grammar and sentence construction in order to discover the author's [writer's] meaning. Study the key words of the passage by comparing their use in other parts of the Bible by means of a concordance and with the help of biblical lexicons and dictionaries.

k. In connection with the study of the biblical text, explore the historical and cultural factors. Archaeology, anthropology, and history may contribute to understanding the meaning of the text.

l. Seventh-day Adventists believe that God inspired Ellen G. White. Therefore, her expositions on any given biblical passage offer an inspired guide to the meaning of texts without exhausting their meaning or preempting the task of exegesis (for example, see *Evangelism*, p. 256; *The Great Controversy*, pp. 193, 595; *Testimonies*, vol. 5, pp. 665, 682, 707, 708; *Counsels to Writers and Editors*, pp. 33-35).

m. After studying as outlined above, turn to various commentaries and secondary helps such as scholarly works to see how others have dealt with the passage. Then carefully evaluate the different viewpoints expressed from the standpoint of Scripture as a whole.

n. In interpreting prophecy keep in mind that:
    1) The Bible claims God's power to predict the future (Isa. 46:10).
    2) Prophecy has a moral purpose. It was not written merely to satisfy curiosity about the future. Some of the purposes of prophecy are to strengthen faith (John 14:29) and to promote holy living and readiness for the Advent (Matt. 24:44; Rev. 22:7, 10, 11).
    3) The focus of much prophecy is on Christ (both His first and second advents), the church, and the end-time.
    4) The norms for interpreting prophecy are found within the Bible itself: The Bible notes time prophecies and their historical fulfillments, the New Testament cites specific fulfillments of Old Testament prophecies about the Messiah,

and the Old Testament itself presents individuals and events as types of the Messiah.

5) In the New Testament application of Old Testament prophecies, some literal names become spiritual: e.g., Israel represents the church; Babylon, apostate religion; etc.

6) There are two general types of prophetic writings: nonapocalyptic prophecy, as found in Isaiah and Jeremiah, and apocalyptic prophecy, as found in Daniel and the Revelation. These differing types have different characteristics:

a) Nonapocalyptic prophecy addresses God's people; apocalyptic prophecy is more universal in scope.

b) Nonapocalyptic prophecy often is conditional in nature, setting forth to God's people the alternatives of blessing for obedience and curses for disobedience; apocalyptic emphasizes the sovereignty of God and His control over history.

c) Nonapocalyptic prophecy often leaps from the local crisis to the end-time day of the Lord; apocalyptic prophecy presents the course of history from the time of the prophet to the end of the world.

d) Time prophecies in nonapocalyptic prophecy generally are long, e.g., 400 years of Israel's servitude (Gen. 15:13) and 70 years of Babylonian captivity (Jer. 25:12). Time prophecies in apocalyptic prophecy generally are phrased in short terms, e.g., 10 days (Rev. 2:10) or 42 months (Rev. 13:5). Apocalyptic time periods stand symbolically for longer periods of actual time.

7) Apocalyptic prophecy is highly symbolic and should be interpreted accordingly. In interpreting symbols, the following methods may be used:

a) Look for interpretations (explicit or implicit) within the passage itself (e.g., Dan. 8:20, 21; Rev. 1:20).

b) Look for interpretations elsewhere in the book or in other writings by the same author [writer].

c) Using a concordance, study the use of symbols in other parts of Scripture.

d) A study of ancient Near Eastern documents may throw light on the meaning of symbols, although scriptural use may alter those meanings.

8) The literary structure of a book often is an aid to interpreting it. The parallel nature of Daniel's prophecies is an example.

o. Parallel accounts in Scripture sometimes present differences in detail and emphasis (for example, compare Matt. 21:33-44; Mark 12:1-11; and Luke 20:9-18, or 2 Kings 18-20 with 2 Chron. 32). When studying such passages, first examine them carefully to be sure that the parallels actually are referring to the same historical event. For example, many of Jesus' parables may have been given on different occasions to different audiences and with different wording.

In cases where there appear to be differences in parallel accounts, one should recognize that the total message of the Bible is the synthesis of all its parts. Each book or writer communicates that which the Spirit has led him to write. Each makes his own special contribution to the richness, diversity, and variety of Scripture (*The Great Controversy*, pp. v, vi). The reader must allow each Bible writer to emerge and be heard, while at the same time recognizing the basic unity of the divine self-disclosure.

When parallel passages seem to indicate discrepancy or contradiction, look for the underlying harmony. Keep in mind that dissimilarities may be due to minor errors of copyists (*Selected Messages*, book 1, p. 16), or may be the result of differing emphases and choice of materials of various authors [writers] who wrote under the inspiration and guidance of the Holy Spirit for different audiences under different circumstances (*ibid.*, pp. 21, 22; *The Great Controversy*, p. vi).

It may prove impossible to reconcile minor dissimilarities in detail which may be irrelevant to the main and clear message of the passage. In some cases judgment may have to be suspended until more informa-tion and better evidence are available to resolve a seeming discrepancy.

p. The Scriptures were written for the practical purpose of revealing the will of God to the human family. However, in order for one not to misconstrue certain kinds of statements, it is important to recognize that they were addressed to peoples of Eastern cultures and expressed in their thought patterns.

Expressions such as "The Lord hardened the heart of Pharaoh" (Ex. 9:12) or "an evil spirit from God" (1 Sam. 16:15), the imprecatory psalms, and the "three days and three nights" of Jonah as compared with Christ's death (Matt. 12:40) commonly are misunderstood because they are interpreted today from a different viewpoint.

A background knowledge of Near Eastern culture is indispensable for understanding such expressions. For example, Hebrew culture attributed responsibility to an individual for acts he did not commit but that he allowed to happen. Therefore the inspired writers of the Scriptures commonly credit God with doing actively that which in Western thought we would say He permits or does not prevent from happening, e.g., the hardening of Pharaoh's heart.

Another aspect of Scripture that troubles the modern mind is the divine command to Israel to engage in war and execute entire nations. Israel originally was organized as a theocracy, a civil government through which God ruled directly. Such a theocratic state was unique. It no longer exists and cannot be regarded as a direct model for Christian practice.

The Scriptures record experiences and statements of persons whom God accepted but were not in harmony with the spiritual principles of the Bible as a whole—for example, incidents relating to the use of alcohol, to polygamy, divorce, and slavery. Although condemnation of such deeply ingrained social customs is not explicit, God did not necessarily endorse or approve all that He permitted and bore with in the lives of the patriarchs and in Israel. Jesus made this clear in His statement with regard to divorce (Matt. 19:4-6, 8).

The spirit of the Scriptures is one of restoration. God works patiently to elevate fallen humanity from the depths of sin to the divine ideal. Consequently we must not accept as models the actions of sinful men as recorded in the Bible.

The Scriptures represent the unfolding of God's revelation to man. Jesus' sermon on the mount, for example, enlarges and expands on certain Old Testament concepts. Christ Himself is the ultimate revelation of God's character to humanity (Heb. 1:1-3).

While there is an overarching unity in the Bible from Genesis to Revelation, and while all Scripture is equally inspired, God chose to reveal Himself to and through human individuals and to meet them where they were in terms of spiritual and intellectual endowments. God Himself does not change, but He progressively unfolded His revelation to men as they were able to grasp it (John 16:12; *The SDA Bible Commentary*, vol. 7, p. 945; *Selected Messages*, book 1, p. 21). Every experience or statement of Scripture is a divinely inspired record, but not every statement or experience is necessarily normative for Christian behavior today. Both the spirit and the letter of Scripture must be understood (1 Cor. 10:6-13; *The Desire of Ages*, p. 150; *Testimonies*, vol. 4, pp. 10-12).

q. As the final goal, make application of the text. Ask such questions as "What is the message and purpose God intends to convey through Scripture? What meaning does this text have for me? How does it apply to my situation and circumstances today? In doing so, recognize that although many biblical passages had local significance, nonetheless they contain timeless principles applicable to every age and culture.

5. *Conclusion*

In the Introduction to *The Great Controversy*, Ellen G. White wrote:
"The Bible, with its God-given truths expressed in the language of men, presents a union of the divine and the human. Such a union existed in the nature of Christ, who was the Son of God and the Son of man. Thus it is true of the Bible, as it was of Christ, that 'the Word was made flesh, and dwelt among us.' John 1:14" (p. vi).

As it is impossible for those who do not accept Christ's divinity to understand the purpose of His incarnation, it is also impossible for those who see the Bible merely as a human book to understand its message, however careful and rigorous their methods.

Even Christian scholars who accept the divine-human nature of Scripture but whose methodological approaches cause them to dwell largely on its human aspects risk emptying the biblical message of its power by relegating it to the background while concentrating on the medium. They forget that medium and message are inseparable and that the medium without the message is as an empty shell that cannot address the vital spiritual needs of humankind.

A committed Christian will use only those methods that are able to do full justice to the dual, inseparable nature of Scripture, enhance his[/her] ability to understand and apply its message, and strengthen faith.

Glossary

Accommodationism/Accommodationists. Accommodationists (or theological moderates) give the appearance of being Bible-believing conservatives, and yet they accommodate conservative beliefs to liberal thought. Unlike radical/classical liberals, accommodationists accept *some* or even *all* of the Bible's miracles and supernatural events, but they maintain that the Bible is not fully reliable in everything. They employ modified versions of contemporary higher criticism to interpret Scripture.

Allegorical Interpretation. A method of interpretation which assumes that a text conveys a hidden, mystical meaning other than its literal, plain, ordinary sense. Its best-known proponent is Origen of Alexandria (A.D. 185-254), who used Greek philosophical categories to spiritualize away the plain meaning of Scripture in his attempt to discover these additional meanings. Allegorical interpretation competed with *Antiochian interpretation* which tended to be rational, historical, and literal.

Canon/Canonical. The word *canon* derives from a Greek word which means "rule." The adjective *canonical* means something that has been accepted as the rule or norm. Applied to the 66 books of the Old and New Testaments, the terms suggest that these inspired books are the Christian's rule of faith and practice.

Canon within the Canon. An expression of higher criticism which implies that certain portions of the biblical canon are more inspired than others. Those portions of Scripture which the critical scholars arbitrarily credit as inspired and trustworthy, and therefore meriting the label of God's Word, are known as the "canon within the canon."

Comparative-Religion Criticism. A higher-critical approach which claims that the Bible writers borrowed from the polytheistic cultures around them. This liberal method seeks to study the evolutionary development of the biblical faith from its assumed polytheistic or primitive forms to its present monotheistic or matured form.

Conservatism/Conservatives. Theological conservatives seek to conserve or preserve the view of Scripture set forth in the inspired Word itself and which formed the consensus of Christendom from its very beginning until the rise of higher criticism. Bible-believing conservatives accept the full inspiration and trustworthiness of the Bible in matters of salvation as well as on any other subject the Bible touches upon. They reject the use of the higher critical methodologies.

Cultural Conditioning. An expression describing higher critical scholars' assertion that at least some parts of the Bible reflect the prejudices or limitations of the inspired writers' culture and times. Since the Bible writers allegedly wrote from ignorance or a distorted view of reality, such scholars argue that the "culturally conditioned" parts are not fully inspired and binding.

Demythologization. A method of interpretation (associated with the name of Rudolf Bultmann) which views much of the Bible as containing primitive forms of thinking and which attempts to translate them into modern categories.

Documentary Hypothesis. A higher-critical theory which maintains that Moses was not the writer of the first five books of the Bible, but that these books can be traced to sources, or *documents,* written later by various unknown authors and compilers. One hypothetical author is called **J** (Yahwist, c. 850 B.C., during the early monarchy of Israel) because he supposedly always called God "Jehovah." Another is known as **E** (Elohist, c. 750 B.C., shortly before Israel's exile) because he allegedly used the Hebrew word *Elohim* for God. There is also **D** (Deuteronomist, 621 B.C.), who is believed to have written Deuteronomy, and **P** (Priestly, time of Ezra) who allegedly belonged to the priestly class after the exile. Based on this hypothesis, higher-critical scholars chop up the Bible into pieces according to whether the section uses the word Jehovah or Elohim, or if it contains references to priestly activity or concerns. The theory was later applied to most Old Testament books and some New Testament books.

Dynamic Equivalence. An approach to Bible translation that seeks to communicate the original meaning in a given text by translating *thought-for-thought.* Because it seeks to make the Bible clear and "alive" in today's language, it often loses many of the nuances of the original language, thereby sacrificing accuracy. Often exhibiting the biases of translators, this approach to Bible translation is most commonly reflected in Bible paraphrases.

Eisegesis (or Imposition). Reading *into* a text a meaning that is not there, by illegitimately imposing onto it the interpreter's own opinion or ideology. *Eisegesis* is the opposite of *exegesis.*

Exegesis (or Exposition). Reading *out* of a text a meaning that is already there, by faithfully explaining the meaning of a text in its original context. Exegesis and hermeneutics are sometimes used synonymously, even though the two terms are distinguishable: *hermeneutics* deals with the underlying assumptions, principles, and methods of interpretation; *exegesis* is the actual practice of interpretation, applying one's hermeneutical principles. Thus, the results of exegesis depend upon the interpreter's (liberal or conservative) hermeneutical foundations. A scholar who does the work of exegesis is called an *exegete.*

Form or Tradition Criticism. A higher-critical approach which seeks to get behind the written sources of the Bible to the period of oral tradition and isolate the oral forms and traditions alleged to have gone into the written sources.

Formal Equivalence. An approach to Bible translation that seeks to preserve *all* of the information in the text, by translating *word-for-word* of the original language as much as possible. Because it seeks accuracy in translation, sometimes the translation may be difficult to understand or awkward to read.

Fundamentalism/Fundamentalist. A point of view characterized by belief in the literal truth of the Bible. Because Bible-believing Christians accept the literal truthfulness of Scripture, rejecting the approach of higher criticism, their liberal counterparts often label them "fundamentalist" to suggest that conservatives are anti-intellectual, obscurantist, reactionary, and authoritarian.

Hermeneutics. From the Greek word *hermeneuein,* meaning to explain, to express, to translate, to interpret. As a science of interpretation, hermeneutics seeks to establish the principles, methods, and rules needed for interpreting written texts, including the Bible. Every hermeneutical method is based on a set of assumptions about the inspiration and trustworthiness of Scripture.

Higher Criticism (Higher-Critical Method). An attitude of skepticism toward the Bible that leads to rejecting those parts of Scripture judged incompatible with the tenets of Enlightenment rationalism. Practitioners of higher criticism refuse to receive the Scriptures as God's inspired and trustworthy communication of His will to all humanity. In this approach, human reason and experience, rather than inspired Scripture, are exalted as the objective, dependable criteria to determine truth. Higher critics question, criticize, dissect, conjecture, and reconstruct God's inspired Word, thus robbing it of its power. Today, higher criticism operates under the various contemporary approaches of the *historical-critical method.*

Historical-Critical Method. An umbrella term that describes the contemporary manifestation of old-fashioned *higher criticism.* As a liberal approach to Scripture, it does not accept the Bible as fully inspired and trustworthy. Maintaining that some things recorded in the Bible are not reliable or accurate accounts of what actually happened, critical scholars have put forward several, often contradictory, approaches touted as "objective" paradigms of Bible interpretation. These include: literary-source criticism, form or tradition criticism, redaction criticism, comparative-religion criticism, historical criticism, structural criticism, etc. These contemporary approaches are established on three major principles: *analogy, correlation,* and *criticism.* The historical-critical method is the opposite of the *historical-grammatical method* (the plain, literal interpretation of Scripture).

Historical Criticism. A historical-critical approach that adopts a skeptical attitude to the historical claims of Scripture. It employs all the other techniques of the various approaches bracketed under the historical-critical method and, in addition, draws upon archeology and secular historical sources to determine authorship, date of writing, and what allegedly led to the writing of the biblical book.

Historical-Grammatical Method. A term dating at least to 1788 to describe a method of studying Scriptures which conducts a detailed analysis of the biblical text in accordance with the original language and historical context. This approach, generally favored by Bible-believing conservatives, recognizes the Bible as fully inspired and trustworthy. In recent times, this expression has been employed as a technical term to describe the traditional Adventist practice of interpreting Scripture according to its simple, literal, plain, direct, or ordinary sense. The historical-grammatical method is the opposite of the *historical-critical method* (contemporary higher criticism).

Illumination. A divine act which enables a person (prophet and non-prophet) in a right relationship with God to understand God's revealed will correctly.

Infallible/Infallibility. Derives from the Latin *infallibilitas,* meaning the quality of neither deceiving nor misleading. Applied to the Bible, the term suggests that Scripture is wholly trustworthy and reliable. The word *infallible* is often used as a functional equivalent to *inerrant* (from the Latin *inerrantia,* the quality of being free from factual, moral or spiritual error). If we press the distinction, *infallible* would indicate "no potential for error" and *inerrant* "no actuality of error." *Infallible* is the stronger word, although many people think that the reverse is true. To declare Scripture as infallible or inerrant means to assert the Bible's divine origin, truthfulness, and trustworthiness, never denying, disregarding, or arbitrarily relativizing anything that the Bible writers teach.

Inspiration. A divine act by which God enables the prophet to grasp and communicate in a trustworthy manner that which has been revealed to him/her in divine revelation.

Liberalism/Liberals (Classical or Radical). Theological liberals deny the full trustworthiness of the Bible. Seeking to accommodate Bible truth to modern culture or science, classical/radical liberals deny the validity of miracles and the supernatural, and they adopt the methods of higher criticism (historical-critical method) as the way to restore the truthfulness of the Bible. Compare **Accommodationism.**

Literal Interpretation. An attempt to understand the Bible in its *plain, obvious,* and *normal* sense. This approach does not allegorize or spiritualize Scripture away in order to find some hidden, mystical, deeper, or secret meaning. The literal or plain meaning of Scripture should not be confused with a "literalistic" interpretation.

Literalistic Interpretation. An interpretation that fails to take into consideration the historical, grammatical, and literary (e.g., poetry, parables, symbol, simile, hyperbole, epistle, etc.) characteristics found in the Bible.

Literary-Source Criticism. A historical-critical approach that attempts to determine the various literary sources presumed to lie behind the present record in the Bible.

Lower Textual Criticism. As distinguished from *higher criticism* of liberal scholarship, *lower textual criticism* is a discipline that compares, analyzes, and evaluates ancient Bible manuscripts to ascertain which reading of a passage is closest to the original.

Mechanical (Dictation) Inspiration. A mistaken theory which claims that the Holy Spirit dictated each single word of Scripture. In this view of inspiration, the Bible writers are perceived as passive "junior secretaries" who merely transcribed what the Holy Spirit dictated to them. Mechanical (dictation) inspiration should not be confused with *verbal (propositional) inspiration.*

Plain Reading of Scripture. Refers to the *literal interpretation* of Scripture by which an interpreter seeks the plain, obvious, normal sense of Scripture. It is the method advocated by the sixteenth-century Protestant Reformers, William Miller, and the Seventh-day Adventist pioneers, including Ellen White. Contemporary scholars sometimes use the technical term *historical-grammatical method* for this plain reading approach to Scripture.

Principle of Analogy. One of the three cardinal principles upon which the historical-critical method is established. This principle holds that past events must be explained on the basis of present occurrences (i.e., *the present is the key to the past*). This principle, for example, suggests that since dead people are *currently* not rising from the grave, the *past* event of Jesus' bodily resurrection recorded in the Gospels could not have been true.

Principle of Correlation. Another of the three foundational principles of the historical-critical method. This principle states that every event must be explained solely by natural causes, that is, by cause and effect in the natural world (i.e., *every effect has a natural cause*). This means that there can be no miracles or supernatural occurrences; therefore, wherever miracles occur in the Bible, we must either reject those sections or give the miracles a naturalistic explanation.

Principle of Criticism. One of the three foundational principles of the historical critical method. According to this principle, whenever you read any account in the Bible, instead of accepting it as truth, treat it with a level of skepticism or at least accept it only tentatively, with the possibility of revision (i.e., *do not believe everything you hear or read in Scripture*). Skepticism is the key to establishing truth. Therefore as one approaches the Bible, one must begin with suspicion rather than trust.

Progressive Revelation. A theological term indicating God's ever-increasing unfolding or expansion of truth that was previously revealed. Each new revelation interprets and amplifies the previous revelation but does not contradict it in any way. Historically, Seventh-day Adventists have referred to this as "present truth."

Proof-text. A verse or a longer passage that is used to establish a point. If the passage in its context supports the point, such use is legitimate. However, the term is used in a pejorative sense for a method that *arbitrarily* uses isolated texts out of context to support or prove positions on which the interpreter has already made up his/her mind.

Redaction Criticism. A historical-critical approach which attempts to study the activity of the "editors" of the Bible as they allegedly shaped, modified and even created the final product.

Revelation. A divine act by which God discloses Himself, enabling the prophet to come to an understanding (about someone, thing, or event) that the prophet could not have discovered or fully understood on his/her own.

Spirit of Prophecy. Also known as the *testimony of Jesus* (Rev 19:10), it refers to the messages of comfort, guidance, instruction, and correction that God commissions His true prophets to deliver to His people (cf. Rev 1:1-2, 9; 22:8-10). It is also an identifying characteristic of God's end-time remnant church (Rev 12:17). True prophetic messages never contradict God's revelations given through earlier prophets and recorded most definitively in inspired Scripture. Because Seventh-day Adventists believe that Ellen G. White was a true recipient of this biblical gift of prophecy, they often refer to her writings as the "Spirit of Prophecy" or the "Testimonies."

Structural Criticism. A historical-critical approach that attempts to investigate the relationship between the surface structure of the writing and the deeper implicit structures that belong to literature as such.

Theological Pluralism. Maintains that no theological or doctrinal truth can ever claim to be absolute or final. Proponents argue that conflicting or contradicting theological views are legitimate and must be allowed to cohabit in the church.

Typological Interpretation. A type of biblical interpretation in which persons, events, and institutions in the Old Testament are understood as foreshadowing persons, events, or institutions in the New Testament.

Vaticinium Ex Eventu. A technical term for the practice of describing what has already happened as though it were a prophecy of something yet to happen. Based on the higher-critical assumption that there can be no miraculous manifestations, including God's ability to foretell the future, this term suggests that wherever there are clear evidences of fulfilled prophecies, the prophecies must have been written after the event actually took place.

Verbal (Propositional) Inspiration. The Holy Spirit's guidance of inspired writers in choosing their own words as they wrote Scripture. When inspiration is described as "verbal," it suggests that despite the inadequacies of human language, because of the Spirit's guidance, the thoughts, ideas, and words of the Bible writers accurately convey God's message revealed to them. Verbal inspiration should not be confused with *mechanical (dictation) inspiration.*